Hollywood and the Baby Boom

Hollywood and the Baby Boom

A Social History

James Russell and Jim Whalley

Bloomsbury Academic
An imprint of Bloomsbury Publishing Inc

B L O O M S B U R Y
NEW YORK · LONDON · OXFORD · NEW DELHI · SYDNEY

Bloomsbury Academic

An imprint of Bloomsbury Publishing Inc

1385 Broadway	50 Bedford Square
New York	London
NY 10018	WC1B 3DP
USA	UK

www.bloomsbury.com

**BLOOMSBURY and the Diana logo are trademarks
of Bloomsbury Publishing Plc**

First published 2018

© James Russell and Jim Whalley, 2018

Library of Congress Cataloging-in-Publication Data
A catalog record for this book is available from the Library of Congress.

ISBN: HB: 978-1-5013-3149-7
ePDF: 978-1-5013-3152-7
eBook: 978-1-5013-3150-3

Cover design by Eleanor Rose
Cover image: Film *Parenthood* 1989 © Universal / Courtesy Everett Collection / Mary Evans

Typeset by Deanta Global Publishing Services, Chennai, India
Printed and bound in the United States of America

To find out more about our authors and books visit www.bloomsbury.com.
Here you will find extracts, author interviews, details of forthcoming events
and the option to sign up for our newsletters.

This book is dedicated to Peter Krämer,
for always encouraging us to see The Big Picture.

CONTENTS

Part Five: Legacy

IMAGES

FIGURES

ACKNOWLEDGEMENTS

Research for this book was funded by a Leverhulme Trust research project grant from 2012 to 2014, and the authors would like to thank the Leverhulme Trust for their support and investment.

We would also like to thank De Montfort University, particularly our colleagues in the Leicester Media School and the Cinema and Television History research centre.

As we explain in the introduction, many people have contributed to this book through interviews and survey responses. We are extremely grateful for their time and thoughtful replies, which have greatly improved the finished text.

James Russell would like to thank Hannah, Ivy and Hugh.

Jim Whalley would like to thank his family, for their love and extreme tolerance, especially Fletch and Charlie, who didn't exist to thank in his previous book, and Kathryn. Rich Glanville, James Brook and David Brook were brilliant sources of information and conversation.

Introduction

At the start of Phil Alden Robinson's *Field of Dreams* (1989), Ray Kinsella, played by Kevin Costner, is walking through the fields of his Iowa farm at sunset, when he hears a mysterious voice whispering 'If you build it, he will come.' Encouraged by radical 1960s author Terence Mann (played by James Earl Jones and loosely based on J. G. Salinger), Ray builds a makeshift baseball field among his corn cobs and is both shocked and delighted when the ghosts of long dead baseball players join him from the afterlife to play. The film is peppered throughout with allusions to the formative cultural experiences of the baby boomers. Ray discusses going to college in voice-over, and claims, 'Officially my major was English but really it was the Sixties. I marched. I smoked some grass. I tried to like sitar music.' Terence Mann's work is described as 'a voice of warmth and reason during a time of great madness. He coined the phrase, "Make love, not war." While other people were chanting "burn baby burn" he was talking about love and peace and understanding'. At the film's climax, Ray is reunited with the ghost of his dead father, and the distinct generational experiences that caused their estrangement are resolved as they find some reconciliation.

IMAGE 1 *Ray Kinsella (Kevin Costner) and Terence Mann (James Earl Jones) meet the ghost of a baseball player in* Field of Dreams *(1989).*

Though based on a novel by W. P. Kinsella (born in 1935), *Field of Dreams* is a quintessential baby boomer movie: it valorizes the 1960s as a high point of progressive social change; it focuses on the different cultures and attitudes of the boomers and their parents' generation; it depicts a regular family man, approaching middle age, living a settled (if not financially secure) life in Midwestern America; and it is infused with nostalgia, both for the sportsmen of the 1920s, and the movie culture of the 1930s and 1940s – indeed, its combination of heartfelt drama with a soupçon of fantasy directly invokes classics such as *Its a Wonderful Life* (1946). Critic Roger Ebert described it as 'the kind of movie Frank Capra might have directed, and James Stewart might have starred in'.[1]

The movie's director, Phil Alden Robinson (b. 1950), saw it as an opportunity to express the triumphs and frustrations of his generation. He told us:

> By the time I got to college we really had a sense as a generation that we were doing something different. And really what we did was we ended the 1950s. The 1950s you had to wear a jacket and tie to everything. To get on an airplane you got all dressed up. To go to a theater, you got all dressed up. We weren't going to do that. I still don't wear ties. It felt like we were saying, 'there's a new way of doing everything' and it eventually seeped into the work that we did when we got older.
>
> And I thought, 'If I'm going to personalise [*Field of Dreams*] and find my way into this story, it's going to be through the 1960s.' So I gave Ray a little backstory, he went to Berkeley and [he] met [his wife] at Berkeley. Because it felt like, this is what our generation is pointing towards: you open yourself up and reject the past but you can't just reject the past, you have to – on some level – embrace the past, because it's where you came from. I thought that the reconciliation with the father, in a way, was the missing piece of the 1960s rebellion.

According to Oliver Gruner, *Field of Dreams* 'treads a careful line between recuperation and rejection', of the 1960s, which are ultimately presented as 'part of a broader historical continuum where universal themes of optimism, despair, dreams deferred and human relationships prevail'.[2] Audiences responded: the film earned $64 million on US release, making it the nineteenth highest earning film for its year; it was nominated for Best Picture at the 1990 Academy Awards; it also helped to establish Kevin Costner as an iconic boomer star.

---

[1] Roger Ebert, Review of *Field of Dreams*, *Chicago Sun-Times*, 21 April 1989, http://www.rogerebert.com/reviews/field-of-dreams-1989.
[2] Oliver Gruner, *Screening the Sixties: Hollywood Cinema and the Politics of Memory* (New York: Palgrave MacMillan, 2016), 74–5.

Twenty-five years later, in February 2015, the American Association of Retired People (AARP) hosted its fourteenth annual 'Movies for Grown Ups' awards gala at the Beverly Wilshire Ballroom. The event was attended by a 'select group of 2014 moviemakers deemed most significant to a fifty-and-over audience'.[3] In his acceptance speech for the Career Achievement Award, Costner sought to rally the audience of ageing baby boomers by invoking the rebellious spirit of their youth:

> I think our generation still has the time to fulfil its promise. Winning and losing are still before us. ... I'm not saying we should go out and build a baseball field in the middle of a cornfield. What I am saying is we were the first generation that knew something was broken, and we weren't afraid to take it on. Something is still broken. We still are the Boomers. We're not just old dogs looking for one last fight. We still have a chance to stand taller than we ever thought was possible. I think we have a chance to still go out with a bang. There's still time. I don't know how much. ... But there's still time.[4]

Channelling the spirit of *Field of Dreams*, Costner reminded his audience of baby boomers that they had changed America in the 1960s and they retained the same political and social power fifty years later. However, Costner also recognized that their power as an audience for his movies was declining. According to the *Los Angeles Times*, Costner gently 'chided the audience for "only paying half" to go to a movie', going on to complain that 'it's very hard to get a gross from baby boomers with half-price movie discounts, "You have to go twice"'.[5]

Both points were true. Since the moment that the baby boom first began in the mid-1940s, the resulting cohort of Americans were at the forefront of profound changes in the nature of public life. The rise of the domestic suburb in the 1950s, the growth of youthful political radicalism and the civil rights movement in the 1960s and 1970s and return of corporate conservatism in the 1980s can all be understood as part of the baby boom experience. In his 'defence' of the baby boom generation, the writer Leonard Steinhorn argues that 'over a single lifetime boomers have accomplished what few generations before them were able or willing to do – to undo many of the accumulated hypocrisies and knotty contradictions that have tangled this

---

[3]Marianne Zumburge, 'Kevin Costner Rallies Baby Boomers at AARP Movies for Grownups Awards', *Variety*, 3 February 2015, http://variety.com/2015/scene/vpage/kevin-costner-rallies-baby-boomers-at-aarp-movies-for-grownups-awards-1201422680/.
[4]Quoted in Zumburge, 'Kevin Costner Rallies', online.
[5]Christie D'Zurilla, 'Kevin Costner at AARP Gala', *Los Angeles Times*, 3 February 2015, http://www.latimes.com/entertainment/gossip/la-et-mg-aarp-movies-for-grownups-awards-kevin-costner-eddie-redmayne-20150203-story.html.

country's history since its earliest days'.[6] Alternatively, the writer Tom Wolfe dismissed them as the 'me' generation, a group who privileged self-regard and narcissism over the community spirit of previous generations.[7]

However we define the world view of the boomers, since the 1950s it has been inextricably linked with film. In the movie theatre and at home, Hollywood provided images, stories and ideas that helped define the baby boomers. It was no accident that, as he sought to inspire, Costner peppered his speech with references to films, from *Field of Dreams* to George Stevens's *Giant* (1956). Equally, according to historian Douglas Gomery, the baby boomers 'alter[ed] all forms of American life, and none more so than moviegoing'.[8] If we look at the broad contours of American cinema history, the life cycle of the baby boomers closely correlates to key shifts in the nature of American movies.

In the 1950s, when the majority of boomers were children, Hollywood focused much of its production resources on epic films that addressed young and old alike, the studios became heavily involved in the production of child-oriented television series, and the Disney Company assumed a position of lasting dominance. In fits and starts, the child audience – which is to say the boomers – became one of the industry's most lucrative audiences for the first time in its history, although only one company really recognized their commercial power at this time: Disney. In the late 1960s, when the boomers entered their teens, censorship laws were relaxed, and Hollywood increasingly targeted teenaged viewers with more 'challenging' movie content that spoke to the emergent counterculture. In the 1980s and 1990s, mainstream film production became increasingly dominated by family-oriented movies, as the baby boomers settled down and started families of their own. Remarkably, the boomers remained a hugely important audience for Hollywood into late middle age. As a result, the movies of the late 1980s and early 1990s (like *Field of Dreams*) continued to address the concerns of baby boomers. In recent years the industry has also experienced a boom in home viewing technologies targeting older viewers. These changes cannot be satisfactorily explained as intentional attempts to exploit baby boomers over and above other audience members. Instead, they indicate that Hollywood, like any other industry or institution, is at the mercy of broad historical, social and demographic processes, and Figure 1 shows the extent to which youth and adult viewers shifted over time as the boomers grew older.

[6]Leonard Steinhorn, *The Greater Generation: In Defense of the Baby Boom* (New York: Thomas Dunne, 2006), xii–xiii.
[7]Tom Wolfe, 'The Me Decade', *New York Magazine*, August 1976, http://nymag.com/news/features/45938/.
[8]Douglas Gomery, 'Motion Picture Exhibition in the 1970s', in David A. Cook, *Lost Illusions: American Cinema in the Shadow of Watergate and Vietnam* (Berkeley: University of California Press, 2000), 397.

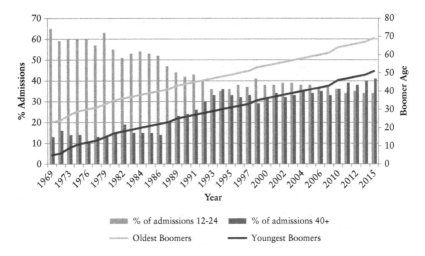

FIGURE 1 *Trends in Age Group Share of Total Annual Tickets Sales at the Domestic Box Office, 1969–2015.* Source: MPAA (See Appendix B)

Relatively little scholarly work has been done to trace the direct impact of the baby boom on Hollywood. Assessing film exhibition in 1970s America, Douglas Gomery argues that the baby boom 'generated more loyal movie fans than in any time in history'.[9] In Peter Krämer's reappraisal of the Hollywood Renaissance, he demonstrates how the demands of the youth market were a contributing factor to changes in the industry's output in the late 1960s and early 1970s.[10] Robert C. Allen has also argued that ageing baby boomers prompted a surge in family entertainment across the home video market in the 1980s.[11] Otherwise, the boomers' importance to Hollywood has been more or less assumed. In this book, we have set out to test that assumption, by looking at the ways that Hollywood has attempted to cater to the baby boom audience, and also at the activities of the baby boomer filmmakers and executives. Speaking at a trade event in 2013, movie marketing guru Catherine Paura reminded her audience that the boomers were still a vital audience, even if they did only pay half price for tickets, and she concluded, 'We feel as if we invented going to the movies. It's a part of who we are.'[12] We tell the story of that relationship.

---

[9]Gomery, 'Motion Picture Exhibition', 398.
[10]Peter Krämer, *The New Hollywood: From Bonnie and Clyde to Star Wars* (London: Wallflower Press, 2005).
[11]Robert C. Allen, 'Home Alone Together: Hollywood and the "Family Film"', in Melvyn Stokes and Richard Maltby, eds, *Identifying Hollywood's Audiences: Cultural Identity and the Movies* (London: BFI, 1999), 109–34.
[12]Quoted in Dave McNary, 'CinemaCon: Boomers Keeping Filmgoing Buoyant, Says Researcher', *Variety*, 16 April 2013, http://variety.com/2013/film/news/boomers-keeping-filmgoing-buoyant-cinemacon-attendees-told-1200375550.

Identifying the baby boom

The baby boom is commonly agreed to have begun in 1946, when the United States experienced an unexpected and unprecedented surge in birth rates, 'reversing a century and half long decline in fertility'.[13] In the mid-1930s, annual birth rates dipped as low as 2.3 million, but in 1947 alone, 3.8 million babies were born, and numbers continued to rise.[14] Between 1954 and 1963 more than 4 million babies were born each year. The result was a 75 million strong generation, which ranked as the largest demographic group in the United States by some margin. By 1964, when birth rates began to decline, 40 per cent of the population were aged under twenty. The baby boomers were followed by a smaller generational group, now commonly known as generation X, which is usually understood to have been born between 1965 and 1984. 'Gen-X' was then followed by a larger group, made up to some considerable degree by the baby boomers' children, known as 'Millennials'.

Since the baby boom was first observed, it has been a constant source of fascination for scholars and media commentators across a wide range of subjects on two grounds. The first is purely demographic: the baby boom means there is an ageing cohort of Americans eighteen years wide that is disproportionately numerous compared to the cohorts around it. In the 1950s and 1960s there were more children, in the 1960s and 1970s there were more teenagers and so on. This is significant because a larger cohort requires more goods and services and therefore costs and spends more money. At every stage of their lives, boomers have demanded special attention. The second justification for focusing on the baby boom is more complex and less easily measurable, and stems from the social conditions that helped create the boom in the first place. In the words of Jane Edmunds and Bryan S. Turner, the baby boom also 'came to have social significance by virtue of constituting itself as cultural identity'.[15] They argue that the baby boom is an example of generational identity performing a comparable function to gender, race and class as a way of uniting and dividing large social groups. In effect, the boomers had an identity that gradually shaped their sense of who they were and who they were commonly understood to be.

We will look in detail at the causes of the baby boom, and the formative experiences of the boomers in Chapter 1, but perhaps the most well-understood aspects of the boomer experience are their perceived sense of

---

[13]Herbert S. Klein, *A Population History of the United States* (Cambridge: Cambridge University Press, 2004), 174.
[14]Klein, *A Population History*, 175.
[15]Jane Edmunds and Bryan S. Turner, *Generations, Culture and Society* (Buckingham: Oxford University Press, 2002), 7.

privilege, and their association with liberal politics. The baby boomers were more attentively parented than previous generations, and grew up in an intense consumerist milieu, with a greater disposable income than almost any previous generation of young people. Political scientist Paul C. Light also argues that the cultural and social proximity of the baby boomers cultivated 'a lifelong commitment to individualism ... a search for space and opportunity'.[16] Both factors have contributed to their status as the 'Me Generation' lampooned by Wolfe.

In terms of politics, the boomers 'came of age in a period of international turmoil, decolonization and Vietnam war [that] saw the formation of movements that tended to be anti-establishment', which shaped their status as a culturally distinctive demographic group.[17] In 1988, Light wrote that 'on issues of social tolerance, there is no doubt that the baby boom are the liberal anchor of American political opinion'.[18] These attitudes to traditional codes of behaviour and morality informed the rise of the 1960s civil rights movement, counterculture, feminism and the peace movement. They also underpin Kevin Costner's vision of the baby boomers' purpose in his 2015 speech to the AARP, but the boomers were and are by no means exclusively liberal in their world view. The boomers lived through social change, but not all of them endorsed that change, and America's highly partisan political culture today is a legacy of deep fractures in the boomer experience.

While the demographic size of the baby boom is undisputed, there is more debate about the date range of the baby boom as a coherent social identity. Some have argued the generation began earlier with the 'victory babies' of 1943, as they enjoyed many of the same advantages as their younger siblings, and that the sense of shared experience began to diminish in those born after 1957. Those born after 1957 were less likely to have clear memories of the unrest of the late 1960s and the draft. They also had to contend with the long line of older boomers ahead of them in establishing a career. Paul Light reports that those born between 1958 and 1964 could expect to earn 10 per cent less in their lifetimes than those in the first years of the boom. As the 1960s progressed, many of the factors that contributed to the boom were undone. The introduction of the pill in 1960 contributed to a fall in birth rates that had begun in 1958. Annual births fell under 4 million in 1964, the start of a dip below long-term trends that was not recovered until 1982. The number of marriages also fell while divorce rose sharply, from under 400,000 annually in 1961, to over 1 million by the middle of the 1970s. At the end of the 1960s, the economy was faltering and the early 1970s witnessed double-digit rises in interest rates and inflation.

---

[16]Paul C. Light, *Baby Boomers* (New York: W.W. Norton, 1988), 131.
[17]Edmunds and Turner, *Generations, Culture and Society*, 25.
[18]Light, *Baby Boomers*, 230.

Our study seeks to address the baby boom as both a demographic and sociological phenomenon, and as such we employ two slightly different sets of dates. For filmmakers we begin with the victory babies of 1943 and include individuals born until 1960. Given the emphasis on change, much of our analysis is centred on the lives and work of filmmakers from the earliest years of the period, such as George Lucas (1944) and Steven Spielberg (1946). The youngest of our interviewees was writer and director Steve Kloves, born in March 1960. He felt sufficiently close to the defining events of the 1960s to consider himself a boomer:

> News was pretty powerful, and you were very aware of the Vietnam War, and Martin Luther King dying and Robert Kennedy dying, I was aware of that. There was a shadow over it all ... I didn't personally feel in peril, but it was always tinged by darkness. ... What was very alive in my family was that my brother was six years older and he was going to be in the lottery, and that was a very real thing.

For audiences, numbers are more important than the nuances of individual experience, and so we focus on those born between 1946 and 1964. In this regard, the baby boom had its greatest impact once members born during the peak years of the boom – the ten years from 1954 to 1963 – reached a new life stage, and so boomers born in the latter years have increased significance.

Our methods

This book uses several different sources of data to paint what we hope is an accurate picture of the baby boom's influence and significance. Our intention is to combine the scope of social history with the focus of cinema history. When scholars try to understand the history of American movies, they invariably focus on the individuals, events and institutional decisions which appear to have had the most obvious impact. In his history of 1930s Hollywood, *The Genius of the System*, Thomas Schatz shows how a small cadre of producers and studio executives collaborated to forge a functioning system for the creation of entertainment movies.[19] In *The Hollywood Studio System*, Douglas Gomery identifies the studio heads of the 1930s, and later Universal's Lew Wasserman as 'innovators and leaders', who determined the future trajectory of American movies over decades.[20] Although historians

---

[19]Thomas Schatz, *The Genius of the System: Hollywood Filmmaking in the Studio Era* (New York: Faber and Faber, 1988).
[20]Douglas Gomery, *The Hollywood Studio System: A History* (London: BFI, 2005), 208.

may repudiate a 'great man' theory of history, the ongoing primacy of the auteur theory, which identifies directors as the 'authors' of films, also encourages us to believe that movies are the product of individual agency. Relatively few people in the film industry have any great belief in the auteur theory, which is now considered mostly passé in critical and scholarly circles too, but it remains an important marketing tool and continues to shape how we talk about movies. We have assumed that a filmmaker's background as a baby boomer will have some effect on the types of movies they seek to produce, and the generational identity of production personnel is one of several factors determining the movie content.

Another way of understanding cinema is to focus on audiences. Through a combination of interviews, surveys and data analysis, scholars have made considerable progress in understanding what movies and moviegoing have meant to large groups of people. Annette Kuhn has uncovered the ways that cultural identity was shaped and reinforced by moviegoers during the 1940s.[21] Peter Krämer has shown how attendance data and opinion polls shed new light on the moviegoing choices of 1960s Americans.[22] Fandom scholars today have tried to make sense of the intense engagement that many feel with certain key film properties, at an individual level in the case of Martin Barker and Kate Brooks's early work on *Judge Dredd* (1994), and at a collective level in the case of Barker's later involvement with the *Lord of the Rings* audience project.[23] Focusing on audiences is an approach that owes much to social history: trying to understand how ordinary people have been affected by the ongoing march of change, and a growing body of work by film scholars aims to explore the societal experience of moviegoing.

Our history brings together these two approaches, and sets out to show that we can trace the impact of impersonal, large-scale trends such as the baby boom on cinema. As an audience, the baby boom made choices about the films they would and would not watch. Hollywood also made certain assumptions about what the baby boomers wanted. When they achieved creative power, the boomers themselves made certain choices about how the industry should be structured and what movies a new generation of moviegoers might want to see. The goal of our project is to reveal why those choices were made, by talking to the people who made them.

We look at the baby boom through three prisms: archival sources, audience opinion and filmmaker interviews. Using archival research, we try to assess what senior figures in the film industry thought about the boomers,

[21]Annette Kuhn, *An Everyday Magic: Cinema and Cultural Memory* (London and New York: I.B. Tauris, 2002).
[22]Krämer, *The New Hollywood*, 67–88.
[23]Martin Barker and Kate Brooks, *Knowing Audiences: Judge Dredd, Its Friends, Its Fans and Its Foes* (Luton: University of Luton Press, 1998); and Martin Barker and Ernest Mathijs (eds), *Watching The Lord of the Rings: Tolkien's World Audiences* (Oxford: Peter Lang, 2007).

and we look at the ways that these assumptions shaped the movies that got made, and the marketing efforts surrounding them. Most of this data has been drawn from production materials and the trade press in the United States and the United Kingdom. Throughout, we pay particular attention to box office charts, because they reveal the films that have resonated with audiences, and because financial success influences wider production trends, and the progress of individual careers. Until 1980, we rely on rental figures reported in *Variety*.[24] This is the amount of money returned to the distributor by exhibitors. Since 1980, it has become the norm for studios to announce gross box office receipts and we have found boxofficemojo.com to provide the most reliable and comprehensive figures. Unless otherwise stated, all financial data relating to movies is taken from this site. Box office grosses tend to be (but are not necessarily) around double the amount of rental returns and make it easier to compare the popularity of different releases. We are particularly grateful to the Margaret Herrick Library in Beverly Hills, and to Sheffield Hallam University in Northern England, who both provided phenomenal support and resources during many visits.

Equally, we wanted to understand what ordinary members of the baby boom thought about cinema, and how they would describe their relationship to Hollywood. To this end we devised an online survey made up of twenty questions – some multiple choice, some free text – and promoted this survey across the web. In designing and disseminating the survey we worked from two guiding principles. First, the survey was designed to be as open as possible, allowing each respondent to bring their own memories and associations while still guiding them to consider the different ways in which they may have engaged with film at various points in their life. Secondly, we were keen to reach beyond academia in finding respondents. While appeals to the academic community have the advantage of finding a sympathetic and articulate audience, it is also an audience that – by definition – has their opinions disproportionately well represented in existing scholarship. To this end we avoided advertising our study on academic forums and mailing lists and instead found respondents through targeted ads on Facebook and Google, engagement with chat forums and respondent panels offered by surveymonkey.com.

The text of the survey, which went through two iterations during the life of the project, can be found in Appendix A, along with a more detailed overview of our approach. We ended up with over 800 responses, a large number for an academic project in film studies, or for a piece of commercial audience

---

[24]Our figures are taken from a comprehensive list printed by *Variety* in May 1993 of all films released before 1981 that had grossed over $3 million at the domestic box office. These figures include rentals from rereleases. Lawrence Cohn, 'All-Time Film Rental Champs', *Variety*, 10 May 1993, C76–108.

research, but a drop in the ocean of the 75 million baby boomers, and as a result our survey cannot be considered representative of the generation as a whole. Still, we believe our sample is large enough – and sufficiently varied – to reveal interesting, if not necessarily numerically significant, patterns. For this reason, some quantitative results are presented. In the main, however, it is the qualitative responses that are most valuable, providing us with some insights into individual experiences, and giving ordinary boomers a voice in this book. We use the memories and opinions harvested in our survey to personalize the sweeping historical narrative we are telling.

Finally, we have interviewed a number of key baby boomers involved in the film industry. We sent out fifty requests to directors, writers and studio executives and were ultimately able to arrange ten interviews of between one and three hours. Throughout 2012 and 2013 we spoke to Nancy Meyers, Jerry Zucker, Ivan Reitman, Lawrence Kasdan, Tim Harris, Jack Epps Jr, Leonard Maltin, Steve Kloves, Phil Alden Robinson and Sean Daniel. Each provided compelling insights into their own careers, and talked at length about their experiences in Hollywood. This data has proved invaluable, and like the audience survey, it has given baby boomer filmmakers the chance to speak in their own voice. Our project was funded by a grant from the Leverhulme Trust in the UK, and we are enormously grateful to them and to all our contributors.

We should also note that while the primary subject of the study is the relationship between film and the baby boom in the United States, on occasion we have felt it necessary to expand into North America, given the close economic and social ties between the United States and Canada. All box office figures used, for example, are from the North American box office. As Doug Owram has shown, Canada experienced a population boom very similar to their neighbours and experienced the same pattern of social change.[25] When asked about his move from Canada to Hollywood, interviewee Ivan Reitman commented, 'I never thought of myself as either Canadian or American, but as a North American. I thought from a point of view of the arts, there are no borders.' It is in that spirit that we have included the likes of Reitman and James Cameron in our narrative, although for logistical reasons, we only conducted the survey in the United States.

Structure

In Part 1, 'Childhood', we start at the beginning, by exploring the early years of the baby boom and the state of the film industry in the immediate aftermath

---

[25]Doug Owram, *Born at the Right Time: A History of the Baby Boom Generation* (Toronto: University of Toronto Press, 1996), 7.

of the Second World War. Over the course of three chapters we explore how the rise of a new kind of family experience, and the emergence of a huge generation of children, affected the production imperatives of American cinema, and the moviegoing habits of the American people. Throughout this part, we use a combination of archival research and commentary from our interviewees to explain how Hollywood initially struggled to notice and effectively capitalize on the baby boom audience, with the exception of one key figure: Walt Disney.

In Part 2, 'Youth', we focus on the 1960s and 1970s, when Hollywood reoriented much of its production schemes to cater more directly than ever before to the baby boom audience, at a time of great social change. Here we explore the complex response of the boomers themselves to the shifting social climate of the period, and we look at the film industry's conception of what young people wanted. The resulting 'New Hollywood' is considered a golden age of artistically challenging and mature mainstream cinema, but the baby boom audience responded in a diverse range of ways to films like *Easy Rider* (1969), *The Godfather* (1972) and *The Exorcist* (1973).

In Part 3, 'Success', we shift attention away from audiences to focus on the baby boomers who gained positions of creative control in the late 1970s and early 1980s. From this point onwards, a growing group of boomers began to shape the content of American movies directly, making films both for the boomer audience and for a new generation of younger viewers. We trace the shifting film market of the 1980s, and argue that the boomers played a determining role in shaping the American entertainment industry, in the process rendering its product more commercial than ever before.

Part 4, 'Maturity', explores the changing preoccupations of boomer filmmakers and audiences entering middle age. Here we move through the 1990s and 2000s, as the boomers who ascended to the most senior positions in the industry, were succeeded by filmmakers from a new generation and began to pay half price for their movie tickets. We conclude the book with Part 5 by looking at the legacy of the boomers and their attempts to create a reputation commensurate with their achievements.

When Kevin Costner chided his audience at the AARP awards for paying only half price for movie tickets, his statement was clearly intended as a joke, but it contained a kernel of truth. The boomers have profoundly influenced American movies, but Hollywood never found it particularly easy to capitalize on them. From the moment they began to appear, the boomers have hardly ever paid full price to watch movies. They caught them on television, or at a Saturday matinee showing, or at the drive-in, or at a midnight movie double feature. As we will discover in Part 1, the boomers almost immediately presented Hollywood with a problem that took three decades to solve: What did they want to watch?

PART ONE

Childhood

1

Hollywood and the Baby Boom in the 1950s

At first, the baby boom's impact on Hollywood was unclear. The social and economic changes that were bound up with the baby boom changed the habits of Hollywood's audiences, but made no great difference to the makeup of that audience, or to the concerns of industry personnel. It took until the mid-1950s for Hollywood to feel the effects of baby boomers as an audience and as a social phenomenon. Consequently, this chapter focuses on the prehistory of the baby boom, and explains how the baby boom fed into wider social changes in America. In the first half, we look in detail at the immediate causes and consequences of the baby boom. In the second half, we examine the structure and operating practices of the Hollywood studios at the end of the 1940s, as the baby boom began to affect the norms of the American movie industry, along with other seismic shifts.

The origins and impact of the baby boom

Just as the end of the Second World War put an end to declining birth rates, it also signalled the end of the two decades of economic and social hardship that had begun with the great depression in the late 1920s. As a result the baby boomers grew up in an unprecedented era of prosperity, which Landon Jones has described as 'a buccaneering orgy of buying and selling that carried all things before it'.[1] Unlike other countries, the war had left America well positioned for economic growth as American ingenuity was turned from producing armaments and waging war on foreign powers to combating more prosaic human problems – getting clothes clean, keeping food cold, moving from A to B. The GIs returned home to a country that was more thoroughly

---

[1]Landon Jones, 'A Booming Baby Explosion', in Stuart A. Kallen, ed., *The Baby Boom* (San Diego: Greenhaven Press, 2002), 33.

modernized and wealthier than ever before. The war had restricted family life while it boosted the country's commercial infrastructure. For the first time in decades, peoples' life prospects were visibly improving. In 1946, *Fortune* magazine celebrated a tangible change in the wind, declaring, 'This is the dream era, this is what everyone was waiting through the blackouts for ... . The Great American Boom is on.'[2]

In his history of the baby boom, Landon Jones observes that the economic impact of the boom was understandably first felt by businesses catering to the very young:

> The spending boom started, literally, at the bottom. Diapers went from a $32 million industry in 1947 to a $50 million in 1957 ... mothers and fathers were paying $5 million annually (twice the pre-boom business) to have baby's shoes bronze plated at L.E. Mason Inc., in Boston. More than one in ten Americans was consuming baby food at a rate of 1.5 billion cans a year in 1953 (up from 270 million in 1940).
>
> As the kids grew up, so did the markets. Throughout the 1950s the 5–13 age group grew by an additional one million baby boomers every year. The toy industry set records annually after 1940, growing from an $84 million stripling, to a $1.5 billion giant. Sales of bicycles doubled, children's toys became a boom market. At its peak, the juvenile market was ringing up a staggering $33 billion annually.[3]

The commercial opportunities of the age weren't limited to the sale of toys and nappies. As more of these new families emerged, they increasingly began to move to a new kind of physical environment, which also encouraged intensified forms of consumerism – the suburbs. Suburbia, of a sort, had been observed since the early nineteenth century.[4] However, the dream of suburban living as a distinct, clearly defined part of the American experience, and landscape, only really came to fruition in the 1950s, in a 'suburban revolution which changed the landscape of urban America'.[5] 'True' rural communities declined, as peripheral urban populations expanded dramatically into the empty lands surrounding urban conurbations across the United States.

The first modern suburb of the period is generally understood to be Levittown, New York, a planned development of 2,000 homes on the southern tip of Long Island, within commuting distance of New York City. The housing industry had been in a slump throughout the war years, but

---

[2]Article quoted in Landon Jones, *Great Expectations: America and the Baby Boom Generation* (New York: Coward McCann, 1980), 20.
[3]Jones, 'A Booming Baby Explosion', 33–4.
[4]Jim Cullen, *The American Dream* (New York: Oxford University Press, 2003), 146.
[5]Klein, *A Population History*, 183.

Levitt and Sons were encouraged to pursue the development by the terms of the GI Bill, which guaranteed government support for veterans seeking to buy homes. All of the homes were sold within days of going on the market, and the firm used assembly line production methods (pre-cut timber, identical blueprints) to keep up with demand. By 1951, the company had established four separate developments, made up of over 17,000 homes, and similar sites were springing up across the country. Levittown was most notable for its uniformity: the homes were uniform in layout and construction, occupied uniform strips of land and provided a relatively uniform social experience.

The fact that Americans had the space and resources to build more and more suburbs helped to sustain the baby boom for so long. Herbert S. Klein argues that the baby boom effectively occurred as a result of a range of interconnected factors, with new housing at the centre:

> New levels of family income, new availability of federal credit to the middle and lower classes for home ownership, the introduction of cheap mass produced tract housing, and increasing economic mobility due to the movement to high status employment on the part of the younger population all had their impact on temporarily reversing the trends in fertility. The space and income for providing for more children was now available, and Americans responded to these opportunities by lowering the age at which they married, beginning their families at an earlier age, and opting for marriage more frequently, thus increasing their overall fertility.[6]

By moving away from the city into sprawling, newly minted suburbs Americans were realizing a primal element of the American dream: heading into (a version of) the frontier. Nicholas Sammond has noted that 'the growth of the American suburbs recapitulated the frontier experience, both in its familiarity and its strangeness ... by 1954, the image of the frontier had become common'.[7] Perhaps unsurprisingly, the suburbs almost immediately drew the attention of social commentators like David Reisman and William Whyte. In his bestseller *The Lonely Crowd*, which decried the emergence of the suburbs, college professor Reisman repeatedly used the frontier as the only viable metaphor to describe places like Levittown.[8] In his equally pessimistic 1956 account *The Organisation Man*, Whyte wrote, 'When suburbanites speak of re-establishing the spirit of the frontier communities, there is truth in their analogy. Our country was born as a series of highly communal enterprises and though the individualist may have opened the

---

[6]Ibid., 176.
[7]Nicholas Sammond, *Babes in Tomorrowland: Walt Disney and the Making of the American Child 1930–1960* (Durham: Duke University Press, 2005), 302.
[8]David Reisman, *The Lonely Crowd* (1961: repr. New Haven: Yale University Press, 2001), 127.

frontier, it was the co-operative who settled it.'[9] For Reisman and Whyte, suburbia and the commercialized culture of the 1950s were dulling the spark of individual agency that had previously defined the American national character. In the suburbs, they claimed, individual liberty gave way to henpecked conformity and groupthink.

For the men, women and children who lived in these suburbs, the situation felt different. After the great depression and the Second World War, the space and leisure opportunities provided by the suburbs must have seemed utopian. Suburbia also evoked the frontier experience more directly, in that it brought millions of Americans into previously unsettled spaces of the American landscape. Levittown and other planned suburban communities were often sold to urban Americans as a wholesome environment to raise a family.

Much has been made of the fact that the suburbs either encouraged, or at least benefitted from, a new kind of intense consumerism:

[In the 1950s] consumer spending helped secure a historic reign of prosperity, longer lasting and more universally enjoyed than ever before in American history ... the purchase of a new single family home generally obligated buyers to acquire new household appliances and furnishings, and, if the house was in the suburbs (as over 80% were) at least one car as well. Consequently, between 1949 and 1979, family income doubled.[10]

Increased consumer spending drove the development of new commercial environments. In 1950, an article in the *New York Times Magazine* observed that 'there is a widely held belief that American households are ready to do more buying than they presently do. ... They would do it more readily but for the difficulty of getting to the downtowns where the full range of goods was available.'[11] The solution was already on its way: pre-planned shopping centres located closer to the suburbs. By 1957, 940 shopping centres had been built across America, and when the political scientist Robert Wood wrote his own account of suburban living in 1959, he was able to confidently declare that 'the shopping center has become as much part of suburbia as the rows of ranch houses, split levels and Cape Cods'.[12]

Like the suburbs, malls depended on the other great commercial development of the 1950s – car ownership. According to Lizabeth Cohen,

[9]William Whyte, *The Organisation Man* (1956: repr. Philadelphia: University of Pennsylvania Press, 2002), 396.
[10]Lizabeth Cohen, *A Consumers' Republic: The Politics of Mass Consumption in Post-War America* (New York: Vintage, 2004), 121–2.
[11]Article quoted in Cohen, *A Consumers' Republic*, 261.
[12]Figures from Cohen, *A Consumers' Republic*, 258; Robert Wood, quoted in Cohen, *A Consumers' Republic*, 257.

'New car sales quadrupled between 1946 and 1955, until three quarters of American households owned at least one car by the end of the 1950s.'[13] Refrigerators and televisions were adopted in boomer households at an equally dramatic rate, and all of these domestic technologies would shape the experiences of the boomers, perhaps none more so than television, which we will return to shortly. Not all of the baby boomers experienced these developments in the same way, because not all were wealthy, not all grew up in the suburbs and many were not born in the 1950s, but it is nonetheless the case that the dominant experience for many boomers included a suburban upbringing and an intense ethic of consumerism. Certainly, many of the young baby boomers who would go on to become filmmakers shared a similar kind of suburban upbringing.

In 1953, Steven Spielberg's family moved to a two-storey, 'colonial style' home in a recently constructed suburb of Haddon Township, New Jersey. Despite the colonial trappings, the Spielberg house was brand new, part of a suburb constructed on the site of a potato farm in 1949. He grew up surrounded by similar families, who had all taken advantage of the GI bill and the boom in suburban construction to build better lives for themselves as the American economy kicked into high gear. His father, Arnold, was an electrical engineer and war veteran, and his mother, Leah, tended house when he was young. Spielberg went to junior school in Haddonfield, and played in the semi-pastoral hinterland of Haddon Township, where gloomy forests and the vestiges of the old farm coexisted with bustling new streets of suburban houses (a world Spielberg would recapture with great aplomb in his 1982 hit *ET: The Extra Terrestrial*).

Although writers, and filmmakers, often characterize suburbia as an isolated (and isolating) environment – Kenneth Jackson memorably wrote that 'there are few places as desolate and lonely as a suburban street on a hot afternoon' – most middle-class baby boomers remember their suburban childhoods quite positively.[14] In his biography of Spielberg, Joseph McBride writes that 'many of the fathers in Stevie's neighborhood were, like Arnold Spielberg, young veterans buying their first homes under the GI bill. [Haddon Township] swarmed with dozens of children'. One of Spielberg's neighbours at the time reported, 'It was a great place for kids to be raised. What made it nice is that it was a new neighborhood and people came in from different areas. Most of them were young people and they got along.'[15] Although Spielberg experienced some bullying, he was nonetheless a pretty regular

[13]Cohen, *A Consumers' Republic*, 123.
[14]Kenneth T. Jackson, *Crabgrass Frontier: The Suburbanization of the United States* (Oxford: Oxford University Press, 1985), 280.
[15]Neighbour, quoted in Joseph McBride, *Steven Spielberg: A Biography* (London: Faber and Faber, 1998), 53.

kid, one of a vast army running riot across this newly minted suburban landscape. Later, critics would describe Spielberg as 'the poet of suburbia'.[16]

In the equally new suburb of Drexel Hill, Pennsylvania, the film director Nancy Meyers (b.1949) was having a similar kind of experience: 'We lived on a street with forty eight children on my block, so even growing up I was aware there were just so many kids in my neighborhood. And a lot of the families in my neighbourhood had ten kids, eight kids, seven kids, twelve kids.' Way across the Midwest, Jerry Zucker, described his childhood in Milwaukee by observing that

> 'it was very *Leave It to Beaver*. I was born in 1950 and we lived in the suburbs of Milwaukee, called Shawood. We lived in a nice neighborhood and they were nice, modest houses. A very clean neighborhood. Everyone mowed their lawn and cleaned up the garbage and was friendly. We had a basketball net on our garage and we played Frisbee. My brother and I were constantly inventing games when we were kids.'

For Spielberg, Meyers, Zucker and many millions of others, the 1950s was a time of childhood adventure, defined by an economic surge with no historical antecedents. In his memoir of growing up in the 1950s Bill Bryson bluntly declared of his own suburban childhood, 'I can't imagine there has ever been a more gratifying time or place to be alive than America in the 1950s.'[17]

On paper, at least, the American movie industry was well positioned to thrive in this new environment. Hollywood had been the primary provider of filmed entertainment in America since the teens, and a 'night at the movies' had been the preferred leisure activity for the majority of Americans for forty years. Hollywood's own system of self-censorship (the Production Code) and the exhibition patterns of most movie theatres (which combined adult-friendly A- and B-movies with child-friendly serial episodes and cartoons) ensured that movies catered to an audience made up of all age groups. In the words of Noel Brown, 'It was widely accepted that Hollywood was, as its advocates insisted, a family institution. That is to say, it was construed as an amusement fitted to serve all facets of the general public, including children.'[18] As young families (with school-aged children) rapidly became the largest group in American society, and levels of personal wealth increased, Hollywood could reasonably expect to benefit from the

---

[16]This quotation is often attributed to Vincent Canby, although James Kendrick believes that it is more likely to have come from a 1982 article by Chris Auty. See James Kendrick, *Darkness in the Bliss-Out: A Reconsideration of the Films of Steven Spielberg* (London: Bloomsbury, 2014), 29.

[17]Bill Bryson, *The Life and Times of the Thunderbolt Kid* (London: Random House, 2007), 5.

[18]Noel Brown, *The Hollywood Family Film* (London: IB Tauris, 2012), 17.

'great American boom' that was supercharging other areas of American industry. Certainly, the prospects for the movie industry looked bright at the start of the baby boom.

The film business after the Second World War

The film industry had entered the immediate post-war period on a high. The restricted market of the wartime years had ensured high grosses for all major studios. Moreover, the end of a tax on excess profits, designed to help fund the war effort, meant that most of the studios recorded substantially higher than usual returns at the close of 1945, which in turn ensured high stock prices.[19] They anticipated further gains in the years to come. By December 1945, the trade newspaper *Variety* was describing the film business as a 'bull market', writing, 'Not even in the lush pre-1929 days has the picture business seen such quick fortunes made.'[20]

The war years hadn't been without problems – many of the Hollywood studios had experienced some disputes with unions, and the war effort had drained resources from the studios in the form of personnel and raw materials, especially film stock. As a direct consequence of a long-running tax on profits, as well as shortages of stock, many of the studios had ended up making more films than they were willing or able to release, building up a glut of pictures which had already been paid for in 1945, but would enter profit in 1946 – hence the short-term reliability of the market.[21] In light of the anticipated stability of audience figures, many in the industry were calling for the construction of new picture houses in 1945 and 1946. At the start of 1946, *Variety* suggested that the appeal of movies was almost total, particularly across ages: 'At the average American family breakfast and dinner table, current movies are the most active topic of conversation. Youngsters know their film stars and stories better than their geography and arithmetic.'[22]

However, 'youngsters' had never been treated as a particularly significant audience by Hollywood executives. In the 1930s, Hollywood had viewed its movies as 'family entertainment', and relied on child stars such as Andy Rooney and Shirley Temple to attract filmgoers, but studios had rarely targeted children with any degree of commitment. Intensified censorship

---

[19]Anon., 'Upped Grosses and Reduced Taxes Bulling Almost Every Picture Stock', *Variety*, 5 December 1945, 5.

[20]Anon., 'Big Pix Profits in Bull Market: Many New Film Millionaires', *Variety*, 12 December 1945, 3.

[21]Anon., 'More Pix but Not Releases Means New High in Inventories', *Variety*, 19 December. 1945, 3.

[22]Anon., 'Everything Follows the Films', *Variety*, 9 January 1946, 33.

requirements and reformist pressure encouraged a brief boom in family-oriented movies throughout the first half of the 1930s, but during this period children were generally catered to with cheap serials and B-movies, which would play alongside a more expensive A-movie targeted at adults.[23] By offering a programme of entertainments, which included some cheaper fare specifically for juveniles, most movie theatres conceptualized of their audience as a diverse group, and never singled out children for special attention. It was assumed that children were part of the audience, especially for westerns, swashbucklers and comedies, but Edward Jay Epstein claims that in the 1940s a child rarely paid more than twenty-five cents for admission, and so was not considered a lucrative patron.[24]

From the 1920s onwards, the major film companies were frequently criticized by exhibitors and lobbying organizations for privileging adult-oriented, 'metropolitan' productions.[25] A few notable exceptions can be identified, such as MGM's *Andy Hardy* series, or Victor Fleming's *Wizard of Oz* (1938; a flop on first release), but for the most part, making movies for kids was left to the smaller, 'poverty row' production houses, which specialized in serials such as *Buck Rogers*, *Tarzan* and *Nancy Drew: Girl Detective*. Only the producer Walt Disney conceived of the value of child consumers differently and his was one of the few prominent film companies struggling when the baby boom began in 1946.

Disney's legacy was built in the 1930s, when his company produced a string of remarkably successful and ambitious films, including the first animated 'talkie', *Steamboat Willie*, in 1928 and the first feature-length animation, *Snow White and the Seven Dwarfs*, in 1937. In his features and short films Walt Disney established a highly recognizable group of animated stars, including Mickey Mouse and Donald Duck, and his films spoke to adults and children in depression-era America with remarkable clarity. According to Steven Watts, while other studios treated family viewers as an ineffective commercial proposition, Disney became 'a folk hero to an adoring American audience', by producing films which 'highlighted important aspects of depression era politics', such as, in *Snow White*, 'the triumph of the underdog, the value of hard work and the virtues of community among common people'.[26] Disney's folksy yet visionary cartoons were defined by their technical ambition, and their homespun, self-consciously naïve vision of the American character. The Disney brothers, Walt and Roy, had moved from Kansas to Hollywood in 1926, and established the Walt Disney Studio

[23]Brown, *The Hollywood Family Film*, 59.
[24]Edward Jay Epstein, *The Big Picture: Money and Power in Hollywood* (London: Random House, 2006), 13.
[25]Brown, *The Hollywood Family Film*, 75.
[26]Steven Watts, *The Magic Kingdom: Walt Disney and the American Way of Life* (Columbia: University of Missouri Press, 1997), 83.

IMAGE 2 *Disney's spectacularly successful first feature-length animation,* Snow White and the Seven Dwarfs *(1937).*

(later Walt Disney Productions). Walt was the visionary, a filmmaker whose interests defined the creative output of the company, while Roy was a gifted manager who was able to fund and make money from his brother's grand visions. Their company took various forms in the years after it was established, but throughout the 1930s and 1940s it was never in the same league as the major studios. Disney produced short animated movies, but it relied on a series of relationships with Columbia, United Artists and then RKO studios to distribute those movies.

Walt Disney Productions was one of many production companies operating at the margins of the industry and its small size, along with its specialization in animation, meant that it was particularly vulnerable to changes in the market conditions of film production and to box office disappointments. It required specialist staff, and its fortunes were dependent on a relatively small number of releases. These two areas of weakness came together in the early 1940s, with the initial commercial failure of Disney's most expensive and ambitious project to date, *Fantasia* (1940), and America's entry into the Second World War in 1941, which radically disrupted the operating conditions of all film studios. Ironically, while Walt Disney bitterly resented the restrictions imposed upon him during the war, his company survived because it depended on government production work, and it entered the post-war period at distinct disadvantage when compared to other major or minor studios.[27]

---

[27]Neal Gabler, *Walt Disney: The Autobiography* (London: Aurum, 2008), 400.

For the other studios, film revenues were healthy during the war years, and continued to rise in 1946, which the industry attributed primarily to the returning GI audience.[28] But already some in Hollywood were beginning to wonder whether or not the reliable business of the war years could be sustained in the longer term, and there were signs that Hollywood's future might be rocky. As attendance grew in the most profitable and luxurious first-run theatres (mainly owned by the majors), it was falling in more affordable second- and third-run chains. Production costs were also rising dramatically, and despite the ongoing boom in profits, the share values of the major studios, which had risen immediately after the war, were beginning to drop in 1946, and fluctuated throughout the immediate post-war years.[29] The sudden unreliability of share prices was one sign that the market for movies was not quite as untroubled as it superficially appeared.

Otherwise, in the immediate post-war period, Hollywood worried more about trade issues than audiences. In the immediate aftermath of the war, the US government had resumed prosecution of a long-standing antitrust action which sought to restrict the major studios' ability to control the market for film distribution and exhibition. The charges revolved around block booking (forcing exhibitors to take inferior product alongside more desirable movies) and ownership of 'first-run' theatres. These were the most lucrative theatres where big movies received their first screening, where ticket sales and profits were the highest and they were invariably owned by the major distributors. In his 1951 report on the antitrust action, Ernest Borneman observed, 'Control of the first-run theaters meant, in effect, control of the screen and the process of doling out licenses designating this theater as first-run and that as second-, third-, fourth- or nth run was the means by which control over the motion picture industry was first achieved and is still maintained.'[30]

In 1948, the legal action was successful, and the major studios were all bound to sign a consent decree which required them to give up ownership of their theatre holdings, and to avoid involvement in other forms of exhibition, including television. (Various other initiatives were devised to open up the film market further, most notably the introduction of tax breaks for independent productions which encouraged many industry personnel to set up their own independent production companies.) For some, including MGM, the antitrust ruling would ultimately prove a disaster because the company relied almost entirely on profits from theatres to fund production. For others, most obviously Disney, it ended up levelling the playing field

---

[28]Anon., 'Film Grosses up 15% over '45', *Variety*, 13 February 1946, 7.

[29]Anon., 'Wall St Lag despite Big BO', *Variety*, 20 February 1946, 3.

[30]Ernest Borneman, 'United States vs Hollywood: The Case Study of an Anti-Trust Suit', in Tino Balio, ed., *The American Film Industry* (rev. ed.; Madison: University of Wisconsin Press, 1985), 451.

much as it was intended to. After the war, Disney's financial situation remained precarious. While the other studios benefitted from the brief boom in ticket sales, Disney did not have a backlog of products to release, and so instead was seeking to cut costs, which meant that Walt could no longer plan grand filmmaking projects without considering the bottom line very carefully. Nonetheless, the conditions of the antitrust ruling opened opportunities for Disney to expand into distribution and new exhibition channels, while the rest of Hollywood would be faced with nothing but restriction. From the moment it began, the legal action affected the majority of studios adversely because it introduced a degree of instability to the standard operating practices that had defined the preceding three decades.

As the antitrust action played out, other headaches arose. The studios fought an ongoing battle with the exhibition sector over the cost and availability of the movie product. Declining supply meant that the majors could charge exhibitors higher rental fees, while exhibitors were asking for more films and lower rentals, accusing distributors of hoarding product to artificially inflate demand. Producers seemed to think that this was the exhibitors' problem, and in turn pushed for the construction of more theatres and suggested that ticket prices be raised.[31] The terms of this debate, which pitted distributors against exhibitors, was a sign of how antitrust would change relationships in the film market.

To make matters worse, the war resulted in significant changes to the international market for American film, especially in Britain (Hollywood's largest market outside the United States), where US investment had been frozen in British banks, and where the government was planning to implement tariffs on film imports. Funds locked overseas encouraged several studios to pursue overseas productions, and over time, the international audience would become a significant focus. Finally, famously, Hollywood was also attracting the attention of anti-communist activists within the US government, which resulted in the notorious HUAC witch-hunts of the late 1940s and early 1950s. All of this meant that in the first few years of the baby boom, Hollywood was more concerned about legal challenges, regulation, international relations and externally imposed restrictions than audiences or film content. Slowly, though, the industry was forced to reconsider long-held preconceptions about the reliability and tastes of movie audiences.

In 1947, despite good ticket sales, *Variety* declared that Hollywood needed to broaden its appeal to capture an estimated 25 million Americans who never watched movies, in order to maintain profitability.[32] It's quite clear at this time – the most stable and successful in Hollywood's history – that the trade press, and presumably the businesses it represented, still didn't

---

[31]See Anon., 'Exhibs, Distribs Yell Foul Play', *Variety*, 4 September 1944, 23.
[32]Anon., 'Wanted: 25,000,000 Pix Addicts', *Variety*, 12 March 1947, 3.

feel comfortable or assured of their ongoing profitability. In a reflective editorial published at the start of the year, *Variety* outlined what it saw as the future of the movie business:

> Skyrocketing production costs are the No. 1 headache of the US film industry today. With picturemaking budgets continuing to mount – and no means in sight of bringing them down – the problem is plainly giving industry toppers qualms about the future. On the other hand, they are pretty much agreed that b.o. returns will remain on high level if general conditions do not too unfavourably affect the nation's and the world's economy.[33]

Among studio heads interviewed for the article, only two, Nick Schenck of MGM and Daryl F. Zanuck of Fox, offered dissenting voices. Schenck said, 'I believe the peak of the boom period in motion picture attendance has been reached and is passing to a more cautious 'shopping' attitude on the part of the public.' He was more right than he, or anyone else in the industry, knew. The year 1946 marked a high point in movie attendance that would never be repeated.

By July 1947, *Variety* reported that 'grosses are off about 10% and attendance considerably more when compared to July last year'.[34] Noting that employment figures were increasing across the United States, *Variety*'s reporter went on to complain, 'There doesn't appear to be any real reason for the slump except a general uncertainty about the future which has Johnny Public hanging onto his grouch bag just in case.'[35] Studio heads generally agreed that the slump might be arrested by cutting costs and improving picture quality. Hence, Jack Warner's insistence that 'this coming year must be the creative year in the motion picture industry. Production must be good, and the public must be convinced that it is good'.[36] Throughout the late 1940s, quality was almost always seen as the main cause of audience decline – if only the pictures were good enough, ran such thinking, audiences would return. Only Paramount president Barney Balaban seemed to recognize that the industry was at the mercy of much larger forces: 'The cost of living kept on rising and there was less money left for pleasure. Some of the easy war cash vanished and a portion of the populations gathered in the big centers for war work purposes dispersed. The increasing numbers and use of new automobiles, the booming of outdoor sports and other forms of recreation

---

[33]Anon., 'Top Drawer Industry Leaders Accent Staggering Production Costs but Fear B.O. Dip', *Variety*, 8 January 1947, 5.

[34]Anon., 'Record Jobs and BO Boomer', *Variety*, 16 July 1947, 1.

[35]Anon., 'Record Jobs', 40.

[36]All of the quotations in this section have been taken from Various Authors, 'Top Industry Leaders Stress Need for More Creative Films', *Variety*, 7 January 1948, 5.

made stronger competition for pictures.' Balaban's solution (cutting costs, better pictures) may have been prosaic, but his analysis of the forces affecting movie consumption was correct.

Over the next few years, declining audiences became part of the background noise of the film industry. Although no one source has ever provided totally reliable figures, every measure of attendance showed an astounding decline. According to the US census, weekly attendance dropped from 90 million in 1946 to 60 million in 1950 and to 40 million in 1960.[37] Surveys carried out by the US Department of Commerce suggest a more modest spike of 79.4 million weekly ticket sales in 1946, which had dropped to 37.7 million in 1957.[38] The decline didn't stop there. Data gathered by the historian Joel Finler shows that weekly ticket sales dropped below 20 million for the first time in 1964, and bottomed out at 16 million in 1971.[39]

The unanticipated post-war decline in movie ticket sales can be attributed almost entirely to the changing social and economic circumstances of those young families who fuelled the baby boom. When they moved to the suburbs, boomer families were also moving away from the established sites of movie exhibition. As their wealth increased, they would often purchase a television alongside their car and refrigerator, which provided entertainment of all kinds for free in the home, a role previously occupied by radio, which had enjoyed a more complementary relationship with the movies.[40] More than 5 million television sets were sold every single year throughout the 1950s (with annual sales often exceeding 7 million), which meant that more than 67 million televisions had been sold by the end of the decade.[41] In 1951, a Warner Bros poll had found that 'television ownership was already responsible for a 3–4% drop in the overall US film audience, with further declines on the way'.[42] Audiences had already started to decline before television ownership became the norm, but purchasing a television clearly discouraged people from going to the movies even further.

Furthermore, a cursory glance at release patterns reveals that the industry was stuck in the past. In some ways, this was hardly surprising. After all, each of the major studios had key stars and filmmakers of the 1940s under long-term contracts, they were operating according to practices that had served them well for many years and they were able to rely on a quantity-over-

---

[37]Data cited in Peter Lev, *Transforming the Screen: The Fifties* (Berkeley: University of California Press, 2003), 7.
[38]Data cited in Michael Conant, 'The Paramount Decrees Reconsidered', in Balio, *The American Film Industry*, 539.
[39]Joel W. Finler, *The Hollywood Story* (London: Wallflower, 2003), 379.
[40]Douglas Gomery, *Shared Pleasures: A History of Movie Presentation in the United States* (Madison: University of Wisconsin Press, 1992), 88.
[41]See Tom Genova, *Television History: The First 75 Years*, available online at http://www.tvhistory.tv/Annual_TV_Sales_39-59.JPG.
[42]Lev, *The Fifties*, 9.

quality ethos, because moviegoing had become a culturally ingrained habit in the United States. For the first fifty years of the medium, people watched movies regularly, and expected those movies to be entertaining rather than spectacular. The industry made most of its profits from ticket sales at first-run theatres, and most studios specialized in providing high volumes of low- or medium-budgeted movies in a range of genres. Occasionally massive hits or flops occurred, and some movies were better than others in artistic terms, but the studio system of the 1930s was not concerned with blockbusters or catering to narrow audience demographics, especially not children.

Hollywood's growing disconnect from its audience was particularly visible in demographic terms, as senior operational roles in Hollywood were filled by older men with little connection to the boomers or their parents. The executive staff at Paramount provide a good example. In 1955, the studio was still nominally being run by Adolph Zukor, its founder, who was then ninety years old; Barney Balaban, the head of production, who was sixty-eight; Edward O'Shea, the head of distribution, who was fifty-nine; and George Weltner, the youngest member of the team, who was fifty-four. The big creative names based at Paramount were equally long in the tooth. The studio's most commercially successful director was Cecil B. DeMille, who was seventy-eight in 1955. Other key Paramount directors included Billy Wilder (forty-nine in 1955) and Alfred Hitchcock (fifty-six in 1955). Across the industry, similar patterns were visible in terms of key stars and industry personnel, the majority of whom had made their names in the 1930s and 1940s, and were now heading towards the end of their careers.

In 1952, *Variety* finally noticed a link between boomers, suburban living and audiences directly, but it focused on the equally bleak fortunes of legitimate theatre rather than moviegoing:

> Close examination of a number of important road cities reveals a hidden factor which may be contributing heavily to the decline of theatergoing in these cities. America's great inland urban empires are moving away from themselves. A major shift in the population centre of gravity has occurred in recent years, and the great residential areas, formally close to the downtown, have gone out to the country.
>
> The residential tide in these cities has gone out and left many famous old theaters, such as the Cass in Detroit and the Hanna in Cleveland, beached in the traffic congested, business, non-dwelling heart of the city. The theater is now an hour or more from the new suburban residential communities which have been five, ten and twenty miles distant from the loop. After 7 pm the downtown city streets of Detroit and Cleveland are virtually empty. The new city has gone home, miles away from its daytime centre of activity.[43]

---

[43]Need Armstrong, 'Suburbia – Key to Legit Future?' *Variety*, 23 January 1952, 1.

Curiously, precisely the same factors were draining audiences from cinemas, but the trade journal didn't notice this connection until 1953, and even then studios seemed reluctant to act upon the information. In August 1953, *Variety* reported on a *Fortune* magazine article which discussed the rapid suburbanization of America, and the concomitant rise in disposable income. Rather than calling for more theatres in suburban areas, *Variety*'s reporters claimed that it was 'difficult to establish' precisely what suburbanization might mean for film distributors, and ultimately used the shift to suburban living to call for a cull of less lucrative small-town theatres.[44]

A few months later, *Variety* reported on a speech given by Arno Thompson, director of the J. Walter Thompson ad agency, which discussed the financial impact of the baby boom. Thompson observed that there had been a 34-per cent increase in under-fives since 1946, and identified teenagers as the smallest demographic group in the United States.[45] Beyond noting that this kind of information was readily available to film producers, *Variety* made no suggestion as to what it might mean for production patterns.

As theatrical audiences declined, exhibitors spotted a change in their patronage, and tried to make the case for privileging family entertainment which might draw boomer parents and kids to theatres. In June 1950, *Variety* observed that exhibitors were 'almost unanimous' in their desire to see 'more family-style entertainment'. According to one theatre owner in New Mexico, 'The business is here – 100,000,000 looking for entertainment. Hollywood should wake up and give it to them. Bring out more comedies and good musicals. Avoid the depressing stuff.'[46] Later in the year, these theatre owners seemed to be proven right, when a brief rise in ticket sales was attributed precisely to this 'lost' family audience:

> Family-type product has provided the backbone of the improvement in grosses which has been felt by most theaters this summer. It's the kiddies and old folks attracted by these pix that make the difference in grosses, exhibs say. The teen-agers and early twenties group can be counted on pretty much in any case, so the family pix get some of that 'lost audience' that has become an industry maxim.[47]

Despite these warnings, the studios, now set at a legal distance from exhibition, generally disregarded signs that boomers and their parents might constitute an important audience for its products. *Variety* sounded a note of caution by pointing out that 'most seasoned trade observers are of the opinion that too much emphasis on the family pix could be as deadly as

---

[44]Anon., 'US Suburbia's Big Pix Role', *Variety*, 5 August 1953, 3.
[45]Anon., 'How Old Is Your Audience', *Variety*, 16 February 1955, 7.
[46]Mike Kaplan, 'Exhibs Sour on Formula Pix', *Variety*, 21 June 1950, 9 and 18.
[47]Herb Golden, 'Family Pix as BO backbone', *Variety*, 6 September 1950, 1.

other cycles have proved'.[48] Despite the usual predictions that things would improve in 1951 (they didn't) *Variety* ended the year by proposing that the industry needed to invest more time and effort in surveying its audience because, in the word of one unnamed producer, 'We'll never know why people aren't going to their theaters the way they used to unless we go out and ask them in person.'[49]

For much of its history, the film industry knew its audience surprisingly little. Instead, in the words of Susan Ohmer, 'Directors, producers, and exhibitors relied primarily on their own observations, on fan mail, or on reports in the trade papers for indications of how audiences felt about a film.'[50] In the early 1940s, pollster George Gallup set up an Audience Research Institute in Hollywood, and started to provide studios with much more detailed information about their audiences. However, he had fallen out of favour by the end of the decade, and most distributors had slipped back into their old habits (with one notable exception – Disney continued to use Gallup's methods as it expanded into new fields).

Several polls into the demographic status of Hollywood's audience were eventually carried out in the 1950s, the most thorough coming in 1957. The survey, commissioned by the Motion Picture Association of America, divided audiences by age range and assessed frequency of attendance (as well as looking at a broad range of other issues). It found that 72 per cent of tickets were sold to moviegoers aged under twenty-nine.[51] These viewers generally went most frequently, and constituted the largest demographic group in the theatre. The survey highlighted the importance of demographic research and encouraged a brief interest in teen audiences, but it also revealed a less well remarked upon fact: children, those aged fourteen or under, attended with greater frequency than almost any other group, and made up a massive segment of the audience – 31 per cent of all ticket sales. Children were watching more movies than ever in the 1950s, but as we will see, the low profits generated by child ticket sales reduced their impact on production planning.

William Goetz, vice president of production at Universal, identified a second problem with polling and surveys: audiences didn't always know exactly what they wanted. As far as Goetz was concerned, making a film involved blending together ingredients that audiences claimed they wanted, but 'it's in blending these known ingredients that something happens. All the things that have gone into the finished product have been carefully weighed, considered and evaluated. Individually, the elements are there but the picture

[48]Golden, 'Family Pix', 1.
[49]Anon., 'Wise Up to Why's of BO Dip', *Variety*, 20 December 1950, 7.
[50]Susan Ohmer, *George Gallup in Hollywood* (New York: Columbia, 2006), 2.
[51]Reproduced in Michael Conant, *Antitrust in the Motion Picture Industry: Economic and Legal Analysis* (Berkeley: University of California Press, 1960), 115.

as a whole creates no more than a ripple'.[52] Goetz's point anticipates a claim made most famously by screenwriter William Goldman in the 1970s – that in Hollywood 'Nobody knows anything,' and nobody can guarantee that a movie will become a hit – not even audiences.[53]

Conclusion

Why didn't all the Hollywood studios quickly reorient production around family-friendly movies in the 1950s? In the main, the answer is pragmatic. While other industries quickly recognized the commercial importance of the young family unit, the boomers on their own were not old enough to constitute a viable audience for Hollywood until the end of the decade. Consequently, at the very start of the 1950s the baby boom slipped out of Hollywood's field of vision, and even as they grew older, their significance remained lost in a mass of conflicting advice about who should be targeted and what should be made. This included some accurate observations about audiences, which often originated with exhibitors, alongside some less accurate suggestions. Presumably it was very difficult for producers, who had previously relied on gut instincts about audiences, to know which advice was correct. Furthermore, exhibitors had been lobbying for more overtly child-oriented product for years, despite the fact that it had rarely proven profitable in the past. Perhaps more importantly, the baby boom began at a time when the film industry was beset by a series of problems and external concerns that distracted and diverted it from focusing on changing audience demographics.

The impact of antitrust was a particularly important factor. The 1948 ruling ensured that none of the major studios could be involved in the construction or management of movie theatres. In effect, they were forced to extricate themselves from the market for film exhibition at almost precisely the moment when attendance at movie theatres began to fall through the floor. In a purely logistical sense, this meant that declining audiences were no longer the studio's problem. Instead, they were a problem for the newly independent exhibition sector to deal with, and throughout the early 1950s, exhibitors robustly complained about rental fees, picture quality and release strategies as they desperately tried to stabilize an ever-declining market.

Crucially, while the studios increasingly operated as global concerns, the exhibition sector was restricted to profits generated on ticket sales in the United States, which effectively meant that they made less money, less

---

[52]William Goetz, 'What Does the Public Want?' *Variety*, 2 January 1952, 13.
[53]William Goldman, *Adventures in the Screen Trade: A Personal View of Hollywood* (London: Abacus, 1996), 40.

reliably, than the studios of which they had previously been a part. From the late 1950s onwards, the Hollywood studios were essentially production/distribution operations licensing content to be screened at movie theatres and on television. These companies were not in a position, legally or financially, to embark on a radical programme of movie theatre construction in the suburbs. Nor were the exhibitors themselves, who were more financially restricted than ever before.

Here, then, is one other key reason why the major studios didn't benefit from the baby boom as other industries did: the 1948 antitrust ruling gradually cut them off from direct contact with their audience, and reconstituted the exhibition sector in a less stable, less financially secure form. None of these companies had the money to build high volumes of new theatres, a problem compounded by the fact that the film industry was relatively unaware of the baby boom anyway. Antitrust, suburbanization and television pushed Hollywood away from the baby boomers, and the baby boomers away from Hollywood.

Other problems also served to distract moviemakers from thinking about demographics, including tax negotiations, strikes, problems in overseas markets and the so-called anti-communist witch-hunts. Producers and distributors may also have felt some prejudice against children's movies, which were often seen as examples of 'low culture'.[54] Each of these affected the structure and operating practices of the major film studios, and so each affected the type of movies that ended up getting made during the 1950s. Hollywood certainly played a major role in shaping the mindset and attitudes of the young baby boomers and their families, but it appears that the baby boom didn't figure much in the mindset of film producers in the early 1950s. As a result, the boomers became movie fans in spite of Hollywood efforts, and their moviegoing habits were often quite different from those of previous generations. The next two chapters explore how boomers watched movies and the movies that they watched.

---

[54]Brown, *The Hollywood Family Film*, 9.

2

Watching Movies

As a child, George Lucas didn't care much for movies. 'Movies had extremely little effect on me when I was growing up,' he said. 'I hardly ever went, and when I did, it was to meet girls. Television had a much larger affect.'[1] The first time Steven Spielberg visited a movie theatre, he also found the experience underwhelming:

> My father told me he was taking me to see a circus movie. Well, I didn't hear the word movie, I only heard the word circus, so we stood in line for an hour and a half, and I thought I was going to see a circus. I'd already been once before to a circus and I knew what to expect: the elephants, the lion tamer, the fire, the clowns. And to go into this big cavernous hall and there's nothing but chairs and they're all facing up, they're not bleachers, they're chairs – I was thinking, 'Something is up, Something is fishy.'
>
> So, the curtain is open, and I expect to see the elephants and there's nothing but a flat piece of white cardboard, a canvas. And I look at the canvas and suddenly a movie comes on and it's *The Greatest Show on Earth*. At first I was so disappointed. I was angry at my father – he told me he was taking me to the circus and is just this flat piece of color. I retained three things from the experience: the train wreck, the lions and Jimmy Stewart as the clown. Everything else just went over my head.
>
> For a while I kept thinking 'Gee that's not fair,' I wanted to see three dimensional characters and all this was flat shadows, flat surfaces. I was disappointed by everything after that. I never felt life was good enough, so I had to embellish it.[2]

---

[1]George Lucas, quoted in John Baxter, *George Lucas: A Biography* (London: Harpercollins, 2000), 25.
[2]Steven Spielberg, quoted in McBride, *Steven Spielberg: A Biography*, 50–1.

Cecil B. DeMille's circus drama *The Greatest Show on Earth* (1952) adopted a documentary-style structure, with a narrator revealing the inner workings of the circus over the course of one year, but much of the story was focused on backstage drama. A young Charlton Heston played the leader of the P. T. Barnum and the Ringling brothers travelling circus, and at the start of the film, Cecil B. DeMille himself appeared on stage to tell audiences:

> We bring you the circus – that Pied Piper whose magic tunes lead children of all ages, from six to sixty, into a tinseled and spun-candied world of reckless beauty and mounting laughter; whirling thrills; of rhythm, excitement and grace; of daring, enflaring and dance; of high-stepping horses and high-flying stars.

Steven Spielberg may have found the movie disappointing, not least because it still very much focused on adults and their concerns, but DeMille's opening monologue tells us something about his presumed audience. As the title suggests, *The Greatest Show on Earth* aimed to be more than just a movie. Instead, it was a grand spectacle, calibrated to provide audiences of all ages with an experience not dissimilar from that of a real circus.

Although they would go on to become the most influential filmmakers of the post-war period, making movies grounded in a fascination with cinema history, Lucas's and Spielberg's early experiences were fairly typical. Like many boomers, they grew up in an era defined by movies, particularly movies shown on television, but they rarely visited the downtown, first-run movie palaces that had been regular haunts for earlier generations of Americans. Instead, they were far more likely to watch movies on television, or at low-cost drive-ins. A trip to the most prestigious movie theatres was an occasional treat, even if the movie itself failed to inspire. They were part of the audience that was slipping out of Hollywood's grip at the start of the 1950s.

This chapter focuses on the early moviegoing experiences of the baby boom generation. We ask what moviegoing choices were available to children in the 1950s and what were the most common experiences? We start by looking at movie theatres themselves, then move on to television and finally discuss the emergence of drive-ins and the financial problems associated with the baby boom audience.

Theatrical viewing, from roadshowing to the matinee

After his early disappointment with *The Greatest Show on Earth*, Steven Spielberg became a more committed movie fan, attending matinees at the Kiva Theatre in Scottsdale, where cartoons, B-movies and 1930s serials would be shown alongside modern movies reaching the tail end of their runs. He also regularly visited the Round-Up Drive-In with his parents, and occasionally took in the classier, prestige blockbuster of the day. Spielberg was particularly affected by the films of David Lean, whom he would describe as 'the greatest influence I ever had'.[3] One Phoenix schoolmate clearly remembers Spielberg showing up to class 'promoting *Bridge on the River Kwai* as the greatest movie ever made because of its stupendous action scenes'. In 1990, he told the American Film Institute that Lean's movies 'made me want to be a filmmaker. The scope and audacity of those films filled my dreams with unlimited possibilities.'

As ever, Spielberg's experience of moviegoing was fairly typical. Boomers occasionally saw the biggest films on prestigious first-run or roadshow engagements, but more commonly caught movies further down the food chain, especially at Saturday morning matinees. In our survey, respondent 482 fondly recalled 'the once a year movies, like *The Ten Commandments* and musicals,' while respondent 192 'also loved the local theater Saturday kids' matinees – a double feature mostly attended by kids only'.

Hollywood's most obvious response to the decline in audiences at the start of the 1950s was to reduce the volume of film productions. In 1948, the major studios released 488 movies between them. In 1952, this had reduced to 253, and by 1963, the number of annual film releases from the major studios hit 142.[4] Despite calls from theatre chains to maintain or increase product volume, the studios consistently reduced the number of films in production, citing 'a lack of acceptable scripts or personnel' as the chief cause.[5] In reality, the combination of declining audiences, the exhibition and ownership complexities introduced by antitrust and rising production costs encouraged the major studios to focus their production budgets on fewer, more expensive movies, which, it was hoped, could command a higher ticket price than conventional releases. We will discuss the nature of these and other releases in the next chapter, but the implications for audiences were dramatic. Within the first few years of the 1950s, the volume of product flowing through movie theatres of all sizes declined, ownership of those theatres was taken on by new national chains and the industry began to privilege the sort of expensive, spectacular movies that performed well in prestigious first-run theatres, where the majors still earned the majority of their revenues.[6] The number of regular movie theatres in the United States declined, from 16,904 in 1950, to 12,291 in 1960, and, worst of all, overall box office takings fell by over $400 million, from $1.3 billion in 1950, to

[3]This and the following statements by Spielberg are quoted in McBride, *Steven Spielberg*, 82.
[4]Finler, *The Hollywood Story*, 364–5.
[5]Anon., 'Prods. Could – If They Would', *Variety*, 24 November 1954, 3.
[6]Sheldon Hall and Steve Neale, *Epics, Spectacles, and Blockbusters: A Hollywood History* (Detroit: Wayne State University Press, 2010), 136–40.

$951 million in 1960.[7] In effect, the decline in audiences that stymied the industry at the end of the 1940s had exactly the effect that studios feared – the revenue potential and cultural reach of the movie industry declined. Only the biggest, most expensive movies had any sort of impact.

In 1954, Lornan Granant, who owned the only theatre in the tiny town of LeRoy, Minnesota, appealed for support from parents by promoting moviegoing as a wholesome activity for their kids. 'If we are going to close,' he wrote in the *LeRoy Independent*, 'where are your children going to spend their evenings? Out on the highways in automobiles or visiting places where you do not want them to be.'[8] In effect, *Variety* observed, Granant 'told the town's mothers and fathers that by remaining away from his showhouse they may drive their children into delinquency'.[9] Granant, like many others, knew that his patrons were staying away as they started to have kids, but according to Walter Reade Jr., president of the National Association of Theater Owners (NATO), producers in the 1950s did not fully understand the problems facing exhibitors. 'They are not getting accurate or reliable information from distribution,' he told a meeting of executives at RKO studios, 'and do not sincerely seek or want it'.[10] As far as Reade and others were concerned, the growing gap between the concerns of producers and the experiences of exhibitors meant that Hollywood was becoming increasingly disconnected from the entertainment needs of a changing audience, which Reade felt required more family films. Hollywood hit back that profits were not sufficient to sustain further investment. One unnamed executive told *Variety*, 'These are not the days when we can afford to make films for a comparatively small sector of our audience. The best we can do is hope to make better pictures that have wider appeal in every respect.'[11] In fact, the baby boom meant that children, and their parents, already constituted the largest demographic group in the United States, but they were still viewed as a 'small sector' of the audience. Concerns over the viability of the studios' output were shared across the exhibition sector, although Hollywood's response did little to assuage the concerns of rural theatre owners.

Rather than focusing on conventional family product, movies like *Samson and Delilah* (1949), *Quo Vadis* (1951), *The Ten Commandments* (1956), *Ben-Hur* (1959) and *Lawrence of Arabia* (1963) became a constituent element of Hollywood's production schedules – spectacular, epic movies which warranted high rentals fees from exhibitors and worked well on the biggest screens, at the best theatres. Almost all of these movies were treated

---

[7]Lev, *The Fifties*, 304.

[8]Lornan Granant, quoted in Anon., 'Lectures Townspeople in Film Benefits', *Variety*, 13 January 1954, 11.

[9]Granant, quoted in Anon., 'Lectures Townspeople', 11.

[10]Hy Hollinger, 'Studios Aloof to Exhib Grief', *Variety*, 10 March 1954, 7.

[11]Anon., 'Little Family Features too Costly, Say Distribs', *Variety*, 24 November 1954, 3.

IMAGE 3 *Epic scale and spectacle in* Ben-Hur *(1959).*

to a form of 'roadshow' release, which meant that they were subject to a 'two a day, upped admission policy' at the most expensive city centre theatres, where they might run for months or even years on 'special engagements'.[12] Roadshowing packaged cinemagoing as a special, occasional experience for all the family and so fitted neatly with the changing geographical and familial situation of the audience. A visit to a big roadshow epic at a prestigious theatre was an occasional cinematic treat for many young baby boomers.

For the major studios, roadshowing was 'the only way left to recoup production costs', and the number of high-budget epics in circulation increased as the roadshow 'habit' of paying more for semi-annual cinema trips overtook more regular viewing, at least for some sectors of the audience.[13] By the end of the 1950s, a relatively small number of highly budgeted movies were frequently earning a disproportionate share of box office revenues.[14] Thus, the movie 'blockbuster' was born.[15] Roadshowing, and the concomitant rise of more spectacular, expensive movies, was therefore an attempt to capture the burgeoning audience of young families who might be drawn back from the suburbs into city centres for a standout release. High-budget movies were sold to exhibitors at a higher rental rate than conventional releases, and their 'must see' status allowed the big studios to retain some control of the exhibition sector even as antitrust legislation played out.

However, spectacular epics did not totally supersede 'normal' genre releases of all kinds, and a 'normal' cinematic experience was still very much

---

[12]Anon., 'More Roadshows to Lick Costs', *Variety*, 9 July 1947, 3.
[13]Anon, 'More Roadshows', 3.
[14]James Russell, 'Debts, Disasters and Mega-Musicals: The Decline of the Studio System', in Linda Ruth Williams and Michael Hammond, eds, *Contemporary American Cinema: US Cinema since 1960* (New York: McGraw-Hill, 2006), 58.
[15]For more on the origins of the term 'Blockbuster', see Hall and Neale, *Epics, Spectacles, and Blockbusters*, 139.

part of 1950s culture, particularly for children. Aside from occasional family trips, young baby boomers were most likely to visit a regular movie theatre as part of a weekend matinee performance. In our survey, for example, respondent 267 'seldom missed a Saturday', recalling that the 'cost was only 9 cents until you turned 13'. Throughout the first half of the twentieth century, 'the children's matinee constituted the most common specialized use of traditional theater'.[16] On Saturday mornings across the United States, Junior Matinees and Junior Motion Pictures Clubs dominated regional movie theatres. Many were coordinated by regional exhibition chains, like the 'Krazy Kat Club' and 'Mickey Mouse Club' in California, or the 'Radio Patrol' in Chicago.[17] For a few cents in admission, each offered a diverse schedule of entertainment, usually including a cartoon, a serial, shorts and a 'child-friendly' feature.

After 1946, matinees were supported by the Children's Film Library, an initiative established by the Motion Picture Association of America (MPAA) which made 'significant family films from all the leading Hollywood studios since the early 1930s available to exhibitors for use in Saturday Matinee shows'.[18] As a result, matinees screened a diverse array of movies, often from the 1930s and 1940s, alongside current releases, but for many young boomers in the audience, the appeal of the matinee was not necessarily dependent on the movies being shown. The writer/director Phil Alden Robinson recalls:

> I remember sometimes going to Saturday matinees, because they would show kids movies on Saturday matinees, but I don't remember a whole lot of what they were. We were more interested in playing baseball and watching television.

Alternatively, writer/director Nancy Meyers, who grew up in the suburbs of Pennsylvania, remembers the ritual of moviegoing much more than the content:

> Here's how the day went: we would stop at the candy store which was doors down and we'd buy a bag of penny candy. It was just very fun. And this candy store was half candy and half bicycles and the bikes were up on the wall, so our parents would take us there to buy bikes, but also they sold candy, so primarily to me it was candy. So we'd buy candy, go to the movies, and then we'd go to the other side of the movie theater for pizza, and that was when our mom would pick us up.

---

[16]Gomery, *Shared Pleasures*, 138.
[17]Ibid., 138.
[18]Brown, *The Hollywood Family Film*, 88.

Taken together, the inexpensive once-a-week matinee, and the highly expensive, occasional trip to a prestigious city centre movie theatre represented the twin poles of many boomers' formative moviegoing experiences, and neatly illustrate Hollywood's shifting priorities in the 1950s. Both were tried and tested strategies that had been in use for many years, and both proved adaptive to changing attendance patterns. However, the baby boomers were the first generation in many decades whose viewing choices were expanding to include new arenas where movies might be consumed. While Hollywood looked for ways to draw audiences back to the traditional movie theatre, audience were enjoying more opportunities to consume Hollywood product than ever before, most notably in the home.

Television

As early as 1949, before television ownership became the norm, writer/director Claude Binyon, in a piece for the *Motion Picture Herald*, voiced concerns over cinema's ability to unify, and hold onto, viewers of all ages:

> Fourteen months ago the Binyon household acquired a television receiver. It became a custom for the family to cluster around the television set, and to stay there if an important sports event or public ceremony were being televised.
>
> All this was the normal reaction to a novelty but as the months wore on, it was observed that the clustering was constant and that the family did not break up but remained in one place, as a unit, throughout the programme period.
>
> He concluded, and not without considerable artistic reluctance, that the motion picture screen must be provided with product as family wide in appeal and interest as that provided by television if the theatre is going to survive the competition for family unit attention that television is certain to offer.[19]

This article, and many others, identified television viewing as a compulsive family activity, and stressed the need for movies that might capture family viewers. Instead, as Hollywood suffered, companies involved in television manufacture, sales and channel ownership all benefitted enormously from the baby boom. As a result, television played a defining role in the cultural life of the boomers. NBC chief Brandon Tartikoff once said, 'Television itself is a baby boomer, it's a baby boom instrument. The baby boom generation

---

[19]William R. Weaver, 'Family appeal Vital to Combat Video: Binyon', *Motion Picture Herald*, 5 February 1949, 35.

has never known an environment where there wasn't a television.'[20] According to the writer director Joe Dante, television played a vital part in his experience of 1950s America:

> My nostalgia [for the 1950s] stems from the fact that I was not an adult then. If I'd been an adult in the 1950s I might have felt stifled, but the 1950s happened to be the best time to be a kid ever. It was after the war, the culture was child-centred, there were all these inventions to make your life better, the media was burgeoning, there was a lot of attention to children's programming on TV, and even adult programming wasn't unsuitable for children.[21]

The film industry had a complex relationship with television. Banned from direct involvement by the 1948 antitrust ruling, during the late 1940s and early 1950s the film industry equivocated between seeing television as a valuable forum for promoting its products (as radio had been) and as a direct threat which would steal away movie audiences. Both views were correct. As the 1950s rolled on, television became established and profits from movies continued to decline. In 1947, Warner Bros recorded net profits of $22 million, but by 1953 this figure had fallen to $2.9 million.[22]

In fits and starts, most of the major film studios developed a workable, lucrative relationship with the television industry by the mid-1950s, although profits from movie theatres remained central to the studios' business model. Filmed material replaced live broadcasts as the dominant form of television content by the middle of the decade, and most of the major studios established production units devoted to shooting television movies and serials.[23] In April 1951, the *Hollywood Reporter* argued that west coast television stations alone required more product than the entire theatrical exhibition sector:

> TV stations in LA are now using filmed product at the rate of nearly 5000 shows per year, counting openly films running a quarter hour or longer. This is equivalent to more than five times the annual output of Hollywood features and shorts combined which means that if video stations used only current product they would have to run each picture five times in order to get by under present output and consumption. The

---

[20]Brandon Tartikoff, quoted in Light, *Baby Boomers*, 41.
[21]Quoted in Bill Krohn, 'I, Robby: The Secret Life of Joe Dante', in Bill Krohn and Jonathan Rosenbaum, eds, *A Gremlin in Hollywood: Joe Dante in Context*, July 1999 (unpublished ms limited to four copies), 149, in 'Joe Dante' file, AMPAS Margaret Herrick library.
[22]Christopher Anderson, *Hollywood TV: The Studio System in the Fifties* (Austin: University of Texas Press, 1994), 2.
[23]Anderson, *Hollywood TV*, 14.

present rate of consumption by no means represents a saturation point here, according to video program executives, but actually is limited by the availability and cost of product.[24]

In a separate report, the paper noted that the 'seven television stations in LA now are showing 273 hours of film weekly', which made up 58 per cent of the total on-air programming.[25] It was not long before Hollywood provided the majority of pre-recorded content shown by television networks.

All of this means that, in broad terms, the Hollywood studios were reaching the baby boomers and their parents. If anything, the baby boomers consumed more filmed entertainment than any previous generation. But boomers grew up watching old movies at home, or watching Hollywood-produced television serials like *Dragnet* (NBC, 1951–9) or *Father Knows Best* (CBS, 1954–5, 1958–60, NBC, 1955–8). Historian Paul C. Light has claimed that 'by the time the average baby boomer had reached age sixteen, he or she had watched from 12,000 to 15,000 hours of TV'.[26] For Steven Spielberg, the influence of television has been almost total, 'I was and still am a TV junkie. I've just grown up with TV, all of us have, and there's a lot of TV in my brain that I wish I could get out of there. You can't help it – once it's in there, it's like a tattoo.'[27]

One of the most influential figures on the television landscape was Walt Disney. As Christopher Anderson observes, 'Unlike many who groped for a response to the dramatic changes that swept the movie industry following World War II, Walt Disney and his brother Roy answered uncertainty with a calculated plan for diversification.'[28] The pair planned to 'transform the Disney studio from an independent producer of feature films and cartoon short-subjects into a diversified leisure and entertainment corporation'.[29] Television would come to form a key pillar of Disney's operation, because it offered 'unparalleled access to a family audience that [Disney] had cultivated more effectively than any Hollywood producer', providing 'the surest route to the lucrative baby boom market'.[30]

The putative television network ABC 'especially valued series that might appeal to the growing demographic of what one ABC executive called "youthful families", and thought Disney, with its appeal to those families,

---

[24]Anon., '5000 Films Yearly on TV Here', *Hollywood Reporter*, 9 July 1951, 1.
[25]Anon., 'Films Fill 50 pct. of TV Time', *Hollywood Reporter*, 3 July 1951, 1.
[26]Light, *Baby Boomers*, 15.
[27]Steven Spielberg, quoted in McBride, *Steven Spielberg*, 62.
[28]Christopher Anderson, 'Disneyland', in Horace Newcomb, ed., *Television: The Critical View* (6th ed.; Oxford: Oxford University Press, 2000), 19.
[29]Anderson, *Hollywood TV*, 20.
[30]Ibid., 19.

was a perfect match for ABC'.[31] In 1954 ABC paid $2 million for twenty
episodes of a show that Disney called *Disneyland*, and purchased a 35
per cent share in Disney's theme park plans for a further $500,000. The
resulting programme was relatively simple for Disney to produce. Its format
involved Disney himself introducing animated shorts from the company's
back catalogue alongside a handful of specially commissioned live action
pieces, such as four episodes focused on frontier hero Davy Crockett in
1955 that were subsequently edited together and released in theatres as
Davy Crockett: King of the Wild Frontier (1955). These segments were
interspersed with behind-the-scenes features about Disney's forthcoming
theatrical productions, and information about the ongoing construction of
the Disneyland theme park in Anaheim, California. For Disney himself, the
show's primary purpose was to ensure funding for, and consumer interest in,
the park, or, as he later joked, 'ABC needed the television show so bad, they
bought the amusement park.'[32] Nonetheless, the show stood as a colossal
hit in its own right.

Disneyland 'delivered viewers like no programme in ABC history' and was
'viewed weekly in nearly 40% of the nation's 26 million TV households'.[33] As
a result it became ABC's most valuable asset in terms of advertising revenue
and encouraged the network to forge a further partnership in the form of
The Mickey Mouse Club in 1955, a magazine programme featuring boomer
children (or 'Mouseketeers') performing alongside prerecorded serials and
variety acts. The show aired on weekday afternoons, after schools had
finished, and quickly came to match *Disneyland* both in its popularity with
boomer audiences, and value for the network.

Disneyland and the *Mickey Mouse Club* served a vital role in familiarizing
young people with Disney's releases, but they also offered a site where movies
and moviemaking were presented to, and discussed by, young people. As a
consequence of appearing so frequently on his shows, Walt Disney became
'the most widely recognised filmmaker in the world', and he was able to
speak directly to a young audience about the 'magic' of moviemaking.[34]
In effect, by exposing the production processes of Disney films and other
ventures, his shows helped to foster an interest in the movies themselves that
television could address in other ways. Just as Disney relied on prereleased
material to sustain *Disneyland*, television also quickly came to constitute the
primary site where baby boomers were able to watch older movies.

Initially the studios resisted licensing their movies to be screened on
television, partly in response to pressure from movie theatre owners, partly

[31]Gabler, *Walt Disney*, 597.
[32]Ibid., 505.
[33]Anderson, 'Hollywood TV', 26.
[34]Gabler, *Walt Disney*, 513.

because the old movies did have some value as potential theatrical rereleases and partly because no one really knew how much the movies were worth as television screenings. The first studios to embrace television sales were minor players such as Monogram and Republic, who made over 4,000 movies available for television in 1950, including Gene Autry's westerns and science fiction serials like *Flash Gordon*. However, the rest of the studios held out, although Dick Williams, writing in the *Los Angeles Mirror* in 1950, recognized that the studios had a narrow window to avoid losing further ground to the television networks:

> It looks as if it is now or never for the film companies to start releasing their own back product for television showing. Because soon the big networks will be engaged in making their own pictures here and the great demand of video stations for full length features will not be nearly as great as it is at present.[35]

In 1955, the producer David Selznick bluntly declared, 'When television is willing to pay more than the amount made in reissues, then we will go into television.'[36] That same year, the industry-wide impasse was broken when Howard Hughes sold his ownership of RKO Studios to the General Tyre and Rubber Company, who in turn sold the rights to screen a block of RKO's pre-1948 releases to the C&C Television Corporation. By 1958, C&C claimed to have made over $25 million from licensing alone – more than it paid for the entirety of RKO's holdings – and all of the other major studios had similar arrangements.[37] Pre-1948 movies quickly came to make up the majority of content shown on many television networks across the United States.

As a result, boomers could watch many, many movies on television, but they were almost all from the 1930s and 1940s – much like the Saturday matinee schedules at small-town movie theatres. Many boomers became cinephiles as a result – but they did so mainly through exposure to an older film culture, and the movies of the 1950s and early 1960s seem to have meant much less to them, at least in relative terms. Writing for the *New York Times* in 1963, Hollis Alpert described the overwhelming volume of movies that circulated on television screens:

> At home it has been possible to see a simply fantastic number of old movies: no fewer than 7500 made in Hollywood before 1948; approximately

---

[35]Dick Williams, 'Editorial', *Los Angeles Mirror*, 18 May 1951, in 'Films Shown on Television,' file, AMPAS Margaret Herrick library.
[36]Selznick quoted in William Boddy, *Fifties Television: The Industry and Its Critics* (Chicago: University of Illinois Press, 1993), 135.
[37]Boddy, *Fifties Television*, 136.

1000 British films; another 700 made in foreign languages and dubbed into English and close to 2000 post-1948 movies made by American producers abroad. If movie theaters have suffered because of this spate of films on television, an additional effect has been to make movie addicts of a new generation.[38]

Certainly this fascination with old movies is clearly reflected in our survey. Respondent 144 vividly remembers 'seeing *Casablanca* on TV and being fascinated; it is still my all-time favorite film', while respondent 67 recalls:

I watched a lot of movies on TV. I remember watching old B&W movies on our local station in the morning (if there was no school), heavily edited movies on TV after school, cut down to fit a 90-minute slot with commercials, and 'Family Classics' on WGN-TV on Sundays (a library of about 30 movies that they repeated annually for at least ten years).

In similar fashion, respondent 212 remembers mostly clearly watching 'the B-list stuff that got put on TV during the day. I remember lots of WW2 movies'. The academic writer Alan Nadel (b.1947) felt that these older movies permeated life for the boomers:

Long before my parents took me to see my first movie, I had seen countless movies at home on television. Watching movies became not only ordinary – in that movies chronically occupied the only real living space our apartment afforded – but also integral to our family life. Hepburn or Bogart, Errol Flynn or Fay Wray were present for our meals, and they spoke to me while I did my homework.[39]

For many filmmakers, the pervasiveness of older movies on television defined their early education in cinema. Phil Alden Robinson recalls:

My first exposure to great movies was on television. In New York City – we had the New York City television channel – there were three network stations, and then there were four or five independent stations, and they tended to run either local programming, or old movies. Literally all day and night you could watch these things. There was always a black and white movie on. Always.

One of the most fondly remembered methods of presenting movies was the show *Million Dollar Movie*, first run by the independent WOR-TV Channel 9

---

[38]Hollis Alpert, 'Now the Earlier, Earlier Show', *New York Times Magazine*, 11 August 1963, 22.
[39]Alan Nadel, *Flatlining on the Field of Dreams* (Durham: Rutgers, 1997), ix.

in New York State in 1955, and then adopted by other independent local stations across the United States. Channel 9 found that they could effectively compete with the larger national networks (and their affiliates) by screening movies every evening over the course of a week. The *Million Dollar Movie* was always a 1930s or 1940s studio picture, never shown on television before (initially drawn from the RKO library), which ran at the same time every night for a week. The first movie shown was William Wellman's 1947 political comedy *Magic Town*, and as the years passed, well-regarded movies such as *Citizen Kane* (1941) and *King Kong* (1933) featured in the slot, alongside a host of otherwise forgotten comedies, musicals and dramas from across the classical era.

It is hard to overestimate the importance of *Million Dollar Movie* and other television screenings for the young boomers, many of whom were far more influenced by their exposure to television than by their occasional visits to the movie theatre. By screening movies repeatedly, night after night, *Million Dollar Movie* didn't just expose the young boomers to a broad range of classic movies, it also allowed them to study those movies, to view them repeatedly and obsessively. As a result, baby boomers were more likely to be conversant with old movies than with current releases. The producer Sean Daniels felt that 'TV was for watching black and white movies, for *Million Dollar Movie*, and a movie would play all week – I'll never forget it'. Or, in the words of Phil Alden Robinson:

> *Million Dollar Movie* was on every night on channel 9, and they would show one movie every night for a week. And often it was *Mighty Joe Young* [1949] or *Yankee Doodle Dandy* [1942], the wonderful James Cagney musical. But you could watch it for a week. *An Affair to Remember* [1957] – I remember that would be on for a whole week, and you'd watch it over and over again.

Across America, children found, in *Million Dollar Movie*, a way to engage with movies unlike anything they might find at movie theatres. Screenwriter Jack Epps Jr put it like this:

> In terms of growing up in Detroit, and especially in the 1950s, what was so different then was you only had three channels, and in Detroit we had four – because we had the Winsor Channel – so it was really great, one extra channel. And what was playing on Winsor was basically a lot of old movies. So we had a channel almost devoted to running old films, because in the early 1950s what they put on television was movies, because they were cheap. So I was raised watching a lot of the 1930s and 1940s movies, just as a kid, and they were black and white movies because there was no colour. So that's what you watched.

Million Dollar Movie was joined by an upscale cousin in 1961, when NBC debuted its *Saturday Night at the Movies* slot, with a big, post-1948 release, *How to Marry a Millionaire* (1953), screened in colour.[40]

As a result of these regular screenings, movies also came to constitute significant family viewing rituals – *It's a Wonderful Life* and *The Wizard of Oz*, neither of which were successful at the box office on first release, found a colossal national audience when they were regularly repeated at Christmastime. Before *Saturday Night at the Movies*, the networks were unwilling to screen movies during primetime, but CBS made an exception for *The Wizard of Oz* in 1957, which became one of the network's most viewed television events.[41] Today these movies have taken on a cultural significance for boomers and their families that vastly outweighs their initial impact at the box office.

In our survey, *The Wizard of Oz* was one of the most commonly mentioned films, with respondent 27 remembering that 'we had the 1st color television in the neighborhood, so everyone came to our house to watch *The Wizard of Oz* so they could see the color in Munchkinland', and respondent 95 remembering that 'we planned the evening around it'. In total, eighty-seven respondents identified the television screenings of *The Wizard of Oz* as a feature of their childhood, with respondent 144 confidently reminding us that 'of course I loved *The Wizard of Oz*'. The movie's primacy in American culture is due almost entirely to its impact as a small screen experience of the baby boomers, rather than its reception in the 1930s. Furthermore, the combination of fantasy, escapism, spectacle and terror in the movie (respondent 212 recalls that 'the flying monkeys scared the hell out of me' when they first saw it aged 6) has arguably had a fairly significant impact on the filmmaking preferences of the baby boom generation. Producer director Ivan Reitman told us, 'I remember seeing *The Wizard of Oz* very early, even though that was from many years before, and by the time I was ten years old, the two kinds of movies that I loved were horror movies and comedies.' For Reitman, and for many others, the movie existed in a continuum of classic musicals, B-movies, noir and horror that defined their understanding of entertainment, at least on television.

Horror in particular was a genre that had a powerful influence on many boomers, who first encountered Universal's classic horror movies on television. Sean Daniel, who would go on to produce the 1996 remake of *The Mummy*, recalls sitting through the *Million Dollar Movie* theme music (actually 'Tara's Theme' from *Gone with the Wind* – another link to 1930s film classics), before he could watch '*Gorgo* [1961] and *The Giant*

---

[40]Douglas Gomery and Clara Pafort-Overduin, *Movie History: A Survey* (London: Routledge, 2011), 247.
[41]Boddy, *Fifties Television*, 139.

Behemoth [1959] and *The Mummy* [1932] and everything I just loved'. In our survey, respondent 320 noted that as a child, 'horror movies were my favorite – *Frankenstein, Dracula, The Mummy*'. Respondent 41 preferred 'scary movies – the Universal movies', and remembered 'these were shown on TV on Saturday nights, and I'd watch with friends at slumber parties'. Respondent 107 was blunt, '*Dracula, Frankenstein, Bride of Frankenstein* [1935]. Horror movies don't get better than them.'

The dominance of horror and also science fiction (in the form of Republic serials) as a home viewing choice was also visible in a new kind of cinematic experience that reached the baby boomers with a degree of success that evaded more conventional movie theatres – the drive-in, where old movies, and B-movie genres like horror and science fiction, thrived.

Drive-ins

Drive-in theatres were known in the trade as 'ozoners', and for many baby boomers, the drive-in was a quintessential part of their formative moviegoing experiences. While they rarely played the most prestigious movies, and received scant support from the major distributors, they nonetheless represented an attempt to reconfigure the cinemagoing experience for suburban families. Like television, these new moviegoing options played an important role in shaping the boomer's experience of movies and moviegoing. For example, survey respondent 256 saw '*Gone with the Wind* at the drive-in with my parents and fell in love with historical dramas and grand narratives'.

While the number of traditional movie theatres in the United States declined from 16,904 in 1950 to 12,291 in 1960, drive-ins boomed during the 1950s, growing from 2,200 sites to 4,700.[42] For the most part, drive-ins were constructed by independent entrepreneurs, such as Robert L. Lippert, a developer who owned numerous drive-ins up and down the West Coast. The established studios treated drive-ins with some disdain, which may have been rooted in a sense that the drive-in provided its customers with an inferior, downmarket experience. Patrons of drive-in theatres would view movies through their windshield, on a screen that was notably inferior to that of a conventional theatre. Sound came through speakers that clipped onto the edge of the car window.

However, drive-ins were successful in the 1950s precisely because they seemed to solve one of the key problems facing the industry – they offered a convenient arena for suburban boomer families (and teens with cars) to watch movies. Peter Lev claims that drive-ins were often situated on

---

[42]Lev, *The Fifties*, 212.

'newly developed suburban areas where open land was still available'.[43] In effect, they could be constructed quickly on cheap tracts of land closer to a relatively captive audience than downtown movie theatres. In his history of American moviegoing, *Shared Pleasures*, Douglas Gomery explicitly makes the link between suburbia and the drive-ins:

> With little suburban growth in the 1930s, and none during the Second World War, the number of drive-ins in 1945 stood at less than twenty five theaters. The [subsequent] development of the drive-in was an American phenomenon because of the huge demand for auto-convenient movie exhibition by the millions of new suburbanites from coast to coast. By 1952, average attendance at drive-ins had grown to nearly four million patrons per week.[44]

In fact, drive-ins were successful because they catered to a mobile audience, rather than because they were springing up at the heart of modern suburbs. The majority of drive-ins built in the early part of the 1950s were located on the edge of small towns and in other rural areas – usually because the real estate value of suitable land for suburban development on the outskirts of cities had been driven beyond what drive-in operators could reasonably afford by the boom in suburban construction itself.[45]

Like so many trends of the period, drive-ins were anecdotally associated in the public mind with teens, a point made by Peter Lev, who notes in his history of the 1950s that while they attracted the family trade, they 'were even more attractive to teenage audiences'.[46] It seems likely that the importance of the teenage audience has been overestimated in relation to drive-ins (although they were certainly part of the audience), and that families dominated drive-in ticket sales. (Gary Rhodes has suggested that drive-ins only became dominated by teenagers in the 1960s, when the actual numbers of outdoor theatres were declining.)[47] Nonetheless, survey respondent 210 recalls, 'When I was in high school (1965–8), the drive-in theater was a popular dating activity. I remember few of the movies.'

In a profile of Robert L. Lippert, and various other drive-in operators, a 1956 article in the *Saturday Evening Post* observed, 'In nine out of ten cars you'll see young children asleep on the back seat and on the floor. That's why the ozoners are going over big. The drive-in movie is the answer to the sitter problem and to the downtown parking problem. It's the answer to

---

[43]Ibid., 212.
[44]Gomery, *Shared Pleasures*, 91.
[45]Paul Monaco, *The Sixties* (Berkeley: University of California Press, 2003), 46.
[46]Lev, *The Fifties*, 215.
[47]Gary D. Rhodes, 'Introduction', in Gary D. Rhodes, ed., *Horror at the Drive-In: Essays in Popular Americana* (Jefferson, NC: McFarlane, 2003), 6.

the young family's night out. It's the neighbourhood theater of the future.'[48] The article went on to profile the owner/operator of 'The Starlite Drive-In theatre on Highway 20 southwest of Chicago', Stanford Kohlberg, and described his operation in detail:

> Admission for adults is $1.25; youngsters under twelve, as many as can be packed in the car, are free, and each gets a door prize. The $1.25 pays for a movie, for dancing under the stars to music from name bands. It includes free milk for babies and free diapers if young mothers forget them. Kohlberg has a kiddie-land for youngsters too small to be interested in cinema drama. He has a miniature golf course and driving range for anyone in the family not interested in the picture.
>
> 'Parents know their youngsters won't wind up in a beer hall,' says Kohlberg, 'We don't even sell alcoholic drinks. The drive-in is the answer to the problem of wholesome amusement for the teenager.'[49]

However, the *Saturday Evening Post* claimed that 'the passion pit problem seems to have resolved itself. The bulk of the patrons are young couples with children', and it quoted Ralph Smitha, proprietor of another Chicago ozoner, who claimed, 'The drive-in attracts brand new movie patrons: young families with children.' Certainly our survey bears this out. For some, like respondent 234, the drive-in formed a primal cinema memory, 'The first movie I remember is *Elephant Walk* [1954] at the drive-in. My parents took us all hoping we would sleep in the car while they watched the movie.' According to respondent 191, 'Almost all my childhood family movie experiences involved drive-in movies. The main thing I remember from these is playing with other kids on the playground beneath the screen, most of us in our pajamas.' Respondent 192 recalls that 'family drive-in nights were great', and, like many of our survey participants, saw the drive-in as a family experience.

Douglas Gomery has made a similar case for treating the drive-in as an environment tailored to the boomers and their families:

> Some drive-ins took direct aim at the suburban family with an ever-growing number of young children by tendering free passes to parents of newborns up to three months of age. Many drive-ins passed out free milk. Children age twelve and below nearly always were admitted free. … What fantasies it held – for teens desperate for a little privacy or for a family hungry for a cheap night of fun – had little to do with the

---

[48]Frank J. Taylor, 'Big Boom in Outdoor Movies', *Saturday Evening Post*, 15 September 1956, 31 and 100 in 'Drive-Ins' file, AMPAS Margaret Herrick library.
[49]Taylor, 'Big Boom', 101 (all subsequent quotations).

movie-viewing experience. The lone attraction of the drive-in seemed to be that it was cheap entertainment for baby boom families wanting the occasional night out – two dollars a car for whoever could squeeze in. The slogan for Pacific Theaters' Southern California customers became: 'Come as you are in the family car.'[50]

Drive-ins, then, can be understood as a concerted effort to reach baby boomers and their families, and they were successful. By the early 1960s, one out of every five viewers was watching a movie at a drive-in.[51]

However, Hollywood continued to treat the drive-ins with some equivocation, and frequently resisted releasing mainstream movies to the drive-in sector, which quickly came to occupy a position at the bottom of the runs system. 'Since drive-in theaters did have problems getting new quality products,' writes Gary D. Rhodes, 'they opened their arms to B-movies.'[52] Meanwhile, Eric Mark Kramer remembered, 'The fancy movies limp into the drive-in worn and tattered if at all, to be projected on the drive-in screen, arising majestically from the midst of corn, soybean and wheat fields.'[53] According to Kerry Seagrave, 'The times that a drive-in would play a first run film from a major studio would always remain relatively rare. Ozoners would always feature distinctly different programming from that shown at indoor houses.'[54] As we will see in the next chapter, this 'different programming' was drawn primarily from independent producers specializing in low-budget exploitation movies: horror, science fiction, rock and roll movies, sensational juvenile delinquent pictures and others. According to Phil Hardy, 'By all accounts, more Science Fiction films were played at drive-in theaters (the growth of which in the fifties coincided directly with the science fiction boom) than were films of any other genre.'[55]

Why did studios resist releasing movies at drive-ins? Why was the bulk of the industry disdainful of a phenomenon that clearly did reconnect with the increasingly 'lost' boomer audience? To some extent, film exhibitors were deterred by resistance from the established indoor theatre chains, who wanted to maintain their dominance in an increasingly restricted market, and so pressured the studios to deal warily with the drive-ins. It is also possible that production executives and high-level creative personnel didn't

---

[50]Gomery, *Shared Pleasures*, 92–3.

[51]Ibid., 91.

[52]Rhodes, 'Introduction', 2.

[53]Eric Mark Kramer, 'Who's Afraid of the Virgin Wolf Man', in Rhodes, *Horror at the Drive-In*, 20.

[54]Kerry Seagrave, *Drive-In Theatres: A History from their Inception in 1933* (Jefferson, NC: McFarlane, 1992), 59.

[55]Phil Hardy, 'Introduction,' in Phil Hardy, ed., *Aurum Film Encyclopedia of Science Fiction* (London: Aurum, 1983), xiv.

see the drive-in theatre as a sufficiently prestigious exhibition site, suitable for the industry's A product.

However, the dominant reason why Hollywood exhibited strong ambivalence towards the drive-in theatre is fairly simple. Drive-ins captured the family audience by keeping ticket prices very low, and instead, relied on concession sales and profits from other ventures, from dry cleaning to barbecue, in order to maintain profitability (Douglas Gomery estimates that 'by 1955, drive-ins sold around four times as much popcorn, candy and soft drinks as the average indoor theater').[56] This meant that the drive-in returned significantly less revenue to exhibitors than other theatres, and so drive-ins occupied a position at the very bottom of the system of runs and clearances that continued to dictate studios release strategies throughout the 1950s and 1960s. They were not anywhere near as profitable for the studios as the audience attending first-run theatres, and so the audience at drive-ins (young families) was not treated as anywhere near as important as the audience at first-run theatres – whoever they may have been. The curious status of the drive-in theatres – which explicitly targeted boomers and their parents – reveals clearly why Hollywood never exploited child and family viewers to the fullest possible extent.

Conclusion

We will see in the next chapter that Hollywood already saw children as a small, relatively unimportant subset of a much larger audience that could be addressed with broadly appealing genre movies. Unfortunately, the demographic structures and audience attendance habits that underpinned these assumptions were, as we have seen, undergoing dramatic change. For Leonard Maltin, who would grow up to become one of the most well-regarded movie critics of his generation, moviegoing in 1950s New Jersey involved watching old movies, at cheap matinee performances:

I was a graduate of the last generation, as far as I can tell, of Saturday Matinee Kiddie shows, to which I was firmly addicted. As I later came to understand, what they would show mainly at the matinees in my part of New Jersey, and I guess elsewhere, was films that the movie exchanges still had prints of. They weren't necessarily that old – some were older than others – so I saw Francis the Talking Mule pictures, Ma and Pa Kettle, Abbott and Costello, some of the science-fiction horror fantasy films, and lots and lots and lots of cartoons.

---

[56]Gomery, *Shared Pleasures*, 92.

Maltin's experience was fairly typical – both in terms of the movies he watched and the circumstances in which he watched them – and it's hard to see how a distributor earned much money from a movie fan like the young Leonard Maltin, no matter how passionate he may have been. And Maltin was certainly passionate: by age fifteen he was editing movie fanzines and laying on screenings of his own for friends. So, if Hollywood couldn't make money by catering to a committed film fan like the young Leonard Maltin, it's easy to see why the child audience was rarely considered important. Children were perhaps the least profitable audience of the period. They never paid full price for a movie ticket, and what's more, they rarely attended the sorts of prestigious first-run theatres where Hollywood distributors could earn substantial profits.

Another good example of this problem can be found in the travails of the Children's Film Library. The library's director Marjorie Dawson, and her team, identified releases it felt would be suitable for children's screenings, and then approached distributors for prints. Films were edited for violence, but, according to Dawson, a key requirement was length: 'Children want action and they can't stand a picture that's longer than an hour and a half,' she told *Variety*.[57] Dawson also felt that child audiences remained reliable in the face of competition for television, but the screening arrangements secured by the library generally negated any chance of generating profit. Children participating in its summer screening series, which ran at theatres across the United States, paid $1 for admission to twelve screenings across the summer school vacation. Any money returned to the distributors was negligible, at best. Although the library was presented to the outside world as a positive move, and at its height was used by over 2,500 theatres, Noel Brown has argued that 'the creation of the Children's Film Library represented a tacit admission on the part of the MPAA that the majority of films were unsuitable for juvenile audiences'.[58] Furthermore, most of the prints used by the library were in a poor state, and the MPAA failed to invest in maintaining supply in the mid to long term. By 1955, *Variety* reported that while NATO president Wilbur Snaper was complaining about 'a tremendous lack of pictures suitable for children', the contents of the library had 'dwindled to the point where it has become difficult to build programmes'.[59] Even at its height the scheme, as with so many attempts to capture the boomers, provided children access to movies, but didn't provide studios access to their money.

The problem occasionally reached extremes. Survey respondent 267 recalled, 'The drive-in was another special way to watch movies. [We] Lived

---

[57]Anon., 'Kid Library Wiggle Tests Films', *Variety*, 19 May 1954, 17.
[58]Brown, *The Hollywood Family Film*, 89.
[59]Anon., 'Kid Film Library Evaporates', *Variety*, 16 March 1955, 7.

on the coast and had to fight the mosquitoes. [We] had to try and sneak someone in by putting them in the trunk of the car.' In June 1954, *Variety* printed a brief story headlined '53 Kids in Bus, $1 Admission', which ran:

> Drive-Ins playing up 'family nite' rates of a buck for each carload should take note of what occurred at Ray David's ozoner in Chadron, Neb., recently. After a day of picnicking, the Chadron school superintendent loaded the school bus with Junior class members into the ozoner, – 53 passengers for $1. However, there was a happy ending: The kids zoomed concession stands sales to a record take.[60]

Needless to say, the studios didn't make any money from the concessions.

---

[60]Anon., '53 Kids in Bus – $1 Admission', *Variety*, 9 June 1954, 7.

3

On the Screen

'Hollywood has its own mystery to cope with these days', ran a 1953 editorial in *Variety*, 'centred on the erratic, unpredictable state of the box office. While the studios are striving to inject commercial values into all films, baffling to execs is why some films click, and others, which are equally stocked with ingredients that normally pay off, bring in unimpressive returns'.[1] As we have seen, this was a familiar refrain throughout the decade – What *do* audiences want? Hollywood's best guesses resulted in a series of film releases throughout the 1950s which helped define the childhood of the baby boomers, but rarely depicted or dealt with the boomers with any degree of commitment.

This chapter looks at the various movies produced between 1946 and 1964, and seeks to identify some of the key trends that arguably resonated with, or reflected, the baby boom experience. In general terms, the period was characterized by a reduction in the volume of film releases, as we saw in the previous chapter, and by growth at the top and bottom ends of the market. The era saw more expensive releases, usually spectacular, roadshow epics or musicals targeted at the largest possible audience, alongside more low-budget science fiction, horror or teen-oriented exploitation releases, targeting the drive-in and second run market. In both cases, these new trends represented an inchoate effort of sorts to cater to young families and baby boomers.

In the main, however, Hollywood continued to provide a broad repertoire of 'normal' mid-to-low-budget releases grounded in the genres of previous decades. Musicals, thrillers, dramas, westerns, crime movies, melodramas and war movies (focusing on both the Korean War and Second World War) were core elements of all the major studios' production schedules. With some exceptions, these releases 'stayed away from political causes and delineated the values of a prosperous and increasingly suburbanised

---

[1]Anon., 'H'wood's Biggest Whodunnit', *Variety*, 21 January 1953, 3.

society',[2] providing entertainment and escapism that was predominantly aimed at an adult audience. While there were fewer of these kinds of movies on release than in previous periods, they still made up the majority of Hollywood movies, and still provided a cultural 'background noise' to the early years of the baby boomers. We start by looking at the biggest movies of the period, the epics that ran on roadshow engagements, before moving on to look at the mid- and low-budget films that filled ordinary movie screens across the United States. Along the way we seek out genres and movies that held a particular appeal for child or family audiences, notably in the form of Disney's key releases during this period, and we end by looking at the ways that Hollywood depicted the American family in the 1950s. In our conclusion we discuss two figures who profoundly influenced the baby boomers – Walt Disney and Billy Wilder. The former capitalized on the baby boom by exclusively targeting children and young families. The latter made no movies for children at all, but nonetheless came to represent the best of Hollywood in the minds of many boomer filmmakers.

Epics

The most significant development in 1950s cinema occurred when the major studios started spending more money on fewer, more spectacular and expensive productions, designed to draw back family groups to high cost auditoriums for a special, one-of-a-kind experience. Early pressure to reduce the number of productions, and privilege 'high value' releases had developed in response to changes in booking practices required by the Paramount decrees. Once films were being sold to exhibitors on an individual basis, *Variety* predicted that 'only the top product will have the best chance in the coming selective buying market'.[3] According to Daryl F. Zanuck, 'That's the future of our film selling: getting everything possible from out top picture. That means the small films are dead.'[4] Zanuck had already begun to reduce production of B-films at Fox in 1946, and he had a very clear sense of what constituted 'top product'. He wanted films with grander thematic ambitions, telling Fox employees, 'We've got to start making movies that entertain but at the same time match the new climate of the time. Vital, thinking men's blockbusters. Big theme films.'[5]

---

[2]Lev, *The Fifties*, 34.

[3]Abel Green, 'Pix Production's Dipsy Doodle', *Variety*, 5 February 1947, 1.

[4]Daryl F. Zanuck, quoted in Green, 'Pix Production's', 62.

[5]Daryl F. Zanuck, quoted in Leonard Mosley, *Zanuck: The Rise and Fall of Hollywood's Last Tycoon* (London: Granada, 1984), 290.

In 1946, *Variety* observed that only thirty-three films had ever exceeded $4 million in domestic rentals (chief among these was the epic historical spectacle *Gone with the Wind*), but that the vast majority of these releases had come in the past five years. The trade journal concluded that the 'challenge of increasing production costs is being met by Hollywood in the b.o. power of the films it is churning out. While the totals on the expense sheets are soaring, coin garnering potentialities of the films they represent are keeping pace.'[6] Although audiences dropped off noticeably in the late 1940s, the earning potential of individual movies continued to increase.

In 1946, both the western *Duel in the Sun* and small-town drama *The Best Years of Our Lives* grossed more than $10 million in rentals, immediately becoming the second and third highest grossing movies of all time. In 1949, Cecil B. DeMille's biblical extravaganza *Samson and Delilah* took fourth place with rentals of $9 million. In each case, these were expensive prestigious movies, made by the industry's leading talent, which performed precisely as Daryl F. Zanuck had predicted. They stayed at first-run houses for long periods, and attracted audiences back to cinemas who were otherwise slowly giving up on movies. MGM struck gold in the early 1950s by following the template of DeMille's *Samson and Delilah* almost to the letter in Mervyn LeRoy's *Quo Vadis* (1951). Produced for a then unprecedented sum of $7 million, *Quo Vadis* told a story of Roman generals and pious Christians during the reign of the Emperor Nero in the first century ad. The film boasted spectacular production values and brought in $10.5 million on its first run. In 1953, the epic historical film met a growing interest in new exhibition technologies, in the form of Fox's *The Robe*, famously the first film shot in the anamorphic widescreen process Cinemascope. Some of the studios had been experimenting with new technologies throughout the first few years of the 1950s, in hope of hitting upon some novelty that might draw viewers back to the cinema. During the summer of 1953, considerable support for stereoscopic 3D emerged, but despite a few hits, the technology never really took off with audiences.

Three trends, then, technical innovation, high-budget and high-rentals productions, and grand historical or biblical themes were combined in *The Robe*, which quickly became a colossal hit. From this point onwards, the widescreen epic became a staple of Hollywood's production schedules. The historian Joel W. Finler suggests that the blockbuster strategy of the 1950s 'worked for a time and the fall in audiences was briefly halted'.[7] In 1953, weekly attendance did indeed rise for the first time since the end of the war (from 42 million in 1952 up to 47 million in 1953, before stabilizing at 50 million in

---

[6]Herb Golden, 'Hollywood's 33 Top Hits', *Variety*, 25 September 1946, 1 and 5.
[7]Finler, *The Hollywood Story*, 14.

1954 and 1955).[8] Cecil B. DeMille's final movie, *The Ten Commandments* (1956), further cemented the biblical epic as a Hollywood mainstay. However, in 1956, audiences again began to decline, even as individual movies shattered box office records. Epics nevertheless remained some of the biggest, most influential releases, and were often marketed targeting children.

According to the press kit for William Wyler's 1959 bestseller adaptation, *Ben-Hur: A Tale of the Christ*:

> Since the opening of *Ben-Hur* special student performances throughout the country have proved a lucrative source of additional revenue. Today, more than ever before, educators, religious leaders and parents are seeking entertainment of a high moral and educational nature for the young people they are guiding. *Ben-Hur* is that kind of entertainment, and for this reason your welcome at various schools and youth organisations will be a hearty one.[9]

The pamphlet went on to suggest various ways that exhibitors might attract the interests of scout groups, girl guides, church youth groups and schools of all sorts. Similar materials accompanied the release of many roadshow epics. *The Ten Commandments* was promoted by another all-important study guide, and a book entitled *The Ten Commandments for Children*, which 'features the figure of Charlton Heston as Moses on its cover, together with picture credits prominently displayed. In addition, inside front cover carries a quotation from Cecil B. DeMille', according to the press notes.[10] Children were also appealed to with a colouring pencil set and book, 'manufactured in three denominations – Catholic, Protestant and Jewish'.[11] Promotional material provided by the studios also usually included a colouring contest, which the press book for *Samson and Delilah* claimed that the movie 'should certainly appeal to children and head them towards your theater to see the film'.[12]

In our survey, William Wyler's *Ben-Hur* (1959) and *The Ten Commandments* were repeatedly cited as formative cinematic memories. Like so many films of the period, both films utilized a biblical setting and told broadly appealing narratives of faith and conversion. Both spoke to the beliefs of a largely Christian country and both told stories that the majority of parents would find agreeable fodder for family viewing. Respondent 744 recalls that 'the first movie I remember seeing was *Ben-Hur*', while respondent 242 'loved big biblical spectacles like *Ben-Hur*'.

---

[8]Ibid., 379.
[9]MGM Pictures, *Ben-Hur* Press Kit, 35.
[10]Paramount Pictures, *The Ten Commandments* Press Kit, 8.
[11]Ibid.
[12]Paramount Pictures, *Samson and Delilah* Press Kit, 4.

However, the most widely beloved movie of the period was Fox's 1965 *The Sound of Music* directed by Robert Wise, starring Julie Andrews. An adaptation of a hit Broadway play from Rodgers and Hammerstein, the movie combined memorable tunes, with a wartime setting and spectacular, widescreen Austrian scenery. It was produced for a budget of $8.2 million and generated rentals estimated at somewhere between $115 and $125 million, making it the highest grossing release of all time, a record previously held by *The Ten Commandments* and then *Ben-Hur*.[13] Survey respondent 107 remembers that 'my father took me to see *Sound of Music* as a child for my first theater experience. We sat in the balcony and I will never forget the opening scenes of the mountains'. For respondent 51 the movie offered an insight into recent history:

> Mom took us to see *The Sound of Music* when I was five, on its second release after its Oscars. I could not follow any of the Nazi theme or its vibe of fear. I was like, 'Mommy, why does the black spider make people nervous?' She told me the story of Hitler and the Nazis and WWII and I was gobsmacked hearing about that for the first time.

Overall, *The Sound of Music* was the most frequently cited movie from the 1950s and 1960s in our survey, often either as a formative moviegoing experience, or as a continuing favourite.

The truth is that the success of epic blockbusters, which often made most of their profits in prestigious first-run theatres and overseas, always remained exceptional in the 1950s and 1960s. Attending was an exceptional activity for most moviegoers – perhaps a once-in-a-year event – and their revenues were exceptional in comparison to all other releases. They only attracted audiences back to the cinema occasionally. They never reignited moviegoing as a habit, and they mostly catered to the boomers by offering opportunities for edification, which was not how they were necessarily received. Survey respondent 63 recalls that his 'first in-theater movie was *Samson and Delilah*, in which a falling column caused blood to gush from the mouth of the guy it landed on. Totally awesome for a kid of six!' Instead Hollywood's lower budget releases offered a broader repertoire of pleasures.

Westerns, swashbucklers and comedies

Epics offered an exceptional alternative to Hollywood's regular content, but while movie executives remained part of an older generation, and while audiences remained relatively unstudied, many of the movies released in the

---

[13]Hall and Neale, *Spectacles, Epics and Blockbusters*, 184.

late 1940s and early 1950s seem much more like a continuation of existing trends rather than a new type of product for a new type of audience. The biggest hits of 1946 were both highly budgeted melodramas: *The Best Years of Our Lives* focused on the fortunes of returning veterans, while *Duel in the Sun* was a western, marketed on the basis of sexualized romance, from producer David O. Selznick. The biggest hit released in 1947 was a Bing Crosby vehicle about a curmudgeonly doctor called *Welcome Stranger*, in 1948 westerns *Red River* and *The Paleface* (a western comedy with Bob Hope) dominated the box office alongside the UK import *The Red Shoes*. In 1949, the biblical epic *Samson and Delilah* pipped the war movies *Battleground* and *Sands of Iwo Jima* to become the number one movie. In 1950, the swashbuckler *King Solomon's Mines* and Disney's *Cinderella* won out over *Annie Get Your Gun* (a western musical) and the comic melodrama *Cheaper by the Dozen*. In these lists it is possible to see signs that the content of Hollywood movies might be changing, but for the most part, the high and low grossing movies of this period relied on the stars, settings and subjects of the wartime era.

The youngest baby boomers had fond memories of many key 1950s releases. Respondent 339, one of the oldest boomers in our survey recalled, 'I went to the movies with my dad, and would go to a few Saturday matinees with my peers. We saw movies like *Cinderella*, *Bridge on the River Kwai* [1957], *Old Yeller* [1956], *King of Kings* [1961].' Respondent 709 recalled that the movies of her childhood were 'happy, light-hearted affairs', and identified Doris Day's musicals and *Singin' in the Rain* (1952) as key memories. The key successes of summer 1950 bear this out. *Father of the Bride* and *Our Very Own* were both lightweight dramas about rural or suburban families, and, as we will see, Disney's various hits of the period in these genres targeted children very successfully. In these early years, a number of westerns, a genre often thought to have an inbuilt appeal to boys, also performed well.

Many of the established genre releases that hit movie screens in the 1950s seem to have had the same broad appeal for kids, just as they had done in the 1930s and 1940s. Effectively, the industry maintained a strategy that had worked well in previous eras, despite the fact that moviegoing habits, and the wider demographic makeup of the country were changing. Early in 1954, *Variety* suggested that low sales over the Christmas period may have been connected to a paucity of product aimed at children (usually referred to as 'Moppets' in the trade press) and looked forward to a bumper Easter. 'Unlike last Christmas week,' ran an editorial published in March 1954, 'bookings for the spring holiday season have been carefully selected to supply the small fry market [and] distribs have made available a number of pictures of sufficient entertainment value to encompass the tastes of the whole family.'[14]

---

[14]Anon., 'Moppet-Aimed Easter Bookings', *Variety*, 17 March 1954, 7.

The range of films perceived as child friendly gives some indication of the how Hollywood understood the tastes of child viewers. The surefire hits of Easter 1954 included reissues of Disney's *Pinocchio* (1939) and Fox's *Heidi* (1937) – both adaptations of classic children's stories. However, they also included a number of recently produced swashbucklers, notably MGM's *Ivanhoe* (1953) and *Knights of the Round Table* (1953), Fox's *Prince Valiant* (1953) and Disney-RKO's *Rob Roy* (1953). Clearly these kinds of films, historical adventures filled with action, adapted from myths, legends and even comic strips, had a clear appeal to children, especially boys. Yet the trade rarely discussed them as 'children's films', and while, 'action adventure' movies were often identified by boomers as a childhood favourite in our survey, relatively few of these movies were recalled fondly, if at all, by any of our respondents.

As well as medieval swashbucklers, Hollywood also produced a series of films about pirates, including Disney's 1950 adaptation of *Treasure Island* and Warner Bros' 1952 *The Crimson Pirate*. More so than the medieval swashbucklers they resembled, these movies were generally understood as having a particular appeal for children. *The Crimson Pirate* was a knockabout parody of the swashbuckler, described by Carl Millikin Jr, Warner's head of research as, 'a good natured melodrama – sort of a child's eye burlesque of pirates and their ways'.[15] The movie begins with Burt Lancaster's title character admonishing the audience not to take the film too seriously, before launching into a display of acrobatic swordsmanship. Arthur Pollack wrote in the *LA Daily Compass* that the movie was made up of 'all sorts of mad and comical doings, mostly acrobatic, all absurd. Children should be spellbound by it. Nothing makes sense'.[16] In the *Hollywood Citizen-Reporter*, Lowell Redelings described it as 'an excellent entertainment recommended not only for adults with a sense of humour but for young people and children'.[17] Warner Bros made little effort to market the film to children, preferring instead to emphasize the appeal of Burt Lancaster and the Italian production (at least according to the press kits they produced). Nevertheless, the studio and movie critics all seemed to tacitly assume that *The Crimson Pirate*, and, one might assume, most pirate movies, were for kids. For better or worse, swashbucklers were children's films of a sort, even if the industry rarely discussed them in these terms. So too, were westerns and broad comedies.

As it worried over the child audience in 1954, *Variety* also hoped that the western *Tarza, Son of Cochise* (1954), would prove successful, alongside the

[15]Letter from Carl Millikin Jr, head of research at WB, dated 12 May 1952, Folder marked 'Story misc.', in '*Crimson Pirate*' file, Warner Bros Archives, University of Southern California.
[16]Arthur Pollock, Review of *The Crimson Pirate*, *Daily Compass*, August 28 1942, in '*Crimson Pirate*' Files, Warner Bros Archives, University of Southern California.
[17]Lowell Redelings, Review of *The Crimson Pirate*, *Hollywood Citizen News*, 27 September 1952, 12.

rural comedy *Ma and Pa Kettle at Home* (1954). Again, *Variety*'s implicit suggestion that these movies might appeal primarily to children gives some indication as to the standing of westerns and comedies in the early 1950s, which were both implicitly perceived as appealing primarily to children and families. The western in particular seems to have held allure for young boys that ensured its popularity throughout the 1950s (a period often seen as a golden age for western film production). In the words of writer/director Lawrence Kasdan:

> I always loved westerns – and *The Magnificent Seven* (1960) which was John Sturges' remake of *The Seven Samurai* [1954], really sort of changed my life. It was a wonderful movie and it represented so many paradigms of heroism and manhood and the pull between darkness and light and courage and fear. They're all sort of embodied in there. That movie just changed everything. I knew that's where I wanted to be: in that world. I came out of there and said, 'I want to make movies.' I was 14 years old.

Westerns were identified as important childhood movie experiences by 112 of our survey respondents – mostly older boomers, born before 1958, and mostly men. For the most part, westerns were identified as favourites, but titles rarely stuck in the memory. Respondent 136 noted that 'they pretty much blur together into whatever was playing at the local theater on Saturday mornings when I was 10 and under. I vaguely remember war movies and westerns.' Respondent 641 tellingly observed that his viewing choices were dictated by his father's interests: 'My dad liked the drive-in movies and we tried to see one every week if there was a new one playing in our area – he liked westerns, military, adventure, sci-fi, action, horror or mystery so I saw whatever he liked and learned to enjoy whatever I saw.' And, of course not every child was a fan: respondent 216 remembers that while 'James Bond films were just awesome in every way, westerns were usually tedious until the Indians attacked'.

As if in acknowledgement of the growing child audience, many westerns became preoccupied with family relationships, and a number of key 1950s releases clearly link homesteaders with boomer families. Perhaps the most famous example is George Stevens's 1953 movie *Shane*, which is focused on the relationship between Alan Ladd's titular gunslinger, and a young boy who comes to idolize him. In effect, the movie dramatizes the relationship between boy viewers and the western heroes they saw at the movies. The boy, Joey, is particularly fascinated with Shane's gun, and sees the gunslinger as a more exciting, proactive figure in contrast to his own father.

The same year, the John Wayne vehicle *Hondo* featured a very similar relationship at its centre. In both movies, and many other releases from Disney's *Davy Crockett: King of the Wild Frontier* through to John Ford's *The Searchers*, the homesteaders making a life for themselves in the wilds of

IMAGE 4 *John Wayne as Hondo Lane teaches six-year-old Johnny (Lee Aaker) in* Hondo *(1953).*

the frontier clearly exist in a milieu with striking similarity to the idealized suburbs of the baby boom. In almost every case the settled world of the homesteader personifies the future, while the gunslingers represent a fading past. More importantly, films like *Shane* and *Hondo* go out of their way to provide an on-screen access point for child viewers, in the form of a child as a central character. Both show an awareness of the importance of children to the appeal of the western movie and the western myth.

Perhaps the most child-friendly western hero of the period was the Lone Ranger, who first appeared on radio in 1933, made the leap to movie serials in 1938 and became a fixture of the ABC early television schedules in 1949. The Lone Ranger married comic book preoccupations with secret identities and vigilante justice to a frontier setting, and the character was a masked man who, accompanied by his Native American sidekick Tonto, fought villains in the American West. The character had been developed by Detroit based producer George Trendle, who sold the rights on to Jack Wrather in 1955, who ceased production of the radio serial, but continued producing new episode of the television serial for ABC until 1957, and developed a movie based on the character for Warner Bros in 1956. According to the *New York World Telegram*, 'Warner decided to film the veteran program after making movies of *Dragnet* [1954] and *Our Miss Brooks* [1956]', and *The Lone Ranger* was clearly part of a concerted strategy to build movie hits out of successful television shows.[18] The publicity kit produced for the

---

[18]Aline Mosby, 'Lone Ranger to Cry Hi-Yo on the Silver Screen', *NY World Telegram and Sun*, 9 September 1955, 24.

film emphasized its status as a movie with all age appeal and huge marketing potential. 'Did you know that of the millions of Lone Ranger fans,' asked the press book, 'adults form 55% of the audience, and children 45%? Add up the audience saturation of *The Lone Ranger* via radio, television, newspaper syndication comic books, fiction, records, merchandisers and other media and you get an audience impact unprecedented for any motion picture.'[19] The movie was little more than an expanded episode of the television show, and was produced at minimal cost, using the existing production crew and cast. It generated a modest $1.5 million at the box office, representing a strong return for Warner Bros, but also indicating at the limited commercial capacity of films aimed squarely at the baby boom market.

Beyond westerns, many key comedies of the age can also be understood as retaining a particular appeal for children. The Ma and Pa Kettle series of films were comedies about a rural family with 15 children, who, in the first movie, *Ma and Pa Kettle* (1949) move to a modern suburban home, and struggle to cope with the proliferation of gadgets it contains. The Kettle movies were one of several long-running comedy series that endured throughout the 1950s, although the most familiar to early baby boomers were probably William 'Bud' Abbott and Lou Costello. Abbott and Costello had been a hugely successful comedy duo throughout the 1940s, and were consistently considered among the most commercially reliable stars from 1940 until 1952.[20] They continued to work in movies and television throughout the 1950s and received mentions from seven participants as childhood memories in our survey.

Their 1952 release *Jack and the Beanstalk* gives some indication of the pair's position as child-friendly performers. Various Warner Brothers' press releases present the movie as part of a concerted effort to speak to younger viewers:

'Kids are getting too many killings and shootings in their entertainment fare these days,' says Costello, 'Bud and I plan to give them something exciting and yet not exciting enough to bring on nightmares when they fall asleep.' Yes Bud and Lou haven't let their juvenile friends down. They know what it means to have them on their side. For it has been the love and affection they have for children – and that children have for them – that has been the real basis of their unprecedented movie success.[21]

On release, *Variety* suggested that the movie had indeed reached its target audience, with some provisos, 'Subject assures hefty response from moppet

---

[19]Warner Brothers Pictures, *Lone Ranger* Press Kit, in '*Lone Ranger*,' file, Warner Brothers Archives, University of Southern California.

[20]Top Ten Moneymakers Poll, reproduced in Lev, *The Fifties*, 306.

[21]Anon., 'Undated Press Release', in '*Jack and the Beanstalk*' file, Warner Bros Archives, University of Southern California.

audiences, but from an adult appreciation standpoint the film probably won't have much appeal.'[22] The movie earned $1.6 million in rentals in the United States – a fairly standard return for a low-budget, child-friendly movie.

By the late 1950s, Abbott and Costello had been replaced in the public's affection by another comedy duo, Dean Martin and Jerry Lewis, who appeared in a series of movies for Paramount. Unlike Abbott and Costello, few of the Martin/Lewis comedies seem to have been designed with child audiences in mind, and they were rarely promoted at the time to children over other demographics, but they remained reliable money spinners for the studios, and they hold an important place in the memories of many baby boomers (receiving eleven mentions in our survey), who clearly went to see them. Respondent 513 told us, 'I love the old Jerry Lewis movies, I can relate to these, and my mother reminded me of Jerry Lewis 'cause she always made me smile.'

In several key respects, Jerry Lewis appealed to younger viewers because he was a relatively childlike performer, who gave broad performances in a series of inexpensive but modestly successful movies. In 1952, DC Comics began a popular spin off comic book called *The Adventures of Dean Martin and Jerry Lewis*, which was published (as *The Adventures of Jerry Lewis*) into the 1970s. In 1957, after his partnership with Dean Martin collapsed, Lewis began making films with the director Frank Tashlin, previously an animator at Warner Bros. Their first film, *Rock-a-Bye Baby* (1957) was a musical comedy which featured Lewis as a television repairman, and bumbling adoptive father to a trio of unruly triplets. While the story was principally an adult affair, focused on Lewis's unlikely relationships, in its own way, it sought to capture the milieu of the baby boom.

Disney

For the majority of Hollywood studios, catering to children and families was a hit-and-miss business. For Disney, it was the only business. In the immediate aftermath of the Second World War, the company's financial situation had been relatively precarious. While the other studios had enjoyed a brief boom in ticket sales, Disney did not have a backlog of product to release, and so instead sought to cut costs, which, as we have seen, placed severe limitations on the scale of the company's ambitions for future feature projects. Furthermore, money that the studio had invested in the UK was suddenly frozen overseas by new financial restrictions imposed to assuage fears of a post-war financial collapse in Europe. In 1946, the company could only continue operating with an emergency loan from RKO, and

---

[22]Anon., Review of *Jack and the Beanstalk*, *Variety*, in *'Jack and the Beanstalk'* file, Warner Bros Archives, University of Southern California.

although a roster of animated productions was revived, Walt Disney never really recovered the passion for animation that had driven him in the 1930s. Films like *Make Mine Music* and *Song of the South* (both 1946) proved commercially successful, but they retained the episodic quality of Disney's wartime releases, and certainly didn't measure up in creative terms to earlier hits such as *Snow White* and *Pinocchio*. *Song of the South* also generated controversy for its essentially benign depiction of African American life in the immediate aftermath of slavery, and so has never been celebrated or rereleased in the same manner as other Disney 'Classics.'

Walt Disney Productions nonetheless invested in a programme of quality animated features, starting with *Cinderella* (1950). In contrast to the pre-war period, budgets were more tightly controlled, and Walt himself was, by many accounts, less involved than before with the production of these new animated films.[23] During production, Disney animator Dick Heumer wrote to his friend, the producer Charles Palmer, declaring, 'Astonishingly enough things are getting done. And they're not bad my boy, not bad: in fact, if things go on as they are, well, we might have another *Snow White* on our hands, hien?' However, Heumer noted that Walt Disney, whom he called 'the grand panjarandrum is now hotly embroiled in a new project. He is building him (as he would put it) a little amusement park.'[24] Later, Disney told one interviewer that, for him at least, *Cinderella* 'was just a picture'.[25]

The film was nonetheless rapturously received by Disney's contemporaries and film critics. Writing to Disney, the director Michael Curtiz described it as Disney's 'masterpiece of all pictures you have done.'[26] According to *Variety*:

Cinderella is one of Walt Disney's top achievements as an animated story spinner. He catches the warm and simple charm of the Charles Perrault classic so effectively and with such easy presentation that film truly is a delight, a cinch to please audiences of all ages.[27]

Mandel Herbstman made a similar observation in his review for *Motion Picture Daily*:

Cinderella holds entertainment rewards for audiences of all ages, but there is something about this tale of the pretty little scullery maid who married the Prince Charming that makes ideal screen fare for the youngsters. For *Cinderella* is the symbol of magic fulfilment to every child.[28]

[23]Gabler, *Walt Disney*, xx.
[24]Undated letter from 'DH,' in 'Charles Palmer files – Correspondence Dick Huemer – folder 33,' AMPAS Margaret Herrick library.
[25]Walt Disney, quoted in Gabler, *Walt Disney*, 477.
[26]Michael Curtiz, quoted in Gabler, *Walt Disney*, 477.
[27]Anon., Review of *Cinderella*, *Variety*, 13 December 1949, 12.
[28]Mandel Herbstman, Review of *Cinderella*, *Motion Picture Daily*, 13 December 1949, 10.

In each case, reviewers made the obvious but undeniable claim that *Cinderella*'s appeal was strongest for child viewers, and the film's astonishing commercial performance provided a clear indication that Disney animation, and the child audience, were powerful forces that other studios were failing to adequately exploit. The film was mentioned as a childhood favourite by seven of our survey respondents, but it clearly connected with a huge audience. Over the course of its run, *Cinderella* generated over $9 million in box office rentals, making it the highest grossing film of 1950, and, on rerelease, it remained one of the most commercially successful films of the period.[29]

Cinderella was followed by *Alice in Wonderland* in 1951, *Peter Pan* in 1953 and *Lady and the Tramp* in 1955. In all, between 1946 and 1964, Disney released eleven feature-length animated movies, most of which enjoyed significant commercial success. For instance, *Peter Pan* earned $7 million in rentals, making it the fifth highest grossing release of 1953 and *Lady and the Tramp* earned $8 million, making it the third highest grossing movie of 1955.[30] Respondents to our survey consistently recalled Disney movies as central elements of their childhood, with 171 of them naming the company as part of their childhood memories. Respondent 173 recalls that *Sword in the Stone* (1963) 'was my first movie experience. My father took me to a really fancy, fashionable, stylish "movie palace" and we stood in line for an hour.' When asked what films he remembered fondly from childhood, respondent 485 echoed many others by declaring, 'A lot of Walt Disney movies.'

Disney's cultural reach broadened as its post-war offering came to include live action features for the first time, initially in the form of short nature documentaries such as 1948's *Seal Island*, the first in the company's True Life Adventure series. In 1950, Disney released its first fully live action movie, an adaptation of *Treasure Island*. The film was a modest hit, earning $3 million in US rentals, but its production had been motivated primarily by operational requirements. Because Disney was unable to realize profits from the UK market as a result of the ongoing post-war trade restrictions, it had instead chosen to re-invest its 'frozen' capital in a UK-based film production. The film's relative commercial success nonetheless encouraged Disney to develop more live action films in a similar vein.

By 1954, live action fiction films dominated the company's production schedules, and by the early 1960s, Disney was releasing six to ten live action films for every animated feature. By 1964 Disney had produced forty-three live action fiction films and seven feature-length documentaries

---

[29]Figures used here are from Krämer, *The New Hollywood*, 111. Box office data relating to Disney releases is complicated by the frequent rereleasing.

[30]Krämer, *The New Hollywood*, 112.

along with many short films. The live action releases were Disney's bread and butter with boomer audiences – generally appealing films focused on a very broad cross section of child-friendly topics – from prestige movies like *Swiss Family Robinson* (1960) and *Mary Poppins* (1964), through to low-budget boilerplate productions like *The Shaggy Dog* (1959) and *Summer Madness* (1963) starring Disney stalwarts Fred MacMurray and Hayley Mills, respectively.

Disney's key release of 1957 was *Old Yeller*, essentially a tragic children's film, focused on a frontier family and their beloved pet dog. The movie was based on bestselling novel by Fred Gipson, and in its review, the *Motion Picture Herald* noted that 'exhibitors who have been clamouring for more family type pictures will welcome Walt Disney's latest outdoor drama, which depicts, in vivid Technicolor hues, homestead life in frontier Texas during the 1860s'.[31] *Variety*'s claim that the movie 'carries strong family appeal which should run up good returns in the general market', proved correct.[32] *Old Yeller* returned rentals of $8 million, making it the fourth highest grossing film of the year.[33] In particular, the film's climax, where the eponymous Old Yeller is put down after contracting rabies, was an iconic moment for many young boomers in the audience. Twelve of our survey respondents identified *Old Yeller* as a childhood favourite, often because the film affected them emotionally. Survey respondent 82 wrote, 'I remember REALLY crying when Old Yeller died,' a sentiment echoed by several other respondents, and succinctly discussed by the writer/director/producer Steve Kloves, who explained:

> I have to say, though, that one of the most devastating experiences of my young movie-going experience was *Old Yeller*, where they shoot the dog at the end. I was inconsolable after that movie. Because I grew up in a place, in the suburbs, where emotions were tamped down, and where things felt very vanilla to me, I was given free rein with my emotions at the cinema, so I was crying at the end of *Old Yeller*. The cinema was a powerful place, a place where anything could happen.

After 1953, all of these movies were released via Disney's newly established distribution wing, Buena Vista Pictures, which freed the company from its reliance on RKO, and established Disney as a studio equivalent in terms of operational capacity to any of the other major players in the US film market. Alongside its movies, Disney's expansion into television allowed the company to develop an intense relationship with its core audience of baby

---

[31]Warren Hart, Review of *Old Yeller*, *Motion Picture Daily*, 14 November 1957, 12.

[32]Whit., Review of *Old Yeller*, *Variety*, 14 November 1957, 10

[33]Figures from Krämer, *The New Hollywood*, 113.

boomers. The company benefitted immeasurably from a reliable, large and growing consumer base that was not being exploited by competitors in any serious way. As a result, Neal Gabler estimates that in 1966 alone (the year of Walt Disney's death),

> 240 million people saw a Disney movie, a weekly audiences of 100 million watched a Disney television show, 80 million read a Disney book, 50 million listened to Disney records, 80 million bought Disney merchandise, 150 million read a Disney comic strip, 80 million saw a Disney educational film, and nearly 7 million visited Disneyland.[34]

These figures give some sense of Disney's impact on the baby boomers, who would have made up the vast majority of these many millions. In our survey respondent 74 remembered preferring 'almost any movie with Disney characters or ones that showed places around the world'. For many boomers, Disney's reach extended way beyond the cinema screen. His ABC television shows had rendered him a familiar figure for millions of young Americans, and his theme park, Disneyland, rapidly became a totemic part of putative boomer culture.

Disney had been toying with the idea of developing a theme park since the end of the Second World War. Initially, Walt conceptualized of the project as a touring exhibition of miniatures, but as he began developing scenes and tableaus of small-town Americana the project grew in scale, coming to incorporate a new-found fascination with robotics, and a lifelong love of small gauge railways.[35] By the end of 1951 as the company began to branch out into new areas on screen, the project had evolved from the miniature Disneylandia to a theme park that rapidly became 'a national amusement park, not a park of local or regional interest like previous amusement parks, but a destination for a nation of television viewers'.[36]

Disney's television production deal with ABC helped to fund the project, the cost of which had ballooned to $17 million by the time Disneyland opened at the terminus of six highways in Anaheim, California, in July 1955. Shortly before the opening, *Variety* reported that 'all showmen agree that the project is of staggering imaginative concept, a sure winner, one of the true wonders of entertainment', even as it worried over the cost to Disney and to patrons.[37] Any fears about the park's financial viability were quickly laid to rest as it generated colossal and growing returns, earning $10 million in its first year of operation alone, fully one-third of the company's

---

[34]Gabler, *Walt Disney*, x.
[35]Ibid., 481.
[36]Anderson, *Hollywood TV*, 30.
[37]Anon., '$17,000,000 Disneyland Preview', *Variety*, 13 July 1955, 1.

earnings for 1955.[38] ABC's *Disneyland* television played a vital role in familiarizing baby boomers with the so-called magic kingdom from the moment construction began. As a result, millions of boomers across the United States were intimately familiar with Disneyland, and their pester power clearly drove the park's burgeoning success. In 1957 one visiting father declared, 'Disneyland may be just another damned amusement park, but to my kids, it's the Taj Mahal, Niagara Falls, Sherwood Forest and Davy Crocket all rolled into one. After years of sitting in front of the television, the youngsters are sure it's a fairyland before they even get there.'[39]

Unsurprisingly, for a huge number of boomers Disneyland was more than a leisure destination – it offered an influential site of imaginative escapism that would resonate throughout their lives, particularly for those boomers who would go on to work in Hollywood. When pitching the movie *Raiders of the Lost Ark* (1981) in 1978, director Steven Spielberg explained, 'What we're just doing here, really, is designing a ride at Disneyland.'[40] Spielberg's later movies, notably *Jurassic Park* (1993), also evince a fascination with games, theme parks and rides that clearly derives from the early allure that Disneyland held for boomers. It is also no accident that since the boomers have assumed positions of creative control in Hollywood, theme parks have become a far more dominant element of the studio business.

Taken together, Disney's operations in the 1950s made the company an outlier in relation to the other major studios, but the films, television shows and parks provided a powerful connection to the relatively untapped baby boom audience. For a huge number of boomers growing up in the 1950s, Disney's productions were a routine part of everyday life, but other, powerful influences also resounded.

Science fiction and horror

One of the most popular genres identified by respondents to our survey born in the 1940s and 1950s seems to have been 'Monster movies,' a term frequently used as a catch-all to describe science fiction films and horror movies featuring fantastical creatures, be they aliens, the product of scientific advances gone awry or supernatural beings. Respondent 120's childhood favourites were 'old classics from the 1930s and 40s' as well as 'monster movies and late-night horror movies'. Respondent 108 recalls 'the Universal monsters especially', and respondent 88 remembered clearly watching 'the

---

[38]Anderson, *Hollywood TV*, 30.
[39]Unnamed parent, quoted in Anderson, 'Hollywood TV', 30.
[40]Steven Spielberg, quoted in Patrick Radden Keefe, 'Spitballing Indy', *New Yorker*, 25 March 2013, http://www.newyorker.com/culture/culture-desk/spitballing-indy.

monster movies at the matinee'. For respondent 85, these movies were life changing:

> I also got into horror movies early, specifically older black and white horror movies like the Universal films. My favorite movie, then as now, was the original *King Kong* from 1933. I saw it at the public library as part of their summer reading program, when I was perhaps 9 or 10 years old. It completely changed my life, sparking my life-long interest in horror and science fiction films. I had never seen anything like that film before; I've often tried to recapture the sense of wonder I felt at seeing that movie, but I've never been able to do so. You could mostly only see movies on television in those days. I can remember scouring the television Guide every week when it came out, looking for some old monster movie that I hadn't seen yet, and often wheedling my mother into letting me stay up past midnight to be able to watch them.

The monster movie had been part of Hollywood's production schedules for a long time, but it became a quintessential 1950s phenomenon. Such films were usually low budget, featuring subjects that would rarely appear in a major studio release in previous decades. Only Universal had specialized with any degree of commitment in producing horror movies during the classical era, and although the genre dealt with potentially grotesque subjects, 'Universal's monster films had always been popular fare for children, even in the 1930s'.[41] The industry as a whole tended to regard the genre as being of low cultural and commercial status. Only a handful of high-budget science fiction films were made in the 1950s, but many low-budget movies were released. Victoria O'Donnell estimates that 'five hundred feature films and shorts were produced between 1948 and 1962', becoming a 'major genre'.[42] O'Donnell has identified numerous causes of the 1950s science fiction boom, including fears of nuclear proliferation, visible technological advances in the nature of American life, a hugely successful rerelease of *King Kong* (1933) and a concomitant boom in science fiction literature.[43]

Fears of extraterrestrial invasion recurred in movies such as *The Thing* (1951), *The Day the Earth Stood Still* (1951), *It Came from Outer Space* (1953), *Invasion of the Saucer Men* (1957) and *The Blob* (1958), among others, while monsters and mutants appeared in *I Was a Teenage Werewolf* (1951), *Creature from the Black Lagoon* (1954), and various others. For the most part, these films can be understood in similar terms to the teen movies

---

[41]Brown, *The Hollywood Family Film*, 91.
[42]Victoria O'Donnell, 'Science Fiction Films and Cold War Anxiety', in Lev, *The Fifties*, 169.
[43]O'Donnell, 'Science Fiction Films', 170.

discussed below, in that they were often produced on the margins of the industry. Boomers are most likely to have seen monster movies on television, where Universal's older films circulated endlessly, while new movies played at drive-ins and in matinees. Furthermore, the films themselves often featured characters with a curiously childlike position in society. A good example is Don Siegel's classic *Invasion of the Body Snatchers*, produced independently by Walter Wanger in 1956. The film tells the story of an ordinary town taken over by shape-shifting alien seed pods, which either take over or replace the bodies of the town's original residents. Once they have been taken over, the townsfolk lose their ability to experience emotions and immediately begin plotting global domination. Their plot is uncovered by Miles Bennell, a local doctor played by Kevin McCarthy.

Like so many monster movies of the period, *Invasion of the Body Snatchers* has been read as a response to the 'threat' of communism, with the emotionless pod people standing in for irreligious, communist menace. However, in its preoccupation with changing (specifically, falling asleep and waking up somehow different), the movie does seem to be partly about growing up. Bennell is a carefree bachelor, who isn't quite integrated into the adult life of the small Californian town where the action takes place. In effect, he is a childlike figure, and his fear of being taken over by the pod people does seem to represent some ambivalence about growing up that may have spoken in some way to children.

Invaders from Mars, produced independently by Edward L. Alpertson in 1953 and distributed by Fox, was one of few films to incorporate a child protagonist at its centre. In it, keen amateur astronomer David (Jimmy Hunt) notices a flying saucer approaching and notifies the authorities who are already being brainwashed by Martian invaders. The same issues of 'mind control' that inform *Invasion of the Body Snatchers* also feature in *Invaders from Mars*, which presents adults as initially untrustworthy and easily brainwashed, while young David has to navigate an increasingly frightening world of coming war and peril. It's not hard to see the film as a meaningful narrative for many young baby boomers.

Whatever its cause, young people's interest in science fiction and horror movies was part of a larger cultural trend for horror and the grotesque in the 1950s, which caused social commentators some concern. In addition to the low-budget monster movies of the age, comic books, magazines and pulp novels sprung up providing similar thrills and chills. Perhaps the best known of these were the horror comics published by EC Comics, such as *Tales from the Crypt* which ran from 1950 to 1955. The growth of horror-themed entertainment led the psychiatrist Fredric Wertham to take up his famous crusade against horror comics, and mass media more generally. Wertham was preoccupied with the effect that media consumption had on children, and feared that reading or watching violent, sexualized or otherwise stimulating media products might contribute to youth crime and mental disorders, an argument most clearly articulated in his 1954 book *The Seduction of the Innocent*.[44]

Following the publication of Wertham's book, and a congressional hearing on Juvenile Delinquency in 1954 that generated many headlines, EC's horror comics were regulated off the shelves by the Comic's Code Authority. However, other outlets catering to children with an interest in horror emerged. The most important of these was the magazine *Famous Monsters of Filmland*, first published in 1958. The magazine was edited by Forrest J. Ackerman, who was seeking to capitalize on growing interest in 'classic' Hollywood horror movies, following block sales of television screening rights. *Famous Monsters* proved hugely successful, and was published monthly until 1983. For many boomers, it transformed their engagement with movies, and in its account of *Famous Monsters'* fiftieth anniversary, the *Los Angeles Times* claimed that Ackerman 'shaped the very essence of horror and science-fiction fandom' in the United States.[45]

According to Jack Epps Jr.:

> I loved those Universal Monster movies. I thought those were the greatest movies ever. I still do think they were just brilliant pieces of work. So I used to get *Famous Monsters of Filmland* every time it came out and it was a fantasy.

The writer Stephen King, another boomer, sees *Famous Monsters* as an iconic part of the boomer's shared culture:

> In the late 1950s, a literary agent and compulsive science fiction memorabilia collector named Forrest J. Ackerman changed the lives of thousands of kids – I was one – when he began editing a magazine called *Famous Monsters of Filmland*. Ask anyone who has been associated with the fantasy – horror – science fiction genres in the last thirty years about this magazine, and you'll get a laugh, a flash of the eyes, and a stream of bright memories. I practically guarantee it.[46]

The significance of *Famous Monsters* is twofold. First, it allowed children to indulge an interest in fantasy and horror that would stay with them throughout their lives. Secondly, it revealed the inner workings of cinema, especially fantastical films, in a way that clearly stimulated the creative impulses of Steven Spielberg, John Landis and many others. At the time

---

[44]Fredric Wertham, *The Seduction of the Innocent* (New York: Rhinehart, 1954).
[45]Jeff Boucher, 'Forrest J. Ackerman Ailing', *Los Angeles Times*, 4 November 2008, http:// herocomplex.latimes.com/uncategorized/forrest-j-ack-1-2/.
[46]Stephen King, *On Writing* (New York: Pocket, 2000), 22–3.

of his death in 2008, Ackerman's massive collection of mementoes and memorabilia included tributes from numerous directors, including a poster for *Close Encounters of the Third Kind* (1977), which director Steven Spielberg had inscribed, 'A generation of fantasy lovers thank you for raising us so well.'[47] The magazine showed its readers that filmmaking was a practical business. It was something you could *do*, not merely something you watched.

Teen movies

For a huge number of boomers, horror movies and drive-ins were a quintessential feature of their youth, but they are most commonly associated with another 1950s phenomenon – the rise of the teenager. Although the term 'teen-ager' had been widely used throughout the first half of the twentieth century, the idea of the teenager as a distinct cultural and social group gained a great deal of currency in the 1950s, so it is perhaps no surprise that Hollywood noticed the teen audience. In the words of Thomas Doherty, '1950s teenagers were strange creatures, set apart from previous generations of American young people in numbers, affluence, and self-consciousness ... they had more money; and they were more aware of themselves as teenagers.'[48] These were not boomers, the oldest of whom would not reach their teens until the very end of the decade, but the growing interest in teens was an early example of movie producers beginning to target viewers on the basis of their age.

In addition to the findings of 1950s audience surveys, Doherty sees the success of Columbia's Bill Haley vehicle *Rock Around the Clock* in 1956 as a key turning point. 'Prior to 1956, there was no industry-wide consensus on the vital importance of the teenage market, much less an earnest assault on it. After *Rock Around the Clock*, the industry campaign to attract teenagers would be concerted and conscious.'[49] The film had been hastily assembled by independent producer Sam Katzman to capitalize on the growing popularity of Bill Haley and the Comets, and it was one of the first releases to depict, and address a subculture of rock 'n' roll music and its teenaged fans.

While *Rock Around the Clock* may have generated solid profits on the back of its low production cost, the film was not a major hit – failing to chart at all in the top thirty highest grossing releases of the year. Rather, Doherty

---

[47]David Konow, 'Remembering the Wonders in Famous Monsters Magazine', in *Tested*, 25 November 2014, http://www.tested.com/art/movies/468170-remembering-wonders-famous-monsters-magazine/.

[48]Thomas Doherty, *Teenagers and Teenpics: The Juvenilization of American Movies in the 1950s* (Philadelphia: Temple University Press, 2002), 34.

[49]Doherty, *Teenagers and Teenpics*, 54–5.

observes, it was significant because it was 'marketed to teenagers to the pointed exclusion of their elders'.[50] More importantly, the film encouraged the major studios to invest in low-budget pop musicals featuring established, teen-friendly stars. The most successful of these was Elvis Presley, who featured in a string of hits in the late 1950s/early 1960s starting with *Love Me Tender* in 1956. He featured as a childhood or teen memory for eighteen respondents, all but one of them female. In his biography, Bill Clinton gives an insight into Elvis's influence on young boomers:

> I loved Elvis. I could sing all his songs, I admired him for doing his military service and was fascinated when he married his beautiful young wife, Priscilla. Unlike most parents, who thought his gyrations obscene, my mother loved Elvis, too, maybe even more than I did. ... Elvis' first movie, *Love Me Tender*, was my favorite and remains so, though I also liked *Loving You* [1957], *Jailhouse Rock* [1957], *King Creole* [1958], and *Blue Hawaii* [1961]. After that, his movies got more saccharine and predictable.[51]

Despite the grand claims made about the importance of the teenagers in the 1950s, and Hollywood's efforts to address them, teens did not really constitute a significant audience in pure demographic terms, and teen films were a minor trend that rarely generated substantial returns. The trade press barely mentioned teenagers in the 1950s, and certainly privileged them no more than any other demographic group as it looked for ways to stop declining audiences. Even if they went to the movies very regularly, the teenagers of the 1950s had been born during a period of low birth rates, and as a result, they constituted a small subset of the overall population. In 1950, there were less than 20 million Americans aged between fifteen and nineteen out of a total population of 150 million, and so they constituted less than 6 per cent of the total population. By contrast in 1970, fifteen- to nineteen-year-olds made up 10 per cent of a significantly expanded population. Demographic historians have described a 'pinch' in the number of teenagers that lasted throughout the 1950s, but which was quickly reversed as baby boomers grew older.[52] Teenagers were then, and remain, frequent moviegoers, but in the 1950s they were less important as a demographic than at any other time in the post-war period.

So, teenagers may have emerged as a recognizable group and discrete stage of human development in the 1950s but the importance of the teen film in the 1950s, for Hollywood at least, can easily be overestimated. Many

---

[50]Ibid., 57.
[51]Bill Clinton, *My Life* (New York: Arrow, 2005), 36.
[52]Frank Hobbs and Nicole Stoops, *Demographic Trends in the 20th Century* (Washington: US Government Printing Office, 2002), 55.

younger boomers saw Hollywood's teen films, and were influenced by them, but for the film industry, focusing on teens was a brief fad that never really worked to reverse declining audiences, because teens did not constitute a large enough audience to make much of an impact on the box office (although they certainly would later, when the boomers entered their teens). As a result, teen films quickly became the preserve of small companies on the margins of the business, and did not return to prominence until the mid-1960s.

Adult life and adult movies

Despite the industry's unwillingness to develop a strategy to engage with suburban viewers, Hollywood did seek to depict shifting trends in family life in the American suburbs in the second half on the 1950s, often in fairly negative terms. Nina Liebman observes that 'in the 1950s, a new type of drama began to dominate major studio output, a drama in which representations of family life began a strange and pronounced journey into stylistic excess, patriarchal omnipotence and the depiction of controversial social issues'.[53] Where television generally depicted family life as benign, a number of movies showed American families to be troubled, sexually repressed and, at times, emotionally destructive. These films include Douglas Sirk's *All That Heaven Allows* (1955) and *Imitation of Life* (1959), Nicholas Ray's *Bigger Than Life* (1956) and *Rebel without a Cause* (1956), as well as Mark Robson's *Peyton Place* (1957) and various others.

Some of these suburban melodramas struck a chord with audiences (notably *Rebel without a Cause*, *Peyton Place* and *Imitation of Life*) and generated impressive returns, while others performed less well. But they were united in their presentation of a troubling vision of the American family and suburban experience that translated the writings of William Whyte and David Reisman onto the screen. The films invariably focused on weak fathers who either hurt or damage their children (*Bigger Than Life* and *Rebel without a Cause*), or they treated suburbia and the family unit as a superficial construct, beneath which lurked sexual misadventure, misery, anxieties over class and race, and all manner of other problems (*Imitation of Life*, *Peyton Place*). Surprisingly few of these films featured children, focusing instead on the romantic or social difficulties faced by teenagers, but a handful found room to include youthful boomers. *Bigger Than Life* focuses on a suburban father (played by James Mason) who becomes addicted to cortisone and fixates on the educational needs (and failings) of his young son. While the son is little more than a cipher in an otherwise lurid

---

[53]Nina Leibman, *Living Room Lectures: The Fifties Family in Film and Television* (Austin: University of Texas Press, 1995), 6.

story of drug addiction and attempted murder, the movie nonetheless gives voice to concerns over child rearing and childhood that increasingly came to dominate 1950s discourse. In a less dramatic fashion, the comedy drama *A Hole in the Head*, directed by Frank Capra in 1958, features Frank Sinatra as Tony, the widowed father of an eleven-year-old boy, and focuses on his life as a hotelier in Miami. The film is predominantly concerned with Tony's romantic travails, but in the character of his son, Ally, the baby boomers are acknowledged, and the pair enjoy a lively father/son relationship.

In a more general sense, the push in the 1950s by filmmakers such as Rey, Otto Preminger, Stanley Kramer and George Stevens to seriously address America's social problems within popular entertainment gave visibility to many of the issues – such as race and sexual freedom – that would become important causes for many boomers as they reached adulthood. Here, the rise to stardom of Sidney Poitier is a good example of the ways in which Hollywood product could engage with (and potentially influence) social debate. Raised in Miami by Jamaican parents, Poitier became a major star in the late 1950s following his role in *The Defiant Ones* (1958). Over the next decade he played a string of 'masterful, restrained, wholly proper, and desexualized hero[es]', winning the Oscar for Best Actor for *Lilies of the Field* (1963), and becoming the industry's top box office star. For Paul Monaco, 'The phenomenon of Sidney Poitier's acting success can easily be perceived as a product of 1960s Hollywood's liberal good intentions, or could be ridiculed as the crass exploitation of a pleasant male stereotype by producers during an era of new consciousness about race in America.'[54] Either way, as Terry Christensen concludes, 'His screen presence surely helped prepare white audiences for integration. He also helped create an audience for virtually all black film.'[55] In our survey, Poitier's films were mentioned by nine respondents. Citing *Guess Who's Coming to Dinner* (1967), respondent 254 – who was twenty when the film came out – said, 'When I look back and think (teens thru twenties), most films that moved me involved race/racism.' *Lilies of the Field* came out when respondent 260 was eleven. On seeing it, she 'fell in love with Sidney Poitier and still am'.

Away from Poitier's films, however, the increasingly challenging melodramas of the 1950s, with their growing focus on sex, drugs and other transgressive topics were part of a wider shift in Hollywood's mid-budget productions, which arguably served to push the industry even further from the child and family market, ultimately excluding children entirely. As television increasingly came to dominate the field of family entertainment, some in Hollywood felt that it was time to pursue an adult audience by presenting the sort of material that could not be screened on television. In a

---

[54]Paul Monaco, *The Sixties*, 149–51.
[55]Terry Christensen, quoted in Monaco, *The Sixties*, 151.

series of films, starting with Preminger's adaptation of stage play *The Moon is Blue* in 1953, the studios all began to produce movies that challenged existing censorship laws, by presenting sexual relationships, violence and drug use with a new-found degree of frankness. Many of these movies look tame in retrospect, but they represent a significant step change in acceptable topics for movies. According to those in the industry, the slow shift to more adult-oriented topics was 'the result of producers moving to satisfy what they conceive to be the public's slowly developing but very real yen for challenging, more adult entertainment'.[56]

Prior to the 1950s, Hollywood movies had been regulated according to the terms of the self-imposed 'Production Code', a document written by Motion Picture Producers and Distributors of America (MPPDA) chief Will Hays and a host of advisers. The Production Code was a set of guidelines, strictly enforced by the Production Code Administration, which sought to regulate the content of all movies in such a way as to render them palatable to viewers of all ages. By the 1950s, pressure to drop restrictions on film content was building. It was generally thought that the need to control the content of American movies limited their appeal in Europe, where ratings were already in place.[57] No studio seems to have developed a concerted strategy for favouring adult-oriented movies. Rather, external pressure in the form of court cases and European imports met internal pressure in the form of filmmakers who wanted to pursue more interesting subjects in more challenging ways. Furthermore, the industry's growing inability to generate profits from established genres encouraged experimentation. In a climate where television was increasingly perceived as the preferred medium of regular family entertainment, movies with adult themes proliferated. In this moment, Nina Liebman observes, 'The film and television industries began to carve out separate content turf', with Hollywood increasingly focusing on adult-oriented movies.[58]

Discussion of the censorship issue was another dominant concern for the movie trade throughout the 1950s, and another distraction from the baby boom. Worrying about movie content and movies for adults actually drew studio bosses and producers away from engaging with demographic data, and certainly discouraged them from making films for children, despite the fact that the challenging, adult-oriented movies of the period rarely generated anything other than modest box office returns. It is also worth noting that it is easy to overestimate the trend for challenging movies. As we have seen, Hollywood remained most successful when it catered to the widest possible audience demographic in the 1950s. It was only as the baby boom grew older,

---

[56]Brown, *The Hollywood Family Film*, 109.
[57]Fred Hift, 'Mature BO no Myth', *Variety*, 28 April 1954, 3.
[58]Liebman, *Living Room Lectures*, 3.

and developed a taste for more experimental movies, that such fare moved to the top of the box office charts. However, in the 1950s, one producer and one director captured the imagination of the boomers more than any others. The producer was Walt Disney and the director Billy Wilder.

Conclusion: Billy Wilder/Walt Disney

Billy Wilder was born in 1906, in the hinterlands between Poland and Austria. He worked in the German film industry during the 1920s, but fled to the United States before the outbreak of the Second World War and began directing in Hollywood in 1942 with *The Major and the Minor*. Throughout the 1950s, Wilder was extremely prolific, directing and writing a series of comedies, melodramas and noir movies, all inflected with a bitter, satirical edge. His story of murder and Hollywood glamour, *Sunset Boulevard* (1950), was followed by the bleak drama *Ace in the Hole* and *Stalag 17*, both in 1953, while later in the decade he directed mostly comedies, including *The Seven Year Itch* (1955) and *Some Like it Hot* (1959), before releasing the movie generally considered his masterwork in 1960, *The Apartment*.

Few of Wilder's movies were aimed at children in any way, and few depicted family life, or younger people, at all. Wilder was principally concerned with the failings, regrets and self-delusion of adults in the 1950s. Nancy Meyers considers him 'The God on the Mountain', and Ivan Reitman told us, 'I remember watching Billy Wilder very early in my life and being really knocked out by his films.'[59] Jack Epps Jr. recalled that he and his writing partner Jim Cash 'both had a great fondness for the work of Billy Wilder, who probably had the greatest influence on me as any one person, and *The Apartment* as any one film. I saw it when it came out, I think I was 11, 12. We loved the romance and the sensibilities of Billy Wilder.' Steve Kloves, who would go on to direct *The Fabulous Baker Boys* in 1986, and adapt Warner Brother's *Harry Potter* films, also claimed that '*The Apartment* is, I realise, very influential to me too'. The writer/director Cameron Crowe was so inspired by *The Apartment* that it inspired him to produce a book-length series of interviews with Wilder. In one interview he explained, '*The Apartment* is my favorite movie,' and he worked with Wilder because 'I had a deep need to pay tribute to this guy. He had really influenced me in my own study of screenwriting.'[60]

[59]Nancy Meyers, quoted in Daphne Merkin, 'Can Anybody Make a Movie for Women?', *New York Times*, 15 December 2003, http://www.nytimes.com/2009/12/20/magazine/20Meyers-t.html.

[60]Interview with Cameron Crowe, 'Talk of the Nation' *National Public Radio*, 20 Dec. 1999, transcription available at *The Uncool*, http://www.theuncool.com/press/conversations-with-wilder-npr-talk-of-the-nation/

Wilder's movies clearly provided a gateway to a richer engagement with cinema, especially for those boomers who would later go on to carve out careers in Hollywood. Far from deterring younger viewers, the 'adult' flavour of Wilder's work provided a hint of the mature possibilities that cinema might offer, and arguably Wilder's acerbic view of the world naturally matched up to the developing sensibilities of the baby boomer generation as they grew older. However, Wilder's films in no way recaptured the 'lost' audience of baby boomers that Hollywood struggled to address throughout the 1950s. Nor did many of the films discussed in this chapter, at least not to any serious degree. Even when movies of the 1950s struck a chord with younger viewers, they rarely generated exceptional box office returns, and the majority of Hollywood studios looked to the past in order to find solutions to the problems of the present.

As we have seen, Walt Disney took a different tack from almost anyone else in the film industry, and like Wilder, Disney was also a totemic figure in introducing boomers to the cinema, despite the very different nature of his movies. Perhaps the most remarkable aspect of Walt Disney Productions' commercial expansion in the 1950s is the lack of competition Disney faced in capitalizing on the baby boomers. Remarkably, no other film studios sought to pursue the child and family audience as Disney's success became clear. Instead, Disney was almost always treated as exceptional by the film industry, and by subsequent writers. Bob Thomas writes in his biography, *An American Original*:

> How could it happen? How could one man produce so much entertainment that enthralled billions of human beings in every part of the world? That is the riddle of Walt Disney's life.[61]

Steven Watts describes Walt Disney as 'arguably the most influential American of the twentieth Century', and makes the point that news stories in the 1950s 'regularly portrayed Walt Disney as a creative figure whose wondrous powers bordered on the magical'.[62] And Neal Gabler begins his exhaustive account of Disney's life by outlining the many ways that Disney 'reshaped the culture and American consciousness. Disney,' he writes, 'was protean', both as a cultural force and as an entrepreneur. Gabler observes 'by managing, almost purely on instinct, to tap into the elemental and the essential in almost every form he ever worked in'.[63] Even the most negative critiques of Disney invariably assume personal culpability.

---

[61]Bob Thomas, *Walt Disney: An American Original* (New York: Disney Editions 1976), 3.
[62]Watts, *The Magic Kingdom*, 397.
[63]Gabler, *Walt Disney*, x.

The trade press in the 1950s and 1960s was certainly less lyrical, but nevertheless often treated Disney with the kind of dismay reserved for outsiders. *Variety*'s report on Disneyland's opening begins by suggesting that the company's share value was probably 'scaled too high', ringing a note of caution over what appeared an outlandish idea. Good or bad, Disney was almost always seen as exceptional. As a result, Disney's success in the 1950s was invariably understood as a result of his 'genius' rather than as a consequence of demographic change.

In reality, Disney's growth in the 1950s was entirely due to the baby boom. Because Disney specialized in catering to child and family viewers, the company was far better positioned than any other film studio to capitalize on the baby boom generation. The sort of products that Disney provided directly targeted the largest demographic group in the United States (a group that only got larger as the 1950s rolled on). Consequently, Disney's films, television shows, theme parks and other products spoke to a large and ever-growing audience, which was mostly ignored by all the other film studios. What's more, Disney's success in the 1930s meant that the studio had already 'proven itself' to the boomer's parents, and so it entered the 1950s as the single most reliable 'brand' for family entertainment in the media marketplace.

The value of Disney's commercial appeal was encapsulated by the colossal success and lasting legacy of the 1964 release *Mary Poppins*, which starred Julie Andrews as a magical nanny to two British children at the turn of the century. In its historical setting, spectacular song and dance numbers, integration of animation with live action, and commercial appeal, the movie not only embodied Disney's address to baby boomers, it also brought together many key trends of 1950s and 1960s Hollywood. It was the second highest grossing release of the year, earning slightly less than the relatively similar, albeit more adult-skewing, *My Fair Lady*, but still generating rentals of over $31 million. Thirty of our survey respondents identified the film as a firm favourite. Respondent 47 (b.1963) recalled that '*Mary Poppins* was the first movie I saw in the theater that I remember'. Respondent 268 (b.1960) told us that 'I loved *Mary Poppins* when I was very young', while respondent 177 (b.1960) remembered that it was a 'Great movie', despite being 'terrified by the chimney sweeps'. Like so many of Disney's other productions, *Mary Poppins* focused on the relationship between children and their caregivers, but also functioned as a neat metaphor for Disney's relationship with his audience. *Mary Poppins* brings a practical magic to the lives of the children under her care, and takes them on adventures to a series of magical realms not entirely unlike the kinds of fun-filled spaces promised by Disneyland.

Despite the film's commercial success, it nonetheless marked a point of transition for Disney and the baby boom audience. Although Hollywood would continue to employ many of the strategies discussed in this chapter into the late 1960s, they became increasingly unworkable. Large-scale epics and musicals were competing for an ever-diminishing share of the audience, and in the late 1960s, attendance finally fell so low that the box office could no longer sustain regular high-budget productions. Furthermore, the baby boomers who now dominated the US population were growing up, reaching their late teens and early twenties. In the late 1960s, the financial crisis that Hollywood had held at arm's length for over a decade – with intermittent success – finally arrived, and for the first time, the baby boomers were seen as the answer.

PART TWO

Youth

4

A Changing Audience

The 1960s were a time of crisis and renewal for Hollywood, marked by the curtailment of earlier production strategies and a more concerted effort to attract baby boom audiences. While the Walt Disney Company continued to pursue child audiences throughout the 1960s, the other major studios slowly increased production of films aimed at teenagers and young people. In the 1950s, teen movies had been a small but important feature of the studios' output. As the boomers entered their teenage years en masse, the settings and subject matter of earlier teen films (pop stars and pop music, delinquent antiheroes, family dysfunction, youth revolt) became more relevant to a larger subset of the audience. As a result, such themes began to recur more frequently, in more commercially successful films. The American movie market did not return to health by the end of the 1960s, but it entered a new phase, during which the assumed tastes and cultural experiences of the boomers became central to Hollywood's production strategies.

This chapter charts the growth of mainstream youth-oriented (16- to 24-year-olds) production during a period when youth values and identity were undergoing radical change. It begins in 1964, when the oldest boomers were eighteen. By this point, there were approximately 73 million baby boomers, who made up almost 40 per cent of the total US population. As overall profit levels declined, the power of that audience finally became obvious to Hollywood executives. In the first section we look at some unanticipated hits that challenged earlier assumptions about youth-oriented material. Throughout the remainder of the chapter, we look at the effect of these hits on production cultures at the time, and we examine the impact of changes to the rating system, which enabled filmmakers to tackle more explicit, challenging subject matter.

A new youth market

Hollywood's courting of the baby boom saw its beginnings in 1964 with the arrival of The Beatles. Just six months after their appearance on the

Ed Sullivan Show (CBS, 1948–71) the group's first feature, *A Hard Day's Night*, was released to US theatres. Little about the film's production hinted at its importance. Its distributor, United Artists, had assumed the group's popularity was a passing fad and so insisted on a brief shooting schedule and a low budget. The director, Richard Lester, was a 32-year-old American with little experience in making feature films, who had worked largely in British television comedy. The studio's uncertainty about the band's screen potential was such that they shared star-billing with ageing sitcom actor Wilfred Bramble.[1]

Yet *A Hard Day's Night* became a critical and commercial success and set a precedent for the next decade of Hollywood production. Neither Lester nor The Beatles were interested in following the relatively well-established formula for teen pop music movies. Instead, they combined equal helpings of European experimentation, British social realism and knockabout humour drawn from the band's personalities. In crisp black and white, *A Hard Day's Night* is a playful, heightened account of two days on tour, culminating in a live television appearance in London. Along the way, the band evades fans, gives impromptu performances and falls victim to comic misunderstandings. One encounter was especially prescient for the years ahead, on both sides of the Atlantic.

IMAGE 5 *George Harrison challenges an advertising executive in* A Hard Day's Night *(1964).*

---

[1]Tino Balio, *United Artists: The Company That Changed the Film Industry* (Madison: University of Wisconsin Press, 1987), 250–1.

Lost in the television studio, George Harrison accidentally wanders into the office of an advertising executive and is mistaken for an auditioning actor. The executive is casting a commercial for teenagers and initially treats the Beatle with undisguised scorn. In his view, teens are targets for exploitation, their 'worthless' opinions easily manipulated into buying 'nasty' fashions. However, when Harrison derides the agency's 'resident teenager' and professional trendsetter Susan ('She's a drag, a well-known drag. We turn the sound down on her and say rude things') the executive's sneering confidence evaporates. He orders Harrison out of the office and frets over the implications of what he has heard, asking his young secretary, 'You don't think he's a new phenomenon, do you?' Though a quick check of the calendar reassures him that the next change in youth fashion isn't due for another three weeks, he still elects to cancel Susan's contract: 'Let's not take any unnecessary chances.'

The scene works as a microcosm of the uncertainty and anxiety that gripped the media industries from the mid-1960s, especially in Hollywood. In the twenty years since the end of the Second World War, young people had become established as the primary market for entertainment and fashion. Blessed with free time and spending money, they were voracious consumers, apparently willing to attend films aimed at their parents and susceptible to gimmicks and trends. This seeming lack of discrimination kept much youth-oriented production cheap and formulaic and at worst bred the kind of contemptuous attitude among producers and executives portrayed in *A Hard Day's Night*. Yet such contempt hid the extent of their dependency, along with a growing suspicion that the young weren't always so easy to influence and predict. The release of *A Hard Day's Night* was a case in point.

With a budget of £189,000, the film returned $6.16 million in rentals in North America alone, making it the seventh most popular film of the year. It was also the first film aimed squarely at the youth market to break into the annual top ten, and it was clearly different from other hits of the period. Not only were The Beatles explicitly presenting themselves as representatives of a new, independent and self-confident youth identity, the film itself looked nothing like anything else in the charts. For survey respondent 216, who was a teenager when it was released, '*A Hard Day's Night* had an irreverence that I had rarely seen except in cartoons'. What little narrative the film contained was overwhelmed with camera tricks, gags and other flights of fancy. It was smart, impudent and exciting, and about as far from the endless Elvis vehicles as it was possible to imagine. *A Hard Day's Night* was an early warning of the massive change that was about to hit both the film industry and America as a whole.

The social and cultural forces that would erupt in the second half of the decade were already building. In his personal history of the 1960s, Todd Gitlin traces the true birth of the youth protest movement to the

Woolworth's sit-in in North Carolina in February 1960, when four young African American men refused to leave their seats at a segregated lunch counter. These four took part on the first day, rising to three hundred by the fifth. In Gitlin's view, 'youth culture might have remained just that – the transitional subculture of the young, a rite of passage on the route to normal adulthood – had it not been for the revolt of black youth, disrupting the American celebration in ways no one had imagined possible'.[2] As protest spread across the South, pockets of white young people were inspired to give their support, and not only to civil rights. Civil liberty, campus reform and peace movements all gained in popularity. The Student Peace Union, for example, grew from 150 members in 1960, to 2,000 by 1962 and 4,000 by 1963. The following year, all universities and campus-based organizations received a boost when the first year of the baby boom began enrolling, lifting freshman numbers by 37 per cent. Yet in 1964 protest and revolt was still not widespread: 'No one expected students to rise up en masse.'[3]

This was certainly true in the film industry. With its pervasive sense of youthful insubordination and invention, A Hard Day's Night may have been a preview of things to come, but at the time the studios could be forgiven for overlooking its significance. Relative to expectation, it had done uncommonly well, but it wasn't in the same league as the year's very top pictures My Fair Lady ($34 million in rentals), Mary Poppins ($31 million) and Goldfinger ($23 million). At this point, high-budget roadshow spectacles with an all-age appeal remained the most lucrative production trend, offering little motive for change. Indeed, when The Sound of Music became the highest grossing film of all time in 1965, the studios embarked on an unprecedented programme of spending on similar productions. In February 1967, a front page Variety story reported that 'every major Hollywood studio is currently involved either in the prepping or releasing of filmusicals'.[4] Sixteen were counted in total. Far from being a priority, youth was noticeable mainly by its absence from studio production between 1965 and 1967. Where teens or young adults did appear they were either deadly earnest idealists, or 'groovy', perpetually dancing funsters, both types evident in Stanley Kramer's 1967 hit Guess Who's Coming to Dinner. Still, in other quarters, people were taking notice, and several of them were to be major players in the years ahead.

At Columbia's Screen Gems television unit, two recently hired producers, Bob Rafelson and Bert Schneider, used the success of A Hard Day's Night to sell a television pilot following the adventures of a young, male four-piece pop group. Screen Gems bought the concept from Raybert Productions in

[2]Todd Gitlin, The Sixties: Years of Hope, Days of Rage (London: Bantam, 1993), 83.
[3]Gitlin, The Sixties, 164.
[4]Anon., 'H'wood Poppin' to Sound of Music With 16 Film Tuners Set by Majors', Variety, 1 February 1967, 1.

April 1965 and *The Monkees* premiered on NBC in September 1966. The series made its creators rich, and Rafelson and Schneider sought to invest their profits in film production.[5]

A Hard Day's Night also inspired a number of younger film writers and directors, including Francis Ford Coppola (b.1939) and William Friedkin (b.1935). Friedkin was a television director who made his feature debut with *Good Times* (1967), a Lester-esque caper that substituted The Beatles for Sonny and Cher. While *Good Times* was a critical and commercial failure, it nonetheless led to further work in features. Coppola was an overachieving graduate student at UCLA, mixing odd jobs for Roger Corman with a writing contract for Seven Arts. 'Undeniably' inspired by *A Hard Day's Night*, he wrote, produced and directed *You're a Big Boy Now* (1966), about zany New York counterculture.[6] It was entered into the Cannes Film Festival and received an Oscar nomination (for actress Geraldine Page), and it also served as Coppola's graduate thesis. It did not, however, have any impact on industry thinking; when the then 29-year-old Coppola returned to Hollywood, he was assigned to the Fred Astaire leprechaun musical *Finian's Rainbow* (1968).

In the box office charts, signs of a cultural shift continued to come from outside the major studios, mainly in the form of relatively popular imports from 'swinging' London. In 1965, John Schlesinger had the twenty-second highest grossing film of the year with *Darling* about the sexual and romantic misadventures of a model, played by Julie Christie. In 1966, *Alfie*, *Georgy Girl* and *Blow-Up* were all top twenty hits in the United States, and combined a new sexual frankness with young British stars and aesthetic choices that were clearly different from Hollywood's norms. *Blow-Up* in particular, though the least commercially popular of the three, became notorious for featuring full-frontal nudity and ambiguous artistic flourishes from its director, Michelangelo Antonioni.[7] The only comparable US production came in the form of a low-budget B-movie from veteran youth exploitation producers American International Pictures (AIP). Directed by Roger Corman (b.1926), *The Wild Angels* starred Peter Fonda and Nancy Sinatra as members of a motorcycle gang who antagonize everyone they encounter. It is a relatively nihilistic, violent film, but the gang justify their behaviour (including killing a policeman and beating up a priest) as some kind of rebellion against social constraint. As Fonda's character puts it, 'We wanna be free. We wanna be free to do what we want to do. We want to be free to ride our machines without being hassled by the man. And we want to get loaded and we want to have a good time.' Such sentiments apparently

---

[5]Peter Biskind, *Easy Riders, Raging Bulls: How the Sex, Drugs and Rock 'n' Roll Generation Saved Hollywood* (New York: Bloomsbury, 1999), 52–60.
[6]Peter Cowie, *Coppola: A Biography* (New York: Da Capo, 1994), 31.
[7]Peter Lev, *The Euro-American Cinema* (Austin: University of Texas Press, 1993), 91–8.

struck a chord, as *The Wild Angels* became the sixteenth biggest hit of 1966, and AIP's most successful film ever.

By May 1967, the cumulative impact of 'off-beat imports' provoked *Variety* to note, 'Many in the trade are asking the same question these days: "why can't we make the same kind of picture here?"'[8] In part, the trade paper had answered this question already. In 1964, its front page had declared that the American film industry was an 'Old Guy's Biz' with the average age of filmmakers standing at fifty-four.[9] As studios cut back their workforces, the various unions conspired to protect their existing members, making it increasingly difficult for outsiders to get a foot on the career ladder. A few high-profile exceptions demonstrated the value of new – usually younger – ideas. The year 1964 saw Stanley Kubrick – still only thirty-six – release *Dr Strangelove*. The following year, Mike Nichols was able to use his stage success and connections to make his directorial debut with *Who's Afraid of Virginia Woolf* (1966) aged thirty-four. While neither film could be accused of being specifically youth-oriented, both were innovative, controversial and successful, *Virginia Woolf* spectacularly so, becoming the third highest grossing film of its year.

As 1967 progressed there were more obvious signs of a larger change in American cultural priorities, which was noticed relatively quickly by independent producers. In the news media, both the counterculture and student protest were prominently discussed, troop deployments to Vietnam increased and the resulting draft was more widely applied. The result was a new wave of anti-war demonstrations. In January 1967, a collection of countercultural groups, including many older boomers, gathered in San Francisco for the 'Human Be-In', an event that set the stage for the city's Summer of Love and provided a convenient visual shorthand for the social changes taking place at the time. In August, AIP announced their upcoming slate would focus on 'the Now Generation', 'a program of films designed for the young adult audience market ranging from college students to age twenty four', the oldest of whom would have been born in 1943.[10] By November, United Artists were making similar noises. Executive Vice President David A. Picker briefed journalists that his company would be 'throwing a bridge over the generational gap' with 'young directors' and 'new ideas'. Apparently bemused by the presentation, *Variety* saw fit to add, 'Possibly without intention the symbol of the "young director" with "young ideas" seemed to be Richard Lester.'[11]

---

[8]Ronald Gold, 'US Can't Get On the Offbeat. But Majors Take the "Risk" Abroad', *Variety*, 10 May 1967, 10.

[9]Anon., 'US Films as "Old Guy's Biz"', *Variety*, 24 November 1964, 1.

[10]Anon., 'AIP Sets Now Generation', *Variety*, 16 August 1967, 7.

[11]Robert J. Landry, 'UA Bridges Generation Gap: Every Age Group Has Understudy', *Variety*, 13 November 1967, 3.

The majors were not far behind. Throughout 1967, author John Gregory Dunne was given extensive access to the day-to-day running of Twentieth Century Fox by Richard Zanuck. His account of the year, published as *The Studio*, painted a fascinating portrait of an organization committed to following its big hit, *The Sound of Music*, but beset with doubt regarding changing market conditions. The main focus was the colossal effort and expense Fox was devoting to three musicals, *Dr Dolittle* (1967), *Star!* (1968) and *Hello, Dolly!* (1969). Darryl Zanuck, Richard's father and boss, estimated the combined cost of the three projects to be $50 million and confided to Dunne, 'Quite frankly, if we hadn't made such an enormous success with *The Sound of Music*, I'd be petrified.'[12] Yet elsewhere in Dunne's account there was an awareness of new audiences and tastes demanding consideration. Richard Zanuck rejected a Henry Koster project about a youth orchestra travelling to Moscow with the comment, 'You'll get the music lovers, no doubt about that, none at all. But how about Beatles fans?'[13] In addition, Dunne reported that

> the enormous success of *Darling, Alfie, Morgan* [1966] and *Georgy Girl* had not been lost on the studio. All had been made with stars then virtually unknown in the US, and, instead of trying for mass appeal, all had appealed primarily to the under-thirty audience. The promise of high return for low investment was irresistible ... and the studio had seven low-budget contemporary English pictures in preparation.[14]

A November industry advert from Fox detailed a new campaign it was running in 'such youth-orientated magazines as *Cheetah*, *Eye* and college publications ... to reach the opinion makers of the young audience'. The tagline was 'Think young! Think Fox!'[15] In December, a short *Variety* article announced that 'related to the notion that the biggest audience for film is the younger generation [Warner-Seven Art's] idea is to 'get with' practically everything that can be pitched to kids'.[16] Implicit in all of this was a suspicion that something had happened to America's young that meant that they could no longer be reached by Hollywood's existing methods and product. Despite the industry's recent run of success, the assumption appears to have been that the likes of *My Fair Lady* and *The Sound of Music* appealed only to families and older audiences, missing out the 'youth' audience who were seizing hold of the culture. This apparent change, usually referred to as a 'revolution', ran the gamut of experience from fashion to politics, social relations

[12] John Gregory Dunne, *The Studio* (London: Vintage, 1998), 242.
[13] Dunne, *The Studio*, 44.
[14] Ibid., 66.
[15] Advertisement, *Variety*, 29 November 1967, 12.
[16] Anon., 'W7 Stress Upon Youth', *Variety*, 6 December 1967, 4.

to entertainment.[17] As David Picker noted, there was a perception that a generation gap had opened, and Hollywood personnel were left stranded on the wrong side. This perception was reinforced by concurrent developments in the MPAA's long-awaited transition from censorship to ratings.

Towards a ratings system

Virginia Woolf and *Blow-Up* were decisive events in the slow demise of the MPAA's Production Code. The voluntary system of self-censorship had functioned relatively well throughout the golden age of the 1930s and 1940s. However, Jon Lewis notes that 'the PCA seemed to lose control of production in the late 1950s', as a combination of more explicit post-war film imports, along with filmmakers seeking greater creative licence, declining studio support and unreliable audiences undermined the viability of the code.[18]

In June 1966, the Production Code Administration (PCA) gave a seal to the expletive-heavy, adult-themed *Woolf* when Warner offered to release the film with the warning, 'No One Under 18 Admitted without Parent'. In September, the MPAA unveiled a revised Code that formalized Warner's innovation with the label 'Suggested for Mature Adults'. The new code had been in place for less than three months when it too was found wanting. When MGM submitted *Blow-Up* for approval, the PCA objected to two scenes of female nudity that included pubic hair. MGM were at first willing to cut the offending shots, but when Antonioni objected, the studio stood by their director, ultimately releasing the film in December without a seal using a subsidiary company, Premiere Pictures.[19] When the film became a hit, it effectively rendered the code irrelevant. The MPAA had only appointed its new chairman, Jack Valenti, in April, and one of his first tasks was to plan the introduction of a new ratings system, which would restrict access depending on age.

Questions of audience became increasingly urgent as the industry adjusted to the two-tier Production Code and the pending arrival of ratings. Granted the option to include 'mature' content in their films for the first time in almost forty years, filmmakers had to weigh up the benefits and drawbacks

---

[17]For example, Anon., '"Visual" Mod & "Verbal" Crix: Kubrick's Sure *2001* To Click', *Variety*, 10 April 1968, 5, which runs, 'Because today's filmgoers are predominantly under 25, it would seem vital for the industry to learn something about this market and its tastes. As many sociological and psychological commentators have already noted, there has been a widespread revolution among today's youth, but little of this change has yet to be reflected in the films produced in the US.'

[18]Jon Lewis, *American Film: A History* (New York: WW Norton, 2008), 242.

[19]Lev, *The Euro-American Cinema*, 95.

of formally limiting their potential audience. To assist their members, in 1967 the MPAA commissioned the Daniel Yankelovich Research Corporation to conduct an unprecedented survey of moviegoing audiences and their habits.[20] Initially presented to top studio executives in January 1968, it served to confirm their suspicions. Valenti released an overview to the public in March that worked hard to put a positive spin on the findings. However, the full report summary was leaked at the same time and it came to very different conclusions.

In both accounts, the headline situation was the overwhelming dominance of youth at the national box office.[21] In 1967, the 28 million 16 to 24-year-olds in America comprised 20 per cent of the population, but nearly half (48 per cent) of movie ticket sales. For Valenti, this was cause for optimism, given that – thanks to the baby boom – the youth demographic was only going to grow in the coming years. Valenti also noted the report's finding that college attendance increased cinema attendance and concluded that – given the boomers' historically unparalleled levels of education – the generation could be counted on to provide a 40 per cent jump in ticket sales by 1975. The report's authors, however, were less convinced of the industry's current and future health. For them, a major area for concern was the 30 per cent of the country who never went to the cinema at all, and the further 18 per cent who 'almost never' attended. Further, the industry was almost totally reliant on a core group of 'frequent' moviegoers: 18 per cent of the population who bought 76 per cent of tickets. In this category the young were even more prevalent, accounting for 54 per cent.

To explain these discrepancies, Yankelovich offered factors familiar and novel. As might be expected, settling down and having a family severely cut into the time and funding people allotted for catching a movie. Equally, few in the industry would have been shocked to hear 'television has apparently been draining off the less discriminating audience which finds the kind of casual diversion it wants readily enough on TV'. More specific to the current moment was respondents' opinion of the films being released. Against the backdrop of the challenges to the Production Code, the survey found a small majority (57 per cent) 'generally approve the recent liberalization of film content and treatment'. Yet within this statistic was evidence of a generational divide. According to Yankelovich, the trend towards increased sex and violence was 'almost completely reflective of young people's opinions', with 83 per cent of 16 to 24-year-olds approving. By contrast, more than half (57 per cent) of those over forty were found to 'actively disapprove' of the

---

[20]According to Valenti, the research was paid for by the major studios, who each contributed $15,000. Wayne Warga, 'Facts of Life about Movie Audiences', *Los Angeles Times Calendar*, 29 December 1968, 4.

[21]This, and subsequent quotations, from Anon., 'Pix Must Broaden Market', *Variety*, 20 March 1968, 1, 78.

same developments. The report concluded that Hollywood would be unwise to ignore the demands of such a massive potential audience and pointed out that a lack of family entertainment in theatres was a frequent lament. Listening to their needs could help enlarge the audience pool, whereas 'the danger we see is that the industry may neglect this longer range and more difficult task in favor of the more immediate opportunities which do not require a coordinated effort towards a long-range industry-wide goal'.

Both the link between filmgoing and college and the impact of new adult content are evident in boomer recollections of the period, in our survey and elsewhere. One important detail is that campus enthusiasm for film was not limited to new releases. A repeated memory is the teenage discovery of art cinema – both American and foreign – and a new appreciation for Hollywood classics, often linked to film societies and campus screenings. From 1964, at McMasters University in Canada, Ivan Reitman became involved in the running of the student union's film society:

> We ran all these series of films: horror movies, comedies, big Hollywood extravaganzas, this was of course the years of the French New Wave and the Italian neorealism from the fifties, and we ran series for everything and sold series tickets, and we were this huge hit and made a tonne of money and we would take all that money and give it to various kids to make movies.

At the University of Michigan, Lawrence Kasdan was an eager patron of a similar programme, having arrived in 1966:

> There were all these film series showing the old films. Not only the American films, which I had known and loved, but all the foreign films I had never been exposed to at all. And also some much older American films that had never been on television. It was like taking a bath. I was seeing five to ten movies a week.

Over at Michigan State a year later, Jack Epps, Jr. recalls:

> You'd go into people's rooms and there'd be posters on the wall of Bogart and Laurel and Hardy and WC Fields, all these people who'd been totally forgotten. They were forgotten people. Humphrey Bogart was just gone. So he became resurrected and people became interested, and then the New Wave, and French films and Fellini and Bergman and all those things became a very big deal.

Our survey tells a similar story. For respondents of all ages, college was a time of expanding cinematic horizons. All of the twenty-two respondents who expressly mentioned a general preference for art or foreign film in their teens and young adulthood also reported they had some experience of college education, even if they did not graduate. Respondent 142, born in 1945, was drawn to 'arty stuff, like foreign films, or comedies like those of Peter Sellers'. A college Buster Keaton festival was particularly memorable: 'I never laughed so hard in my life.' For respondent 240, born in 1953, 'There was only one theater when I was growing up; when I went to college, there were dozens available. ... By my senior year ... I was watching fifty films a year (I kept track).' Respondent 166 (b.1961) remembers, 'In college, I had two film societies on campus that showed a ton of movies. The huge metropolitan area that I was in also added a few artsy movie theaters. That led me to seeing three or more movies [a week] for most of my college life. Those were rarely new releases, but mostly older movies and often foreign.'

As will be discussed in more detail below, accounts from the time and written since find a connection between cinephilia and the leading edge of social and political change. Noting in 1966 that 'film is the art for which there is the greatest spontaneous appetite in America at present',[22] critic Stanley Kauffmann excitedly labelled the youth of the day 'The Film Generation' for their 'uniquely responsive' attitude towards cinema. Among the reasons given for this development, 'The film form seems particularly apt for the treatment of many of the pressing questions of our time: inner states of tension or of doubt or apathy.'[23] Such a reading fits with a recollection of Todd Gitlin from 1962, in a period of personal uncertainty before he became president of Students for a Democratic Society (SDS):

I went to Bogart movies (the two-week Bogart festival had become an exam-time institution at the Brattle Theatre): I was overpowered by *Casablanca*, of course, but also by *To Have and Have Not* [1944] and even the hypersentimental *Key Largo* [1948] and *Passage to Marseilles* [1944], all allegories about the passage from cynicism to political commitment. I also loved Truffaut's *Shoot the Piano Player* [1960], I think because it illustrated so brilliantly how things don't work out as you plan.[24]

SDS held their first meetings at the University of Michigan, where Kasdan recalls,

The entire time I was there – from 1966 and I actually stayed on to '72 because I got a master's degree – that was the hottest moment in American student radicalism. The movies were absolutely the thing that was happening culturally. The anti-war movement was happening

[22]Stanley Kauffmann, *A World on Film: Criticism and Comment* (New York: Harper and Row, 1966), 415.
[23]Kauffmann, *A World on Film*, 417.
[24]Gitlin, *The Sixties*, 103.

politically, but there was plenty of mixing and crossing over in terms of what the zeitgeist was. The zeitgeist was: the world is changing. We're going to change it. And look: the movies are different to how they've ever been.

As well as new ideas, films in the mid-1960s were also providing youth with hitherto unimaginable access to taboo subject matter and graphic imagery. In effect, films intended for 'Mature Audiences' in the language of the PCA were most appealing to viewers in their teens. As filmmakers home and abroad increasingly pushed at the boundaries of acceptable content, boomers became the first generation of young people to have nudity, adult language, discussion of sexual issues and bloody violence as part of mainstream entertainment. They made quite an impression. For respondent 750, born in 1946, 'Who's Afraid of Virginia Woolf will always stand out. That was an extraordinary experience and it taught me that film can be more than fluffy entertainment'. Respondent 648 (b.1945) also remembered seeing Virginia Woolf 'multiple times'. Respondent 210 (b.1950) said of her teen years, 'I remember few of the movies, but do remember seeing Alfie and Georgy Girl. Note that I was still in the conservative Midwest at that time, and racy or controversial movies never came to town.' For respondent 236 (b.1955), the most memorable film of his youth was The Blue Max (1966), for affording him 'my first view of female breasts', a fleeting drop of Ursula Andress's towel. Speaking in 1985, filmmaker John Hughes (b.1950) vividly recalled the impact of Blow-Up:

> Sex is much more exposed now. When I was a kid, Playboy was looking at boobs – that was it. There were rumors hinted that photos had been taken of completely naked people. I remember when I saw Blow-Up for the first time. I saw it about twenty five times, moving closer to the front row. Then when it came out on videocassette, I went and looked at it. I remembered the scene where David Hemmings and the two girls are rolling around on the paper as being at least four hours long. But it was "Wham!" – it was a flash, it was gone. But it was burned in on my brain.[25]

At the same time as executives were digesting the implications of the Yankelovich survey, a series of events made the pace of change – and the extent of national division – appear more urgent. In America, just as in Europe, amusement at the free spirit and eccentricity of young people was giving way to concern, as alternative lifestyles became more prominent and protest commonplace. In October 1967, 100,000 people had marched on the Pentagon in protest at the war in Vietnam. In April and May 1968,

---

[25]John Hughes, quoted in Chris Willman, 'The Kids Are Alright', Bam, 29 March 1985, 21.

students staged an occupation of buildings at Columbia University. In August 1968, there were violent clashes between police and protesters outside the Democratic National Convention in Chicago. In Hollywood, a series of unexpected hits and flops rocked the industry, ushering in a period that has since been seen as a high point of artistic and culturally significant filmmaking. The first of these films, Arthur Penn's *Bonnie and Clyde*, was released in 1967. By focusing on the experiences and world view of young antiheroes, and making use of the licence afforded by the new ratings system, the movie appeared to offer a new kind of experience, geared much more directly to the tastes of the boomers than anything that had preceded it.

A break with the past

As almost every history of the period delights in telling, *Bonnie and Clyde* was not an immediate triumph. Its producer-star Warren Beatty had to plead with studio head Jack Warner to get financing, and when Warner sold his studio to Seven Arts, the low-budget project got lost in the shuffle, receiving little support during a half-hearted 1967 release. Those that did see it, though, took notice. In the *New York Times*, Bosley Crowther was so appalled by the film's graphic violence and (as he saw it) flippant tone that he subjected it to two separate mauling reviews.[26] In the *New Yorker*, Pauline Kael was equally spirited in its defence, writing 9,000 words of detailed praise.[27] Against this backdrop of clashing opinion, the film acquired must-see status, to the extent that Warner-Seven Arts agreed to a rerelease in January 1968, where takings were often double what they had been in the same theatres first time around. By the end of its second run, *Bonnie and Clyde* had taken nearly $23 million in domestic rentals having cost just $1.6 million.

The Graduate, another key hit with younger viewers, was an equally small-scale production (it cost $3 million), but from early in production its independent producer/distributor Joseph Levine suspected he had something special. In April 1967, Levine's company Embassy had announced an ambitious slate of films, but most effort and expense was devoted to publicizing *The Graduate*'s Christmas debut. Early reviews vindicated this decision, with *Variety* concluding, 'The young market, particularly will dig [it], and older audiences also will be amused.'[28] Tellingly, Levine focused his

---

[26]Bosley Crowther, 'Bonnie and Clyde', *New York Times*, 14 April 1967, http://www. nytimes.com/movie/review?res=EE05E7DF173CE361BC4C52DFB266838C679EDE; Bosley Crowther, 'Run, Bonnie and Clyde', *New York Times*, 3 September 1967, 57.
[27]Pauline Kael, 'Bonnie and Clyde', *New Yorker*, 21 October 1967, 147–71.
[28]A. D. Murphy, 'The Graduate', *Variety*, 20 December 1967, 6.

campaign on his director, writing a lengthy press release that declared, 'The real star of *The Graduate* is Mike Nichols, a star you never see, even though you do see him in every frame of the film.'[29] At the box office, the film began spectacularly and never looked back. By July it had sold 20 million tickets,[30] and it ultimately brought in $40 million in rentals, third for the decade and by far the best return compared to cost.

At first glance, *Bonnie and Clyde* and *The Graduate* were very different productions, the former a period gangster film, the latter a contemporary coming-of-age comedy. But under the surface, the two shared sources of inspiration and presented similar visions of America. Both drew upon Hollywood tradition, augmented by ideas taken from European art cinema. Both films flaunted their own authorship, using unconventional techniques such as rapid zooms, jump cuts and slow motion that were designed to be noticed. Both presented young protagonists driven to extreme action by a disappointing and unfair society. And both challenged taboos with their content. In *Bonnie and Clyde*, the violence that angered Bosley Crowther is designed to upset viewers, shocking them with its suddenness, or sickening them with its drawn-out detail. In *The Graduate*, the lead character embarks on an affair with the wife of his father's business partner that, while not graphically portrayed, was still unusual for a mainstream release. As Nancy Meyers, who was born in 1949 and saw *The Graduate* on New Year's Eve of her last year at high school, remembers, 'The concept of having an affair with your mother's friend was so out of my realm of possibility of what life could have in store for anybody, it was mind blowing.' For Meyers, *The Graduate* marked the moment she became aware that films were changing: 'you just started to see such an interesting take on life and not just a typical Hollywood movie ... things weren't told so simply.'

Both films received repeated mentions in our survey.[31] In the case of *Bonnie and Clyde*, several were struck by its violence. Respondent 787 (b.1954) saw the film when he was thirteen, prior to the introduction of the ratings code. He 'was extremely shocked at the violence, having never seen anything like it before'. Respondent 99 (b.1958) credits *Bonnie and Clyde* and movies by Sam Peckinpah for her 'seeing graphic violence for the first time ... They seem tame now but were shocking to me then.' For respondent 150, who was fifteen in 1968, the film was his 'first exposure to that much

---

[29]Joseph Levine, 'I Do Believe in Stars', 1967 Press Release from Embassy Pictures, in 'Tom Miller' file 6-f.81, AMPAS Margaret Herrick library.

[30]According to a full-page advertisement run in *Variety* by Embassy on 8 July 1968, 19.

[31]Thirteen respondents mentioned *The Graduate* (seven male, six female, born between 1941 and 1960, the seventh most referenced film of the 1966–75 period), eleven respondents mentioned *Bonnie and Clyde* (seven male, four female, born between 1946 and 1967, joint eleventh with *Blazing Saddles*, *Rocky Horror Picture Show*, *Easy Rider*, *MASH* and *Young Frankenstein*).

bloodshed and to bluegrass music'. Memories of *The Graduate* were often less detailed, although respondent 251, who was born in 1951 and saw it with an older friend, remembers it was 'quite scandalous at the time'. Both respondents 745 (male, b.1947) and 210 (female, b.1950) pinpoint 1967 as a year when their interest in filmgoing increased, 745 citing *The Graduate*, *Bonnie and Clyde* and Paul Newman's prison rebellion drama *Cool Hand Luke*. Respondent 210 says that 'prior to 1966, I saw very few releases. Starting in 1967, I saw most of the popular movies. ... Everyone my age loved *The Graduate*'.

The Graduate and *Bonnie and Clyde* showed that cinema that was artistic, young and challenging could not only be successful, but could out-gross more conventional product, a conclusion reinforced by a trio of 1968 releases. Stanley Kubrick's *2001* was originally intended to be a family roadshow attraction, but during production the director made a number of changes that took the project in a more challenging, narratively ambiguous direction. Reporting on reactions to a first week showing, *Variety* commented, 'Discussions in the lobby afterwards were of the "what does it mean" variety that in the past few years have usually suggested a [box office] winner.' Kubrick also encouraged associations with a younger audience, telling reporters, 'People over forty aren't used to breaking out of the straightjacket of words and literal concepts, but the response so far from younger people has been terrific.'[32]

At Paramount, two directors with pedigrees in European art cinema turned apparently unpromising material into major hits. Roman Polanski – known for a series of intellectual thrillers – made Ira Levin's novel *Rosemary's Baby*, about a mother's struggle against Satan worshippers, into a surprisingly restrained but deeply unsettling experience. Franco Zeffirelli, who had worked for Visconti and Rossellini before moving to America, filmed *Romeo and Juliet* using teenage leads. Though it would later receive a G rating (then revised to PG), marketing emphasized the film's sexuality, showing the couple lying in a naked embrace. *Romeo and Juliet* had the fifth highest rental returns for the year, and *Rosemary's Baby* the eighth. Both were also critical successes, including Oscar wins.

Beyond the rise of new and unexpected hits, 1968 also saw the production methods that the studios had adopted in the mid-1950s begin to look decidedly unstable. As with the New Hollywood hits, the Old Hollywood flops started late in 1967. *Dr Dolittle* opened three days before *The Graduate* in December 1967 and was supposed to be Fox's seasonal blockbuster. Instead, it finished eighteenth for the year with $6.2 million in rentals, only a fifth of what the film cost to produce and market. Many of the musicals and other expensive projects the studios had put into production following

---

[32]Anon., '"Visual" Mod & "Verbal" Crix', 5.

the success of *The Sound of Music* were relative failures. The problem was not necessarily that these films had become unpopular (though some undoubtedly were); it was that far too many were being made, all competing for the same pool of occasional filmgoers who went to see only one or two movies every year. When the number of lavish roadshow productions went up, attendance didn't follow suit, making it less and less likely any one film would be the runaway smash that their budgets all but required.

Other casualties included *Chitty Chitty Bang Bang* (1968), *Star!*, *Hello, Dolly!*, *Paint Your Wagon* (1969), *Sweet Charity* (1969), *Goodbye, Mr Chips* (1969) and *On a Clear Day You Can See Forever* (1970). As Sheldon Hall and Steve Neale have pointed out, the case of Fox's *Hello, Dolly!* is a particularly good example of the madness gripping the industry. Desperate for a bankable release, Fox began making their version of the hit musical in 1967, despite having given assurances that the finished film wouldn't be released until the original stage production had ended its run. This didn't happen until late 1969, meaning that Fox ran up a year of interest payments on an already costly production. In the end, *Hello, Dolly!* was the fifth biggest hit of its year, but it still managed to lose over $13 million.[33] Of the late 1960s musicals to feature in our survey, *Chitty Chitty Bang Bang* and *Camelot* (1967) received most mentions, but only one (for *Camelot*) came from a respondent who was over sixteen at the time of the films' releases. Columbia's hit *Funny Girl* (1968) was mentioned four times, but again, only one came from a respondent who fit within Hollywood's sixteen to twenty-five 'youth' category at the time. Among respondents who mentioned genres, nineteen remembered musicals as being a key genre during their teens and young adulthood, compared with forty-two who mentioned romance, seventy-one who mentioned horror, ninety-six who mentioned action/adventure and ninety-seven who mentioned science fiction. For these ordinary boomers, the mega budget family musical was not as memorable or relevant as a host of other production types.

Conclusion: Exclusive cinema

A sense that the audience was splintering was reinforced by the introduction of the MPAA's ratings system in November 1968. With ratings came – theoretically at least – confirmation that filmmakers in America had creative parity with the freedoms long enjoyed by European productions. Instead of relying on the PCA to police film content at the point of production, ratings allowed filmmakers to make whatever movie they wanted, which was then policed at the point of consumption, excluding audiences on the basis of age.

[33]Hall and Neale, *Epics, Spectacles, and Blockbusters*, 195.

Though the MPAA originally intended its 'G' rating to be a continuation of the original Production Code, it was soon being awarded to only a small minority of productions. Above G were M, R and X, and the next few years saw jockeying between filmmakers, the MPAA and audiences regarding the different ratings' limits and social meaning. This was most clearly apparent with the 'M' for Mature rating, as the label initially created some confusion among parents about whether Mature meant unsuitable for children. In 1970, it was relabelled GP, indicating 'parental guidance suggested' and in 1972 became PG. Yet there was equal uncertainty about the boundaries between the higher ratings. Respondent 195 remembers, 'When I was 11 my father took me and my sister to a double feature of *Patton* (released 1970 and rated GP) and *MASH* (1970, rated R). There was lots of war violence, but in the scene where Houlihan is shown naked in the shower, he tried to cover our eyes.' The first X rating was given to *Birds in Peru*, a French-language import, but *Variety* reported confusion within the industry about how the decision had been reached, particularly as the film appeared to have a similar level of sexual explicitness to *The Fox*, which received an R.[34]

The failure of high-profile mega-musicals, and the unexpected success of challenging low-budget films about young people finally turned Hollywood's attention to the baby boom generation as a distinct and commercially viable audience. The end of the Production Code further renegotiated the relationship between Hollywood and its audience, making age a determining factor in access. Ratings became a tool to address boomers, because they allowed movies to be targeted at one group, distinct in terms of age and cultural experience, while older and younger viewers were tacitly or explicitly excluded. If much of Hollywood's output had deterred older boomers by fostering movies that seemed old fashioned, or prim, then ratings opened up the prospect of new content. The challenge for studios and filmmakers was to balance the obvious sensational attraction that previously taboo material would have for some audiences, with the repelling effect it would have for others, as well as the negative impact the aggressive pursuit of such material could have on public relations. In the next chapter, we will see how these challenges were met.

---

[34]Anon., 'MPAA Ratings to Now: G(43), M(29), R(22); Puzzle: X for Birds but R for The Fox', *Variety*, 4 December 1968, 18.

5

Movies and Youth Revolt

In November 1968, *Variety* reported 'an atmosphere of confidence and optimism' at the National Association of Theater Owners' annual conference:

> If anything, the theatre men are more bullish about the future than are those supposedly eternal optimists, the picturemakers. The youth of the country – up to 25 years – are the backbone of the reviving film industry, and they represent an army of customers that, based upon statistics, will increase in numbers during the next five years. There is an almost unbounded confidence that this time the film business is attuned to the desires of this vital young audience.[1]

Bonnie and Clyde and *The Graduate* may have alienated some audiences, but they drew others with such force that it didn't seem to matter, and furthermore they were cheap. In the context of the new demographic information furnished by the Yankelovich report, it is understandable that Hollywood preferred to bet on younger audiences and ignore Yankelovich's warning against dependency on youth. Consequently, after 1968 the studios redoubled their efforts to understand and cater for what suddenly appeared to be their most reliable demographic.

This chapter explores some of the ways that Hollywood sought to address the boomers, with politically and artistically challenging productions designed to cater to an alternative, 'countercultural' mindset. As in previous decades, Hollywood studios knew relatively little about their audience, and frequently relied on a set of assumptions about young people that movies themselves helped to foster. The first part of this chapter looks at the changing values and opinions of the boomers. We then move on to explore the key releases of the late 1960s, by looking at some of the more

---

[1]Thomas M. Pryor, 'Youth With 'Em, Exhibs Grin: Clergy Helps on Film Morals', *Variety*, 13 November 1968, 1.

challenging, alternative productions of the period, and comparing these to more traditional genre releases.

Youth values

The studios' sudden focus on young audiences was more risky than it sounded, because 'youth' was often treated as a single, stable category, when in reality, the outlook and experiences of the boomers remained diverse. By 1968, the boomers watched far more movies than any other group, but they were not uniformly engaged in rebellion or artistic discovery. As Paul Light has argued, the popular image of the boomers as a horde of campus revolutionaries was one of a series of oversimplified caricatures, and in Light's view, 'each caricature describes a slightly different version of the same white, affluent baby boomer'.[2] In addition to their work for the MPAA, the Yankelovich Corporation were also engaged in an ongoing series of studies on youth opinion during the 1960s and 1970s, and their conclusions highlight a number of fundamental differences within the 16- to 25-year-old age group. For them, the most important split was between college and non-college attending youth, although significant differences also existed within each category, and along lines of gender and race.[3]

In the late 1960s, revolution was largely confined to college campuses, and even then unevenly so. Future film critic Leonard Maltin, who arrived at New York University in 1968, is a good example of a student who was caught off-guard by the pace of change. He remembers, 'I was about as ignorant and apolitical as one could imagine, so this was a rude awakening to a new reality. During my four years at school I had a crash course in societal change. It was also the era of women's lib. Everything was a learning experience then, including the movies.' Asked about whether he considered himself part of the popular image of the 1960s, he replied, 'I would say I was an observer. Sometimes a perplexed observer. *Often* a perplexed observer.'

Though it wasn't necessarily apparent at the time, there was not one revolution but two, both of which underpinned the emergent American 'counterculture' often associated with the boomers. The first was a shift in social values towards liberal ideas of self-fulfilment, equality and opposition to traditional notions of family, religion and patriotism. The second half of the 1960s saw a sudden increase in the pace of change, beginning in California. Tim Harris, who would go on to write *Trading Places* (1983) and *Twins* (1988), was born in 1946 and spent his summers in Big Sur.

[2]Light, *Baby Boomers*, 20.
[3]See Daniel Yankelovich, *The New Morality: A Profile of American Youth in the 1970s* (New York: McGraw Hill, 1974).

He remembers, 'It was so much fun. It just felt that the world had become completely different but in a very positive way.' According to Yankelovich, the holders of these 'new values' were 'never a majority of the college population' but thanks to their 'unfortunate tendency to demean the old values' they were both highly visible and somewhat removed from the rest of society.[4]

The second revolution was political and was fuelled by what its proponents saw as the unjust war in Vietnam. In Yankelovich's analysis, discontent began with a 'small core' of political radicals, never more than 15 per cent of students, who were temporarily able to enlist the support of the college majority based on their 'loathing, fear, and revulsion' of the draft.[5] After graduate student deferments ended in 1967 – meaning the entire male college class of '68 could be drafted – there were 221 major demonstrations on 101 campuses.[6] Until anti-war sentiment peaked in 1970 and 1971, it seemed to be part of the same movement upending other aspects of American life, so that for a time at the end of the 1960s, it looked like college youth were at war with everything their parents stood for. For the most visible members of the counterculture, political dissent, opposition to the war and support for civil rights of all kinds sat alongside a willingness to explore alternatively lifestyles, new fashion, drug use and new forms of popular music.

Off campus was a different picture. An October 1968 Gallup poll found that, overall, 45 per cent of respondents under thirty years of age self-identified as 'hawks' regarding the war, compared with 43 per cent who considered themselves 'doves' and 12 per cent who had no opinion.[7] A 1969 Yankelovich survey highlighted the difference between college and non-college opinion on war, with 69 per cent of non-college youth under twenty-five saying that 'containing communism' was a reason for which it was worth fighting a war, compared with only 43 per cent of college youth. In the same survey, 59 per cent of non-college youth said that 'fighting for our honor' was a reason for which it was worth fighting a war, compared with 25 per cent of college youth.[8] As Landon Jones notes, 'One of the ironies of Vietnam is that the opposition to the war was led by college students, who were safely deferred, whiles its support often came from young laborers ... who were doing the actual fighting.'[9]

---

[4]Yankelovich, *The New Morality*, 9.
[5]Ibid., 8.
[6]Jones, *Great Expectations*, 96.
[7]Yankelovich, The New Morality, 94.
[8]Richard M. Scammon and Ben J. Wattenberg, *The Real Majority* (New York: Coward, McCann & Geoghegan, 1971), 49.
[9]Jones, *Great Expectations*, 98.

Similarly, in the late 1960s, non-college youth's social values were still significantly closer to those of their parents than to trends on campus. In 1969, a clear majority still considered premarital sex and homosexuality to be morally wrong, and judged religion and patriotism to be very important values, all minority opinions among college youth. Unfortunately for the film industry, non-college youth were also more like their parents in going to the cinema less frequently – rarely to the extent of not going at all (in the 1967 poll, just 3.5 per cent of all 16 to 24-year-olds said they never went to the movies), but certainly less than college kids. Worse, even though Jack Valenti was right to highlight soaring college admission rates (from 3.6 million in 1960 to almost 8 million in 1970), university attendance was still in the minority.[10] Eventually, 22 per cent of baby boomers graduated from college.[11] Even allowing for high dropout rates, less than half the generation ever enrolled.

By pursuing a production policy, therefore, that pandered to radical college youth, the Hollywood majors were effectively privileging a vocal minority of a minority of a minority of the American population. As Valenti argued, there was good reason for this – in terms of the frequency of their cinema attendance, this group were undoubtedly the industry's most reliable customers – and accordingly the studios stepped up their attempts to understand their target demographic. In 1968 it had been a novelty when MGM hired a temporary 'scholastic' representative to help sell *2001* to students, but by the middle of 1970 all of the major studios had full-time campus contacts collecting youth opinion.[12] Throughout 1969 and into 1970, both the trade press and representatives from the studios continued to talk up specifically youth-oriented production as a viable and cost-efficient replacement for the mega-budget general audience spectaculars they could no longer afford. To those who suggested such a policy would further alienate older customers, Valenti countered that it was the older generation that needed to change: 'One way to bridge today's generation gap is for the older generation to see the new movies and see them in the company of young people.' Nor did he accept criticism that the studios were failing to cater for families: 'I could show you a lot of G movies that died horrible deaths. There's no lack of family movies; there's a lack of family audiences.'[13] The resulting tranche of releases targeted boomers more directly, but also more narrowly than ever before, and were made by a new group of often younger filmmakers – not boomers, but members of the interwar generation

---

[10]Steve Gillon and Nancy Singer Olaguera, *Boomer Nation: The Largest and Richest Generation Ever, and How It Changed America* (New York: Free Press, 2004), 19.
[11]Light, *Baby Boomers*, 41.
[12]Eric Spilker, 'Majors Staff Up for Youth', *Variety,* 24 June 1970, 3.
[13]Anon., 'Valenti Sez Sex Becoming Old Hat in Pix, But There's No Family Audience', *Variety,* 15 October 1969, 3.

who were clearly sympathetic to the burgeoning youth culture, like Arthur
Penn (b.1922), Mike Nichols (b.1931) and Dennis Hopper (b.1936).

Youth movies

In January 1969, MGM announced the appointment of 39-year-old Louis
Polk Jr as company president. According to *Variety*, Polk 'cast himself into the
mold of the "new breed" youth-oriented film man – a type common among
young producers or even cinema professors, but so far unknown in the top
reaches of major company management'. Adopting a tone that awkwardly
attempted to reconcile revolutionary zeal with corporate interests, Polk told
reporters that 'the opportunity is to meet what the younger people of our
society are demanding from the filmmaker by introducing stimulating and
challenging as well as entertaining productions at a profit commensurate
with the stockholders' expectations'.[14] The task proved beyond Polk, who
was replaced in October by 50-year-old James Aubrey, but 1969 did see
a large number of relatively low-budget and unconventional productions
appear among the highest grossing releases.

   Three films portraying different aspects of youth culture made the top
twenty. Adapted from Philip Roth's novella, *Goodbye Columbus* examined
class relations in Jewish New York with its story of a young, aimless army
veteran (played by Richard Benjamin) dating a wealthy, spoiled college girl
(Ali MacGraw). *Alice's Restaurant*, from *Bonnie and Clyde*'s director Arthur
Penn, was a freewheeling, somewhat comic look at the counterculture from
the perspective of twenty-year-old Arlo Guthrie. Based on one of Guthrie's
songs, the singer played himself being expelled from college, joining a
commune and escaping the draft among other adventures. *The Sterile
Cuckoo*, the directorial debut of producer Alan J. Pakula, was a college
romance between two lonely outsiders, played by Liza Minnelli and Wendell
Burton. In addition, Paul Mazursky had a top ten hit with his debut, *Bob
& Carol & Ted & Alice*, a comedy about two middle-aged couples who
flounder in their attempts to embrace countercultural values. Slightly further
down the charts, independent release *Last Summer* made a success of the
darker side of teen sexuality. Depicting the shifting relationships between
two girls and two boys on holiday, it ends with a gang rape and had the
twenty-sixth highest rentals total for the year.

   The year 1969 also saw a number of hits featured taboo-breaking
material, European influence or both. *Midnight Cowboy* was a gritty tale
of male prostitution in New York from UK director John Schlesinger and

---

[14]Anon., 'Polk ("Now" Generation) Begins; McLuhan-Quoter, Gal-Charmer', *Variety*, 15
January 1969, 3.

costarring Dustin Hoffman. When it became the most expensive film to date (at $2.3 million) to receive an X rating, *Variety* reported the industry 'will now follow the film's career with added interest, as it had been assumed that UA was counting on garnering to the feature much of the teenybopper audience which responded to Hoffman's smasheroo *The Graduate*'.[15] *Midnight Cowboy* beat all expectations, taking over $20 million in rentals (third highest for the year), and winning the Oscar for Best Picture. Below it, *Z*, a French-language political thriller from Costa-Gavras, was the fourteenth biggest success. Two sexually explicit dramas from Sweden, *I am Curious (Yellow)* and *Fanny Hill*, were similarly popular. Sam Peckinpah's ultra-violent western *The Wild Bunch* was probably more discussed than seen, but still placed twenty-first for the year. Even a cheap 'how-to' sex documentary – purportedly for married couples – titled *Man and Wife* managed to crack the top thirty.

The film to make the biggest impact, however, was a by-product of the surge of imitation that followed *A Hard Day's Night*. After wild initial success, The Monkees faded fast and their television show was cancelled by NBC in February 1968. By all accounts, the group had become an embarrassment to their creators, Rafelson and Schneider, who decided to finish the job NBC had started by thoroughly trashing the group's image in a feature film produced by their company Raybert. The resulting *Head* (1968) was a critical and financial failure, but Raybert was still flush with Monkees money and its founders went looking for new projects. The first was a low-budget biker film that friends Peter Fonda and Dennis Hopper had been trying to get off the ground at AIP. Despite Fonda's star-turn in *The Wild Angels*, AIP were stalling over the proposed content of the new project, and the involvement of the notoriously unruly Hopper. Raybert were more accommodating and put up the $360,000 needed to make their film, eventually titled *Easy Rider*. It follows two bikers (played by Fonda and Hopper) riding across the American South with funds from a cocaine deal. Across several episodic encounters the pair take drugs, contend with hostile locals and consider their place in society – in the process betraying a curious nostalgia for some unspecific agrarian past – before perishing in a violent, random confrontation.

Innovatively edited and featuring a climactic subjective 'trip' sequence, *Easy Rider* was enthusiastically received as the next step towards a new American cinema, winning the First Film Award at Cannes. More than any other film mentioned in the survey, the film was associated with the counterculture and social change by respondents. Respondent 408 remembers, 'I adopted the typical world view of growing up in the 1960s

---

[15]Anon., 'UA's Midnight Cowboy Most Costly Film to Be Marked X for Youth', *Variety*, 21 May 1969, 26.

and early 1970s, hence movies like *Easy Rider*.' For respondent 94, *Easy Rider* 'drove home the sense of alienation'.

In theatres, it earned $19 million in rentals, making it the fourth biggest hit of 1969. In relation to its paltry cost, such returns were astounding, and the majors fell over each other in attempting to replicate *Easy Rider*'s success. In doing so, they would have been spurred on by Columbia's involvement in the film's release. Despite the recent youth-associated hits, there was still a sense that what youth would respond to was dangerously unpredictable. In September 1969, *Variety* ran an article lamenting,

> The trouble is, more often than not, that showmen who find a release is loaded for youth are taken by surprise. A good many of the films later touted as surefire for the young crowd (under thirty) – and there have not been that many of them, in the aggregate – have been unexpected bonanzas to (when they're frank) puzzled, even red-faced producers. With the possible exception of some of the American International product starting with Beach and Motorcycle frolics, few producers have, until very recently, consciously planned for the young. There's a consequent feeling in the trade that there is actually no such thing as a planned youth blockbuster, though sometimes claimed after the box office proves it.[16]

Few films from the original 1967 attempt to intentionally embrace youth had found an audience. For all their courting of the 'Now Generation', AIP struggled to replicate the level of *The Wild Angels'* success. The company only had two further top thirty hits, *The Trip* (twenty-fifth for 1967) and *Three in the Attic* (twenty-fifth for 1968) until *Macon County Line* – a violent rural revenge picture – in 1974. Equally, it seemed as though few who thought young, thought Fox, as only one of the studio's announced youth roster, *Prudence and the Pill*, managed to scrape over $3 million in domestic rentals.

The legend around *Easy Rider* is that Columbia hated the film until its Cannes success, but the reality is more complicated. An internal marketing memo following a preliminary screening of an unfinished cut in January 1969 shows the film did have supporters. Writing to marketing executive Richard Kahn, Bob Quinn (position unknown) admitted it would be a difficult sell, but emphasized, 'It is, in my opinion, an *important* film', and lavished praise on almost every aspect of the production.[17] It was Columbia who came up with the film's iconic poster and tagline ('a man went looking for America and he couldn't find it anywhere') about which Peter Fonda has

[16]Robert F. Hawkins, 'Youth Slant as Accident: Producer Often Quite Surprised', *Variety*, 3 September 1969, 3.
[17]Bob Quinn, 'Easy Rider Preliminary Analysis', 27 January 1969, in 'Easy Rider Promotion' file 3.f-128, AMPAS Margaret Herrick library.

said, 'When we, the hippies, all arrived up at the sales office at Columbia, we thought, "What are these guys going to know?" We walked in and saw that [and we said,] "That's got to be it. You came up with that? Far out, put it in."'[18] The marketing campaign was completed in time for a double-page advert in *Variety* announcing *Easy Rider*'s Cannes entry, before its festival screening.[19] *Easy Rider*, therefore, demonstrated that the studios could still play an active role in youth exploitation, and over the next year all the majors rushed to exploit the youth demographic more than ever.

In August 1969, *Variety* reported that Fox were 'eager' about five new productions, each costing under $4 million, that offered either 'provocative sexual angles' or '"knock the establishment" satire'. The five – *Myra Breckinridge* (1970), *MASH* (1970), *Move* (1970), *Hello-Goodbye* (1970) and *Run, Shadow, Run* (1970) – were contrasted with the studio's upcoming Second World War epic *Tora! Tora! Tora!* (1970) as each required only $7–$10.6 million at the box office to make a profit, compared with *Tora! Tora! Tora!*'s $35 million to break even. The article concluded that Fox executives were 'feeling that these five upcoming films can no longer be designated "little films" and that in today's market they may be as significant to the upbeat fiscal picture as the advance mass audience interest in something like company's fall debuting *Hello Dolly* Filmmusical'.[20]

By December it was Universal who were 'taking some rapid, some say frantic, steps to catch up with other majors' flair and success in the area of youth appeal and/or art market product, specifically as to domestic US production'.[21] While the studio postponed or abandoned 'upwards of fifteen' of its existing projects, executive Ned Tanen was charged with leading an entire youth division. Demonstrating the allure of *Easy Rider*, Tanen signed the follow-up films of both Hopper (*The Last Movie*, 1971) and Fonda (*The Hired Hand*, 1971). Other releases had similarly recent inspiration. *Diary of a Mad Housewife* (1970), from director/writer team Frank and Eleanor Perry, could have been *The Graduate* from Mrs Robinson's point of view. *Taking Off* (1971), a Milos Forman comedy about parents trying to reclaim lost youth, starred *The Graduate*'s writer Buck Henry. Monte Hellman's *Two-Lane Blacktop* (1971) also had a superficial *Easy Rider* resemblance. Former ad director Michael Cimino was signed to make his debut feature for the studio and was in no doubt that Hopper's and Fonda's success was at the root of his good fortune. As Cimino asserted in a January 1970 interview, 'The 27-year-old New Yorker is convinced that the commercial success of this one film has turned the blind and deaf among the major studio execs

---

[18]Peter Fonda, quoted in the documentary *Easy Riders, Raging Bulls* (2003).
[19]Advertisement, *Variety*, 7 May 1969, 12.
[20]Anon., 'Taking Note Of Youth-Slanted Clicks Of Others, Fox Eager About 5 Newbies', *Variety*, 13 August 1969, 6.
[21]Anon., 'Universal Bathes in Youth Fountain', *Variety*, 10 December 1969, 3.

into "seeing and hearing new" men willing, even eager, to listen to almost anyone's "far-out" notion of what could make a feature film.'[22]

At Columbia, Schneider and Rafelson were rewarded for the success of *Easy Rider* with a six-picture deal for Raybert productions, soon renamed BBS. They began with *Five Easy Pieces* (1970), directed by Rafelson, which was followed by *Drive, He Said* (1971), directed by Jack Nicholson, *A Safe Place* (1971) from Henry Jaglom and *The Last Picture Show* (1971) by Peter Bogdanovich. Columbia also had two 1970 movies depicting campus unrest: *Getting Straight*, the first studio film for former AIP man Richard Rush, and *RPM*, from veteran Stanley Kramer.

At Warner Brothers, Francis Ford Coppola had quickly followed *Finian's Rainbow* with *The Rain People* (1969), a road movie about a disillusioned housewife that impressed critics but failed commercially. Coppola was still able to convince the studio to finance a company to make films by his young friends (including 'victory baby' boomers George Lucas and John Milius, both born in 1944), all film school graduates. Lucas had moved from Modesto, California, to Hollywood in 1964 to enrol on the film programme at USC. Few members of the faculty had any real experience of the film industry, and, according to Lucas, they generally advised students to leave USC out of their resume when looking for work in the business.[23] Coppola was one of the first film graduates to reach a position of authority and overturn this thinking. Coppola named his company American Zoetrope. Its first production was Lucas's *THX 1138* (1971), an expansion of his 1967 student film THX 1138:4EB (Electronic Labyrinth). Suddenly, projects such as Michael Wadleigh's *Woodstock* documentary were considered highly commercial properties. Warner acquired the rights two days prior to the festival and pressured Wadleigh hard to complete editing as quickly as possible. When *Woodstock* was released in March 1970, the studio set ticket prices between $4 and $5 dollars, at that point the most ever charged for a Hollywood release.[24]

In the first half of 1970, MGM had two films – Michelangelo Antonioni's $7 million *Zabriskie Point* and *The Strawberry Statement*, directed by Stuart Hagmann – focusing on student protest and a third, *The Magic Garden of Stanley Sweetheart*, about a college dropout discovering New York's counterculture. Paramount's youth productions that year included *Little Fauss and Big Halsy*, starring Robert Redford and *Bonnie and Clyde's* Michael J. Pollard, Bernardo Bertolucci's *The Conformist* and an X-rated adaptation of Henry Miller's *Tropic of Cancer*. Paramount also funded the

[22]Aubrey Tarbox, 'Universal Act of Faith in 'Youth' Slants: Frank Perry, Mike Cimino Get Remarkably Free Pacts', *Variety*, 28 January 1970, 7.
[23]Baxter, *George Lucas*, 50.
[24]Aniko Bodroghkozy, 'Reel Revolutionaries: An Examination of Hollywood's Cycle of 1960s Youth Rebellion Films', *Cinema Journal* 41, No. 3 (Spring 2002), 38.

most expensive youth-oriented production of the period, an $18 million adaptation of Joseph Heller's *Catch 22*, directed by Mike Nichols. Research commissioned by the studio revealed that while there was a large audience familiar with the book, it was 'concentrated among men, those under 25, the high educated and frequent moviegoers'.[25]

But here there was an irony. The young people Hollywood were increasingly targeting were openly hostile to American institutions and big business, and Hollywood was clearly both. A 1969 survey conducted for Paramount at the National Student Association Congress in August offers a particularly extreme example of the views the studios were confronting. In a section on the limitations of the report, the authors noted, 'The suspicion and repugnance of many attending students to corporations as establishment symbols resulted in not only a disappointingly low response rate in self-administered questionnaire returns but in partial and often perversely presented information when the questionnaire was returned.'[26] Regardless, the authors felt they had enough responses to characterize 'the college activist' (though they covered their backs with the proviso, 'Unless the information received was a complete put-on').

In the late 1960s, then, the student politician was:

> The hyper-consumer of cinematic sight. His [*sic*] taste in film is in drama, comedy and suspense; musicals, westerns and science-fiction are in low esteem. His concern about the local college theater is in getting in at a reasonable price and seeing better films than a concern in the number or luxury of theaters. He is much more aware of the story and message and much less concerned with the media aspects of production.

In terms of specific recent Paramount productions, respondents were more impressed with the timeless qualities of *Romeo and Juliet* than the 'dated now' of *Goodbye Columbus*, despite the latter's star Ali MacGraw being singled out as best new actress. More troubling was the report's account of widespread unrest at the congress, culminating in a physical takeover of the rostrum on election night. As the 1960s drew to a close, the leading edge of the youth movement was extremely volatile. That a simple election couldn't be held without physical confrontation speaks to the many factions within this group of young people. It also says something of the desperation of

---

[25]A Fishman, '*Catch 22* Telephone Survey 1970, Report Date 30 February, 1970', in 'Communikon audience test reports', file 2.f-3, AMPAS Margaret Herrick library.

[26]This and subsequent quotations are from Arnold Fishman and Lin Gladstein, 'Communikon Audience Survey Conducted at the Annual Congress of the U.S. National Student Association in El Paso, Texas, August 20 through August 26, report date 29 October 1969', in 'Communikon audience test reports', file 2.f-15, AMPAS Margaret Herrick library.

the studios at the time that this actively hostile, far from unified group was being courted as potential saviours of the industry.

The gamble did not pay off. While the period has been celebrated as a time of unusual artistic achievement (including in our survey – respondent 779 remembers 'the early 1970s just exploded with creativity ... there was always something coming out that I wanted to see'), the studios struggled to win large audiences with their new direction. The first signs of doubt were evident when *Zabriskie Point* returned less than $1,000,000 in rentals to MGM. In April 1970, the studio's sales vice president Doug Netter was still talking up their relationship with Antonioni, telling journalists that their deal with the director promised two more film and would 'probably be extended'.[27] By August the studio was cancelling youth-oriented projects, including films by Sam Peckinpah and *The Strawberry Statement*'s Stuart Hagmann and a proposed adaptation of Abbie Hoffman's book *Revolution for the Hell of It*.[28] Antonioni ultimately made one more film for MGM, 1975's *The Passenger* with Jack Nicholson.

The other studios fared little better. Few of the 'youth cult' movies produced in 1969 and 1970 returned a profit. Most of those that did (including *Diary of a Mad Housewife* and *Getting Straight*) were only modest successes and so failed to cover the costs of the many failures. *Catch 22* was the ninth biggest hit of its year, but rentals of $12.25 million still translated into a substantial loss for Paramount. Just as with the fad for musicals three years earlier, the studios were confronted with a period where it was widely accepted that the industry had misjudged its audience but much of the resulting product was still waiting for release. In 1971 alone, *Variety* counted twenty-three 'juve-oriented' major company releases that brought in less than $500,000. 'It was a year', the paper concluded, 'in which distribs wished they had never heard of the Yankelovich Report that apparently first put the youth bug in their ear'.[29] While the vast majority of these films were on a far smaller scale than the musicals they replaced, they were also more numerous and each new release took a toll on studio resources.

There were exceptions. Alone among the low-budget studio productions, Fox's *MASH* delivered on the promise of marshalling countercultural sentiment into blockbuster takings. Again aided by a well-judged advertising campaign that invited comparison between its Korean War setting and events in Vietnam, the Robert Altman directed comedy about army surgeons clashing with their superiors took $36.7 million in rentals,

---

[27]Addison Verrill, 'MGM Thinks Young and Big: 18–25 Features a Year as Goal', *Variety*, 8 April 1970, 3.
[28]Anon., 'When "Youth" Pix Bore Young: Metro's Rule Is Forget It Fast', *Variety*, 26 August 1970, 1.
[29]Anon., 'Youth Film Market a BO Mirage', *Variety*, 29 November 1970, 1.

the third biggest hit of 1970.[30] Below it, despite (or perhaps because of) high ticket prices, *Woodstock* was the year's fifth biggest hit with $16.4 million. In sixth, Arthur Penn demonstrated that he, at least, appeared to be in-tune with audience tastes with *Little Big Man*, a western that also worked as a Vietnam allegory. Made for CBS's short-lived film division and starring Dustin Hoffman, the $15 million production just managed to earn back its costs in domestic rentals. At Columbia, the BBS operation had hits with two of their first four releases, but neither bore much resemblance to *Easy Rider*. Rafelson's *Five Easy Pieces* (fourteenth for 1970 with $8.9 million) borrowed *Easy Rider*'s breakout star Jack Nicholson but placed him within a delicate, low-key drama about the personal frustrations of a thirty-something former piano prodigy. *The Last Picture Show* (ninth for 1971 with $14.1 million) featured teenage protagonists, but the setting was 1950s small-town Texas, and director Bogdanovich shot the film in black and white, deliberately evoking the style of John Ford.

Audiences almost uniformly rejected films that attempted to capture the protest movement or counterculture directly. This was in keeping with the earlier New Hollywood hits. For all their later association with the revolution of the youth movement, it is notable how little radical youth culture the early hits contain. *The Graduate*, for instance, is much more about what is wrong with the parents' culture than depicting any sort of viable alternative. Although the second half of the film prominently features a romance between its 21-year-old protagonist and a college girl, the audience is never privy to their conversation. When the couple talk in the car at the end of their first date, the viewer is left outside, unable to hear. Indeed,

IMAGE 6 *Benjamin Braddock (Dustin Hoffman) engages Elaine Robinson (Katharine Ross) in conversation in* The Graduate *(1967).*

[30]Cook, *Lost Illusions*, 89.

the common interpretation that the film was 'about' contemporary youth caught the production team by surprise. Nichols has said, 'At that particular moment, "the generation gap" was everything. It never even entered our minds!'[31] At the end of the film, Benjamin is seen disrupting the wedding of his former girlfriend, whisking away the bride moments after the exchange of vows. The reunited couple make their escape by bus, collapsing onto the back seat still caught up in the exhilaration of the moment. Yet instead of ending on this note of giddy revolt, Nichols allows his camera to linger as the smiles fade and the couple silently begin to contemplate the implications of their actions. J. W. Whitehead has argued that the significance of those final frames was overlooked by many who saw and discussed the film during its original release, with audiences and critics preferring the anarchic action to the sober reflection that followed.[32] This certainly chimed with the experience of director Phil Alden Robinson, who was seventeen in 1967:

> I remember understanding the first part of that ending, and not understanding the second part and wondering, 'Why is that?' And it was before I was aware there was a director or a screenwriter with a point of view. I just thought it was a story. I remember being thrilled by the breaking up of the wedding, because it did feel like what our generation was doing everywhere: breaking up convention and tradition. The using the cross to lock the doors, we cheered that. And they get on the bus and I remember being all caught up: 'Hey this is really cool' and then you do get that sense of ... 'What do we do now?' That actually is a very emblematic thing for our generation. We tore stuff down before we thought about what we were going to replace it with.

Even *Easy Rider* and *Alice's Restaurant*, the two successes which clearly feature the counterculture, are at best ambivalent about the ways of living they portray. In *Easy Rider*, the two bikers disagree about the viability of a commune they visit. Fonda's character is the more optimistic, but later he famously concludes, 'We blew it.' Late in *Alice's Restaurant*, Guthrie realizes he has been living a negative existence: 'It's weird, good things in my life always seem to come out of not doing what I don't want to do. Now that they're not after me to do what I don't want to do, what *do* I wanna do? It may take me some hard travelling to find that out for my own self.'

Among hit films, this sense of negativity reached a crescendo in 1970 with *Joe*, an independent release directed by John Avildsen that came twelfth

[31]Sam Kashner, 'The Making of *The Graduate*', *Vanity Fair*, March 2008, http://www.vanityfair.com/news/2008/03/graduate200803.
[32]J. W. Whitehead, *Appraising* The Graduate: *The Mike Nichols Classic and Its Impact in Hollywood* (Jefferson: McFarland, 2010), 4.

for the year. Originally titled 'The Gap', it is an unflinchingly bleak portrayal of contemporary America. When his daughter is hospitalized by a drug overdose, Bill, a wealthy businessman angrily confronts her boyfriend and accidentally kills him. Horrified by his actions, he retreats to a bar, where he finds Joe, a metal worker who rails against the counterculture. Caught up by Joe's invective, Bill confides his crime to him, creating an unlikely partnership, driven by Joe's envy and Bill's fear that Joe could turn him in. When Bill's daughter disappears, Joe and Bill team up to find her, eventually tracing her to a commune. There, Joe begins shooting the occupants and urges Bill to join in to eliminate witnesses. The film concludes when Bill guns down a fleeing woman, not realizing that she is his daughter. No social group depicted in *Joe* emerges with any credit. The working class are bigoted and violent; the middle class are isolated hypocrites; youth is alternately pathetic, ridiculous and parasitic.

Traditional genre releases

Another factor in the turn away from youth productions was the continuing popularity of more traditional, genre releases. A decisive moment was the March 1970 release of Universal's *Airport*, an all-star drama that behaved as if the 1950s had never ended. The top-billed performers were Dean Martin and Burt Lancaster, playing a pilot and airport controller who must contend with a snow storm and bomb plot. *Airport*'s one concession to social change is its male leads' complicated love lives; both are married but also involved with much younger women. Produced by Ross Hunter for $10 million, the film was an immediate hit, the second highest earning release of the year with $45 million. According to *Variety*, *Airport* was a throwback 'to the days to the Hollywood dream factory so recently pronounced forever extinct', and for the rest of the year, *Airport* was repeatedly cited by the press and executives as evidence that the studios must continue to offer a varied production slate.[33] Though *Airport*'s success was attributed to the 'lately neglected older generation of film goers', the film received three mentions from respondents in our survey as a childhood memory. Respondent 686 (b.1958), for instance, still considers the film a favourite, remembering, 'It was one of my first movies with a date, I loved the excitement of the film, the special effects (for 1970).'

Yet even before *Airport*, the studios' rush to embrace youth and new ideas belied the fact that such productions were invariably outnumbered by more familiar product. The year 1968 may have been notable for the

---

[33] Addison Verrill, 'Oracles Edgy, Buffs Scoff: As Old Format Films Big BO', *Variety*, 15 April 1970, 5.

success of *2001*, *Romeo and Juliet* and *Rosemary's Baby*, but the top release of the year was still Broadway adaptation *Funny Girl*, and the rest of the top ten included an array of established genres and stars: Jack Lemmon and Walter Matthau in adult comedy *The Odd Couple* (third), Steve McQueen in police thriller *Bullitt* (fourth), musical *Oliver!* (sixth), Charlton Heston in science fiction *Planet of the Apes* (seventh), Henry Fonda and Lucille Ball in family comedy *Yours, Mine and Ours* (ninth) and Peter O'Toole and Katharine Hepburn in historical drama *The Lion in Winter* (tenth). Given the much publicized youth dominance of ticket sales, it seems unlikely that these films could have out-grossed all others without a degree of support from audiences under 25, and indeed, all of the top ten were mentioned in our survey with the exception of *Yours, Mine and Ours*.

The pattern continues in 1969, only with mounting evidence that audiences could be responsive to attempts to incorporate aspects of the New Values and a degree of formal experimentation within major studio releases. Three films in particular indicate a less polarized audience than is commonly acknowledged. By far the biggest hit of the year was western *Butch Cassidy and the Sundance Kid*. Coming from established director George Roy Hill, whose previous two films, *Thoroughly Modern Millie* (1967) and *Hawaii* (1966), were the epitome of mid-1960s studio production. *Butch Cassidy* has rarely featured in accounts of Hollywood's creative and cultural revolution. Yet in several respects, Hill's adaptation of William Goldman's script invited comparison with the leading drivers of change, *The Graduate* and *Bonnie and Clyde*. From Nichols, Hill borrowed female lead Katharine Ross, placing her character in a similar bind between social convention and the rebellious inclinations of her romantic partner(s), as well as a specially commissioned pop-music score (Burt Bacharach replacing Simon and Garfunkel). The debt to Penn and Beatty was more extensive. Beginning with opening credits that substituted *Bonnie and Clyde*'s hushed, sepia slideshow of its protagonists' early years for silent movie clips, *Butch Cassidy* matches the earlier film almost beat for beat, albeit with greater emphasis on capers than violent action. In both, the outlaw heroes are drawn to robbery through a playful desire to avoid social constraints rather than material gain, a premise that renders law enforcers spoilsports, if not outright villains. Matters take a serious turn when the male lead (Beatty/Paul Newman) is cornered and forced to kill for the first time, an abrupt and graphic event that has a lasting impact on the perpetrator. From there, the heroes find their odds of escape rapidly reducing as the law closes in, culminating in a lengthy, one-sided, innovatively presented shootout in which they perish. Highlighting the difference between the productions, where *Bonnie and Clyde* uses slow motion to prolong its heroes' suffering, *Butch Cassidy* uses a freeze-frame to avoid it.

On release, *Butch Cassidy* had a mixed reception from critics, with several highlighting its derivative elements. In the *New York Times*, Vincent

Canby complained that 'you keep seeing signs of another, better film behind gags and effects that may remind you of everything from *Jules and Jim* to *Bonnie and Clyde* and *The Wild Bunch*'.[34] In the *Chicago Sun-Times*, Roger Ebert was unimpressed by the conclusion, which he felt 'was a misguided attempt to copy *Bonnie and Clyde*'.[35] However, the film's studio, Fox, clearly believed it had youth potential as Yale University was selected to host the premiere.[36] The reception from audiences was ecstatic.

Butch Cassidy's domestic rentals of $46 million were double that of any other film that year, more than double that of *Bonnie and Clyde* and topping even *The Graduate* as the most successful film of the late 1960s. While it didn't feature in our survey as frequently as its predecessors, *Butch Cassidy* was mentioned by five respondents and for some at least it caught the spirit of the times. Respondent 178 (b.1955) considered *Woodstock* a 'very big deal' and found *Z* 'politically relevant' and also listed *Butch Cassidy* among her teen experiences. Respondent 256 was born in 1952 and she remembers, 'Movies with a counter-culture edge were popular when I was maturing. I saw *Butch Cassidy & the Sundance Kid* about a dozen times. *Easy Rider* and *Bonnie and Clyde* were also favorites. ... *Butch Cassidy* and *Easy Rider* were the anthem movies of me and my boyfriend.'

Also in the top ten in 1969, *The Love Bug* and *Cactus Flower* demonstrated that interest in the counterculture wasn't restricted to the young. *Cactus Flower* has all the hallmarks of a production that was intended to attract older viewers. Based on a Broadway play, it was not mentioned in our survey and at its centre is a formulaic mismatched romance between a philandering dentist (played by Walter Matthau) and his prudish secretary (Ingrid Bergman). However, the major obstacle to the couple's happiness is the dentist's ongoing relationship with a much younger woman, played by television comedian Goldie Hawn in her film debut. Hawn, born in 1945, had made her name as a zany, body-painted hippie on NBC's variety show *Rowan and Martin's Laugh In* (1967–73). Her character in *Cactus Flower* retained her 'far out' language and mannerisms from television, but overlaid a new vulnerability, quickly established in the film through a suicide attempt. Hawn won the Oscar for Best Supporting Actress, making her one of the first boomer stars. *Cactus Flower* was the ninth biggest hit of its year, taking over $1 million more in rentals than the much-discussed 'youth' hit *Goodbye Columbus* in tenth.

More successful still, *The Love Bug* was the second biggest hit of the year, one place ahead of *Midnight Cowboy* and arguably as big a surprise.

---

[34]Vincent Canby, '*Butch Cassidy and the Sundance Kid*', *New York Times*, 26 September 1969, http://www.nytimes.com/movie/review?res=EE05E7DF173CEE61BC4D51DFBF668382679EDE.
[35]Roger Ebert, '*Butch Cassidy and the Sundance Kid*', *Chicago Sun-Times*, 13 October 1969, http://www.rogerebert.com/reviews/butch-cassidy-and-the-sundance-kid-1969.
[36]Advertisement, *Variety*, 20 August 1969, 13.

Since the huge success of *Mary Poppins* in 1964 and the death of their founder in 1966, Walt Disney Productions had maintained the lucrative routine established in the 1950s whereby its infrequent costly animations were balanced with more regular mid-budget, live-action, family-oriented comic fantasies. With industry figures such as Jack Valenti loudly preaching the family audience's demise, Disney more than ever had the territory to themselves. Between 1965 and 1968 the company placed at least two and usually three new productions in the annual top thirty, and continued to systematically rerelease titles from their vault. Among survey respondents, those born in the late 1950s and early 1960s were the most likely to associate Disney with their childhood film viewing.[37] Though families remained their main focus, Disney films were not impervious to cultural trends; 1967's animated *The Jungle Book*, for example, featured a quartet of mop-haired singing vultures who looked and sounded suspiciously like a certain Liverpudlian pop group.

The Love Bug was a move in the same direction. Based on a story by Gordon Buford, the film's concept – a racing driver discovers his car has a personality and life of its own – was little different from Disney's live-action releases from the late 1950s and early 1960s. The execution, however, added several contemporary details, not least making the car (given the name Herbie) a Volkswagen Beetle. By the late 1960s, the Beetle's unusual shape and irreverent marketing had established the car as an iconic symbol of the counterculture. Disney built on the connection by locating the driver (played by company regular Dean Jones) in San Francisco, a decision that enabled encounters with the residents and ideology of Haight Ashbury. At traffic-lights Jones is challenged to race by a young hippie couple in an open-top custom car. At a drive-in restaurant, two middle-aged hippies brand Jones and his date (Michele Lee) 'a couple of weirdos' as they attempt to wrestle Herbie under control. Throughout all their adventures, Jones and Herbie are accompanied by Jones's mechanic/artist housemate who has visited Tibet and explains the car's behaviour in terms of Eastern philosophy.

The Love Bug is also notable for the inclusion of exceedingly mild libidinous content, a recurring feature in Disney movies of the period, presumably intended to appeal to adults and older teens. Lee is first introduced in the film when Jones walks past a car dealership and sees a sign reading 'May we direct your attention to these', with a pair of woman's legs in a mini-skirt protruding below. We then discover the legs belong to Lee, who is in the process of attaching the sign's lower half: 'new arrivals

---

[37]A total of 143 respondents born between 1961 and 1964 answered the question on childhood tastes and memories and 47 mentioned Disney by name. Among respondents born between 1956 and 1960, it was 47 out of 189. Among other age groups, the next most likely were those born between 1951 and 1955, where 30 out of 135 mentioned Disney.

from Europe'. While such humour hardly rivalled the sexual explicitness evident in the output of other studios, it still suggests the culture as a whole was reconsidering its boundaries. In theatres *The Love Bug* made over $23 million in rentals. Together with its sequels, it was also the most mentioned Disney film in the survey from the period, and the third most mentioned Disney title overall. Not surprisingly, all but two of its twelve appearances came as childhood memories. The exceptions were respondent 80, who was twenty-three when *The Love Bug* was released and saw the film as part of a day out with her mother and grandmother, and respondent 671, who was born in 1958 but associates the franchise with negative memories of his teens: 'I was forced to watch movies like *Gone with the Wind* and Herbie movies when we would go to the drive-in or because we grew up with just one TV. Those kind of movies I detest today.'

One of the most interesting aspects of our survey results from this period is the way in which respondents label and group releases, often in ways that run counter to the prevailing wisdom at the time and in historical accounts. Respondent 150 describes *Bonnie and Clyde* as a crime film, while for respondent 99 it is 'historical' along with *Barry Lyndon* (1975). Respondent 96 lists it as 'action', equivalent to *The Poseidon Adventure* (1972) and the James Bond franchise. In the case of *The Graduate*, respondent 144 considers it a 'blockbuster' together with *Jaws, Indiana Jones, 2001* and *Star Wars*. Respondent 248 included *The Graduate* with *Exodus* (1960) and *King of Kings* (1961) as the most memorable films of her youth, but added it was *Exodus* that affected her most. For respondent 260, the film is a love story, listed with *Love Story* (1970), *Funny Girl* and *A Star Is Born* (1976).

Other landmark films of the late 1960s are similarly linked to more routine, genre-based studio productions. *2001* was the second most mentioned film from the 1966–76 period in our survey and several responses indicate that while for some it had the 'visceral, emotional and psychological' impact that Kubrick intended, others enjoyed it as the science fiction spectacle MGM had originally hoped for and emphasized in marketing.[38] Respondent 254 remembers seeing it as a teenager and the experience left him 'nearly speechless, musing for days after about the nature of man, the universe, where we came from and where we're going'. For respondent 132 however, the film was memorable 'mostly because of how matter-of-fact it was about space travel. I didn't like the ending ... I didn't understand what it was trying to say'. Between those responses, respondent 102 was excited about the production on the basis of Arthur C. Clarke's companion novel and even organized a school trip to see a Cinerama presentation. He recalls 'it was every bit as good as I had hoped for'. Six of the film's twenty-eight mentions came as childhood memories or experiences. Respondent 377 still considers

---

[38] Anon., '"Visual" Mod & "Verbal" Crix', 5.

it his favourite: '[It was the] first science fiction movie I saw, and at my age (about 7–8) it was amazing. It hooked me on Strauss and classical music in general as well.'[39]

For respondent 381, the difference between the movies of his childhood and those of his teens was 'more color and action movies'. His examples include *Dirty Harry* (1971), westerns and *Easy Rider*. Respondent 376 wrote that his teens involved 'more socially relevant films, such as *Easy Rider*, *The Godfather* [1972], *The Exorcist* [1973], [and] *The Good, the Bad and the Ugly* [1966]', while adding that he 'still watched sci-fi'. In listing his favourite films, respondent 726 elected to compare *Gone with the Wind* with *Midnight Cowboy*, noting the latter could be considered 'a great love story in a different matter'. Respondent 412 still considers *MASH* to be a favourite because 'I have always loved good, well-written humor'. *MASH* registered as a teen memory for respondent 251, who wrote, 'It is difficult to recall movies that "stood out" during this time – maybe because I was more interested in relationships. However, I do remember going to see *MASH* on a double date. *Love Story* stands out as well.'

Conclusion

This last comment raises another often overlooked issue: that there were many young people who continued to view the cinema as a social rather than cultural activity. A number of respondents made the point that specific films were less important than the general experience (or excuse) of going to the movies. For respondent 162, 'During my teens, I watched more movies, but really 'going to the movies' was just an excuse I told my parents so I could go hang out with my friends or boyfriend. NOT at the movies ... I can't remember any movies I liked as a teenager/young adult.' Respondent 216 remembers he saw 'many more movies in the theater, as they were associated with date nights'. Similarly, for respondent 729, 'Dating increased frequency of seeing movies and going to the theater. We lived outside of town so this also increased contact with other people.' Respondent 123 remembers his teens as 'the dating years and movies were selected with my date in mind'. For respondent 95, 'Dating took me to movies I mightn't otherwise have been interested to see.'

As these responses indicate, it was hard to quantify exactly what elements of any movie ensured success with the youth audience, whose tastes were clearly more diverse than many in the industry assumed. As we have seen, and as we continue to explore in the next chapter, the popularity of films

---

[39]Such memories support Peter Krämer's analysis of *2001*'s release and reception in Peter Krämer, *2001: A Space Odyssey* (London: BFI, 2010).

such as *Butch Cassidy*, *Cactus Flower* and *The Love Bug* in 1969 did little to dampen industry speculation that the future lay in cheaper, more divisive material. At the same time, it is arguable that both the trade press and studio executives overemphasized the 'new' elements of the films that were associated with youth, and underplayed their more traditional appeals. As already noted, while *The Graduate* and *Bonnie and Clyde* introduced unfamiliar approaches and ideas, they also continued to offer many of the pleasures of established Hollywood genres. As we will see in the next chapter, these more conventional traits would become the focus of Hollywood's output as the boomers grew older.

6

Towards the Modern Blockbuster

At the end of 1970, Paramount released *Love Story*, a low-budget college-set romance that became the biggest hit of the year. With domestic rentals of $48.7 million it not only made more than *Airport* ($45.2 million) and *MASH* ($36.7 million), but also more than any other film since *The Sound of Music* in 1965. The film had had a convoluted journey to the screen: originally written as a screenplay by Harvard professor Erich Segal, it was unsuccessfully shopped around every studio before Paramount's studio chief Robert Evans bought it as a vehicle for Ali MacGraw. During pre-production, the project's fortunes improved markedly when a novelization of the script, written by Segal at Evans's request, became a bestseller. Now in possession of a 'pre-sold' property, the studio put more effort into marketing, but the level of success still came as a surprise.

Like *Airport*, *Love Story* was received in the press as a major departure from current trends, yet it had clear precedents in Paramount's recent output. Like *Sterile Cuckoo*, it showed a side of campus life untouched by social unrest, in *Love Story*'s case a relationship between a rich jock and a scholarship musician. Like *Romeo and Juliet*, it presented generational conflict in personal terms (the jock clashes with his father over his choice of partner) and ended tragically. *Love Story* also confirmed the star appeal of MacGraw, who played the musician opposite Ryan O'Neal as the jock. In our survey, the film received only one mention less than *The Graduate*. Eleven of its thirteen mentions were from women, all as either a favourite or teen experience. Like respondent 251 quoted in the previous chapter, several watched on a date or, as in the case of respondent 770, clearly wished they had: '*Love Story* ... made every teenage girl want to fall in love, and hold her boyfriend's pinky finger!'

Unlike *Joe*, or *Easy Rider*, *Love Story* was a broadly appealing film, which depicted young people without the trappings of the counterculture. It set the tone of the filmmaking climate of the early 1970s, as studios increasingly reverted to traditional appeals such as stars, adaptations of already popular material and increased production values. In this way, Hollywood sought to develop a more nuanced relationship with the boomers. As a result, the 1970s can be understood as a period of change and experimentation. On the one hand, highly explicit films were being made and released. On the other hand, the blockbuster movies of the 1970s were slowly being recalibrated to reflect the shifting values of Hollywood's audience, as the boomers grew older.

This chapter starts by looking at the outlook and executive culture of the 1970s, and tries to assess how the industry's preoccupation with youth audiences played out. We then move on to look at the key releases made during this uncertain period, before focusing on the stars and filmmakers whose work resonated with boomer audiences as they headed towards their teens and twenties.

Executive culture in the 1970s

Reflecting on *Love Story*'s production, former Paramount executive Peter Bart said in 2000, 'Other studios had turned it down as being not only soft but downright "icky". At a time when movies were supposed to be "hip", this was the mirror opposite. Indeed, Robert Evans ... and I had a tacit understanding that, while we both felt this could be a hit movie, we wouldn't embarrass ourselves by talking much about it.'[1] Bart's comments go some way to explaining the disproportionate enthusiasm for productions aimed at radical youth between 1968 and 1971. While the standard explanation for the experimental turn of the late 1960s is simple youth demographics, the way in which executives perceived and targeted the youth market had as much to do with self-image and corporate culture as actual conditions among America's young. In this regard, the movie industry was not alone.

According to Thomas Frank, during the late 1950s and early 1960s the advertising industry had undergone a cultural revolution that pre-dated and then ran parallel with the change in American society. Beginning with small, upstart agencies such as the legendary Doyle Dane Bernbach (DDB), advertising executives had increasingly rebelled against the rigid company hierarchies and research-led campaigns of the 1950s, favouring instead more creative approaches that acknowledged audiences' growing disdain for the established tricks of their trade. In the early 1960s, the resulting ads tended towards self-deprecating humour and minimalist design, typified by DDB's campaigns for Volkswagen's Beetle. Then, in 1966, just as the likes of *Alfie* and *Blow-up* were finding audiences in theatres, advertising developed a 'strange and sudden infatuation with countercultural imagery'.[2] As with

---

[1] Peter Bart, 'Better Laid Than Never', *Variety*, 1 May 2000, 1.
[2] Thomas Frank, *The Conquest of Cool: Business Culture, Counterculture and the Rise of Hip Consumerism* (Chicago: University of Chicago, 1998), 105.

film, the focus on the counterculture made limited demographic sense, given that those involved were 'clearly a minority' of young people.[3] Yet Frank argues that the industry's adoption of the counterculture's language and symbols was justified on two counts.

First, the counterculture's rejection of post-war America's priorities and customs was a natural fit with the 'new consuming vision that [advertisers] had been espousing for a number of years already'.[4] As DDB vice president E. B. Weiss commented, 'Isn't changing lifestyles what marketing is all about?'[5] Importantly, advertisers didn't only adopt the counterculture in their adverts; among Madison Avenue executives, 'by 1967, longer hair, beads, loud colors, and wide ties replaced the infamous "gray flannel suit"'.[6] Their co-option was based on a perceived sense (within the industry if not the counterculture) of shared purpose. Secondly, the target of countercultural ads was generally not the counterculture. As early as 1966 it was well established that 'images of youth were simply not appropriate for the youth market'.[7] Instead, 'for admen, "youth" was a sort of consumer fantasy they would make available to older Americans'.[8] As evidence, Frank notes that 'symbols of rebel culture' were ubiquitous in automobile advertising, where youth accounted for only 9 per cent of the market.[9]

At the start of the 1970s, the situation in the film industry was at once strikingly similar and hopelessly reversed. The box office turmoil of 1965–9 had provoked a rapid turnover in top-level executives, often in the wider context of company takeovers and reorganizations. Many new arrivals came from outside the studio system. At Fox, Darryl Zanuck had brought in his son Richard after only a brief spell as an independent producer. At MGM, Louis Polk had no previous film experience. In 1966, Robert Evans had been installed as head of production at Paramount by its new owner Charles Bluhdorn of Gulf and Western. At the time of his appointment Evans's chief credentials for the job were his successful pursuit of the film rights to Roderick Thorpe's novel *The Detective* followed by a brief spell in charge of the studio's European operation. In 1969, Warner Brothers was bought by Kinney National Service and independent producer John Calley was brought in as production head. According to Peter Biskind, Calley first received word of Warner's interest while on *Catch 22* for Paramount.[10]

---

[3]Frank, *The Conquest of Cool*, 109.
[4]Ibid., 110.
[5]Ibid., 123.
[6]Ibid., 111.
[7]Ibid., 120.
[8]Ibid., 119.
[9]Ibid., 109.
[10]Biskind, *Easy Riders, Raging Bulls*, 83.

Faced by the implosion of the roadshow production model that had originated in the 1950s, the new executives, like DDB and their ilk, saw it as their mission to inject fresh creativity and change into their organizations. Like the ad men, several seemed to feel an affinity between their battle to reinvigorate film production and the youth revolt that was a constant presence in the media, and altered their styles accordingly. In his autobiography, Evans baldly states, 'I was in the middle of a revolution' and emphasizes his lack of training: 'An executive I was not. That's why Bluhdorn hired me.'[11] When he was required to present Paramount's upcoming release slate to the Gulf and Western board, Evans proudly recounts the reaction of Bluhdorn associate Martin Davis to his long hair: 'You look like a Woodstock reject.'[12] Describing the atmosphere at Warner under Calley's leadership, Biskind quotes casting director Nessa Hyams: 'Once you got to Warners, you were in the middle of Woodstock. Five o'clock in the afternoon, instead of the clinking of ice in a glass would be the aroma of marijuana wafting down the first floor.' Warner story editor Jeff Sanford agreed, 'We were all hippies.'[13]

In this context, Hollywood's brief dalliance with radical youth (and correlated embarrassment about continued more traditional productions) seems understandable. Yet unlike advertisers, the results of executives' decisions were intended for and reliant upon the youth market. Though studios did make attempts to interest older audiences in their youth product (Paramount, for example, ran an ad in the *New York Times* suggesting readers watch *Goodbye Columbus, Romeo and Juliet* and *If ...* (1969) to 'see the great change that is happening'), youth dominance of the box office remained stubbornly high throughout the early 1970s with 12 to 24-year-olds accounting for around 60 per cent of all tickets sold.[14] When young people failed to turn out for the innovative new productions, takings plummeted. Since the end of the Second World War, Hollywood had become accustomed to shrinking audiences, but 1971, the year when the youth trend had the greatest influence on the studios' output, proved the nadir. From the post-war average weekly attendance high of 90 million, Hollywood's popular appeal bottomed out with an average of just 15.8 million.[15] The strategy Hollywood had adopted at the end of the 1960s – focusing on transgressive films about youth culture – was clearly failing to engage a mass audience. As we will see in this chapter, the 'Hippies' at Warner Bros and elsewhere needed to find a more commercially viable product that connected with the boomers 'as they were', rather than as Hollywood understood them.

---

[11]Robert Evans, *The Kid Stays in the Picture* (New York: Hyperion, 1994), 109 and 171.
[12]Evans, *The Kid Stays in the Picture*, 192.
[13]Biskind, *Easy Riders, Raging Bulls*, 86.
[14]Advertisement, reprinted in *Variety*, 30 April 1969, 16.
[15]Cook, *Lost Illusions*, 489. For MPAA audience share figures, see Appendix B.

Renegotiating the blockbuster

All of the top five most successful films of 1971 were genre films, flavoured to greater or lesser degrees by adult themes and disillusionment with social institutions. Top for the year was the most traditional release, Norman Jewison's faithful, three-hour adaptation of the Broadway musical *Fiddler on the Roof*. It was followed by two police thrillers, *The French Connection* and *Dirty Harry* (second and fifth), period coming-of-age drama *The Summer of '42* and the seventh film in the James Bond series *Diamonds Are Forever*. In their own ways, both *Fiddler on the Roof* and *The Summer of '42* did present youth-themed stories that were relevant to the contemporary moment; *Fiddler's* narrative involves daughters in conflict with their father and *Summer of '42* portrays a young teen's first exposure to sex framed within the wider context of America's involvement in a foreign war. Yet like *Love Story*, neither was considered sufficiently hip to be discussed as part of the youth production trend. Lower in the top ten, three other films also featured teen protagonists from different times, but their success was primarily attributed to their exceptionality (credited to or blamed upon their directors), rather than their positions within general trends. Kubrick followed *2001* with *A Clockwork Orange*, an X-rated literary adaptation about youth delinquency in the near future. Nichols rebounded from *Catch 22* with *Carnal Knowledge*, a bleakly comic drama charting two friends' dysfunctional sex lives from college in the 1940s to the present. Bogdanovich exploited the freedom won by BBS to deliver *The Last Picture Show* as an exercise in classicism, albeit combined with adult themes and nudity.

	Title	Domestic rentals (millions)
1	Fiddler on the Roof	38.2
2	Billy Jack	32.5
3	The French Connection	26.3
4	Summer of '42	20.5
5	Diamonds are Forever	19.8
6	Dirty Harry	18.1
7	A Clockwork Orange	15.4
8	Carnal Knowledge	14.07
9	The Last Picture Show	14.1
10	Bedknobs and Broomsticks	11.4

FIGURE 2 *Domestic Rentals Chart, 1971.* Source: Variety.

Here it is worth noting that film content was not the only factor keeping older audiences from theatres. At least two other trends were important. First, the 1960s and 1970s saw a decline in the standards of film exhibition. As their audiences moved to the suburbs, long-established urban theatres lacked the revenues for refurbishment. According to exhibition historian Douglas Gomery, the late 1970s found viewing conditions reach 'an all-time low' with 'too many sticky floors, too many noisy patrons, and too many films that seemed alike'.[16] Where new theatres were built in the suburbs, they were cheap and offered only the bare minimum viewing experience. Into the 1970s, they were also increasingly likely to be multiplexes.

In effect, the multiplex was the first major attempt to solve the problem of geographical distance that had first began the process of separating Hollywood from its audience with the rise of suburbia in the 1950s. Far more so than the relatively rural drive-ins, multiplex screens were enmeshed in the consumerist lifestyle of the American suburban experience. However, while the introduction of multiple screens in a single venue theoretically had the potential to cater to different audiences, Douglas Gomery has argued the practical reality favoured younger patrons. The new cinemas were often built in or near malls and so became haunts for teenage shoppers with time to kill. To cut costs and maximize space, screens were small, cramped and poorly sound-proofed. During the 1970s, multiplexes were still a relatively small section of the overall marketplace, but where they did exist, as Gomery concludes, 'The multiplex put an end to people over thirty-five going to the movies regularly.'[17] In effect, the multiplexes came too late to stave off audience decline among older generations of viewers, but offered new opportunities for movie consumption to the boomers.

Secondly, older, more casual film fans had less incentive to overlook declining conditions as recent theatrical releases were now a staple of network television programming. William Lafferty reports that by the end of the 1960s, up to fourteen network hours per week were devoted to feature films. Blockbusters could draw massive audiences. When *Love Story* was first shown by ABC in October 1972 (less than two years after its theatrical debut) it became the most watched network movie of all time to that point. Its 42.3 Nielsen rating was more than double the combined ratings of the rival networks.[18] In addition, the networks had begun developing their own feature-length productions to combat the rising costs and explicit content of theatrical films. These television movies proved as popular as Hollywood releases; at the time of *Love Story*'s television premiere, four of the top ten highest rated films had been produced for television.

---

[16]Gomery, *Shared Pleasures*, 100–1.
[17]Ibid., 101.
[18]Bob Knight, 'Love Conquers All, Lifting ABC to No. 1 in Third Week', *Variety*, 11 October 1972, 33.

And yet, chastened by recent results, by 1972 the industry had all but abandoned their direct pursuit of boomers as a separate audience group. A *Variety* front page headline from November that year declared 'Youth Shuns Youth-Lure Films'. Suddenly, art-oriented, inexperienced filmmakers were no longer welcome. Oliver Stone graduated from film school in 1971 and found Hollywood to be a hostile place. He later told Peter Biskind, 'The *Easy Rider* period was over. You couldn't make those films anymore. They really nailed us.'[19] Even as the contours of the baby boom ensured the size of the youth audience continued to grow, the studios turned away from projects dealing with young peoples' lives, especially with a contemporary setting. This was despite signs that the deep divisions of the recent past were healing.

When the Yankelovich Corporation surveyed youth in 1973, they found very different results to 1969. On campuses, the movement for political revolution lost support after 1970. Students moved away from attempting to overthrow the system towards finding ways to bring their different values into the existing social structure. From 1970 to 1973, the number of students who considered economic security an important criterion for work rose from 33 per cent to 58 per cent.[20] Support for the New Values continued to spread, however, with a steady rise in students who wanted more sexual and social freedom, and rejected traditional ideas of patriotism, religion and materialism. Crucially, values among non-college students were moving in the same direction. Across a range of topics, Yankelovich found the non-college majority of 1973 to have reached the point college youth were at in 1969.[21] On many political and institutional issues, opinion across the two groups was all but uniform. 61 per cent of college students in 1973 felt that political parties required fundamental reform, a view expressed by 64 per cent of non-college youth; 79 per cent of college and 77 per cent of non-college young people agreed with the statement that America was basically a racist nation; fully 94 per cent of college and 92 per cent of non-college youth felt that American businesses were too concerned with profit. This liberalization of values was integral to the experience and legacy of the baby boomers, who adopted 'new and powerful egalitarian norms', at this time, that were derived from the rebellious spirit of the counterculture, but more restrained in expression.[22]

Consequently, the majors found other, less direct ways to interest young people in their product. Out of the confusion of the previous five years, producers and executives settled on a handful of practices, combining elements of new and old wisdom that would serve them to mid-decade

---

[19]Biskind, *Easy Riders Raging Bulls*, 137.
[20]Yankelovich, *The New Morality*, 18.
[21]Ibid., 23 (see also subsequent data).
[22]Steinhorn, *The Greater Generation*, xxi.

and in some cases beyond. There was renewed interest in the appeals of familiar material, through genre and presold properties such as novels and plays. While the industry found less time for new voices, directors who had demonstrated a commercial artistic touch were increasingly sought after and treated like stars. These filmmakers were often associated with two further trends: the continued inclusion of adult content that had proved so divisive in the previous decade, and critical portrayals of American society and institutions. Finally, from the early 1970s it was apparent that a new constellation of stars had emerged, incorporating both long-established veterans and a new generation of performers.

All of these trends were clearly evident in the biggest hit of 1972, *The Godfather*. Much like *Love Story*, Paramount's development of the project involved a mixture of good judgement and luck. Evans had bought the rights to Mario Puzo's novel while it was still being written. Only when the novel became a bestseller did it become a priority for the studio, who turned to Francis Ford Coppola as writer and director after failing to recruit several bigger names. Coppola's main credentials for the project were his Oscar for co-writing 1970's successful *Patton* and (according to Evans) his Italian American background.[23] Coppola added class and vision to the production. He streamlined Puzo's plotting and insisted on creative choices that were not obviously commercial, including the casting of Marlon Brando, James Caan and Al Pacino, and encouraging Gordon Willis's stately, under-lit cinematography. He also did not shy away from the violence of mafia life, including graphic scenes of murder and milking a memorable scene from the novel where a bloody horse's head is left in an adversary's bed as a message.

Paramount commissioned research into *The Godfather*'s readership at the same time as *Catch 22*. While the audience for Puzo's much more recent work was not yet as large as Joseph Heller's, the report concluded that *The Godfather*'s readers were 'more evenly distributed by sex, age education and moviegoing frequency', although both books enjoyed 'especially strong' interest from men and frequent moviegoers.[24] Encouraged by their success with *Love Story*, the studio devised an ambitious distribution plan. The popularity of Puzo's novel was used as leverage to book the film into a record number of first-run theatres and impose a higher-than-usual ticket price. They then spent heavily on advertising with the intention of turning a profit as quickly as possible. The plan worked better than anyone could have hoped, to the extent that within months *The Godfather* became the highest grossing film of all time to that point, ultimately returning more than $80 million in rentals to its studio.

---

[23]Evans, *The Kid Stays in the Picture*, 220.
[24]A. Fishman, 'The Godfather – Catch-22 Telephone Awareness Survey', February 1970, 'Catch-22' File f.3, AMPAS Margaret Herrick library.

The film (together with its 1974 sequel) was also, by some distance, the most mentioned from the 1966–76 period in the survey. Overall it was mentioned by forty-four respondents, eighteen of whom were female and thirty-five were born between 1946 and 1964. Twenty-one boomer-age respondents listed it as a favourite, making it the fourth most-liked among boomers behind only *Star Wars*, *Gone with the Wind* and *The Wizard of Oz*. What is most striking about the survey comments is the wide variety of ways in which people responded to the film. The most common response was simply to praise the film's quality, either generally (referring to its greatness or classic status as did respondents 254, 348, 260, 298 and 278), or pinpointing specific elements including the story (respondents 777, 406, 587, 66, 296, 246 and 229), acting (107, 146 and 246) and characters (78 and 66). Respondents 652 and 689 singled out *The Godfather* for its portrayal of history, while two respondents (18 and 472) referred to it as a gangster film. Three respondents (587, 480 and 19) emphasized the impact of the film's violence, and three more (785, 245 and 36) specifically referred to the horse's head. As noted above, respondent 376 included the film in a list of releases from the time he considered 'socially relevant'. For two respondents, *The Godfather* had more personal relevance. According to respondent 301, on seeing the film in her teens she 'realized for the first time that some of my neighbors were very likely in the mafia'. Respondent 649 considers *The Godfather* his favourite because 'it symbolizes the good and bad of a culture. Growing up in a similar culture, the family and dinner scenes were especially significant in my life as I grew. Fortunately, I did not have the negative part of the culture in my family'.

With its insistence that corruption and violence were endemic in American society, *The Godfather* both fit within existing trends and encouraged their continuation. The first half of the 1970s saw Hollywood producing a high number of films that validated negative views of aspects of American life. Government, public institutions and corporations in particular were popular targets. *The French Connection* (1971), *Dirty Harry* (1971), *Klute* (1971), *Shaft* (1971), *Sweet Sweetback's Baadasssss Song* (1971), *New Centurions* (1972), *Superfly* (1972), *Magnum Force* (1973), *Serpico* (1973), *Walking Tall* (1973), *The Seven-Ups* (1973), *The Longest Yard* (1974), *Freebie and the Bean (1974)*, *Chinatown* (1974) and *Hustle* (1975) were all top thirty hits that presented the police as corrupt or dysfunctional, often at an institutional level. *MASH*, *Catch 22*, *Kelly's Heroes* (1970) and *The Last Detail* (1973) did the same for the military, while *Hospital* (1971) and *One Flew Over the Cuckoo's Nest* (1975) presented harrowing accounts of life within medical facilities. A frequent theme across these films is the obstructive nature of bureaucracy, with rules and regulations preventing individuals from achieving results. A related trend, dating back to *Bonnie and Clyde*, *Midnight Cowboy* and *Butch Cassidy* was for films that glamorized – or at least sympathized with – criminals and outlaws. These remained popular well into the 1970s, with top thirty examples, including *The Getaway* (1972), *The Sting* (1973), *Paper Moon* (1973), *The Longest Yard, Lenny* (1974), *Thunderbolt and Lightfoot, One Flew Over the Cuckoo's Nest, Dog Day Afternoon* (1975), *Lucky Lady* (1975) and *Silver Streak* (1976).

As the decade progressed, hit films increasingly dwelt upon the corrupting power of money. *The Godfather* was the first of a series of films across a range of genres that found success by demonstrating systemic links between different combinations of organized crime, business and politics and blurring the distinctions between them. Others included *Chinatown, Shampoo* (1975), *Three Days of the Condor* (1975), *Nashville* (1975), *All the President's Men* (1976) and *Network* (1976). Even disaster movies, the cycle of films usually credited with reconnecting Hollywood with more mature audiences, found space to give their narratives of destruction an ideological edge. As already discussed, *Airport* was widely heralded as a throwback picture, resistant to recent social and industrial developments. In some respects it was a sprawling, ungainly production, with characters based in several locations and facing numerous, unrelated threats including extreme weather, a passenger with a bomb and unpopular plans to build a new runway. It was followed by Irwin Allen's *The Poseidon Adventure* (1972), which streamlined *Airport*'s appeal, creating a single location, a single threat and a single source of blame. On an ocean liner's final voyage, its new owner insists that the captain forego taking on ballast in order to increase speed and profit, despite warnings it will put the ship and passengers at risk. When the ship is hit by a tidal wave, the lack of ballast results in it capsizing, killing all but a handful of survivors. This group must then find their way up through the rapidly sinking ship to stand any chance of rescue.

Like *Airport, The Poseidon Adventure* has middle-aged stars playing traditional authority figures, with Gene Hackman as a priest and Ernest Borgnine as a policeman. In keeping with other early 1970s hits, the only youth character is a ditzy woman, a nightclub singer who mainly impedes the progress of her companions. Yet the film is more sharply critical of its leading men. Hackman's priest is undergoing a crisis of faith, and he sacrifices himself at the end with his doubts unresolved. Borgnine as the policeman is aggressive, argumentative and struggling to work through issues with his wife, stemming from her former life as a prostitute. Ultimately, *The Poseidon Adventure* appears more interested in its characters' failings and suffering due to the excesses of big business than their ability to overcome lengthening odds, an impression underlined by the abrupt conclusion, where the final rescue is shown in a single, desultory longshot, with no scenes of relief, celebration or reflection.

The film provided the template for subsequent disaster movies. *Earthquake* (1974) is critical of both the LA police department and cost-cutting builders and concludes in a similar manner to the *Poseidon Adventure*. As *Variety*'s review put it, 'The film ends, not on an upbeat note of civic rebirth, but with [the surviving leads] just standing in the ruins looking bushed.'[25] Allen's *The Towering Inferno* (1974) found more of a balance between punitive suffering and heroic action, but the negative influence of money remained. Hundreds of people are trapped in a burning building because of cost-cutting on safety regulations and the film concludes with a speech from a fire chief played by Steve McQueen to the building's architect played by Paul Newman railing against corporate greed and vanity.

On the one hand, the disaster movies represented a relatively inclusive mode of blockbuster cinema that eschewed graphic violence and countercultural excess in favour of thrilling tension and action. On the other hand, they mostly featured older stars, and retained a critical focus on contemporary issues, especially intergenerational concerns. In effect, the most commercially successful movies of the early 1970s exhibit uncertainty about their audience and appeal. They represent an attempt to recalibrate movies to more mainstream tastes, without a clear sense of what those tastes might be.

Talent and creative freedom

The presence of the likes of Brando, Borgnine, McQueen and Newman – all stars by 1960 – in the top hits of the early 1970s is a powerful demonstration of the undercurrent of continuity beneath the headline upheavals of the era. The established stars who were able to maintain or in some cases improve their standing with audiences were those whose personas best expressed disillusionment and a degree of moral ambiguity. Others included Richard Burton, Clint Eastwood, Jack Lemmon, Walter Matthau, George C. Scott and John Wayne. Yet the period did also see new stars emerge, and in keeping with the spirit of change, they were often noticeably different to their predecessors. The new faces can be divided into two broad groups. A few, notably Hackman and his *French Connection* costar Roy Scheider built personas similar to the veterans. The second group was much more numerous and younger, born between the late 1930s and early 1940s. Though slightly older than the baby boom, several made their names playing teen or young adult characters and even when playing their age, their personas continued to draw upon idealism and rebellion. The oldest, Donald Sutherland, was born in 1935. He was followed by Robert Redford in 1936, Dustin Hoffman, Jack Nicholson, Warren Beatty and Jane Fonda in 1937. Jon Voight and Elliott Gould were born in 1938, Al Pacino in 1940, Ryan O'Neal in 1941 and Barbra Streisand in 1942. Until the late 1970s, these stars specialized in characters whose life situations were

---

[25]Murf., Review of *Earthquake*, *Variety*, 13 November 1974, 18.

broadly in keeping with youth experience: single, either yet to find a career or inexperienced in their profession, and brought into conflict with older authority figures. Notably, when the time came to cast the roles of early boomers Bob Woodward (1943) and Carl Bernstein (1944) in *All the President's Men*, Redford and Hoffman were selected despite each being almost a decade older than the journalists had been at the time of their Watergate investigation.

Much has been written about the elevated profile of filmmakers in the 1970s, resulting in an 'auteur cinema' (to use Cook's phrase) where directors gained more control over production and became important factors in their films' marketing and critical reception.[26] There is certainly evidence that some directors were feted by the studios. Following *The Godfather*, Coppola became the most sought after figure in Hollywood. At Paramount, he was quickly signed for a *Godfather* sequel and this time given greater creative control. When the studio selected *The Great Gatsby* (1974) as the next test of their *Godfather* release strategy, Coppola was hired to do the adaptation, a task that reportedly took him three weeks. Together with Friedkin (who had directed *The French Connection*) and Bogdanovich he was also persuaded to join The Director's Company, an initiative whereby Paramount would pay to make any script of each participant's choosing as long as the budget didn't exceed $3 million. Over at Universal, Ned Tanen's youth division was winding down and one of the final projects under consideration was George Lucas's *American Graffiti* (1973). Tanen only gave the greenlight when Coppola agreed to lend his name to the production as producer.

However, there is much more limited evidence that the industry's pursuit of auteurs reflected audience demand. While figures such as Coppola, Friedkin and Robert Altman were able to follow their own creative agendas, the results rarely proved popular with audiences. After *MASH*, Altman worked at a prolific rate, completing a further eight productions by the end of 1976. Of these just two – *McCabe and Mrs Miller* and *Nashville* – featured in the top thirty hits for their years, finishing twenty-seventh in 1971 and 1975 respectively. In the case of *McCabe*, a western which teamed Altman with Warren Beatty in his first role since *Bonnie and Clyde*, its takings of $4.1 million in rentals were considered a considerable disappointment. Coppola's record was also erratic. The longer, more complex *The Godfather Part II* was a critical triumph and commercial success, although its domestic rentals of $30.7 million meant that nearly two-thirds of *The Godfather*'s audience had been lost. *Gatsby* more straightforwardly failed to live up to expectations, barely making the top twenty. Despite Paramount president Frank Yablans's assertion that The Director's Company could be an area of 'growth potential', only three films were made, two from Bogdanovich

---

[26]Cook, *Lost Illusions*, 68–157.

(his *Paper Moon* was the lone hit), and *The Conversation* from Coppola.[27] *The Conversation* was another critical favourite (it was nominated for three Oscars including Best Picture and Best Screenplay), but on release struggled to earn back its production costs. As we will see, *American Graffiti* was a huge success, but one in which Coppola had no creative stake. Notably, while a number of filmmakers were mentioned in the survey, most were associated with earlier (Hitchcock, Wilder, Bergman, Truffaut) or later (Spielberg, Demme) periods.

One area in which auteur directors did make a sizeable impact on audiences was in exploring the boundaries of the rating system. In the early 1970s there was a series of controversies surrounding explicit sexual and violent content in mainstream Hollywood releases and – like *Virginia Woolf* and *Blow-Up* in the 1960s – each was closely associated with a leading filmmaker. In 1971, Kubrick's *A Clockwork Orange* received an X rating for its portrayal of sex and violence, later reduced to an R when the director agreed to trim a graphic rape scene. The same year, Nichols's *Carnal Knowledge* was released with an R but that didn't prevent a theatre manager from being prosecuted in Albany, Georgia, for distributing obscene material. In 1973, Bernardo Bertolucci's *Last Tango in Paris* was the subject of protests and media condemnation for its X-rated portrayal of a couple's sexual relationship. All three films were nominated for major Oscars and were among the top ten releases of their years. *A Clockwork Orange* was mentioned as a memorable teen experience by seven respondents. Respondent 107 linked it with *The Wild Bunch* and John Waters's *Pink Flamingos* (1972) for its extreme content, while respondent 178 found it 'disturbing'. Respondent 15 saw *Carnal Knowledge* with her boyfriend when she was seventeen, having told her parents they were going to see the family-oriented *Willy Wonka and the Chocolate Factory* (1971). She now recalls, 'That was an eye opener for my little naive self.'

In time, the X rating became closely identified with hard-core pornography, which often used the X as a major part of its promotion. But even before X acquired this stigma, more effort was put into testing the outer limits of the R rating. By common consensus, these were found in Warner Brothers' 1973 release *The Exorcist*. Featuring numerous scenes of sacrilegious, sexualized violence, the film provoked an extraordinary reaction, and it quickly replaced *The Godfather* as the highest grossing film of all time. Itself no slouch when it came to graphic gore, *The Godfather*'s success had still been explained through its ability to pull a wide audience.[28] *The Exorcist*, by contrast, seems to have prospered through intense interest from specific audience groups.

---

[27]Frank Yablans, 'Bold Approach to Pix BO, and TV's Production Virility Yet to be Tested', *Variety*, 3 January 1973, 24.
[28]Abel Green, 'Godfather Boon to All Pix', *Variety*, 5 April 1972, 3.

According to reports from cinema managers gathered by Warner Bros, the film principally attracted young adults, especially college students.

According to Tom Bussell, manager of the Hiland Theater in Albuquerque New Mexico, 'The college kids ... braved that horrendous weather the first week, standing in horrendous wind ... in line up to 2 hours. They're the ones who came back to see it. (But) the high school kids who've seen it ... tell me they wouldn't recommend it to their friends ... most of the older people tell me they wouldn't recommend it to their friends ... they just didn't feel good after seeing the film.'[29] As far afield as Miami and Wisconsin it was the same story. Chris Firth, the manager of the Coral Theater in Miami, reported that 70–75 per cent of *The Exorcist*'s audience was under thirty. At the East Town Cinema in Madison, manager George Haasi said his regular adult crowd had dropped by 75 per cent: 'The people I have got in here have been mostly the young people in the 18–24 age group.'[30] The film was the third most mentioned from the 1966–76 period in our survey, with eighteen of its twenty-three mentions from respondents born between 1951 and 1960. Both respondents 530 and 577 expressly remember watching it when they were thirteen. By far the most frequent comment was the intensity of the experience, with respondents describing the film as exceptionally scary or giving them nightmares.

As Krämer has shown, the peak for explicit representations of sex and sexual violence came in 1973, when *The Exorcist* and *Last Tango in Paris* were among the biggest hits of the year. Krämer suggests that one possible explanation for the relatively sudden disappearance of such themes after 1973 relates to the lifting of the Production Code five years earlier. The restrictions of the code appears to have created a 'pent-up demand' for more explicit material among certain audience groups, resulting in a rapid escalation between viewers and the industry, each wondering how far the other would go.[31] As the 1967 MPAA survey and *Exorcist* theatre reports indicate, the audience for such films was predominantly young, but it was also more likely to be male. A 1974 survey found significantly more women across all age groups objected to extreme content than men, with 43 per cent listing X-rated movies as their least preferred type of film. While 25 per cent of men felt the same, a further 10 per cent also placed X-rated movies among their favourites.[32]

In other ways too, the late 1960s and early 1970s witnessed a significant realignment in the industry's thinking about gender. Until the 1960s, Hollywood focused on the tastes of mature women, based on the assumptions

---

[29]'Taped Conversations with Theatre Managers', in 'Paramount Production' file, AMPAS Margaret Herrick library.
[30]'Taped Conversations with Theatre Managers', in 'Paramount Production' files.
[31]Krämer, *The New Hollywood*, 54.
[32]Ibid., 54.

that the majority of filmgoers were women and that wives and mothers were in charge of family film selections.[33] This assumption was clearly still in place as the studios spent heavily on musicals in the mid-1960s, but it didn't survive into the 1970s, for several reasons. First, the new executives and filmmakers who were able to enter the industry after the mid-1960s broke continuity with the studio system. Left to pursue their own agendas, the overwhelmingly male elite favoured male-centred stories. Secondly, at a corporate level, there appears to have been a culture that prized aggressive, masculine filmmaking. Even when *Love Story* proved one of the biggest hits of all time, there was little enthusiasm for building on its popularity, certainly in comparison to the less successful and more expensive *Airport*. When Universal produced *The Other Side of the Mountain* in 1975, their campaign played heavily on the lack of similar features over the previous five years. Posters featured the tagline, 'Not Since *Love Story* ...' in a font much larger than the title, and the film went on to become the tenth biggest hit of the year.

At the same time, the greatly increased awareness of audiences' youth seems to have encouraged the widespread adoption of thinking akin to what AIP termed 'Peter Pan Syndrome'. Whereas the major studios had long based their production model on married couples and families, since the 1950s AIP had specialized in the teenage market. From observing the behaviour of young ticket buyers, the company reached two conclusions. First, younger children would watch anything an older child would watch, but not vice versa. Second, girls would watch anything a boy would watch, but not vice versa. AIP tailored their projects accordingly, aiming at the tastes of nineteen-year-old boys.[34] As the average age of their imagined ideal viewer decreased, the studios gradually came around to AIP's approach. Not surprisingly, the period saw a widening gap between male and female viewing habits. In 1957, men went to the cinema 'slightly more often' than women. By 1973 there was a significant difference, with 61 per cent of women over eighteen identifying themselves as infrequently or never going to the cinema, compared to 45 per cent of men.[35]

And yet on the few occasions that the baby boom was portrayed on screen in commercial successes between 1971 and 1974, women outnumbered men. In marked contrast to the earlier widespread view of the young as a distinct active group, where contemporary youth featured after 1970 it was almost exclusively as isolated individuals, either lovable kooks or physically and mentally exploited victims. In the first category were Goldie Hawn and Barbra Streisand. After *Cactus Flower* Hawn played variations of her ditzy,

[33]Richard Maltby, *Hollywood Cinema*, 2nd ed. (Oxford: Blackwell, 2003), 10.
[34]Doherty, *Teenagers and Teenpics*, 128.
[35]Krämer, *The New Hollywood*, 7.

free-spirited persona in a number of releases, of which *Butterflies Are Free* (1972) made the top thirty. Though Barbra Streisand was born in 1942, her characters often stood in for a younger generation, and *What's Up Doc?* (in which she played a college student) and *For Pete's Sake* were both hits with present-day settings. Like Hawn, Streisand's characters found themselves at odds with social convention but in pursuit of love rather than social change. In the second category were Maria Schneider (b.1952) in *Last Tango in Paris*, Marilyn Burns (b.1949) in *The Texas Chainsaw Massacre* (1974) and Linda Blair (b.1959) in *The Exorcist*. Boomer men were seen less frequently and tended to be victims. In *The Last Detail*, Randy Quaid (b.1950) plays a naive young sailor sentenced to eight years in prison for stealing $40 from a charity box. In *Thunderbolt and Lightfoot*, Jeff Bridges (b.1949) plays a young carjacker taken under the wing of master-thief Clint Eastwood, but when a heist goes wrong Bridges is beaten to death. In *Butterflies Are Free*, Hawn becomes romantically involved with a young blind man (played by Edward Albert (b.1951)) who struggles to escape the smothering care of his mother.

Only two projects found top thirty success by focusing on wider boomer youth culture. The first, released in 1972, was actually set on a college campus, but coming from the Disney Company, its target audience was at once younger and older than college students. In 1970, Disney had followed *The Love Bug* with *The Computer Wore Tennis Shoes*, a comedy about a college student Dexter Riley (played by Kurt Russell (b.1951)) who accidentally acquires superior intelligence when his brain is merged with a computer. Fittingly for the time, the film portrayed its students as at odds with faculty. More unusually, the conflict is shown to be largely caused by paranoia on the part of the college's dean, who in an early scene complains of 'unrest – everywhere you look, unrest'. In reality while Riley and his friends sport countercultural fashions they are eager and community-minded students, to the extent that they uncover and prevent a plot to defraud the college. The film was a minor hit, taking $6 million in rentals to finish as the year's twenty-fifth most popular release. This was enough to warrant a sequel, 1972's *Now You See Him, Now You Don't*, in which Riley discovers an invisibility potion. It copied the tone of its predecessor almost exactly and was the year's thirtieth biggest hit with $4.61 million.[36]

Given that the Dexter Riley films were clearly aimed at a family audience, their modest success appears to validate Frank's contention that depictions of youth culture were most attractive to those outside the demographic being portrayed. The second – and far larger – youth culture hit of the early 1970s neatly sidestepped this issue by venturing into the recent

---

[36]A second sequel, *The Strongest Man in the World*, followed in 1975. Despite higher collections ($6.87 million), it did not finish in the top thirty.

past. With *American Graffiti*, George Lucas was selling the experiences of the oldest boomers to the youngest. There is general agreement that the film was a conscious response to the failure of *THX1138*. Those close to Lucas – including his wife, Marcia, and Coppola – encouraged him to make something more personal. Lucas took their words as a challenge and turned for inspiration to his upbringing in Modesto, California. In 1977, he told *Rolling Stone*,

> I thought: we all know what a terrible mess we have made of the world, we all know how wrong we were in Vietnam. We also know, as every movie made in the last ten years points out, how terrible we are, how we have ruined the world and what schmucks we are and how rotten everything is. And I said, 'What we really need is something more positive.'[37]

Set on the final Saturday before the new school year in Modesto in 1962, the finished film presents teen culture as a whirl of constant music and movement. After dark, the adults of the town abandon the streets to their children, who have their own set of rules and customs. But the film is also clear-eyed about the limitations of the world it recreates. Over the course of the night its four protagonists (all male) question their relationship to small-town life. Three stay, but one (played by Richard Dreyfuss (b.1947)), leaves for college, an acknowledgement that Modesto did not hold all the answers. Vietnam also hangs heavily over events, the nearest Lucas comes to explaining why this vibrant culture came to an end. At the film's conclusion,

IMAGE 7 *A 1962 night in Modesto, California, in* American Graffiti *(1973)*.

---

[37]George Lucas, quoted in Paul Scanlon, 'George Lucas: The Wizard of Star Wars', *Rolling Stone*, 25 August 1977, http://www.rollingstone.com/movies/news/the-wizard-of-star-wars-20120504.

blocks of text inform the viewer about what happened next to the four leads. One died in Vietnam, and Dreyfuss's character is in Canada, presumably avoiding the draft.

Though it cost just $750,000, *American Graffiti* made Universal more than $55 million in rentals. With the exception of Artie and Jim Mitchell – brothers whose hard-core pornographic feature *Behind the Green Door* was the twenty-eighth biggest hit of 1972 – Lucas was the first boomer director to have a top thirty hit at the American box office. The film was mentioned by seven respondents in our survey, including respondent 216 who remembers, '*American Graffiti* spoke directly to me as a teen.' In the 1977 *Rolling Stone* interview Lucas described receiving numerous letters from young fans telling him *American Graffiti* had changed their lives. 'I became very aware of the fact that the kids were really lost, the sort of heritage we built up since the war had been wiped out by the 1960s, and it wasn't groovy to act that way anymore, now you just sort of sat there and got stoned.'[38] Whether Lucas's reading was correct or not, the reaction chimed with a science fiction project he had been developing. As a child he had loved watching *Flash Gordon* and other space serials on television, and he wondered if today's children would respond to that kind of adventure as well: 'I began to stretch it down to younger people, 10- to 12-year-olds, who have lost something even more significant than the teenager. I saw that kids today don't have any fantasy life the way we had – they don't have westerns, they don't have pirate movies, they don't have that stupid serial fantasy life that we used to believe in.'[39] Lucas's observation, soon to be repeated by other filmmakers of his generation, would have widespread and lasting impact upon the entire film industry. Before that, however, Lucas's star Dreyfuss was chosen by an even younger director to appear in the latest development in the disaster movie cycle. The director's name was Steven Spielberg and the film was called *Jaws*.

---

[38]Scanlon, 'George Lucas', online.
[39]Ibid.

PART THREE

Success

7

Boomer Filmmakers

By 1975, the oldest boomers were in their late twenties. For most of their lives, they had constituted an important audience for Hollywood's product but played little direct role in shaping the content of American movies. Now, though, the tide was shifting, as a new group of boomer writers, directors, producers and stars reached positions of genuine creative control. For the first time, Hollywood wasn't just making movies for the boomers, it was making movies with the boomers.

The baby boom's arrival was announced in spectacular fashion by the unprecedented success of two films from boomer directors: *Jaws* from Steven Spielberg in 1975, and *Star Wars* from George Lucas in 1977. Each smashed the previous record for the highest domestic box office gross, setting new standards for how profitable a single film could be. Although they were closely associated with the slightly older first group of film school graduates who benefitted from Hollywood's flirtation with auteur cinema in the 1970s (Francis Ford Coppola, Martin Scorsese, etc.), Spielberg and Lucas were the first baby boomers to have a distinct and discernible impact on American cinema as directors. Their success was significant not only because of the numbers, but also because the films themselves were recognizably different from other recent hits. With *Star Wars* in particular, Lucas fulfilled his promise to break with existing trends, drawing on his upbringing and exposure to B-movies, Disney, television and classic Hollywood during the 1950s and 1960s to create a model for a distinctive new form of commercial cinema.

Spielberg, too, discussed his film in terms of its B-movie potential (during production he called *Jaws* 'a horror story') and emphasized its simplicity and audience appeals: 'just the essential moving, working parts of suspense and terror'.[1] In the wake of the success of *Jaws* and *Star Wars*, he articulated

---

[1] Andrew C. Bobrow, 'Filming the Sugarland Express: An Interview with Steven Spielberg', in Lester D. Friedman and Brent Notbohm, eds, *Steven Spielberg Interviews* (Jackson: University of Mississippi Press, 2000), 27; Richard Combs, 'Primal Scream: An Interview with Steven Spielberg', in Friedman and Notbohn, *Steven Spielberg Interviews*, 36.

a view of the film marketplace very similar to Lucas's. In a 1978 interview with *Variety*, he said: 'People are going to films more than they did in the era of lavish disasters. That was a time when people didn't want to be entertained. Negativism was symbolized by *Bonnie and Clyde* and *Easy Rider*, films like that. Now, people want to see pictures that are 99 per cent escapist, and are demanding more on screen than ever before.'[2]

For some, the arrival of these figures was nothing short of a tragedy. As Peter Biskind puts it:

> When all was said and done, Lucas and Spielberg returned the 1970s audience, grown sophisticated on a diet of European and New Hollywood films, to the simplicities of the pre-1960s Golden Age of movies, the era Lucas memorialized so well in *Graffiti*. They marched backwards through the looking glass, producing pictures that were the mirror opposite of the New Hollywood films of their peers.[3]

Yet as we have seen in the previous chapters, Biskind reduces the films and audiences of the late 1960s and early 1970s to a single, misleading ideal. Relatively few of the 'sophisticated' movies produced in the baby boomers' name drew large audiences, resulting in the lowest attendances in the industry's history.

Further, the exclusive focus on 'Spielberg and Lucas' is doubly misleading, in that it overstates the similarity of their outlook and films while simultaneously ignoring the extent to which the common ground that they did share was actually typical of many younger filmmakers seeking to break into the industry at the time. For example, in 1976, the year between *Jaws* and *Star Wars*, the top grossing film was *Rocky*, written by and starring Sylvester Stallone. Although Stallone would go on to be best known as an action movie star, his upbringing, and career as a writer/director, closely paralleled other boomers. He was born in 1946 in New York City, the child of Italian immigrants, and received a college education at the University of Miami. He worked in small roles throughout the early 1970s, but found success with *Rocky*, which he reportedly wrote in a matter of days in 1975. *Rocky* earned rentals of $56 million, and went on to win three Academy Awards, including Best Picture and Best Director. It also transformed Stallone from a struggling bit-part player to one of Hollywood's most significant new talents. About his script, Stallone said,

> I am really sick of everybody's anti-Christ, anti-society, anti-government, anti-people, anti-life, anti-happiness. That everything has got this

---

[2]Dale Pollock, 'Spielberg Cuts 1941 17 Mins. Also Reduces Trade Guess on Cost – He Is Sanguine about His Next Six Pix', *Variety*, 17 December 1978, 4.
[3]Biskind, *Easy Riders, Raging Bulls*, 343.

Hemingway fatalism about it ... If I could summarize *Rocky* I would say he is an all-American cornball. ... I wanted to get down where it is real – a celebration of the human spirit. I plan on doing it in all my films. It's too easy to write a downer.[4]

Stallone's comments reflect a wider sense that Hollywood had lost its way as a producer of entertainment. The group of baby boomers who made up the vanguard of creative talent in the late 1970s helped change that. The most commercially successful did favour populist, often spectacular movies with broad emotionally engaging themes, over more artistically challenging work. They brought greater fiscal stability, higher profits and a willingness to treat film principally as a mode of pleasurable mass entertainment, arguably without completely abandoning the principles of creative freedom championed by the filmmakers of the 1970s. Not all of the boomers fit this model, but the writers and directors who emerged from the baby boom generally brought with them a focus on the pleasures of movie viewing that distinguished them from the filmmakers that Hollywood had looked to for their potential 'youth appeal' in the 1970s.

Undoubtedly, the popularity of *Jaws* and *Star Wars* set a precedent for the kinds of new filmmakers and stories the industry was prepared to welcome, but their influence was neither all consuming nor necessarily predictable. The process of deciding which elements of hit films to embellish, repeat or discard is never simple, and there is evidence that even Spielberg himself was unsure of how to proceed. This chapter traces the impact and development of baby boomer filmmakers in the late 1970s and early 1980s, as they achieved positions of creative control in the film industry. It begins by looking in more detail at *Jaws* and *Star Wars*, including Spielberg's route to *Jaws* and the demographic trends that fed into each film's success. A second section then addresses the opportunities and limitations they created for young filmmakers between 1977 and 1981, presenting a complex web of influence and professional and personal connections. The final section turns away from directors to producers and production executives to consider how changes in personnel and industry conditions contributed to new trends.

Jaws and *Star Wars*

On paper, at least, *Jaws* looked very much like a culmination of several pre-established trends. Like *The Godfather* and *The Exorcist*, it was based on a bestselling novel; it brought together trappings of the disaster movie with the gore and terror of the horror film (albeit in PG-rated form); it featured

---

[4]Louise Farr, '*Rocky*: It Could Be A Contender', *New York*, 18 October 1976, 70.

a burnt-out cop as its central character, and took place in modern, small-town America. In their history of blockbuster filmmaking, Sheldon Hall and Steve Neale note that '*Jaws* was part of a new wave of blockbusters, not the beginning of one'.[5] However, while Hollywood was becoming habituated to high grossing hits after *The Godfather* and *The Exorcist*, *Jaws* demolished the record-breaking achievements of those films, earning domestic rentals of $130 million, making it the first film ever to pass $100 million (unadjusted for inflation). The unprecedented success of *Jaws* has been attributed to a number of factors: it was heavily marketed on television and opened in multiple theatres on the same day, rather than being shepherded through the runs and clearances system, and it benefitted from intensive cross-promotion. More than anything it offered viewers a new kind of spectacular moviegoing experience.

Jaws combined stylistic naturalism and genre elements from a whole host of earlier movies, with a propulsive, thrilling plot. Although the film features sequences of intense graphic violence, it nonetheless retains a relatively wholesome view of American life. The film's central character is Chief Brody, played by Roy Scheider, who has traded his life as a big city cop in New York to run the tiny police department of Amity in New England – an island community dependent on tourism, where Brody feels that 'one man can make a difference'. This proves literally true, when the people of Amity are threatened by a man-eating great white shark. After a series of horrifying attacks, Brody teams up with the oceanographer Hooper (played by Richard Dreyfuss) and salty shark hunter Quint (played by Robert Shaw) to track down and kill the great white. Along the way, Brody is transformed from a relatively meek family man, scared of water and easily cowed by the town's mayor, to a more proactive, effective protector of the island, who is able, eventually, to put paid to the shark.

By depicting Brody as a regular guy, and focusing on the ordinary American townsfolk of Amity, the film also strikes a different note to previous hits of the 1970s. Amity feels like a real place: prosperous, full of characters, homely and charming. If movies like *Easy Rider* and *The Godfather* implicitly viewed America through the oppositional prism of the counterculture, *Jaws* takes a different tack. The people of Amity live regular, conservative lives. This is particularly true of Chief Brody. In Peter Benchley's original novel, Brody's marriage is troubled, and one key subplot focuses on an affair between Brody's wife and the visiting Hooper. In the movie, no affair takes place, and Brody's relationship with his wife and children is sweeter, and more settled. Brody is not a boomer, but teens and twenty-somethings feature throughout, especially in the famous opening sequence (when a boomer girl is killed). The oceanographer Hooper (played

---

[5]Neale and Hall, *Epics, Spectacles, and Blockbusters*, 212.

IMAGE 8 *Hooper (Richard Dreyfuss), Quint (Robert Shaw) and Brody (Roy Scheider) overcome their differences to battle a killer shark in* Jaws *(1975).*

by Richard Dreyfuss) stands in for the boomers, and much of the movie is concerned with three different generations of men trying (with limited success) to work together.

Jaws converged with the baby boom perfectly. In 1975, boomers were between 11 and 29 years old, exactly matching the demographic group that Hollywood correctly considered its most important customers. That year, boomers accounted for 74 per cent of tickets sold in the United States. Within that larger group, sales were not evenly split, 12- to 15-year-olds, 21- to 24-year-olds and 25- to 29-year-olds each purchasing 14 per cent and 16- to 20-year-olds accounting for 32 per cent of tickets. This remains an unprecedented concentration of ticket sales within such a limited age range.[6] Not coincidentally, 1975 was also the year that the children of the peak years of the baby boom were in their teens. The children of the years with the very highest number of annual births (1956–9) fell within the 16–20 age bracket. There have never, before or since, been as many American-born teenagers in the United States as there were for the summer of *Jaws'* release.

The film was mentioned by forty-four respondents to our survey, often as a favourite movie or as a memorable viewing experience. For several, watching *Jaws* in the theatre was as big a draw as the movie itself. Respondent 62 recalled the 'thrills, chills, and the weird bits of humor', while watching it, 'in 1975 in a PACKED theater'. For respondent 747 'going to see *Jaws*, in a packed theater, was a standout', while respondent 108 'saw *Jaws* at the drive-in. The crowd reactions were memorable'. Often those reactions, especially for younger viewers, included terror. Respondent 55 (b.1965)

---

[6]For MPAA audience share figures, see Appendix B.

remembered that '*Jaws* scared me to the point of nightmares for weeks', while respondent 103 (b.1965) agreed that '*Jaws* gave me nightmares!'

In its depiction of a functional domestic America, and in its keenness to entertain with grand suspenseful scenes of horror and action, *Jaws* has to be seen as a defining example of boomer filmmaking. From the moment that *Jaws* became a hit, the press began to focus on its director, Steven Spielberg. In his review for the *New York Times*, the critic Frank Rich wrote, 'Spielberg is blessed with a talent that is absurdly absent from most American filmmakers these days: this man actually knows how to tell a story on screen.'[7]

By the time he took on *Jaws* in June 1973, Spielberg had already had plenty of practice. From the age of twelve he made increasingly ambitious amateur films, about alien invasion and the Second World War, culminating with the feature-length science fiction *Firelight* in 1963. *Firelight* was hardly up to the standard of a commercial cinema release, but it contained clear signs of Spielberg's ability, and it was enough to impress family friend Chuck Silvers, who was head librarian at Universal. In 1964, shortly after Spielberg's family moved to California, Silvers offered Spielberg what amounted to an unpaid internship at Universal's script library while he was finishing high school in Saratoga, which allowed him to see Hollywood films being made first-hand. According to biographer Joseph McBride, Spielberg's time spent at Universal was an informal form of 'professional training, much the same as he would have had working his way up the ladder from B pictures to A pictures at MGM or Warner Bros during the Golden Age of Hollywood in the 1930s'.[8]

At the same time, he enrolled at Long Beach State College, but never completed his education – the allure of the movies was too great. Spielberg had continued to make amateur movies while he was working at Universal and in 1968, the independent producer Dennis Hoffman agreed to fund Spielberg's first semi-professional short movie, *Amblin'*. Over the course of twenty-six minutes, the film wordlessly depicted a young man with a guitar case breezily drifting through Southern California, picking up a girl, smoking dope and eventually reaching Santa Monica beach. *Amblin'* was a mood piece more than anything else (Spielberg would later describe it as 'a great Pepsi commercial, with as much soul and content as a piece of driftwood'), but it was a hugely effective calling card for the young director.[9] After he saw it, Chuck Silvers showed the film to Universal's Sid Sheinberg, then head of television production, who almost immediately offered Spielberg a contract to work as a director for television, with the opportunity to branch out into movies.

---

[7]Frank Rich, quoted in McBride, *Steven Spielberg*, 238.
[8]McBride, *Steven Spielberg*, 113.
[9]Ibid., 160.

Spielberg built a reputation as a leading television director, turning in episodes of *The Name of the Game* (NBC, 1968–71), *Night Gallery* (NBC, 1969–73) and *Columbo* (NBC, 1971–8), before taking on *Duel* (1971) for ABC's Movie of the Week series. *Duel* was a powerfully effective thriller, which showcased many of Spielberg's defining qualities as a filmmaker – particularly in the way that it placed its everyman central character in a fast-moving and spectacular conflict. For survey respondent 79, the experience of watching *Duel* on television was intense: 'I couldn't stop watching. I was at my aunt's house for the night and stayed up by myself to watch the entire thing. What a powerful movie.' *Duel* is not 'powerful' because it deals with serious or challenging themes in the manner of many well-regarded theatrical releases of the 1970s, but because it provides an intense, pleasurable and visceral experience that seeks to engage the viewer's senses. More than any filmmaker of the baby boom, Spielberg would claim this quality of pleasurable sensory engagement as his *metier*.

The film's success opened the door for Spielberg to develop his first theatrical feature, *The Sugarland Express* (1973), a road movie that was loosely based on a true story, and focused on a young couple, played by Goldie Hawn and William Atherton (both boomers), who escape police custody and go on the run across the South to 'rescue' their baby daughter who is about to be placed in social care. *The Sugarland Express* clearly fits into 1970s filmmaking trends. It has the pace and naturalism of Spielberg's later work, but its focus on two, ultimately doomed, youngsters on the run from the law clearly derives from *Bonnie and Clyde*, *Easy Rider* and other counterculture-inspired movies. Unlike those films, it seems to have little sympathy for its protagonists, with Hawn's character in particular seen to be selfish and delusional. The pursuing police and the media circus that surrounds them are treated little better, so that, when the chase ends in bloodshed and failure, a sense of waste hangs over the whole narrative.

While he had been working in Universal's television department, Spielberg had treated *The Sugarland Express* as a personal film, an opportunity to express himself more fully than he had been able while working on the more tightly controlled projects assigned to him for television. And, like almost every 'auteur' film of the period that was not based on a bestselling novel, *The Sugarland Express* fared poorly at the box office, despite positive reviews. For Spielberg, the movie's failure to engage viewers was a profound disappointment: 'It did get good reviews', he said, 'but I would have given away all those reviews for a bigger audience'.[10] In this spirit, Spielberg took on the challenge of *Jaws*, in much the same way that George Lucas followed the commercial failure of *THX 1138* with *American Graffiti*.

---

[10]McBride, *Steven Spielberg*, 224.

By the mid-1970s, Lucas was still more clearly associated with the auteur turn than Spielberg. During his time with Francis Ford Coppola, Lucas had been developing an adaptation of Joseph Conrad's novella *Heart of Darkness*, set during the Vietnam War. This concept ultimately became Coppola's *Apocalypse Now*, released in 1979. When Lucas began work on the space fantasy that would eventually become *Star Wars*, these ideas informed his writing:

> A lot of my interest in *Apocalypse Now* was carried over into *Star Wars*. I figured I couldn't make that film because it was about the Vietnam War, so I would essentially deal with some of the same interesting concepts that I was going to use and convert them into space fantasy.[11]

An early pitch was shopped around several studios in the run-up to *American Graffiti*'s release, before it was acquired by Twentieth Century Fox under the steerage of Alan Ladd Jr., (son of the actor; b.1937) – who was uncertain about its commercial prospects, but was encouraged by the positive buzz around *American Graffiti*. At almost every stage of the film's production, the 31-year-old Lucas struggled to achieve support – from studio executives, crew members and even his peers. Fox equivocated over developing the project; Lucas's contract wasn't finalized until a week before shooting; throughout the shoot, the introverted Lucas struggled to motivate a baffled production team.[12]

Star Wars brought together the narrative concerns of 1930s B-movies and serials, westerns, samurai movies and Lucas's directorial interest in textures, surfaces and production design (over and above storytelling) into a relatively unique kind of movie. More than anything, it retained an upbeat family-friendly quality, and Lucas went to some effort to ensure that it reached young filmgoers – pushing for a Memorial Day release because 'I want the kids to be able to see the movie and then talk about it [in school] so we can build word of mouth'.[13] Famously, Lucas also retained a share of licensing rights to *Star Wars*, which made his fortune.

Crucially, this was achieved without alienating the core twelve to twenty-four 'youth' audience. When *Star Wars* was submitted to the ratings board, the panel was evenly split over whether the film should receive a G or PG, prompting Fox to request the higher rating. The official line was that the PG reflected scenes 'that might be frightening to small children, unaccompanied by adults', but *Variety* reported from 'unofficial sources' that the studio

[11]George Lucas, quoted in J. W. Rinzler, *The Making of Star Wars: The Definitive Story behind the Film* (London: Aurum, 2002), 10.
[12]Rinzler, *The Making of Star Wars*, 44.
[13]George Lucas, quoted Rinzler, *The Making of Star Wars*, 284.

'feared a backlash effect from teenagers if the film were to receive a G, which is sometimes considered an 'uncool' rating in teenage circles'.[14] The two explanations are not incompatible and indicate that the studio, if not Lucas, was more focused on attracting teens than prioritizing young children.

Star Wars was a colossal success, making $193.7 million in rentals. The film had an indelible impact on global culture. Less than eight months after its release, *Variety* declared:

> Probably not since David O. Selznick's Metro sensation *Gone with the Wind* has the American public taken a film to its heart as it did 20th Century Fox's *Star Wars* in 1977. One of those rare films that not only appealed to every age and type of filmgoer, it proved to be one of the greatest 'repeat trade items' in screen history, some viewers going back for the third and fourth time.[15]

By 1977, teen numbers (based on annual American births) had begun a fall that would continue almost without interruption until 1989, picking up pace from 1978, when the generation after the boomers began entering their teenage years. But if *Star Wars* had fewer teenagers to draw upon, its suitability for a younger audience meant it was able to connect with baby boomers from a different angle. It is well known that boomers did not have children at the same rate as the previous generation, but millions still did. In the late 1960s and early 1970s, the median age of mothers having their first child hovered around twenty-two, an age women born in 1946 reached in 1968.[16] By the late 1970s, therefore, there was a considerable, and still increasing, number of boomers with children under the age of thirteen.

Ever since the 1940s at least it was an acknowledged fact that filmgoing dropped off considerably with age. As people settled into adult life, their desire (or ability) to attend the cinema diminished. From the time the small adult audience was first seriously discussed as an industry problem in the late 1960s, the primary reason given was the demands of having a family. The 1968 Yankelovich report, for example, considered Hollywood's failure to meet the needs of young married couples with children to be 'the single biggest weakness of the industry today'.[17] The 1975 MPAA report, however, indicates that such conclusions were either off-base, or habits were changing extremely quickly. As the overall attendance figures show, adults were still a disproportionately small part of the cinema audience, but having children, and especially young children, made cinemagoing more rather than less likely.

---

[14]Anon., 'Star Wars Shunned G Rating As "Uncool" For Young Crowd', *Variety*, 1 July 1977, 6.
[15]Robert B. Frederick, '*Star Wars*; What Else Was News in 1977', *Variety*, 4 January 1978, 21.
[16]National Center for Health Statistics, *Vital Statistics of the United States, 1988, Vol. 1, Natality* (Washington: Department of Health and Human Services, 1990), 15.
[17]Anon., 'Pix Must Broaden Market'.

Among all adults (eighteen and over) in 1975, fully 40 per cent claimed to never attend the cinema, regardless of whether they were married or single. This figure fell to 36 per cent among parents with children between thirteen and seventeen, and to just 24 per cent among parents with children under thirteen. When it came to frequent moviegoers, the picture was slightly more complex. Understandably, single adults were the most likely to be frequent moviegoers, with 32 per cent reporting they went to the cinema at least once a month. In comparison, only 19 per cent of married adults said the same. Among parents, just 13 per cent with children between thirteen and seventeen said they attended the cinema at least monthly, but this rose all the way to 26 per cent for parents with children under thirteen. In a marked reversal of Valenti's 1969 statement regarding 'a lack of family audiences', the MPAA clearly believed that family outings to the cinema were behind the strong figures for the parents of young children, noting that they tended to be 'more involved with their children's activities, and presumably more willing to accompany them'. Conversely, the low frequency of moviegoing among parents with older children was because 'children over thirteen turn to their peers for outside activities and probably discourage parents from joining them'.[18]

Star Wars's success was rooted in its ability to appeal to three audience groups simultaneously: children, the wider twelve to twenty-four 'youth' category and adults. As Peter Krämer has argued, it is the combination of the first and third groups that was most significant: by making a film where parents were happy (even eager) to accompany their children in large numbers, Lucas made a virtue of exhibitors' long-standing gripe that children didn't pay full price for their tickets. Being able to charge the whole family – including older children attending separately with their friends – resulted in the highest grosses in film history.[19]

By far the most emphatic outcome of our survey was the popularity of *Star Wars*. In total, it was mentioned in 170 answers, far ahead of *The Wizard of Oz* (86 mentions), *Gone with the Wind* (62 mentions) and *The Sound of Music* (55 mentions). Time and again, it was referenced as a memory of childhood (by forty-seven respondents, forty-one of whom were born between 1965 and 1970), as a memory of teens or young adulthood (by 69 respondents, 45 of whom were born between 1956 and 1964) or as a personal favourite (by 51 respondents, 28 born between 1940 and 1960). What is most astonishing is the undimmed enthusiasm for the film (and to

[18]Motion Picture Association of America, *Summary of Remarks by Jack Valenti, President, Motion Picture Association of America to the Convention of National Association of Theater Owners*, Press Release, 3 October 1975, 4.
[19]Peter Krämer, 'The Best Disney Film Disney Never Made': Children's Films and the Family Audience in American Cinema since the 1960's', in Steven Neale, ed., *Genre and Contemporary Hollywood* (London: British Film Institute, 2002), 185–200.

a lesser extent its sequels) regardless of age. Among younger respondents, recurring themes were the sense of anticipation and the film's cultural importance. It was 'a major event', a 'social phenomenon' that 'everyone was talking about'.[20] Respondent 92 was 'seven or eight' when she saw it. 'I had never seen anything like it. I loved that it was in space. I loved funny R2-D2. I loved a strong princess that nevertheless needed rescuing by TWO male leads.' Respondent 163 (b.1968) recalled 'waiting in line for hours with my younger brother and sister to watch the first *Star Wars*. It may possibly have been the very first movie I ever saw. Oh wow! I still remember to this day the smell of the popcorn, the colour of the burgundy drapes and walls. There was the scents, the crowds, the way my stomach was "humming"'. For some it had a lasting impact. Respondents 25 (b.1967) and 226 (b.1969) described it as 'life changing'. For respondent 169 (b.1969), '*Star Wars* was pivotal. [It] defined my youth'.

Among those who recalled it as a teen or young adult experience, the most common recollections were seeing the film with groups of friends and returning multiple times. Respondent 173 (b.1956) 'saw it dozens of times'. Respondent 192 (b.1962) considered *Star Wars* and its first sequel *The Empire Strikes Back* (1980) 'epic, novel movies seen multiple times with groups of fans'. Respondent 87 (b.1963) recalled, '*Star Wars* and its sequels were mind-boggling. I know that I saw *The Empire Strikes Back* six times in the theater. I think I love it because it was so all-encompassing, with comedy, drama, romance and adventure.' Among older audiences who consider it a favourite, the tone is hardly less breathless. For respondent 527 (b.1949) 'I love the Star Wars trilogy IV–VI! There's a theme of purpose, growth and redemption in these movies and the characters actually have character.' For respondent 744 (b.1950), 'I think the old Star Wars Trilogy will be my favorite of all time, simply because it led the way for other artistic special effects.' Over all age groups it is striking that the film is valued both for its 'groundbreaking' special effects and the quality of its story, characters and fictional world.

Landis, Reitman and a new generation of filmmakers

Hollywood worked fast to build on the success of *Jaws* and *Star Wars*, yet other baby boom directors were not initially part of these plans. Sequels to both films were immediately commissioned, but when Spielberg and Lucas

---

[20]Quotations from (in order of appearance) respondents 125 (b.1967), 146 (b.1966) and 92 (b.1969).

declined to direct them, older filmmakers were brought in, Jeannot Szwarc (b.1937) for *Jaws 2* (1978) and Irvin Kershner (b.1923) for *The Empire Strikes Back*. More generally, similarly themed productions that were either started or modified to resemble *Jaws* or *Star Wars* were also handed to older directors. Examples include *King Kong* (1976, directed by John Guillermin (b.1925)), *The Deep* (1977, directed by Peter Yate (b.1929)), *Star Trek: The Motion Picture* (1979, directed by Robert Wise (b.1914)), *Alien* (1979, directed by Ridley Scott (b.1937)), *Moonraker* (1979, directed by Lewis Gilbert (b.1920)), *The Black Hole* (1979, directed by Gary Nelson (b.1934)) and even *Popeye* (1980, directed by Robert Altman (b.1925)).

Spielberg followed *Jaws* with *Close Encounters of the Third Kind*, an original science fiction story that appeared to confirm his embrace of B-movie inspired entertainment. However, the details of the project were less clear-cut. To produce a screenplay, Spielberg went first to Paul Schrader (b.1946), who had written *Taxi Driver* (1976) for Martin Scorsese.[21] Spielberg was not happy with the result, and eventually received sole credit for the script, about a father whose life is overturned after he witnesses a UFO. Spielberg again cast Richard Dreyfuss as his protagonist, Roy Neary, who goes to more and more extreme lengths to prove that what he experienced is real. Whereas *Sugarland Express* was made on a tight budget and *Jaws* saw its costs spiral during production, on *Close Encounters*, Spielberg was given a virtual blank cheque by Columbia Pictures. Much of the film's eventual $20 million cost was due to the film's extended climax where aliens land and make contact before taking Neary with them into space.

Like *Sugarland*, *Close Encounters* is a film caught between two modes of filmmaking. On the one hand, there is a spectacular adventure, as Neary follows the clues that lead him to the alien landing site. On the other, there are ambiguous character motivations and anti-establishment themes strongly reminiscent of 1970s auteur cinema. Notably, Spielberg chose to cast New Wave legend Francois Truffaut in a major role, despite little acting experience. Though their intentions are ultimately benign, government agencies are seen to be secretive and untrustworthy. As he becomes obsessed with his quest, Neary is often far from sympathetic, first driving away his family and then abandoning the entire human race. Eventually released in December 1977, *Close Encounters* drew mixed notices. *Variety*, for example, found the climax to be 'an absolute stunner' but expressed doubts about the 'uneasy tension' of the first 100 minutes. In theatres, it attracted massive audiences, ultimately taking $82.75 million in rentals, not quite matching *Jaws*, but still among the highest returns of the decade. It was mentioned by fourteen respondents in the survey, all as either a childhood or teen memory.

---

[21]McBride, *Steven Spielberg*, 228–9.

That 1977 ended with two filmmakers just in their thirties at the very top of the box office charts was a powerful incentive for the Hollywood studios to reconsider their wariness regarding young, inexperienced talent. Yet given the costs involved in those productions, it is understandable that a new generation was not immediately handed control of similar projects. In terms of style and subject matter, the most important hit for boomer directors in the late 1970s proved to be *American Graffiti*. In 1978, a mini wave of films was released from directors born in 1944 or later that were clearly intended to replicate *American Graffiti*'s success, offering different combinations of youth cultures, period settings and pop-heavy soundtracks. Several were also made by graduates from USC who were personally connected to Spielberg and/or Lucas, including *Corvette Summer* (1978, directed by Matthew Robbins (b.1945)), *Big Wednesday* (1978, John Milius (b.1944)), *Grease* (1978, Randal Kleiser (b.1946)) and *I Wanna Hold Your Hand* (1978, Robert Zemeckis (b.1952)). Of these, only *Grease*, a cartoonish, 1950s-set musical was successful, finishing as the year's top grossing film. It was mentioned by eleven respondents, mostly as a teen memory. Respondent 68 saw it thirteen times at the theatre. For respondent 631 it remains a favourite because of its 'fun and carefree' nature. In terms of box office trends, *Grease* affirmed two developments indicated by the success of *Saturday Night Fever* (1977, also from Paramount) the previous year: the arrival of John Travolta as a major boomer star, and the potential for a hit soundtrack to cross-promote a successful film.

Two places below *Grease*, another film with *American Graffiti*'s DNA proved more widely influential, though none of its boomer creative team went to USC. Director John Landis (b.1950) and producer Ivan Reitman (b.1946) took very different routes to making *National Lampoon's Animal House* (1978). Landis had grown up in Los Angeles and dropped out of high school to work in the mailroom at Twentieth Century Fox. He took every opportunity to learn about the industry, including travelling to Europe to work as a production assistant on *Kelly's Heroes*. By 1971, he had saved enough money to make his own feature, *Schlock* (released in 1973), a low-budget homage to the monster movies he had loved as a child. Landis's age was central to *Schlock*'s promotion, but, as he told the *Los Angeles Times*, this approach caused problems:

My youth is more of a disadvantage than an advantage. You encounter an incredible amount of hostility. A reporter in Sacramento panned me for my age. He liked the picture but he hated my age. What am I supposed to do? Apologise for being young? I spoke at a university here. It was a horrifying experience. They asked me questions like, 'You had the opportunity to make a feature, why didn't you make a political statement?' I don't question the question, but I question the questioner. Movie-making is one of the most expensive of the arts. One of my reasons for making *Schlock* is that there is a solid monster movie audience that goes to the movies whether they're good or whether they're bad.[22]

Landis's promotional tour brought him to the attention of a trio of comedians who had recently arrived in Los Angeles from Milwaukee. David Zucker (b.1947), his brother Jerry (b.1950) and their friend Jim Abrahams (b.1944) wrote and performed a stage show called *Kentucky Fried Theater*, which parodied popular culture. Like Landis, they found their endeavours didn't always fit with conceptions of what 'youth' should be doing. Jerry remembers, 'We got a lot of knocks in reviews in the college newspapers and others, that we weren't political. We just wanted to make people laugh and be silly.' They took their show to California and began to explore moving into other media. After David saw Landis talking about *Schlock* on *The Tonight Show* (NBC, 1954–), they contacted the young director for advice:

> John was very nice to us. He came to the show and loved it and then we had lunch the next week. We just said, 'Hey, how do you write a script?' We didn't know anything. We didn't even know what a script looked like. None of us had ever read a screenplay. So John went to his car and gave us a screenplay he had to look at. The screenplay he gave me was *American Werewolf in London* [1981]. This was years before it was made.

Landis joined the Zuckers and Abrahams to create *Kentucky Fried Movie*, a series of short sketches, mainly parodies of film and television, with a thirty-minute spoof of kung fu movies titled 'A Fistful of Yen' at its centre. With considerable nudity and explicit language, it was awarded an R rating upon release in 1977. *Variety* recognized that the film likely held a particular appeal for younger boomers, observing, 'The filmmakers correctly perceived that the youth audience today, having been weaned on television, loves seeing the tube spoofed … but there is a more substantive undertone of satirising American cultural values.'[23] While the film was not a major hit, it proved extremely lucrative for its distributors, earning $15 million on a $650,000 budget.

It also brought its makers to the attention of the studios. The Zuckers and Abrahams went to Paramount, where they developed *Airplane!*, a spoof of 1950s disaster films (among other things) that was 1980's fourth biggest hit. It was listed by eleven respondents as either a teen memory or favourite. Landis went to Universal, where executives Ned Tanen, Thom Mount and Sean Daniel were looking for a director to work on a project

---

[22]John Landis, quoted in Gregg Kildare, 'Film-maker, 23, Throws Scares into the Monster Biz', *Los Angeles Times*, 13 December 1973, 14.
[23]Mack., '*The Kentucky Fried Movie*', *Variety*, 3 August 1977, 22.

they had been brought by producers Matty Simmons and Ivan Reitman. Simmons was the business manager of *The National Lampoon*, a satirical magazine first published in 1970 by former staff members of *The Harvard Lampoon* Henry Beard (b.1945) and Doug Kenney (b.1946). It specialized in articles that found comedy in the darker side of American institutions such as family, education and business as well as parodies of popular culture and deliberately featured relatively taboo content. By 1974, the magazine was selling up to a million copies per issue and the brand expanded into radio and theatre.[24] To present (and help generate) material for broadcast and stage, the *Lampoon* writers recruited performers including John Belushi (b.1949), Chevy Chase (b.1943), Gilda Radner (b.1946), Bill Murray (b.1950), Harold Ramis (b.1944) and Christopher Guest (b.1948).

Ivan Reitman had a slightly different background to Spielberg, Lucas or his comedic contemporaries. He was born in Czechoslovakia in 1946, but raised in Toronto:

I don't remember living in Czechoslovakia. My memory basically begins with the escape, when I was four and a half in 1950. They bribed a tugboat captain to take us out of Czechoslovakia. We had money in Czechoslovakia, but literally, we came from one kind of life, and then in Toronto, none of us spoke the language, my mother, within a month or so, found out she was pregnant, and there was no money. We were very poor. But ours was the classic great immigrant's story: first you work for somebody. Then after a while you scrape some money together, and my parents bought a dry cleaning store, then they bought a few dry cleaning stores, and they ended up buying a car wash property. It's now the site of the Toronto International Film Festival.

Reitman attended McMaster University in Ontario:

There, I joined all these clubs and in the first year of university I directed a bunch of plays, I was doing reviews for the newspaper, and by the second year I directed a full-scale musical. I studied on the music programme, but there was a film club that was quite controversial. The club was closed down and I made a deal with the student union that I would take it over and make it into a self-reliant organisation again and we would make films. So I directed a film called *Orientation*, which followed the first few days of a university student. I screened it at a film festival in Montreal, and I won. One of the judges was the Canadian head of 20th Century Fox, and I was always a little bit precocious, and I went up to him and

[24]Tony Hendra, *Going Too Far: The Rise and Demise of Sick, Gross, Black, Sophomoric, Weirdo, Pinko, Anarchist, Underground, Anti-Establishment Humor* (New York: Doubleday, 1987), 378.

he was very complimentary and I said, 'you think it would be possible to show this in a movie theatre?' And he said, 'why don't you show the movie to one or two of our bosses', and that was Zanuck and Brown who were running 20th Century Fox at the time.

The film received a limited release in Canada, and marked the beginning of Reitman's career as a director and producer. He found himself working in what he describes as the Toronto 'microclimate', made up of 'people like Gilda Radner and John Candy and David Cronenberg – it was a small enough community, and we were all the same age – it was the baby boom generation sort of hitting its early twenties'. After graduating college, Reitman extended his work as a producer, making stage shows and low-budget movies with a team he had first established at university. His big break came in the form of *The Magic Show*, which originated in Toronto and ran on Broadway from 1974 to 1978. The show's success bought Reitman, with growing connections to the movie industry, the opportunity to produce one of *The National Lampoon*'s stage shows with Belushi as director and Murray and Radner among the cast. Reitman's deal stipulated that he would be a producer on any script based on the show.

The stage production, *The National Lampoon Show*, debuted early in 1975 and was a critical and commercial success. Several of its cast (Chase, Belushi and Radner, followed by Murray a year later) were recruited as performers for NBC's new late-night variety show, *Saturday Night Live* (1975–), which first aired that October. Reitman began working with Harold Ramis, Doug Kenney and *Lampoon* writer Chris Miller to fashion a film script. Rather than film the sketch show, they drew upon their respective college memories to produce a narrative based on campus fraternity life. Like *American Graffiti* (which was a reference point in their writing process, as can be seen in film's similar concluding captions), the team elected to set their story in 1962, the last year before the assassination of JFK signalled the beginning of 1960s unrest.[25]

But where *American Graffiti* portrayed early 1960s youth as separate from the culture of the protagonist's parents, but essentially benign, *Animal House* presented something more disruptive. It focused on Delta House, a notorious fraternity more interested in hedonistic fun than academic achievement. In the version of the script Reitman and Simmons sold to Universal, the Deltas' antics lacked structure and – in keeping with the tone of the *Lampoon* – could be intentionally repellent. Landis was brought in to oversee revisions: 'My major contribution in working with the writers was to say that there had to be good guys and bad guys. They couldn't all be pigs. Bluto [the Delta House member written for and played by Belushi], as he was originally written,

---

[25]Jim Whalley, *Saturday Night Live, Hollywood Comedy, and American Culture: From Chevy Chase to Tina Fey* (New York: Palgrave, 2010), 46.

was essentially a thug rapist.'[26] The finished film presents an escalating clash between the Deltas and the elitist Omega House, who are supported by the college dean. Rather than attempting any sort of reconciliation, the film ends with the Deltas attacking and demolishing the annual homecoming parade.

Sold with the tag line 'It was the Deltas against the rules ... the rules lost!', *Animal House* recasts the youth-oriented social division of the 1960s as a battle against propriety. It presents the members of a counterculture taking on authority and winning, but for no cause greater than their own amusement. Notably, the members of Delta House are all white, middle-class males. While there is some indication they have a more egalitarian attitude regarding gender, race and class than the white, middle-class males they oppose, at no point are their actions intended to create opportunity for anyone but themselves.[27]

Like *Star Wars*, *Animal House* offered a blueprint for other filmmakers, albeit with a very different attitude to building an audience. Both were conceived as entertainment, but where *Star Wars* found its inspiration in childhood experience and appealed to all ages, *Animal House* was rooted in the boomers' divisive teenage years, and its audience could reasonably assumed to be primarily drawn from the younger end of that generation. It was mentioned by nine respondents in the survey, with six explicitly tying it to their teen experience. Respondent 152, for example, remembered 'going to see *Animal House* when I turned seventeen (it was R rated). It was a popular movie and most of my peers in school had seen it'. *Animal House* revelled in the changes that had taken place in America's recent past and used new attitudes towards social freedom as the basis for comedy. Its R rating allowed it to present humour its makers knew some would find objectionable, drawing some viewers at the expense of others.

Animal House was not the only boomer-related hit to take such an approach at this time. Also in 1978, John Carpenter had a surprise hit with *Halloween*, a low-budget horror film that relentlessly focused creating an intense, scary viewing experience, the horror equivalent of *Animal House*'s lowbrow humour. Though both were relatively restrained compared to the excesses of films to come, *Animal House* and *Halloween* have been identified by William Paul as progenitors of what he calls 'gross-out' comedy and horror: 'movies quite happy to present themselves to the public as spectacles in the worst possible taste'.[28]

Carpenter was born in 1948 and, like Spielberg, began making short films at an early age. He attended USC where a short film (*The Resurrection*

[26]Judith Belushi-Pisana and Tanner Colby, *Belushi: A Biography* (New York: Ruggedland Books, 2005), 132.
[27]William Paul, *Laughing Screaming: Modern Hollywood Horror and Comedy* (New York: Columbia University Press, 1994), 128–36.
[28]Paul, *Laughing Screaming*, 4.

of Bronco Billy, 1970) he worked on as writer, editor and composer won an Academy Award for Live Action Short Subject. Together with Dan O'Bannon (b.1946), Carpenter made a 68-minute science fiction comedy called *Dark Star* inspired by Kubrick's *Doctor Strangelove* and *2001*. It was seen by Jack H. Harris – also the distributer of Landis's *Schlock* – who paid for the production of additional scenes and gave it a theatrical release in 1974. Carpenter followed this with *Assault on Precinct 13* (1976), a police thriller that cost $100,000. *Halloween* cost $300,000, and told the story of an escaped killer who returns to his hometown to murder a fresh group of local teenagers. Like *Animal House*, its focus on teen experiences was indicative of its target audience. Carpenter, however, chose a female central character (played by Jamie Lee Curtis). In showing the teens' lives and deaths, the film featured nudity and gore, although the main focus was on a series of suspense sequences and shocks as the killer stalks his victims. *Halloween* eventually returned $18.5 million in rentals, making it the fifteenth biggest hit of the year. In the context of its tiny budget, this was extraordinary and *Halloween* did eventually inspire many imitators. However, as Richard Nowell has shown, the film's slow release meant that the extent of its popularity did not become clear until the early 1980s.[29]

There was no such delay with *Animal House*. In 1978, Spielberg was already working on his next project, a big-budget comedy that had been developed by John Milius with writers Robert Zemeckis and Bob Gale (b.1951). Originally called 'The Night the Japs Attacked' but later renamed *1941* (1979), it was very loosely based upon various reports of panic and unrest in Los Angeles during the Second World War. Biographer Joseph McBride describes how Spielberg 'was uncomfortable seeming too far out of step with his generation'.[30] After *Animal House* became a hit, Spielberg made production choices that indicate he wanted to make *1941* more like Landis's film. He cast two of *Animal House*'s stars, Belushi and Tim Matheson, and even found space for Landis to make a cameo (the following year, Landis would return the favour, casting Spielberg in his similarly gargantuan Belushi vehicle *The Blues Brothers* (1980)).[31] Belushi's character, a pilot named Wild Bill Kelso, was only in the conclusion of

[29]Richard Nowell, *Blood Money: A History of the First Teen Slasher Film Cycle* (New York: Bloomsbury, 2010), 104.

[30]McBride, *Steven Spielberg*, 300.

[31]At this point in their careers, the link between Landis and Spielberg appeared as potentially significant as that between Spielberg and Lucas, an impression strengthened when the two filmmakers agreed to jointly produce and each direct a segment of *Twilight Zone: The Movie* (1983). However, during the filming of Landis's segment, an on-set helicopter accident resulted in the death of three actors, Vic Morrow, Myca Dinh Le and Renee Shin-Yi Chen. According to Joseph McBride, Spielberg immediately disassociated himself from Landis, who faced charges of involuntary manslaughter. Though acquitted in court in 1987, the case undoubtedly affected Landis's career. McBride, *Steven Spielberg*, 350.

Zemeckis and Gale's original drafts, so new scenes were created in which Belushi performed chaotic slapstick reminiscent of his work as Bluto.[32]

Yet *1941* missed the mark. Its destruction lacked *Animal House*'s lightness of touch and its wartime setting was ill-at-ease with the celebration of social irresponsibility found in the earlier film. Instead it was Reitman who demonstrated how the *Animal House* blueprint could be followed. He had returned to Canada to shoot *Meatballs*, a low-budget, PG-version of *Animal House* starring another *Saturday Night Live* cast member Bill Murray. Set in the present day at an American summer camp and co-written by Harold Ramis, it again followed a misfit, fun-loving community in competition with an elitist rival. Whereas *1941* cost at least $26 million and grossed $23.2 million in domestic rentals, *Meatballs* cost $1.6 million Canadian dollars and returned $21.2 in rentals. The following year, Ramis turned director to make *Caddyshack* (1980), which repeated the basic set-up (with Murray as star along with fellow *Saturday Night Live* graduate Chevy Chase), this time at a golf club and found a similar level of success. In 1981, Reitman, Ramis and Murray changed setting again (to the army) for *Stripes*, which was the year's fifth biggest hit.

Outside of the films already discussed, the number of top thirty hit films with boomer directors was still extremely small. In 1979, beside *1941* (fifteenth) and *Meatballs* (seventeenth), Stallone had the fourth biggest hit of the year with *Rocky II*, and Martin Brest (b.1951; a graduate of the American Film Institute's Conservatory graduate programme) came twenty-seventh with *Going in Style*, a comedy about three senior citizens who plan a bank heist. In 1980, *Airplane!* (fourth), *The Blues Brothers* (tenth) and *Caddyshack* (seventeenth) were joined by *The Blue Lagoon* (ninth), a romance between stranded teenagers directed by Randal Kleiser, *Little Darlings* (twentieth), a comedy drama following two teen girls competing to lose their virginity at summer camp, directed by Robert F. Maxwell (b.1949), *The Elephant Man* (twenty-fifth), a black-and-white biopic of disfigured Victorian John Merrick, directed by David Lynch (b.1946) and *Xanadu* (twenty-eighth), a fantasy musical starring *Grease*'s Olivia Newton-John directed by Robert Greenwald (b.1945).

Of this group, the Reitman/Ramis/Murray *Animal House* follow-ups and other 'gross-out' successors were a logical source of inspiration for other upcoming filmmakers in three respects: they were relatively inexpensive, they were consistently successful, and their focus on teen and young adult tastes and experiences (particularly male) fit both the experience and taste of many entering the industry after college *and* the industry's post-Yankelovich understanding of its primary target audience. As we will see in the next

---

[32]Discussed by Gale and Zemeckis in 'The Making of 1941' Documentary available on the blu-ray edition of *1941* (Universal Pictures, 2015).

chapter, such films became the most likely route into the industry, and it wasn't long before their creators were responsible for much more expensive productions.

By 1980 the verdict was in on the first wave of action and adventure films produced after *Jaws* and *Star Wars*. Though several were profitable and some were among the highest grossers of their years, none approached the popularity of the earlier films and most were plagued by high production costs that diminished their achievements. The difficulty of maintaining control of effects-heavy films was also a familiar story for Spielberg and Lucas, who were now working together. Spielberg had considerably overspent on *Jaws*, *Close Encounters* and *1941*. Lucas as producer struggled with the increased size and ambition of *The Empire Strikes Back*, eventually requiring additional loans from Fox that compromised his ownership of the finished film.[33] The two had first met in 1967 when Spielberg attended a screening of Lucas's short *THX 1138:4EB (Electronic Labyrinth)*. By the mid-1970s they were friends and jointly sold a new film series to Paramount, based on a concept from Lucas. For *Raiders of the Lost Ark* (1981) and proposed sequels, Lucas again drew on childhood memories, this time of adventure films, serials and comics set before or during the Second World War. In his pitch to Spielberg, Lucas also invoked the James Bond series for its spectacle, exotic locations and suave protagonist.[34] To Paramount, the pair stressed fiscal responsibility as well as thrilling set-pieces. The deal Lucas constructed promised stiff penalties if production costs overran, in return for greater profit participation, rights and control.[35]

With a budget of $20 million, *Raiders* was still an expensive production, but with the two most successful filmmakers in history involved it was expected to be a blockbuster, and did not disappoint. *Raiders* was by far the biggest hit of 1981, taking $209 million at the domestic box office. Together with its sequels, it was mentioned in fifty responses to our survey, thirty-three of which also mentioned *Star Wars*, a sign of how it aimed for and delivered a similar experience. Respondent 274 recalled

> I was in college and didn't see many films – but films I liked, I'd see multiple times. The original three Star Wars films, *Raiders of the Lost Ark*, etc. ... I remember *Raiders of the Lost Ark* in particular because I saw it four times the week it came out with different people. One of them was my father, who I seldom did social things with much (my mom died when I was fourteen and we stopped going to family films.) He loved the film, btw.

---

[33] J. W. Rinzler, *The Making of Star Wars: The Empire Strikes Back* (New York: Del Rey, 2010), 40.
[34] A transcript of the pitching session is accessible via Keefe, 'Spitballing Indy', http://www.newyorker.com/culture/culture-desk/spitballing-indy.
[35] McBride, *Steven Spielberg*, 311.

For the industry, *Raiders* provided renewed impetus to find more filmmakers who could offer similar results. It had been written by Lawrence Kasdan (b.1946), who had first come to Spielberg's attention with his script for *Continental Divide* (1981), which, with Spielberg's help, was made with John Belushi. According to J. W. Rinzler, 'What initially attracted both Spielberg and Lucas to Kasdan was his ability to channel a certain 1930s and 1940s sensibility, à la Howard Hawks.'[36] He was soon writing both *Raiders* and *The Empire Strikes Back*. Afterwards, he told us:

> Everybody wanted me to write for them as a screenwriter for hire. I had never had that intention, and I said, 'I'm not taking any writing jobs. I want to write my own things and direct my own things.' Alan Ladd, Jr, who I had met through George Lucas, said, 'Alright tell me your story,' I told him the story of *Body Heat*, and he said, 'I'll give you a deal to write it. I won't tell you I'll make it.' He put me in a building on the Fox lot, and on that floor were a lot of young filmmakers: Barry Levinson [b.1942], Franc Roddam [1946, UK], Steven Spielberg. ... Lucas and Zemeckis were part of that group. There was a real feeling, not just there, but as a generation, that we were going to try to do the best work possible. It was the best kind of competition because you wanted to be excited by what the other person was doing. You wanted to be inspired by it.

Boomers and the film business

The impact of the young boomer filmmakers was mirrored and made possible by similar changes among producers and production executives. Compared to directors and writers, the new generation of deal makers were a diverse bunch, both in their backgrounds and their attitude towards the medium. Those who achieved success, however, were united in their understanding that the industry's future lay in the trends exemplified by *Jaws*: wide, heavily marketed releases based on clearly identifiable genres. Sean Daniel came from a considerably less conservative background than many of the directors discussed above:

> I was born in 1951 and I grew up on the Upper West Side of Manhattan in New York City, my family without money and both parents always working, and I grew up in a very left-wing household. My father was a blacklisted television writer. We would go to political movies as a family; we would go to anti-war demonstrations as a family. As we got older

---

[36]J. W. Rinzler and Laurent Bouzereau, *The Complete Making of Indiana Jones: The Definitive Story behind All Four Films* (New York: Del Rey, 2008), 21.

I would go with my high school friends and they would go with their veteran friends. Political demonstrations were a big part of life.

I was obsessed with movies, and I saw everything. I just saw everything I could get my hands on. Every ticket I could buy. It was a glorious time to be a film watcher. Because, if you're me, and in 1960 I'm nine, well, by then, what's playing at the art houses as they were called was just this endless, unstoppable, bottomless well of inspirational movies. Saturday morning would be Marx brothers and Saturday afternoon would be Rossellini.

Nonetheless, Daniel's route into the film industry was similar to his contemporaries, and he translated his childhood fascination with film into a place in college on the West Coast:

I went to a wonderful public school in New York called the High School of Music and Art. I was an art student and I began to take my first film classes as little electives inside school. Just little Super 8 millimeter shorts. I just knew that somehow I wanted to work in film. There was a new school opening called the California Institute of the Arts, and I tracked it down and applied and got a full scholarship, and that was my ticket to come here. So in September 1970 I arrived at LAX to become a sophomore in undergraduate school in the first class at this new film school, CalArts. It was very hands-on. You worked on your own films, you worked on others students'. It was 16mm. The experimental films didn't have any pull, for me.

At CalArts, Daniel found himself working in close proximity to a new generation of young film directors and producers, which ultimately resulted in a job at Universal:

I had always worked. I had worked when I was in film school. So I secured a job for $125 a week as the second AD on possibly the cheapest movie that Roger Corman ever made. And then a guy who had been a graduate student at CalArts had secured a job at Universal and told me that there was an assistant job opening, a production assistant, that was the title. But to go upward I had to meet the president of production, a guy called Ned Tanen. Now there was no IMDb then, you sort of gleaned what you could, and I'd learned that Tanen had been in charge of the youth unit at Universal and had, if fact, financed *American Graffiti*.

So I become a production assistant at Universal Studios. It paid $300 per week, which was fantastic, and I chose the Universal Studios job. I would go to the studio every day. I would do whatever I could get my hands on doing, and I was on a movie lot, and that was a dream. There weren't many young people working at the studio at the time. It was still older executives from an earlier generation. Tanen was the young person. He had given me some scripts to read, and I gave him my coverage, my synopses and opinion, and he liked what I wrote, so he started to send me scripts. I became sort of his reader.

At the same time I'm working my way up as a junior executive and I'm meeting young agents, and I meet a young agent named Mike Markus and one of his clients is this kid John Landis, so I meet John Landis and we do get on and we do hit it off. And I said, 'John, I'm going to give you this script for this project, *National Lampoon's Animal House*.' He, of course, knew all about the *National Lampoon* and it had been written for Belushi.

The success of *National Lampoon's Animal House* helped Daniel gain a position as a producer at Universal and made him part of a small but select group of young producers identified in 1978 by Maureen Orth in her much-quoted article for *New West* magazine, 'Hollywood's New Power Elite: The Baby Moguls'. In the piece she detailed the defining characteristics of a new generation of industry personnel rapidly attaining influence. While the article included directors, with quotations from Landis and Amy Heckerling (b.1954), the main focus was executives: Daniel, Don (then Donald) Simpson, Paula Weinstein, Mark Rosenberg, agent Michael Black, Claire Townsend and Thom Mount (who Orth credits with alerting her to the trend). As described by Orth, this group shared an intensive work ethic, modest tastes, a passion for cinema, university education and 'their common cultural experience of growing up in the sixties'.[37] Most had been actively involved in the New Left and in them Orth saw the potential to reverse the 'creative disappointment' and 'blockbuster mentality' that had set in during the mid-1970s.

While the article had a high hit rate for identifying individuals who would remain relevant into the 1980s and beyond, it was also highly selective in who it included and the aspects of their lives it chose to highlight. Even in 1978, Simpson was not a good fit for Orth's thesis, and he would go on to typify another strain of executive entirely: he focused on film not for its artistic and social potential but as a product to be easily consumed by as large an audience as possible. Though the likes of Weinstein, Rosenberg and to some extent Daniel would continue to push to expand the range of films the industry produced, those who shared Simpson's outlook (if not his tastes) proved more influential.

The forerunners were producers Michael and Julia Phillips and Jon Peters and they began from opposite ends of the commercial spectrum. The Phillips were born in 1943 and 1945 and began dating in college. While Julia was working as a story editor, they acquired the script for *Steelyard Blues* (1973) by David S. Ward (b.1945) and produced it with former actor Tony Bill. In her autobiography, Julia Phillips emphasized the trio's lack of experience and commitment to film as art, commenting that they 'matriculated at the BBS/Harold Schneider school of filmmaking. Get the money on the screen, and protect your director'. Their principles were compromised during post production, 'The second we [saw] the impact ... recutting ... had on the movie'.[38] Their next project, *The Sting*, also from a Ward script, was much more commercial and much more successful, the second biggest hit of 1973 and winner of that year's Oscar for Best Picture. In 1976, the couple had more luck with an auteur project, backing Martin Scorsese to make *Taxi Driver*, but they came undone the following year, when the scale and pressure of Spielberg's *Close Encounters* overwhelmed them.

Peters was born in California in 1945 and his formal education extended only until the seventh grade. At fourteen he enrolled in beauty college and by his early twenties had built up a successful Beverly Hills hairdressing business, which is how he came to meet, and romance, Barbra Streisand. In 1975 Peters joined with Streisand to produce *A Star Is Born*, a second remake of the 1937 film about a young starlet whose career rise is accompanied by the decline of her older lover's. Despite his inexperience, Peters was closely involved in all aspects of the production, including its release and promotion. He designed *A Star Is Born* as a multimedia event, coordinating the soundtrack, a novelization and a television special and it became the second biggest hit of 1976. In 1980, Peters partnered with like-minded producer and former-Columbia executive Peter Guber (b.1942). The pair maintained a constant presence in the credits of major productions during the 1980s, although their actual contribution to the likes of *The Color Purple* (1985) and *Rain Man* (1988) has been disputed. There is no doubt that Peters was a major creative force on *Batman*, which marked the evolution of his *Star Is Born* formula, and became not only the biggest hit of 1989, but one of the defining films of the era.[39]

In the late 1970s and early 1980s, the studios were scrambling to capitalize on the extraordinary revenues that the likes of *Jaws* and *Star Wars* had demonstrated were possible. One outcome was the continued rapid turnover of executives, creating openings for a diverse range of individuals to begin their motion picture careers. At the very top, a notable trend among the most successful executives was prior experience in television. Frank Price (b.1930) had been president of television at MCA/Universal

[38]Julia Philips, *You'll Never Eat Lunch in This Town Again* (New York: Random House, 1991), 120.

[39]Nancy Griffin and Kim Masters, *Hit and Run: How Jon Peters and Peter Guber Took Sony for a Ride in Hollywood* (New York: Simon & Schuster, 1996).

when he moved to become president at Columbia, later becoming CEO until his exit in 1983. At Warner Brothers, Robert (Bob) Daly (b.1937) was brought from a 25-year career with CBS to become CEO in 1980, a position he held until 1999. Among the notable careers that began or significantly advanced during Daly's early tenure were Terry Semel's (b.1943), who had risen through Warner's distribution arm and was made vice chairman in 1981, Rosenberg's, who became president of Worldwide Theatrical Production in 1983, and Mark Canton's (b.1949), who joined Warner in 1980 as an executive vice president, having previously worked at Fox and United Artists.

Most famously, in 1974 Barry Diller was made CEO at Paramount aged just thirty-two. At ABC he had been closely associated with the introduction of television movies, where he emphasized the need for ideas that could be sold in a thirty-second advertisement.[40] In 1976 Diller hired his former ABC colleague Michael Eisner (b.1942) as president. Eisner also had a reputation for commercial, populist instincts. On his early career, Kim Masters says, 'Even then, in the tumult of the late sixties, Eisner wasn't concerned about creating art or making socially important television. He had only a marginal interest in establishing his bona fides or showing off his taste. He wanted the kind of success that Wall Street understood.'[41] Neither Diller's nor Eisner's impact was immediate. When the studio started a run of hits, several of the biggest (including *Saturday Night Fever* and *Grease*) were put into production by David Picker, a survivor of the Renaissance years who had arrived at Paramount in 1976. Masters reports that Picker's philosophy (developed during his time at United Artists) was 'to pick filmmakers and leave them alone'.[42] Picker was out by 1979, but his films helped define the studio's style and strategy going forward, along with *Heaven Can Wait* (1978), *Foul Play* (1978) and *Star Trek* (1979).

In his place, three young executives came to prominence. The first was Simpson, who also joined Paramount in 1976. According to biographer Charles Fleming, behind Simpson's tales of juvenile delinquency and academic achievement lay 'an ordinary American childhood', reading comics and watching television and movies in Anchorage, Alaska.[43] At Paramount, Simpson quickly rose to become president of production, where he was tasked with implementing Diller and Eisner's concept of a more hands-on approach to the development and production of films. His greatest success was *An Officer and a Gentleman* (1982), in which a working-class

---

[40]Kim Masters, *The Keys to the Kingdom: The Rise of Michael Eisner and the Fall of Everyone Else* (New York: Harper, 2001), 30.
[41]Masters, *The Keys to the Kingdom*, 26.
[42]Ibid., 57.
[43]Charles Fleming, *High Concept: Don Simpson and the Hollywood Culture of Excess* (New York: Bloomsbury, 1999), 24.

rebel navigates the physical and emotional hardships of officer training in the US navy. However, Simpson was fired shortly afterwards and given a production deal. Simpson's replacement was Jeffrey Katzenberg (b.1950) who had joined Paramount as Diller's assistant in 1974 after a precocious first career in politics with New York mayor John Linsday. By the end of decade he was an executive with responsibilities including oversight of the studio's vastly expensive *Star Trek* film and the acquisition of independent productions, such as Ivan Reitman's *Meatballs*.

The third key figure was Dawn Steel (b.1946). Steel's background was in marketing, notably a stint promoting *Penthouse* magazine as a lifestyle brand to compete with *Playboy*. She was initially hired by Paramount to help find commercial partners for *Star Trek* and joined full-time in 1978. Steel was not a film fan. Rachel Abramowitz records that, prior to entering the industry, Steel had 'precisely one transcendent moviegoing experience: *Rocky*'.[44] Still, Steel thrived in Paramount's competitive environment where, she described, 'The zeitgeist of the second floor of the administration building was, "If you can't pitch it in one sentence, it's not worthwhile".'[45]

Conclusion

In the six years between *Jaws* and *Raiders of the Lost Ark*, hits from a relatively small group of boomer filmmakers were instrumental in reversing two filmmaking trends that had developed in the early 1970s. First, they brought a new confidence in Hollywood's traditional function: providing entertainment for large audiences. This was achieved by placing viewer pleasure ahead of personal artistic goals in terms of aesthetics or message and in doing so, they demonstrated audiences were willing to embrace stories that positively represented a variety of American lives and values. Second, the extent of their success made studios reconsider their recently acquired reticence regarding the support and nurturing of new talent.

Yet as the details of this chapter make clear, the studios' doors were not thrown open to everyone. The new boomer directors were mostly drawn from a relatively narrow pool – university-educated white men, with suburban backgrounds in the United States or Canada, who wanted to make similar kinds of movies. While it was possible to build a career in the industry if you didn't fit this profile, the path was significantly less straightforward. This can be seen in the experiences of two women who found their first successes during this period.

[44]Rachel Abramowitz, *Is That a Gun in Your Pocket? Women's Experience of Power in Hollywood* (New York: Random House, 2000), 241.
[45]Abramowitz, *Is That a Gun in Your Pocket*, 236.

The year prior to *Stripes*, Nancy Meyers co-wrote and produced another army-set comedy, *Private Benjamin* (1980), starring (and executive produced by) Goldie Hawn. Where *Stripes* concluded with Bill Murray's character happy and successful in a military career, *Private Benjamin* focused on the social and institutional obstacles facing women attempting the same. Meyers had graduated from American University in Washington before moving to Hollywood where she worked as a reader for producer Ray Stark. She remembers,

And one day he had a meeting with Goldie Hawn, but he was an hour late, so I chatted for an hour and started a life-long friendship. When I left working for him, I decided to become a writer. Goldie heard that I'd stopped working for Ray and asked me to be her partner, and this was unusual because actors weren't really doing this. I came up with the idea for *Private Benjamin* and I wrote it with my [then] husband Charles Shyer and Harvey Miller. I just thought Goldie would be great in that movie, so we pitched the idea. She loved it, so we wrote it for her.

However, selling the concept proved difficult:

Everybody turned it down. We were selling that movie in 1979 and Goldie was a movie star, but she had been on TV for years in a bikini, playing that sort of dumb girl with body paint all over her, and now we were out trying to sell a script with a clearly feminist slant, and one studio read it and called her and said, 'This will end your career, if you make this movie.' And she said, 'Well I don't agree.' Everybody turned it down, every single place we went to turned it down, and Warner Brothers was the last place we submitted it to.

Private Benjamin became the sixth highest grossing film of 1980, but did not inspire successful imitators.

In the Baby Moguls, Orth described Paula Weinstein as 'the only woman that Hollywood is even willing to bet on to run a studio someday'.[46] Within two years, Fox became the first studio to appoint a female president and her name was Sherry Lansing. Lansing was born in 1944 and tried her hand at modelling, teaching and acting (costarring with John Wayne in Howard Hawks's last film *Rio Lobo* (1970)) before beginning a career as a script reader at MGM. Soon, she moved to Columbia as vice president of production. There, she was closely associated with two adult-oriented hits: conspiracy thriller *The China Syndrome* (1979) and divorce drama *Kramer vs Kramer* (1979). These successes were key to her appointment at

---

[46]Orth, 'The Baby Moguls', 20.

Fox in January 1980 and once installed as president she continued to favour 'middlebrow, safe adult comedies [and] issue-oriented dramas that could be politically risky and controversial'. However, Fox's CEO Alan Hirschfield soon became frustrated that Lansing was not pursuing 'the kind of action-adventure genre that the other studios were doing'[47] and increasingly undermined her authority with new appointments and blocked decisions. Finally, Lansing quit in December 1982. Both Meyers and Lansing would go on to further major successes in the 1990s and beyond. But first, the industry trends that hindered their progress intensified into the mid-1980s.

---

[47]Abramowitz, *Is That a Gun in Your Pocket*, 196.

8

Popular Genres and Popular Movies

In 1982, Michael Eisner sent around a memo to his staff at Paramount reminding them that 'we have no obligation to make history. We have no obligation to make art. We have no obligation to make a statement. To make money is our only objective'.[1] The early and mid-1980s found studio executives increasingly confident in their understandings of and ability to cater to their audiences. For filmmakers of the baby boom generation, this was a double-edged sword. On the one hand, it offered routes into the industry, as their formative experiences were seen as central to two highly profitable trends: the fantasy adventure and the teen-focused comedy. On the other, opportunities for boomers with interests that lay outside these genres were limited, and even within them studio interference was common.

For some, these limitations were unacceptable. John Sayles was born in 1946 and modelled his early career on John Cassavetes: self-financing his first features as a director with work on other people's films.[2] He started with *Return of the Secaucus Seven* (1980), a drama about the reunion of a group who were friends in college in the late 1960s. Between the small profit from that and the proceeds of several writing jobs for Roger Corman, Sayles was able to make his second film *Lianna* (1983). He also came to the attention of young producers Amy Robinson (1948) and Griffin Dunne (1955), who hired Sayles to write and direct *Baby It's You* (1983) based on Robinson's high school experiences in the mid-1960s.

Robinson and Dunne had a contract with Paramount to distribute the film, and Sayles clashed with the studio repeatedly over the final cut and

---

[1]Masters, *The Keys to the Kingdom*, 103.
[2]John Sayles and Gavin Smith, *Sayles on Sayles* (London: Faber and Faber, 1998), 51.

overall tone of the project. He remembers, 'They disagreed pretty much 180 degrees from me. This was Jeff Katzenberg and Michael Eisner. My distanced opinion on it is that they had seen *Valley Girl* [1983] and *Porky's* [1981] and *Fast Times at Ridgemont High* [1982] and felt, "Jeez, we could have a big hit high school comedy." And *Baby It's You* just was never going to turn into a high school comedy.' Finally, when Sayles threatened to remove his name from the credits, 'they just gave up on the picture'. For Sayles, his treatment made sense in the context of Eisner's then recent mission statement: 'Right when we were coming out, *Trading Places* [1983] and *An Officer and a Gentleman* [1982] were making so much money that it was crazy for them to try to make their money back on this $3 million picture, when the same people who were doing the marketing could be maximizing their profit on these other movies.'[3]

That four of the five films Sayles mentions were the work of boomer directors – and the fifth, *Porky's*, from writer-director Bob Clark (b.1939), was heavily influenced by *Animal House*[4] – demonstrates that this was a period of studio filmmaking characterized by extremes: as executives chased projects that could bring in blockbuster returns, it was once again possible to reach the very top of the industry with relatively little experience. Equally, though, filmmakers like Sayles, uninterested in producing the kinds of films executives thought could be blockbuster hits, were increasingly shut out.

Yet not all trends during the first half of the decade were in the same direction. Away from the headline figures of the box office charts, the industry was facing two developments that would have significant impact in the years and indeed decades ahead. The first was the start of a long-term shift in moviegoing age demographics, as for the first time since the MPAA began regularly measuring audience statistics in 1967, there was a consistent fall in the percentage of tickets sold to 16 to 24-year-olds, and a consistent rise in the percentage of tickets sold to 30 to 39-year-olds. The second, and most immediately influential, was the rapid adoption by consumers of video cassette recorders (or VCRs). At first seen by many as a threat to Hollywood's business model, instead, home video had two effects: it massively increased studio revenues while simultaneously providing funds for the rapid expansion of independent film production. As we will see, both the rise of video and the demographic shift can be attributed to two now familiar traits of the baby boom generation: their refusal to behave as the industry expected and their ongoing love of watching movies.

---

[3]Sayles and Smith, *Sayles on Sayles*, 92–3.
[4]Thomas Schatz, *Hollywood: Critical Concepts in Media and Cultural Studies* (London: Routledge, 2003), 323.

Boomers and the box office

In the period between 1982 and 1986, the Hollywood majors maintained a varied slate of releases, and with good reason. Some of the top grossing films were adult-oriented comedies and dramas that explicitly dealt with difficult subject matter including gender equality (*Tootsie*, 1982), cancer (*Terms of Endearment*, 1983) and slavery (*The Color Purple*, 1985). With the exception of *The Color Purple*, which is discussed in the next chapter, these films remained the preserve of directors, and, to a large extent, writers born before 1943 who had established careers in film (or television) by the mid-1970s. Many were vehicles for the ageing male stars who rose to prominence in the 1960s and 1970s, such as Dustin Hoffman and Jack Nicholson, but a surprising number provided high-profile and complex roles for boomer actresses. Twenty-two different actresses born in 1943 or later received Oscar nominations during this period working with directors born before 1943 (led by Sissy Spacek and Meryl Streep, each with three nominations), compared with six men. Women also received more acting nominations than men in films directed by boomers (seven versus four), but the overwhelming tendency among younger directors, particularly in box office hits, was to focus on male experience.

For directors (and, again, to a large extent, writers) born in 1943 or later, box office success (a top thirty release) was to be found in just four trends: spectacular adventures, often with a science fiction or fantasy element in the vein of *Star Wars* and *Raiders of the Lost Ark*, teen or comedian comedy after *Animal House*, horror after *Halloween*, and sports, dance or military-themed stories of individual achievement, best typified by early examples *Rocky*, *First Blood* (1982) and *An Officer and a Gentleman*. These categories were far from exclusive, and the different ways in which they were combined allowed for a relatively wide range of tones, themes and appeals to different audiences.

In 1982, for example, boomer directors were responsible for seven top thirty science fiction or fantasy hits, compared with just two (*Blade Runner* and *Firefox*) from directors born before 1943, both of which were box office disappointments in relation to their budgets.[5] In part this may have been due to the cult of youth that Spielberg, Lucas and Landis had created; studios were keen to uncover the next big thing. Now that the door had been opened, the industry was essentially flooded with new talent. Furthermore, younger filmmakers had more interest in producing films of this kind, may have been considered more controllable given the high costs, and also would

---

[5]The seven were *E.T.*, *Star Trek II*, *Poltergeist*, *The Dark Crystal* (co-directed by Frank Oz (b.1944)), *Conan the Barbarian* (John Milius (b.1944)), *The Sword and the Sorcerer* (Albert Pyun (b.1953)) and *Tron* (Steven Lisberger (b.1951)).

not have to 'unlearn' their approach to filmmaking in order to pick up the fast pace and complex effects these movies increasingly required.

The most notable boomer successes were science fiction films *E.T. the Extra-Terrestrial* and *Star Trek II: The Wrath of Kahn*. Both were PG rated and contained appeals to a range of age groups. While *Star Trek II* took slightly less at the box office than its predecessor, its writer-director Nicholas Meyer (b.1945) made it for only a fraction of the cost, having impressed Paramount executives with his debut, the time-travel thriller *Time after Time* (1979). By far the biggest hit – and, indeed, the biggest hit in history to that point – was Spielberg's *E.T.* This was a film Spielberg had conceived as a small, more personal project after the crowd-pleasing *Raiders*, informed by his memories of childhood and his parents' divorce when he was in his teens. The story involves a boy, Elliot (played by then ten-year-old Henry Thomas), who meets and befriends a stranded alien. *E.T.* allowed Spielberg to revisit the sense of wonder evident at the climax of *Close Encounters*, but integrated with a much more sympathetic and nuanced view of life in the suburbs. Elliot's parents have recently separated, and the film goes to great lengths to show that he, together with his older brother and younger sister, struggle as much with their father's departure as with the arrival of a visitor from another planet.

E.T. was a hit the moment it arrived in theatres in June 1982, opening at number one with a weekend gross of $11.8 million. What was remarkable was its staying power. In total, it spent sixteen weekends at the top of the box office, a record that still stands. Six times it relinquished its position to a new release, before climbing back into first place. Its last weekend at number one was in December, six months after its release. When it

IMAGE 9 *Spielberg's suburbia in* E.T. the Extra-Terrestrial *(1982).*

finally left theatres after more than a year, it had grossed $359.2 million. In the survey, it was mentioned by eighteen respondents, seven of whom still consider it a favourite. Despite its focus on childhood experience, the responses make it clear that *E.T.* was not just an experience for children. It received a majority of its mentions (eleven out of eighteen) from boomers who were over eighteen years old when it was released. Respondent 114, who was twenty-four in 1982 said, 'I remember being *very* upset when *E.T.* "died" (although I was much too old to let that bother me).' Respondent 509, who was thirty-two, said she considered it a favourite for 'its emotional impact'.

Elsewhere, however, the trend was to take fantasy, science fiction and adventure stories associated with B-movies and comics and make them as adult as possible without crossing an invisible cultural line that would repel families from theatres. This often involved incorporating horror and comedy elements. After *Halloween*, R-rated horror films were frequent and profitable, but rarely troubled the upper reaches of the charts. The highest positions were achieved by sequels; *Friday the 13th Part III*, directed by Steve Miner (b.1951) was the twenty-first biggest hit of 1982, while *Psycho II*, directed by Richard Franklin (b.1949 in Australia, studied at USC), was the twentieth biggest hit of 1983. Spielberg was instrumental in bringing attractions from these films (scares, and shocking or grotesque imagery) into the PG realm. As a producer, he hired directors of low-budget horror Tobe Hooper (b.1943) and Joe Dante (b.1946) to make *Poltergeist*, the eighth biggest hit of 1982, and *Gremlins*, the fourth biggest hit of 1984, respectively. As director, Spielberg again teamed up with George Lucas to make *Raiders* sequel *Indiana Jones and the Temple of Doom* (1984), which paired the hero with a child sidekick but significantly upped the focus on graphic gore. *Temple of Doom* was the third biggest hit of 1984, but together with *Gremlins* caused 'heated criticism' of the level of violence in Hollywood films marketed to children, a debate that led directly to the MPAA introducing a new PG-13 rating that cautioned 'some material may be inappropriate for young children'.[6]

Across the period, two distinct strands of boomer comedy emerged. The first was a renewed focus on teen experience, increasingly with a contemporary setting. In 1982, Amy Heckerling had a minor hit (twenty-ninth for the year) with her first feature, *Fast Times at Ridgemont High*. This was based on a book and script by Cameron Crowe (b.1957), who at twenty-two years of age had spent a year 'undercover' as a pupil in the California school system. Crowe's script offered a more balanced and emotional – though still R-rated – view of teen behaviour than *Animal*

---

[6]Stephen Prince, *A New Pot of Gold: Hollywood under the Electronic Rainbow* (Berkeley: University of California Press, 2000), 367.

House, but in their commentary for the film's DVD release, both Crowe and Heckerling describe the pressure exerted by Universal executives to make the finished film more like the studio's earlier hit. Heckerling remembers, 'The constant question people had, if they were noticing us at all on this movie, of what we were doing on this movie, which was, "it's too edgy, it's too sexual but not sexy and it's not funny, it should be much funnier, it should be lighter, it should be more pornographic."'[7] Universal insisted *Fast Times* conclude with a series of captions detailing the future lives of the main characters, 'because it worked so well for *American Graffiti* and *Animal House,* so why not us?' Along with the aforementioned success of Bob Clark's *Porky's*, the low-budget *Fast Times* indicated that teen-oriented hits were possible without comedian stars. This situation was confirmed the following year by *Risky Business*, an R-rated comedy written and directed by Marshall Brickman (b.1949) about a high school student (Tom Cruise) who opens a brothel in his home while his parents are away. It was the tenth biggest hit of 1983, taking $63.5 million.

The year 1983 saw the continued development of a distinctive brand of boomer adult comedy, associated with group of male performers whose star personas combined (in varying proportions) a sense of self-aware superiority with a chaotic disregard for social convention. In a series of films they encountered and disrupted different aspects of the adult American experience. They included former *Saturday Night Live* comedians Dan Aykroyd, Chevy Chase, Bill Murray and Eddie Murphy (Belushi died of a drugs overdose in March 1982) as well as Steve Martin (b.1945), Michael Keaton (b.1951), Steve Guttenberg (b.1958), Kurt Russell, John Candy (b.1950) and Tom Hanks (b.1956). In *Trading Places*, directed by John Landis, Aykroyd and Murphy are shuffled between the worlds of homelessness and high finance, before beating the system to earn millions. A Paramount release, *Trading Places* was also a demonstration that studio interference was not inevitable for filmmakers with established box office track records. The film's writers, Tim Harris and Herschel Weingrod, were present throughout production and Harris now recalls, 'It gave me such an unrealistic expectation of what the film industry could be like, because it had it got made instantly, the cast was seamless, easy and full of wonderful surprises. The studio was barely aware of it while it was being shot.' It was the year's fourth biggest hit with a domestic gross of $90.4 million.

Chevy Chase had the year's eleventh biggest hit with *National Lampoon's Vacation*, directed by Harold Ramis, about a father taking his family on a disastrous cross-country road trip to a Disney-style theme park. *Vacation* was written by former *Lampoon* staff writer John Hughes (b.1950) and was based on an article he had written for the magazine, which was set in

---

[7]Amy Heckerling, Audio Commentary on *Fast Times at Ridgemont High* DVD (2003).

1958 and narrated from the point of view of the father's bewildered son.[8] For the R-rated film version, Hughes updated events to the present day, and focused on the father, who is trying to recreate the holiday memories of his childhood. The same year, Hughes also wrote the PG-rated *Mr Mom*, 'a semi-autobiographical account of his own adventures as a househusband' starring Michael Keaton.[9] Directed by Stan Dragoti (b.1932), it was the ninth highest grossing film of 1983. *Vacation* and *Mr. Mom* were the first successful (again, top thirty) family-themed comedies at the North American box office since *Yours, Mine and Ours* in 1968.

In 1984, Hughes switched tracks to teen films, making his directing debut with *Sixteen Candles*, a raucous – though PG-rated – comedy detailing the complex social life of a high school girl on her sixteenth birthday. It was only a very minor success (forty-fourth for its year, taking $23.6 million), but set Hughes off on a run of similar productions, writing, producing and directing *The Breakfast Club* (the sixteenth biggest hit of 1985), *Weird Science* (thirty-eighth for 1985) and *Ferris Bueller's Day Off* (tenth for 1986) and writing and producing *Pretty in Pink* (twenty-second for 1986,

	Title	Box office gross	Director (birth year); Writers (birth year)
1	Beverly Hills Cop	$234,760,478	Brest (1951); Bach (1944), Petrie Jr (1952)
2	Ghostbusters	$229,242,989	Reitman (1946); Aykroyd (1952), Ramis (1944)
3	Indiana Jones and the Temple of Doom	$179,870,271	Spielberg (1946); Huyck (1945)
4	Gremlins	$148,168,459	Dante (1946); Columbus (1958)
5	The Karate Kid	$90,815,558	Avildsen (1935); Kamen (1947)
6	Police Academy	$81,198,894	Wilson (1943); Wilson, Israel (1945), Proft (1947)
7	Footloose	$80,035,402	Ross (1927); Pitchford (1951)
8	Romancing the Stone	$76,572,238	Zemeckis (1951); Thomas (1946)
9	Star Trek III: The Search for Spock	$76,471,046	Nimoy (1931); Bennett (1930)
10	Splash	$69,821,334	Howard (1954); Friedman (1930), Ganz (1948), Mandel (1949)

FIGURE 3 *Domestic Box Office Chart, 1984.* Source: boxofficemojo.com.

---

[8] John Hughes, 'Vacation '58', *National Lampoon*, September 1979, 42.
[9] Anon., 'Name a Movie He Didn't Write', *LA Herald-Examiner*, 17 May 1984, B1.

directed by Howard Deutch (b.1950)). Though set in the present day, these films also drew heavily on Hughes's youthful experiences. About *Sixteen Candles*, for instance, he said, 'It was really a portrait of myself, but I told it from the girl's point of view because of the embarrassment.'[10]

The year 1984 was also marked by a trio of successful *Animal House* imitators – *Police Academy* (sixth for the year, directed by Hugh Wilson (b.1943)), *Revenge of the Nerds* (sixteenth, directed by Jeff Kanew (b.1944)) and *Bachelor Party* (nineteenth, directed by Neal Israel (b.1945)) – and the start of a highly successful move into spectacular adventure by boomer comedy directors. Seven of the top ten highest grossing films of 1984 had boomer directors, and all except one (*Star Trek III: The Search for Spock*) was credited to at least one boomer writer. Both Robert Zemeckis and Ron Howard (b.1954) had attempted their own R-rated farces after *Animal House*, but neither Zemeckis's *Used Cars* (1980), in which Kurt Russell plays a corrupt car dealer and aspiring politician, nor Howard's *Night Shift* (1982), where Michael Keaton opens a brothel in a morgue, made the top thirty for its year. In 1984 and 1985, they joined *Animal House*'s Landis and Reitman in making a succession of PG-rated hits that retained their earlier films' comic obsessions with sex and social irresponsibility, but toned these elements down and incorporated spectacular action. Reitman had 1984's second biggest hit with *Ghostbusters*, teaming Murray, Aykroyd and Harold Ramis as paranormal investigators who save New York from evil spirits. *Ghostbusters* is another example of the freedom and resources that were available to young directors the studios considered commercial. The production came together unusually quickly. According to Reitman:

Dan Aykroyd came to me with an old treatment he had always wanted to do with John Belushi and said, 'this would work with me and Murray' and I looked at it, but his treatment wasn't really a comedy, it was just a big, impossible sci-fi extravaganza. I immediately thought: let's reduce what is fundamentally a brilliant idea to a movie that speaks to me and my generation. I remember taking him to a delicatessen and pitching him, 'ok, it's in New York, it's today, 1984, they're working at Columbia University. They get kicked out for whatever reason, but there's ghosts coming, for whatever reason, in the city, and they decide to start a business.' For me it was a starting a business story, because that's something we can understand and would hold this fantastical story together.

So Harold [Ramis], Danny and I basically, with our families, moved to Martha's Vineyard for two and a half weeks, and wrote *Ghostbusters*, using that pitch. Before we went I went to the studio and said, 'Here, I

---

[10]John Hughes, quoted in Eve Babitz, 'Taking a Change on Love: The New Wave', *Vogue*, September 1984, 86.

want to do this movie *Ghostbusters*', and I'd just done *Stripes*, so I was kind of the golden haired boy and it was a different era – people don't believe now how movies got made; I remember, in not much more time than I just spent describing what I pitched to Dan Aykroyd, I pitched to the head of the studio, Frank Price at Columbia. I said, 'Bill, Dan, Harold, this is the story.' He said, 'How much?' and I just picked a number out of my head – because who knows? – and I said, 'I hope I can do it for about $30 million.' *Stripes* was made for about $10 million, finally. I figured if that's ten, this'll be thirty. That's really the math that I did. And they said 'Fine. It's good so long as you can deliver it by ...' and they actually gave me the June date and we had to go and write the script and build an effects company because there was only one effects company, [George Lucas's] Industrial Light and Magic, and it was basically all tied up, so they weren't even available. So we created our own effects company that was financed by Columbia as part of the budget.

Zemeckis had the eighth biggest hit of 1984 when he was selected by producer/star Michael Douglas (b.1944) to direct *Romancing the Stone*, an action comedy written by Diane Thomas (b.1946) starring Kathleen Turner as a timid romance writer who must travel to Columbia and team up with a smuggler (Douglas) to save her kidnapped sister. Before *Romancing the Stone* was released, Zemeckis was working on an adaptation of *Cocoon*, a science fiction novel about alien powers rejuvenating the residents of a retirement home, but was removed from the project by the studio, Twentieth Century Fox.[11] Instead, he was able to direct *Back to the Future* for Universal, a script he had been developing for several years with Bob Gale in which a teenager (Michael J. Fox) travels back in time to 1955 and has to intervene in his parents' high school courtship. Released in July 1985 – with Spielberg as executive producer and given a 'Presented by' credit – it became the top grossing film of the year, taking $210.6 million.

Howard was a former child star, with leading roles in *The Andy Griffith Show* (CBS, 1960–8) and *Happy Days* (ABC 1974–84), who had starred in *American Graffiti*, and began his career as a director working for Roger Corman. After *Night Shift* he directed *Splash*, bringing in *Night Shift*'s writers Lowell Ganz (b.1948) and Babaloo Mandel (b.1949) to rewrite Bruce Jay Friedman's original script about a man (played by Tom Hanks) who falls in love with a mermaid (Daryl Hannah). It was 1984's tenth biggest hit. After *Splash*, Howard replaced Zemeckis as director of *Cocoon*, which featured Steve Guttenberg among its cast, and it became the sixth highest grossing

---

[11]Charles Champlin, '$1 Billion in Grosses? It Takes Gumption', *Los Angeles Times*, 28 December 1994, http://articles.latimes.com/1994-12-28/entertainment/ca-13836_1_robert-zemeckis.

film of 1985. Meanwhile, Landis had the year's tenth biggest hit, *Spies Like Us*, teaming Chase and Aykroyd as incompetent secret agents. Aykroyd co-wrote the script.

The top grossing film of 1984 was *Beverly Hills Cop*, an action comedy directed by Martin Brest in which Eddie Murphy plays a police detective from Detroit who travels to Los Angeles to solve the murder of a friend. Murphy, born in 1962, was from the trailing edge of the baby boom, connected to older comedy stars by the extraordinarily young age at which he achieved major stardom. The aggressive anti-authoritarian attitude he shared with his *SNL* predecessors made him a very different proposition to previous African American stars such as Sidney Poitier and Richard Pryor (in terms of his film persona) and helped the R-rated *Beverly Hills Cop* out-gross *Ghostbusters*, *Temple of Doom* and *Gremlins*.

In other ways too, *Beverly Hills Cop* had a different set of influences: it was produced by Don Simpson and Jerry Bruckheimer (b.1943) and was originally intended to star Sylvester Stallone. During the early 1980s, Simpson/Bruckheimer and Stallone were on separate but similar paths, making propulsive, action-filled stories of working-class characters achieving success through dedication and physical endurance. Stallone wrote, directed and starred in *Rocky III* (the fourth biggest hit of 1982), co-wrote and starred in *First Blood* (thirteenth for 1982) – which introduced the character of John Rambo, an angry, highly skilled Vietnam veteran who clashes with a local sheriff – and directed and co-wrote *Saturday Night Fever* sequel *Staying Alive* (eighth for 1983). As noted in the previous chapter, as an executive, Simpson had worked closely on *An Officer and a Gentleman*. After leaving Paramount with a production deal, he joined Bruckheimer to make *Flashdance*, a project first brought to Simpson's attention by Dawn Steel, about a steelworker (Jennifer Beals) who wants to be a ballet dancer, which became the third biggest hit of 1983.[12]

The story for *Beverly Hills Cop* (by Danilo Bach (b.1944) and Daniel Petrie Jr. (b.1951)) continued Simpson's earlier films' focus on working-class characters breaking their way into elite society. Stallone was cast in the lead, but he attempted to make script revisions that would have taken the film in a more serious, violent direction and parted ways with the production, to be replaced by Murphy.[13] Simpson and Bruckheimer followed *Beverly Hills Cop* with *Top Gun*, another tale of an outsider in elite society, directed by Tony Scott (b.1944, UK) and written by Jim Cash (b.1941) and Jack Epps Jr (b.1949). Epps remembers, 'We were watching everything. And feeling what was going on. *Top Gun* was a Paramount film so it was influenced by

---

[12]Abramowitz, *Is That a Gun*, 242–3.
[13]Events described in 'Beverly Hills Cop: The Phenomenon Begins' Documentary on *Beverly Hills Cop* DVD (2002).

Saturday Night Fever ... *Officer and a Gentleman,* even *Flashdance* ... *Top Gun* was written with a sense of "we're going to write this for Paramount. How can we get this movie made? Let's do exactly what Paramount like to make. Let's give them this very tight, little movie with this little drama at the centre of it."' Set in a navy flying school, *Top Gun* exchanged the earlier films' class dynamic for a focus on its lead character's journey to emotional maturity, a connection to the era's teen films made stronger by the casting of Tom Cruise. It was the highest grossing film of 1986, taking $176.8 million.

Stallone used his *Beverly Hills Cop* revisions as the basis for *Cobra*, the fifteenth biggest hit of 1986, but his greatest successes remained with the Rocky and Rambo franchises. *Rocky IV*, which Stallone again wrote and directed, took the boxer to Russia where he beats the Soviets' drug-enhanced champion. It was the third biggest hit of 1985. The Soviet Union also provided some of the villains for *Rambo: First Blood Part II* – 1985's second biggest hit – which Stallone rewrote after commissioning a first draft from upcoming Canadian filmmaker James Cameron (b.1954).[14] Like many others, Cameron had begun his career working for Roger Corman. In 1984, he co-wrote and directed *The Terminator*, a low-budget R-rated science fiction thriller that was the twenty-second biggest hit of its year. In 1986 he wrote and directed *Aliens*, the sequel to *Alien*, adding military themes absent from the original. The script for *Rambo* also took its hero back into the military, as Rambo is sent back to Vietnam to find prisoners of war. He locates them, but also discovers the Vietcong are now working for Russia, and that the US government intended for him to fail.

In both the Rocky and Rambo sequels – and *Top Gun*, which also used Russian pilots as adversaries – there were clear links to the *Star Wars*-inspired fantasies of the era, with an increasing focus on spectacular action, technology and binary good versus evil narratives, with Americans as heroes and Russians as villains.[15]

Boomer attitudes and attendance habits

As boomer filmmakers gravitated towards projects that presented uplifting, ultimately positive stories of American life aimed at 16 to 24-year-olds and families, the oldest of the generation were approaching forty while the youngest were leaving their teens. Lawrence Kasdan's *The Big Chill* (1983) was one of the few top thirty boomer films of the 1982–6 period that did

---

[14]Rebecca Keegan, *The Futurist: The Life and Films of James Cameron* (New York: Three Rivers Press, 2010), 48.
[15]Stephen Prince, 'Introduction', in Stephen Prince, ed., *American Cinema of the 1980s: Themes and Variations* (New York: Berg, 2007), 12.

not fit with prevailing trends. A comedy drama with an ensemble cast of boomer stars including Tom Berenger, Glenn Close, Kevin Kline, William Hurt and Meg Tilly, it portrays a weekend reunion of former college friends who find their lives and aspirations have altered considerably since the late 1960s. For Kasdan it continued a theme he had first explored in his directing debut, *Body Heat*:

> That my generation wanted to succeed and succeed rapidly. We had had the slightly illusory idea that we had stopped the war, we were terribly important, our numbers were so great, we influenced the culture. There was a sense of importance that came out of people my exact age, graduating 1970, 1972, 1969, that we could change the world. But the truth was, once you got out there, you didn't have much impact on the world and a lot of people were going to law school, they didn't even know why they were going. They were lost. College had been full of glittering prizes, in terms of excitement, in terms of sex, in terms of drugs. And now you go out in the real world and it was kind of dull.

As might be expected, as the baby boom generation moved into adulthood, opinion polls suggested a mixture of continuity and change, both in relation to the baby boom's past, and to the opinions of previous generations at the same life stage. Undoubtedly, the generation's biggest impact, as Leonard Steinhorn and others have argued, was the continued support of social equality and tolerance of alternative lifestyles. Steinhorn credits the boomers with creating 'an America that is more free and equal than at any other time in our nation's history', a conclusion that is supported by survey data (with one exception – financial equality).[16] In his study of public opinion between 1960 and 1988, William G. Mayer describes a long-term shift in attitudes towards racial and gender equality as well as acceptance of premarital sex, beginning in the late 1960s. Through systematic comparisons of the answers given by different age groups over time, Mayer concludes that between a third to one-half of the total change of opinion in these areas can be attributed to generational replacement (people born after a certain date holding different values to those born before it that become more significant proportionally as older age groups die off).[17]

In other areas, there was also a lingering influence of the late 1960s. Since then, the boomers maintained a lack of faith in the federal government and big business. On attitudes towards Reagan's push for deregulation of businesses in the 1980s, Mayer suggests it was a question of competing negatives: 'which was stronger, the public's growing distrust of business or

[16]Steinhorn, *The Greater Generation*, 10.
[17]William G. Mayer, *The Changing American Mind: How and Why American Public Opinion Changed between 1960 and 1988* (Ann Arbor: The University of Michigan Press, 1992), 299.

its increasing hostility toward big government?' In this case, 'the answer appears to be that government worried people more than business did'.[18] Light reports that in 1985, boomers were on average 10 per cent less trusting than older and younger American towards their leaders and institutions.[19]

Mayer concluded that there was no challenge to 'the old American dream – one of equal opportunity within the competitive, free-market system'.[20] As boomers became a larger segment of the adult population, there was little sign of declining religious belief levels or church attendance.[21] Across the period as a whole, Mayer found few consistent patterns (and certainly no generational patterns) of change in attitudes to government spending or taxation, with the exception of a shift in support from federal to state or local control that suggested a generalized distrust of Washington. Despite fluctuations, the American public remained in favour of maintaining or increasing the spending levels introduced in the 1960s while they also consistently pressed for lower taxes.[22] On the issue of crime and punishment, Mayer reported strong support for the enforcement of law and order, with an increase of 30 per cent in support for the death penalty, less lenient courts and prison as punishment since the 1960s.[23] In short, the boomers' impact on American public opinion was neither straightforwardly 'liberal' nor 'conservative', a state of affairs we will address in more detail in the next chapter.

In several respects, films by boomer filmmakers reflected these trends. Discussing the writing of *Back to the Future* in the early 1980s, for example, co-writer Bob Gale has described shared attitudes held by himself and Zemeckis that closely match the prevailing trend of their generation as a whole:

We decided early on that if there was going to be a working time machine, one of the problems we had to solve writing-wise was where did it come from? We said, 'well, it could come from the government' and we thought about that and said, 'Nah, if the government built it, it wouldn't work.' Then we thought some major corporation could be working on it and we said, 'No, we don't like the idea that some major corporation could be working on time travel.' That opens up a big can of worms that we didn't want to deal with. We thought that the American myth is that there's a guy who in his garage invented an automobile engine that gets 200 miles to the gallon, he invented the reusable match that the match

---

[18]Mayer, *The Changing American Mind*, 101.
[19]Light, *Baby Boomers*, 174.
[20]Mayer, *The Changing American Mind*, 128.
[21]Ibid., 30–3.
[22]Ibid., 327.
[23]Ibid., 263.

companies won't let us have because it'll put them out of business. The
car companies won't let us have the engine. That's the guy that would
invent time travel.[24]

More generally, *Back to the Future* quite clearly makes the case for a
synthesis of attitudes from the past and present. The 1950s' attitudes to
race are criticized, with characters in 1955 unable to believe the town could
have a black mayor in thirty years' time. However, the film was also typical
in that these issues are only present at its margins, with the vast majority of
screen time taken by white, male actors. Particularly in comedy, the drive
to push at social boundaries with the antics of white, male protagonists
could result in demeaning representations of other social groups. Essentially
uncritical – even celebratory – representations of prostitution were common
in films such as *Used Cars* and *Bachelor Party*. *Night Shift*, *Trading Places*
and *Risky Business* all feature prostitutes as their primary female characters
and love interests of their male leads.

While boomer filmmakers increasingly came to occupy dominant creative
positions in the industry, their status as an audience in the 1980s was more
difficult to parse. Assessing overall developments in the composition of
Hollywood's audience is complicated by the MPAA's decision (recently
changed) not to report statistics for children under 12. What can be said
with some certainty is that the apparently 'juvenile mythos' some have
detected in Hollywood's output of the period did not result in a more
juvenile audience.[25] Despite fluctuations, MPAA audience surveys from
1976 to 1986 reveal three key trends.[26] First, across the period as a whole,
numbers among the very youngest and very oldest ticket buyers remained
stable. In 1976, 12 to 15-year-olds bought 14 per cent of tickets and this
was still the case ten years later. Given that the proportion of Americans
in this age bracket was shrinking (by 3.4 million over the ten years, a 20
per cent drop), this stability suggests the industry was more successfully
targeting younger teens than in previous years. At the same time, there was
an increase in the percentage of ticket buyers over 40, from 11 per cent in
1976 to 14 per cent in 1986. There was also little change (a two-point drop)
in the 25–29 age group, even though by the mid-1980s this demographic
included the peak years of the baby boom. Over the forty-five years the
MPAA has measured audiences it has been the 25–29 age group that has
been most resistant to change.

Secondly, the percentage of tickets bought by 16 to 24-year-olds began to
fall, with a slow but fairly consistent slide from 46 per cent in 1976 to 38 per cent

---

[24]Bob Gale, Audio Commentary on *Back to the Future* DVD (2005).
[25]Cook, *Lost Illusions*, xvi.
[26]For MPAA audience share figures, see Appendix B.

in 1986. This fall was almost matched by the third trend, a 7 percentage point rise in the percentage of tickets sold to 30 to 39-year-olds, although the two changes did not exactly coincide. In the older category, growth did not begin until 1981, when the first five years of the boom were over 30. The decline in the dominance of the 16–24 demographic over ticket sales began in 1977, even though that demographic continued to grow as a percentage of the population until 1979. With no correlating pattern in the number of overall ticket sales (one group's percentage of the market was not simply increasing because of the decline of another), it would appear these changes (which, as we will see, were the beginning of a long-term trend towards targeting movies at older audiences) were the result of two related factors. On the one hand, there were the continuing shifts in America's demographic profile caused by the ageing of the baby boom. On the other, there were variations in the habits within specific groups, with younger people going to the cinema less and older people going more.

Returning to the survey, among boomers who were over thirty by 1986 (so born between 1946 and 1955) the 1976–86 period was neither especially popular nor unpopular. When discussing their favourite films, fifty respondents listed titles released between those years, compared with fifty-five for the 1950–65 period and forty-four for both 1930–49 and 1966–75. Once again, the big fantasy adventures featured most, with *Star Wars* a favourite of sixteen, *Indiana Jones* a favourite of nine, *Star Trek* a favourite of five and *E.T.* a favourite of four. Among other early films from boomer filmmakers, *Airplane, Animal House, The Goonies* (directed by Richard Donner (b.1930), but produced by Spielberg, who also wrote the story), *Rocky, The Blues Brothers, The Adventures of Buckaroo Banzai* (written and directed by W. D. Richter (b.1945)) and *This is Spinal Tap* all received single mentions while Simpson/Bruckheimer's *Top Gun* was mentioned twice. Yet there was space for a diverse range of films from older filmmakers which, as already noted, tended towards more explicitly adult themes and subjects. The titles included *The Outlaw Josey Wales* (1976), *Taxi Driver* (1976), *Days of Heaven* (1978), *Being There* (1979), *Alien* (1979, three mentions), *Apocalypse Now* (1979), *Kramer vs Kramer* (1979), *All That Jazz* (1979), *Star Trek* (1979, five mentions), *Somewhere in Time* (1980), *The Big Red One* (1980), *Excalibur* (1981), *First Blood* (1982), *Scarface* (1982), *Blade Runner* (1982), *The King of Comedy* (1982), *A Christmas Story* (1983), *The Natural* (1984, two mentions), *Streets of Fire* (1984), *Ladyhawke* (1985), *Brazil* (1985) and *Out of Africa* (1986, two mentions). Spielberg's first 'adult' film, *The Color Purple*, featured twice as did Spielberg's and Lucas's expressed inspiration for Indiana Jones, the James Bond franchise. There were also mentions for three historical dramas produced outside the United States: *Gallipoli* (1981), *Das Boot* (1981) and *Gandhi* (1982).

In addition to filmmaking and demographic trends, the nature of the moviegoing experience itself continued to evolve in the 1980s. As we have

seen, the 1970s were a notoriously poor time for standards in the business
of film exhibition. Multiplex cinemas were making cinemagoing more
convenient, but at considerable cost. Often built either within or adjacent
to malls, the new multiplexes were nearer the suburbs and theoretically
offered more choice than older, single screen movie palaces. Gone, though,
was any sense of a trip to the cinema as a special experience. Multiplexes
were stripped down to – and often below – the bare essentials necessary
to project the film and sell concessions. Screens were generally small and
poorly maintained by low-wage skeleton staff. A by-product of the drive
to cut costs and squeeze in more screens and seats was inadequate sound-
proofing between theatres, so that the soundtrack of one film could be
heard by patrons watching another. While *Star Wars* drove improvements
to theatre sound, the increased power only served to intensify the sound
bleeding problem. As Timothy Shary has suggested, mall locations meant
that patrons were more likely to be teenagers and films were selected
accordingly.[27] Teenage audiences supervised by a handful of often teenage
staff also impacted upon cinema etiquette. During the 1970s, talking and
other disruptive behaviour became more commonplace, a state of affairs
our survey indicates has remained a feature of US theatres into the present
(see the concluding chapter). As described by the *New York Times*' film
critic Vincent Canby in a 1982 article, moviegoing had become 'frequently
inconvenient, unpleasant, unfriendly and depressing'.[28]

Canby's article concluded with the warning that 'movie theaters may be
closer to extinction than I want to believe'. Yet as Gomery has described,
'there was a reaction',[29] and it was led by a Canadian boomer named Garth
Drabinsky, born in 1949 in Toronto. He studied law and initially went into
independent film production. However, in 1979 he teamed with long-standing
exhibitor Nathan Taylor to launch the Cineplex theatre chain. The first venue
was in Toronto and boasted twenty-one screens – then a world record – and
the business model was based on offering its patrons choice in a high-quality
environment. By 1982, Cineplex had twenty Canadian locations and was
expanding into America. Their first US site was a fourteen-screen cinema at
the Beverly Center shopping mall in Los Angeles. The foyer featured a thirty-
six-foot mural by Gerald Gladstone and individually decorated theatres
ranging from 75 to 250 seats. A *Los Angeles Times* story on the opening
noted that 'Cineplex intends to offer a cinematic mix, including first run,
subsequent run, foreign, art and specialty films (including retrospectives

[27]Timothy Schary, *Generation Multiplex: The Image of Youth in Contemporary American
Cinema* (Austin: University of Texas Press, 2002), 21.
[28]Vincent Canby, 'Film View; When Movie Theaters and Patrons are Obnoxious', *New York
Times*, 7 February 1982, http://www.nytimes.com/1982/02/07/movies/film-view-when-movie-
theaters-and-patrons-are-obnoxious.html.
[29]Gomery, *Shared Pleasures*, 101.

and children's films)'. At the concession stand popcorn and soft drinks were joined by Perrier, cappuccino and espresso. Drabinsky was quoted assuring prospective customers, 'It will be a very classy way to see a movie.'[30]

Initially, the company's upstart status meant that access to major studio releases was limited. During the Beverly's first week of operation its top film was *The Secret Policeman's Other Ball* (1982), a British comedy concert film independently distributed by a tiny, recently founded company called Miramax run by brothers Harvey and Bob Weinstein (b.1952 and 1954, respectively).[31] A 1983 antitrust ruling in Canada opened competition, and there followed a series of acquisitions. In 1984, backed by the Seagram Company's Bronfman family, Drabinsky purchased Canada's Odeon chain, retitling his company Cineplex Odeon. By 1987, the *Wall Street Journal* estimated Drabinsky controlled '40 percent to 60 percent share in North America's four most important movie markets – New York, Chicago, Los Angeles and Toronto'.[32] Not all of the Cineplex's press was positive. Despite Drabinsky's classy intentions, *LA Weekly*'s architecture critic dismissed the Universal City multiplex as 'a monument to mediocrity and confusion'.[33] Perhaps more significantly, when the company began to struggle with the cost of its leader's ambition, it pioneered unpopular on-screen advertising and record ticket prices.[34]

By improving the standard of a trip to the movies, Cineplex had 'tapped into the market of grown up baby boomers'. Gomery reports that by 1990, their methods 'had become common industry practice'.[35] As the 1980s progressed, such developments were necessary to combat not only demographic change, but also the growing importance of new technology that was promising (or threatening, depending on your point of view) to alter the nature of the industry, and even the nature of film. In 1987, Jack Valenti summarized what was at stake: 'Unless theater owners make their theaters fresh, clean and airy, and provide an epic viewing experience that can't be duplicated on a VCR, they're going to be out of business.'[36]

VCRs and the expansion of consumer choice

The introduction and rapid adoption of home video was the second and most profound change to the boomers' relationship with Hollywood. By the

---

[30]Deborah Caulfield, 'Cineplex – A Medley of Movies', *Los Angeles Times*, 14 July 1982, 1.

[31]Gregg Kilday, 'Sampling a Cinematic Smorgasbord', *LA Herald-Examiner*, 30 July 1982, D6.

[32]Leonard Zehr, 'Screen Giant', *Wall Street Journal*, 16 March 1987, 1.

[33]John Pastier, 'Losing It at the Movies', *Los Angeles Weekly*, 14 August 1987, B1.

[34]Vincent Canby, 'Real Butter and Big Bucks', *New York Times*, 13 December 1987, 31.

[35]Gomery, *Shared Pleasures*, 113.

[36]Leonard Zehr, 'Screen Giant', *Wall Street Journal*, 16 March 1987, 1.

mid-1970s, films in the home were the accepted norm. The networks now regularly screened recent box office hits, sometimes within two years of their theatrical presentation. In addition, the decade saw the introduction of pay-cable channels such as Home Box Office and The Movie Channel that made new films more available more quickly to those who were able to pay their subscription fees. Yet the films were still controlled by the studios: films could only be shown when and where their owners wanted. If a prospective viewer missed the start time, they'd have to wait until it was shown again. Screenwriter, producer and director Steve Kloves vividly remembers the situation:

> When *The Great Escape* would be on in the 1960s it would spread like wildfire in the playground, it was like, '*Great Escape* is on tonight and tomorrow night, it's going to be split up in two parts' and we all watched it to see Steve McQueen jump over the barbed wire fence, but it was so special, and now movies aren't special because they're so available every single second. It's kind of like how record collections were when I was a kid: you could always have the record, you could listen to the radio, but film was always a little bit more rare. You'd have to watch the edited version at night, you know like at midnight they'd show *Rosemary's Baby* and it'd be on once every three years, so that's a big deal.

HBO began broadcasting nationally in 1975, within months of the American debut of a new video cassette recording system called Betamax from the Japanese electronics firm Sony. As Frederick Wasser has detailed, for at least fifteen years prior to Betamax's arrival, a host of companies from different countries and with different agendas had been attempting to interest consumers in devices that played video content from physical formats such as discs or cassettes, but none caught on with the public.[37] Sony, and other Japanese firms, approached video with an emphasis on its recording capabilities. With the Betamax, Sony found a price the public were willing to pay (initially $1,300) and a marketing strategy that got them to pay it. The recorder was marketed for its 'time-shifting' abilities. In the view of Sony executives, the public had become trapped by television schedules, forced to arrange their lives around airings of favourite programmes and films. The Betamax, with its recording and timer functions, would set them free.

In 1976, 55,000 machines were sold to American dealers. Within two years, competition arrived from JVC's VHS (video home system). JVC had three advantages: a powerful US partner in RCA, tapes capable of four hours of recording and a lower price. Sony quickly responded with price-

---

[37]Frederick Wasser, *Veni, Vidi, Video: The Hollywood Empire and the VCR* (Austin: University of Texas Press, 2002), 22.

drops and new features, triggering a decade-long format war from which VHS emerged victorious (Sony began producing VHS machines in 1988). In the meantime came unexpected developments in how purchasers of both formats were choosing to use their new machines. The American public may have rejected formats that prioritized prerecorded content, yet once they had the ability to play such content in their homes, they embraced the concept with enthusiasm. None of the major studios anticipated the demand for their films on video. The market was found by entrepreneurs such as Andre Blay, a Detroit businessman who essentially cold-called the major studios asking to license their films to sell on video. Incredibly, Fox responded to his request and negotiated the release of fifty popular titles from their pre-1973 catalogue, beginning with *Patton*, *MASH* and *The Sound of Music*. Tapes were priced between $50 and $75, and individual customers could purchase directly from Blay's company, Magnetic Video, if they paid a $10 fee to join a mail-order club. By 1980 it had 60,000 members.

Again, consumers did not behave as expected. Given the high cost of tapes, it was assumed that Blay's main audience would be collectors, especially as his contract with Fox expressly forbade sale for rental purposes. Yet no one actually enforced this clause, even when Fox purchased Magnetic Video for over $7 million after less than a year of operation. Small businesses sprang up almost immediately, enabling people to borrow tapes at a much lower cost. The service proved so popular that it quickly (but not uncontentiously) became the accepted primary use of prerecorded tapes. The original shape of the video market was dictated by the demands of consumers, not the strategies of powerful industry forces. At each stage of home video's initial evolution, from the introduction of hardware, to the embrace of prerecorded content and the creation of the video rental market, the successful approach was always that which best met consumers' desire for flexibility, value for money and choice. In these early stages, video was still the preserve of early adopters and many of them were older boomers, especially men. By 1980, VCRs were in less than 2 per cent of American homes. Research for RCA conducted in 1981 indicated that 'VCR buyers are overwhelmingly male (70 per cent), generally from 25 to 36 years old, make a "reasonably good income" and are predominantly single or married without children.'[38] Like television in the 1950s, video was yet another domestic technology which relied on the baby boomers as primary consumers, and ultimately shaped their viewing habits.

At the major studios, reactions ranged from Fox's cautious welcome to fear and anger. For Disney and Universal, their main concern was the implications of home recording. Once individuals taped their own copies of

---

[38] Anon., 'Getting Involved with your Machine', *Variety*, 17 June 1981, in 'Video' file, AMPAS Margaret Herrick library.

films from television broadcasts, the studios lost control of their property, a particular worry for Disney, who had long benefitted from carefully timed rereleases of their back catalogue. Further, the ability VCRs gave their owners to manipulate and edit recordings had the potential to decimate revenues from television. In Valenti's words, 'If ... VCRs can erase those commercials, and the fast forward button can skip over them, what happens to our business?'[39] Within a year of Betamax's launch, the two studios had taken Sony to court for supplying the tools for copyright infringement on a mass scale. From 1981, Disney and Warner led the way in a more pragmatic and arguably petty disagreement with the ballooning rental industry. From a standing start in 1977, by the middle of 1983 there were 7,000 stores offering video, with combined rental and retail revenues of just over $1 billion.[40] Here the studios' complaint was that once they'd sold a tape to a store owner, their interest in it ended, so that they wouldn't participate in the proceeds if that tape proved popular. Several schemes were proposed to change the relationship, including that stores rent rather than purchase their inventory. Store owners reacted angrily as the studios were attempting to dominate a market they had done little to create and had even actively opposed.

In each case, the studios' plans didn't so much fail as they were rendered unnecessary by the extent of the public's appetite for movies. The legal case against Sony took years to resolve, going as far as the Supreme Court where Sony won a narrow victory in 1984. By this time, it was clearly apparent that video was both here to stay and a potentially colossal source of new money. In 1984, VCRs were in 17 per cent of American homes.[41] Just a year later, that number had almost doubled to 30 per cent, and video rental and retail revenues had hit $4.5 billion from around 30,000 stores.[42] There was also little evidence that video's growth was having a negative impact at the box office. Ticket sales remained over one billion annually throughout the decade, reaching a peak of 1.26 billion in 1989.[43] In 1986, 30 to 39-year-olds – now a demographic entirely consisting of the baby boom – were still the largest group renting films, and they also accounted for a rising proportion of ticket sales, hitting 20 per cent for the first time.[44] Far from replacing trips to the cinema, it appears that video did the opposite, reigniting or maintaining people's interest in film in general. At least one

---

[39]Morrie Gelman, 'No Place For Advertising on Homevid Agenda', *Daily Variety*, 5 March 1982, 16.

[40]Nancy Rivera Brooks, 'Video Stores – a Record Revolution', *Los Angeles Times*, 30 June 1986, 1.

[41]Will Tusher, 'VCR's Picture Getting Brighter', *Variety*, 14 May 1986, 1.

[42]Tusher, 'VCR's Picture Getting Brighter', 1.

[43]Prince, *A New Pot of Gold*, 2.

[44]Tusher, 'VCR's Picture Getting Brighter', 1.

survey of VCR owners, from 1989, indicated a connection between renting and cinemagoing; 70 per cent of respondents who had not visited a theatre in six months also hadn't rented a video in that time.[45]

Equally, the studio's solution to their exclusion from rental returns was simply to reach out to consumers directly. In 1982, Paramount experimented by releasing *Star Trek II* at the reduced price of $39.95. It became the biggest seller of the year, shifting 290,000 copies. In 1985, Paramount's *Raiders of the Lost Ark* became the first title to sell over a million copies, again with the price at $39.95. Around 75 per cent were sold direct to consumers.[46] Again, the arrival of a new way to consume films did not necessarily hurt existing methods. Cassettes sales to the public increased by 61 per cent from 1986 to 1987, but rentals also continued to grow, up 16 per cent over the same period.[47] 1987 was also the year that video revenues conclusively outstripped domestic theatrical grosses, $7.46 compared with $4.2 billion. Summing up the impact of video in Hollywood around mid-decade, Jeffrey Katzenberg, now chairman of production at Disney, gave his accurate if rather understated assessment: 'Video has become a very important "after" market. ... It is not the tidal wave some anticipated.'[48]

In the next chapter we will see that video ultimately served to amplify the commercial power of the major studios, but in the mid-1980s, it was also instrumental in opening up space for smaller, more independent-minded filmmakers and film producers to reach an audience. The year 1984 was significant not only for the boomer domination of the box office charts, but also as the beginning of a particularly fruitful era in American independent cinema. Given the enormous costs involved, the concept of cinematic independence has always been fuzzy. For some it can be simply a case of sourcing financing and sometimes distribution from outside the majors. For others, a degree of artistic or ideological separation is also a necessary component.[49] The 1980s were a boom time for both definitions, and the new revenues of video were an important catalyst. In 1983, 335 feature films were produced in the United States. By 1987, this number had risen to 550, and the increase was entirely located in the independent sector.[50]

John Pierson begins his history/memoir of American independent cinema as a distinct and artistically motivated alternative to Hollywood with a

---

[45]Anon., 'Survey Says Vid Rentals No Big Drain on Pic BO,' *Variety*, 27 March 1989, in 'Video' file AMPAS Margaret Herrick library.

[46]Wasser, *Veni, Vedi, Video*, 132–3.

[47]Anon., '1987 Video Grosses Outstrip Theatrical by Nearly 2-1', *Boxoffice*, March 1988 in 'Video' file, AMPAS Margaret Herrick library.

[48]Julia Cameron, 'The Panic Faded, Hollywood Comes to Grips with the Brave New VCR World', *Chicago Tribune*, 3 November 1985, 8.

[49]An issue explored in Yannis Tzioumakis, *American Independent Cinema: An Introduction* (Edinburgh: Edinburgh University Press, 2006).

[50]Prince, *A New Pot of Gold*, 45.

handful of influential films made or released in 1984, including Jim Jarmusch's *Stranger Than Paradise*, Joel Coen's *Blood Simple*, Bill Sherwood's *Parting Glances* and John Sayle's return to independence following his Paramount troubles, *Brother from Another Planet*.[51] All were directed by boomers born between 1946 and 1954, and these directors' motivations, themes and subject matters served to define the parameters of independent film for the next decade in much the same manner as Spielberg and Lucas dictated the shape of the blockbuster movie. As we will see in Chapter 10, 'independent' films were to become an important element in the studios' continuing efforts to reach boomer audiences.

Jarmusch (b.1953) and Coen (b.1954) were graduates of New York University's film school and in different ways set out to establish distinct individual cinematic voices. Jarmusch was heavily influenced by the personal filmmaking of international and domestic 'auteurs'. Though he contributed his own hip sense of humour and fascination with life at the margins of American city life, *Stranger Than Paradise* borrowed the minimalist aesthetic of Yasujirō Ozu, a debt acknowledged with an explicit reference to Ozu's masterpiece, *Tokyo Story* (1953). Coen, working with his younger brother Ethan (b.1957) as co-writer and producer, was more comfortable working with Hollywood conventions, even if he routinely subverted them with an idiosyncratic flair for character, dialogue and unusual camerawork. The Coens' feature debut, *Blood Simple*, brought all these qualities to film noir, with a story of adultery and murder in a small Texas town. Sherwood (b.1952) and Sayles, however, rooted their independence in their desire to represent and explore aspects of American life that were ignored by Hollywood production. With *Parting Glances*, Sherwood made a romantic drama involving three gay men living in New York. It was one of the earliest theatrically released productions to deal with the threat of AIDS within the gay community. A homosexual relationship – this time between women – was also the subject of Sayles's second film, *Lianna*. For *Brother from Another Planet*, he turned his attention to questions of ethnicity and identity, giving them a science fiction twist. Joe Morton plays a mute alien who crash lands in upstate New York and, mistaken by the police as a homeless African American, is transported to Harlem and left to fend for himself. In terms of style and tone, such productions took a very different tack to the blockbusters of Spielberg, Lucas and Landis, but some nevertheless exhibited a similar nostalgia for, or interest in, classic genres such as film noir and science fiction, as well as suburban life.

While production financing for these films was scraped together from a variety of sources (including, in Sayles's case, a MacArthur genius grant), all

---

[51]John Pierson, *Spike Mike Reloaded: A Guided Tour across a Decade of American Independent Cinema* (New York: Hyperion Books, 2004).

were bought by companies such as Island, Cinecon, The Samuel Goldwyn Company and Circle Releasing either created or given new confidence and resources by the popularity of video. As Pierson points out, 'Home video was exploding and the video distributors were beginning to throw cash around to acquire rights as if there were no tomorrow.'[52] The films' success and visibility proved inspiring to others. When, a year later, another NYU graduate named Spike Lee (b.1957) completed his first feature, *She's Gotta Have It*, he 'wanted to follow in Jarmusch's exact footsteps', taking the film to Cannes and the New York Film Festival en route to landing a distributor.[53] The plan worked. The domestic rights to *She's Gotta Have It* were sold to Island for $250,000 (more than double the film's cost), who pushed it to a gross of over $7 million. In many ways Lee, as a filmmaker with an instantly recognizable style and persona but whose work was also deeply invested in serving the African American community, was the epitome of independent filmmaking in the 1980s, even if the extent of his success meant he was almost immediately signed up by the majors.

The riches of video were such that it didn't only impact upon low-budget productions. The rapid adoption of VCRs, as well as cable, provoked a range of companies to become involved in film production to meet demand for content. Some attempted to compete with the majors on their own ground with varying success. New Line, who had begun as a distributor of art films, began producing genre films in the early 1980s and had a notable hit with *A Nightmare on Elm Street* in 1984. Carolco, a production company founded by Hungarian Andrew G. Vajna and Lebanese Mario Kassar, was more ambitious, launching straight into a series of expensive action films and thrillers, including Stallone's *Rambo* series. Others, perhaps mindful of the home market's older demographic, invested in dramas and adult-oriented comedy. In the early 1980s, HBO contributed around 25 per cent of the budgets for *On Golden Pond*, *Tootsie* and *Sophie's Choice*, the first two of which were the highest grossing adult-oriented releases of the period.[54] Hemdale Films, originally set up to import British cinema, took a similar route, although they also financed the likes of *Return of the Living Dead* (1985) and *The Terminator*.

In 1985 Hemdale produced *Salvador*, the third feature of writer/director Oliver Stone. Despite coming from a relatively wealthy background, Stone was something of an outlier among baby boomer filmmakers. Born in 1946 and raised in New York, Stone spent a considerable proportion of his youth at private school and visiting family in France, especially after his parents divorced. In 1965 he won a place at Yale University, but dropped out to

[52]Pierson, *Spike Mike Reloaded*, 19.
[53]Ibid., 53.
[54]Wasser, *Veni, Vidi, Video*, 117.

teach English in Saigon, before enlisting in the US army, and requesting combat duties. After his tour, he returned to the United States, and in 1970 he graduated with a degree in Film from New York University. In 1974 he directed a low-budget film, *The Seizure*, before getting his first big break in Hollywood as writer of the 1978 prison drama *Midnight Express*, directed by Alan Parker. Stone then wrote and directed *The Hand* (1981), another horror movie for Warner Bros, which proved a commercial failure, before making *Salvador*, a critical but not commercial hit about a US journalist (played by James Woods) caught up in the Salvadoran civil war, and *Platoon* (1986), a partially autobiographical movie about Vietnam, which starred Charlie Sheen as a naïve young enlistee, faced with the horrors of war and the stark divisions among US ranks.

Despite its uncomfortable subject matter, *Platoon* proved a genuine hit, winning seven Academy Awards, and earning $138 million at the US box office, making it the third highest grossing release of the year. Along with other Vietnam-themed major successes *Rambo II*, *Good Morning, Vietnam* (1987) and *Forrest Gump* (1994; the latter two are discussed in the next chapter), *Platoon* helped to demonstrate the continuing public interest in the divisive war, well over a decade after its conclusion. For all that these are very different films, each found a large popular audience by focusing on individuals' experiences and asking viewers to see those experiences as distinct from the wider motives behind the war. In the words of Steven Prince, *Platoon* 'found American heroism in the ability of its soldiers to endure suffering and privation while participating in a venture whose purpose and ideals few felt good about'.[55] At the 1987 Video Software Dealers Association,

> Stone pointed out that he'd failed for 10 years to get the film made before the vid rights deal proved to be key to securing a financing package. Stone told the assembly of vid retailers that as recently as 1984, it was virtually impossible to get theatrical distribution for a film such as *Platoon*, but that the rise of the vid market meant the rise of stronger, more numerous indie theatrical distribs, and the ability for alternative types of pix to be seen.[56]

The more intensely political and challenging nature of Stone's films, which explicitly criticized American culture and foreign policy, were grounded in the countercultural politics that had defined the youth of the baby boomers, but placed him at odds with the focus on entertainment that featured in

---

[55]Prince, *A New Pot of Gold*, 333.
[56]Anon., 'Video Retailers Receive Stone's Thanks, Warnings', *Variety*, 19 August 1987, in 'Video' file, AMPAS Margaret Herrick library.

the work of his contemporaries. As a result, it is perhaps no surprise that Stone found funding for his projects beyond the major studios, in the newly emergent video market. *Platoon*'s outstanding commercial performance was a testament to the commercial impact of the video retail sector, to the ongoing cultural potency of the Vietnam War, especially for baby boom audiences, and to an ageing audience, actively seeking more mature movies.

Conclusion

Once again, the fortunes of the Disney Company work as a useful snapshot of the baby boom generation's impact on the industry, both through its filmmakers and as an audience. The early 1980s were a difficult time for new Disney productions. As Peter Krämer has shown, the company joined the rest of the industry in pursuing *Star Wars*–style blockbusters.[57] However, Disney's strong association with childhood made it difficult for them to use the same strategy. In 1979, studio president Ron Miller lamented, 'When a studio gets a reputation for making a certain kind of movie and that movie is considered kiddie stuff, you lose your entire audience when it turns fifteen. Those people don't come back until they have kiddies of their own.'[58] *The Black Hole, Popeye, Dragonslayer* (1981) and *Tron* (1982) – the latter two from boomer filmmakers – were all unsuccessful attempts to 'break out of the children's ghetto' and draw in the youth crowd. In 1984, the company changed approach, first creating a new division, Touchstone, to produce and distribute adult-oriented content free from the Disney brand, and then recruiting new leadership. In the wake of the 1983 death of Paramount's owner Charles Bluhdorn, the studio's high-profile executive team dispersed around Hollywood. By the end of 1984, Diller had moved to Fox and Eisner had become CEO at Disney, installing Katzenberg as chairman of the company's film studio.

Three of Touchstone's first four releases were PG-rated fantasy: *Splash* (1984), plus *Baby: Secret of the Lost Legend* (1985) about the discovery of a live dinosaur in Africa and *My Science Project* (1985), in which high school students acquire UFO technology. The remaining release was *Country* (1984), a drama from director Richard Pearce (b.1943) about the hardships of contemporary farmers that starred Sam Shepard and Jessica Lange. Though Lange was nominated for the Best Actress Oscar, the film was not a hit. Yet once Katzenberg was installed as chairman, more emphasis was placed on mature themes, albeit within obviously commercial packages. After a poor start with *Offbeat*, an action comedy looking to capitalize on

---

[57]Krämer, *The Best Disney Film*, 185–200.
[58]Ron Miller, quoted in Krämer, *The Best Disney Film*, 192.

star Judge Reinhold's appearance in *Beverly Hill Cop*, Katzenberg's strategy of targeting older viewers proved successful, with three R-rated hits in 1986. Two were loud, aggressive comedies that focused on marital infidelity and death. *Ruthless People* (the year's ninth biggest hit), from the Zucker brothers and Jim Abrahams, and *Down and Out in Beverly Hills* (eleventh), from Paul Mazursky, were filled with recognizable faces. Costs were kept to a minimum by recruiting, in Katzenberg's words, 'stars on the downward slope of their career'.[59] Since *Close Encounters*, Richard Dreyfuss's career had fallen off a cliff, dragged over the edge by personal problems and poor career choices. His appearance in *Down and Out*, now white haired and playing a businessman with teenaged children, was some distance from the restless outsiders he portrayed for Spielberg and Lucas in the 1970s and marked the beginning of a professional resurgence. *The Color of Money* (twelfth for the year) bought back Paul Newman to play 'Fast Eddie' Felson, his character from *The Hustler* (1961). In the belated sequel, Felson comes out of retirement to coach a young protégé, played by Tom Cruise. Unlike the rest of Katzenberg's initial releases, *The Color of Money* was not a modest production and was sold with its costly star names in a typeface much larger than its title. It was directed by Martin Scorsese, who has since described his involvement as an 'experiment' into whether he could make 'a commercial movie'.[60]

In addition, Eisner and Katzenberg had to address the future of Disney's animation division. *The Black Cauldron* (1985), the studio's first animated release since 1981, was an expensive failure, taking just $21.2 million and placed forty-second on the annual chart. In 1986, the much more modestly produced *Basil: The Great Mouse Detective* scraped into the top forty with $25.3 million. While this was hardly spectacular, by the mid-1980s the potential for the Disney brand to shift video units was established.[61] Industry analyst Jeffrey C. Ulin explains that 'the ultimate accelerant for the sell through market were kids' videos, in particular the emergence of Disney as a dominating force via its video division'.[62] While most adult viewers are relatively unlikely to rewatch movies repeatedly, children were much more likely to watch their favourite films over and over again, making it much more likely that parents would purchase videos for them. As Ulin puts it, 'It does not take brain surgery to recognize as a parent that buying a cassette for $20 that your kids will watch seemingly a hundred times is a good

[59]Jeffrey Katzenberg, 'The World Is Changing: Some Thoughts on Our Business', Unpublished Internal Memo, 11 January 1991, 14, obtained from http://www.lettersofnote.com/2011/11/some-thoughts-on-our-business.html.
[60]Quoted in David Thompson and Ian Christie, eds, *Scorsese on Scorsese* (London: Faber and Faber, 1996), 108–10.
[61]Wasser, *Veni, Vidi, Video*, 152.
[62]Jeffrey C. Ulin, *The Business of Media Distribution*, 2nd ed. (New York: Focal, 2010), 173.

investment.'[63] As home viewing became popular to the point of dominance, Disney remained a force to be reckoned with. The first animated release of the new regime was *Oliver and Company*, an animal version of *Oliver Twist*. When it was released in 1988, it grossed $53 million domestically, the seventeenth biggest hit of the year. Together, the success of Touchstone's adult focus and the resurgence of Disney's 'kiddie stuff' were early indicators that the baby boom were about to change Hollywood again.

---

[63]Ulin, *The Business of Media Distribution*, 173.

PART FOUR

Maturity

9

Mature Movies

Initially, Steven Spielberg's identity as a filmmaker had been defined by his youth. As Spielberg approached forty in the mid-1980s, his story needed a new chapter. The process had begun in 1984, when he signed to direct an adaptation of Alice Walker's acclaimed novel *The Color Purple*. Dealing with race, gender and sexuality in the deep South of the 1930s, the project was not an obvious fit for the director, a situation he was happy to address in interviews, stating, 'It's as if I've been swimming in water up to my waist all my life – and I'm great at it – but now I'm going into the deep section of the pool.'[1] While the film was a commercial hit upon release in December 1985, in some quarters Spielberg's depiction of Walker's politics drew criticism, with the *New York Times* complaining that 'the combination of his sensibilities and Miss Walker's amounts to a colossal mismatch'.[2] More generally, an indication of Spielberg's perceived disconnection from the project's themes came when *The Color Purple* was nominated in virtually every major category at the fifty-eighth Academy Awards, with the exception of Best Director.

Instead, the story of Steven Spielberg growing up as an artist would have to wait until 1987's *Empire of the Sun*. Again based on a prestigious book and rooted in a child's introduction to the adult world, Spielberg was able to sell the film in much more personal terms. In a *New York Times* interview which ran with the title 'Spielberg at 40: The Man and the Child', he drew parallels between the protagonist's experiences, and his own journey through Hollywood:

Hitting 40, I really had to come to terms with what I've been tenaciously clinging to, which was a celebration of a kind of naiveté that has been reconfirmed countless times in the amount of people who have gone to

---

[1] Steven Spielberg, quoted in Glenn Collins, 'Spielberg Films *The Color Purple*', in Friedman and Notbohm, eds, *Steven Spielberg Interviews*, 121.
[2] Janet Maslin, Review of *The Color Purple*, *New York Times* 18 December 1985, http://www.nytimes.com/movie/review?res=9F06E5DC153BF93BA25751C1A963948260.

see *ET*, *Back to the Future* and *The Goonies*. But I just reached saturation point, and I thought that *Empire of the Sun* was a great way of performing an exorcism on that period.[3]

Throughout the interview, there is a sense of ambivalence from Spielberg about his role in the industry as he strives to reposition his career without denigrating his work to date. Noting that he was scheduled to make a second Indiana Jones sequel ('I'm still a showman') there remains a clear dissatisfaction with his recent output: 'I can't eat any more candy or it will ruin my health. I have been in the candy factory for the last three years as a producer making sugar substitutes, and I've gagged on it myself – even though I'm proud of most of the stuff I've given a green light to.' Equally, though, he doesn't see an answer in compromise: 'I have that real pull between being a showman and being a filmmaker and there is a tough netherworld between both titles. It's filled with contradictions and bad choices.'

Elsewhere in recent months, Spielberg had struck a similar tone, bemoaning the state of the industry and his own responsibility for recent trends. At the fifty-ninth Academy Awards, he received the Irving G. Thalberg Memorial Award for creative production, and used his speech to implore filmmakers to reconnect with plays and books in the manner of previous generations. Speaking of 'our romance with technology and our excitement at exploring all the possibilities of film and video', he went on to admit, 'I'm as culpable as anyone in having exalted the image at the expense of the word.'

As with his work of the previous decade, Spielberg's passions and concerns were mimicked by others of his generation as boomers increasingly dominated Hollywood production in the late 1980s and 1990s. Like Spielberg, other established boomer filmmakers sought to alter their focus to address more 'mature' themes and genres. While reaching the age of forty is stereotypically understood as a transformational moment of maturity, it seems significant that for filmmakers who began major careers in their late twenties and early thirties, ten years in the industry meant their youth had been exhausted as a source for inspiration, just as they were consolidating their influence and positions of power. The result was – at least for a time – a suspension of the youth-oriented trends that their generation had imposed on Hollywood since the mid-1960s.

Instead, the day-to-day pressures of adult life – whether work, relationship or family related – became the basis for a succession of hit films, encouraged and in some cases inspired by the changing lives of baby boomer filmmakers, as well as changing audience tastes and demographics. This chapter

---

[3]Myra Forsberg, 'Spielberg at Forty, The Man and the Child', in Friedman and Notbohm, eds, *Steven Spielberg Interviews*, 129 (all subsequent quotations).

documents the emergence of more adult-oriented, or adult-fixated, movies between the late 1980s and early 1990s, by looking closely at the films which achieved commercial success at this time. We also look at the impact that home video and speciality movie producers such as Miramax continued to have on boomers' movie habits and choices.

Growing pains

As we have seen, the first half of the 1980s saw a gradual increase in the ratio of tickets bought by Americans aged between thirty and fifty. Having accounted for no more than 21 per cent of annual ticket sales in the 1970s, by 1986, 30- to 50-year-olds accounted for 28 per cent of tickets sold.[4] That year, Ivan Reitman elected to frame the release of his new film *Legal Eagles* in terms of both his own personal development and recent box office results. Citing *Out of Africa* and *The Color Purple* as examples, he said,

> The baby-boom audience is hitting forty. And unlike previous generations, they're still going to the movies or renting movies that they like. ... What I'm seeing now is that every year a couple of films do really well, and they're the more mature ones ... You know, I'm getting to be forty myself. ... What's interesting to me now is different from what was interesting ten years ago.[5]

Legal Eagles was an ambitious but ungainly combination of murder mystery, romantic comedy and pyrotechnic action starring Robert Redford and Debra Winger. In the film Redford's character is pulled in two directions, at once boyish (he is seen riding around his apartment on a bicycle in the middle of the night) and jaded. This was the first time that Redford – fifty at the time of the film's release – had played a father, and his character struggles with parental responsibility. His daughter is in her early teens and coaches her father on organizing his life and starting a new relationship (with Winger). By most measures, *Legal Eagles* did well at the box office, making almost $50 million, the fourteenth highest grossing film of the year. But a difficult production meant it was also extremely expensive (it cost around $40 million), a factor that, coupled with high expectations and poor reviews, left it labelled a misfire.

Nonetheless, Reitman's understanding of audience trends proved accurate. By 1990, 30 to 50-year-olds were purchasing 32 per cent of tickets annually, and they continued to purchase more than 30 per cent each year

---

[4]For MPAA audience share figures, see Appendix B.
[5]Joy Horowitz, 'From Slapstick to Yuppie Fantasy', *New York Times Magazine*, 15 June 1986, 30.

throughout the 1990s, reaching a high for the decade of 36 per cent in 1995. The boomers' continued presence at the box office enabled filmmakers to keep putting their lives on screen. An inevitable consequence was the fuelling of debates surrounding what kinds of lives should be presented and how they should be viewed. Hollywood product, therefore, was at the centre of ongoing struggles to define the boomers' place in American society, a process that took on a new visibility and urgency as boomers reached the highest positions of influence. On a national level, this was best represented by the election of Bill Clinton as the first boomer president. In Hollywood, the creation of DreamWorks SKG, the first new major movie studio for sixty-five years, by boomers Spielberg, Jeffrey Katzenberg and David Geffen (b.1943), was a particularly ambitious demonstration of the generation's power. Commentators were quick to accuse the industry of being both far to the left and far to the right of public opinion. As we will see, a close look at opinion polls and the content of popular movies suggests the reality was less controversial and more significant. Throughout this period, movies largely kept within touching distance of essentially stable – though far from straightforward – widely held mainstream opinion. In part this was due to the considerable continuities the boomers had maintained with America's past, but it was also down to the mass acceptance of the core new values established in the late 1960s.

	Title	Box office gross	Director (birth year); Writers (birth year)
1	Top Gun	$176,786,701	Scott (1944, UK); Cash (1941), Epps Jr. (1949)
2	Crocodile Dundee	$174,803,506	Faiman (NA, Aus); Hogan (39, Aus)
3	Platoon	$138,530,565	Stone (1946); Stone
4	The Karate Kid Part II	$115,103,979	Avildson (1935); Kamen (1947)
5	Star Trek IV: The Voyage Home	$109,713,132	Nimoy (1931); Meyer (1945), Bennett (1930)
6	Back to School	$91,258,000	Metter (NA); Kampman (1947), Ramis (1944)
7	Aliens	$85,160,248	Cameron (1954); Cameron
8	The Golden Child	$79,817,937	Ritchie (1938); Feldman (NA)
9	Ruthless People	$71,624,879	Abrahams (1944), D. Zucker (1947), J. Zucker (1950); Launer (1952)
10	Ferris Bueller's Day Off	$70,136,369	Hughes (1950); Hughes

FIGURE 4 *Domestic Box Office Chart, 1986.* Source: Box Office Mojo.

That the late 1980s was a time of change in Hollywood can be seen through a comparison of the top grossing films of 1986 and 1987. The top hits of 1986 featured an even spread of PGs (three), PG-13s (four) and Rs (three), in a list heavy on action, adventure and slapstick comedy. First was Don Simpson and Jerry Bruckheimer's *Top Gun*, which in its mix of high-tech thrills and collegiate drama set the tone for the year. Below it *Karate Kid II* (fourth), *Back to School* (sixth) and *Ferris Bueller's Day Off* (tenth) all dealt with teen life and problems while *Star Trek IV* (fifth), *The Golden Child* (eighth), *Aliens* (seventh) and *Platoon* (third) offered spectacular action. With *Ruthless People* (ninth), Jim Abrahams and the Zucker brothers did not shy from their tale's adult themes of divorce, kidnap and business ethics but presented them at such a pitch of blackly comic frenzy that the film had obvious appeal for even the youngest audiences not excluded by its R-rating.

By contrast, seven of 1987's top ten movies were released with an R-rating and most unashamedly privileged older viewers, as did the PG-rated hits. Top for the year was the PG-rated *Three Men and a Baby*, a remake of a recent French comedy about a trio of bachelor friends who must learn to take care of an abandoned baby. The unexpected success of this unassuming film was all the more noteworthy because two of its three

	Title	Box office gross	Director (birth year); Writers (birth year)
1	Three Men and a Baby	$167,780,960	Nimoy (1931); Orr (1953), Cruickshank (NA)
2	Fatal Attraction	$156,645,693	Lyne (1941, UK); Dearden (1949, UK)
3	Beverly Hills Cop II	$153,665,036	Scott (1944, UK); Ferguson (1940), Skaaren (1946)
4	Good Morning, Vietnam	$123,922,370	Levinson (1942); Mitch Markowitz (NA)
5	Moonstruck	$80,640,528	Jewison (1926); Shanley (1950)
6	The Untouchables	$76,270,454	De Palma (1940); Mamet (1947)
7	The Secret of My Success	$66,995,879	Ross (1927); Carothers (1931), Cash (1941), Epps Jr. (1949)
8	Stakeout	$65,673,233	Badham (1939, UK); Kouf (1951)
9	Lethal Weapon	$65,207,127	Donner (1930); Black (1961)
10	The Witches of Eastwick	$63,766,510	Miller (1945, Aus); Cristofer (1945)

FIGURE 5 *Domestic Box Office Chart, 1987.* Source: Box Office Mojo.

leads, Tom Selleck and Ted Danson, were known primarily for starring in long-running television shows – *Magnum PI* (CBS, 1980–8) and *Cheers* (NBC, 1982–93) – that were not aimed at a youth demographic. Like *Three Men*, the other major PG success of 1987, *Moonstruck* (fifth), was a comedy that received its rating simply because of a lack of objectionable content, rather than because of any specific attempt to woo the young. Indeed, its story of a forty-year-old woman (Cher) dealing with her elderly relatives while looking for love harked back to the pre-television days when older women were considered the industry's prime audience.

Among 1987's top R-rated movies, only *Beverly Hills Cop II* (third for the year) unapologetically followed the youth-oriented formulas from the first half of the decade, along with the lone PG-13, *The Secret of My Success*, a Michael J. Fox comedy. *Stakeout* (eighth) and *Lethal Weapon* (ninth) were both action comedies but each placed an unusual emphasis on the experiences of their older protagonists. *Fatal Attraction* (second) and *The Witches of Eastwick* (tenth) combined genre pleasures (thriller and comic fantasy respectively) with a degree of social inquiry into gender roles, albeit greatly reduced compared to their source materials, a British short film and a John Updike novel. Together with *Three Men and a Baby* and *Moonstruck*, the latter four productions share recurring themes of personal reflection and the reconsideration of goals by their boomer protagonists.

The final two films in the top ten, *Good Morning, Vietnam* (fourth) and *The Untouchables* (sixth), went beyond the personal to address matters of boomer history. *Good Morning, Vietnam* was sold by its makers as the first comedy to address America's involvement in the Vietnam War. Like *Three Men* and *Stakeout*, it was a product of the new Disney regime's focus on modestly budgeted adult entertainment. By using the genuine experiences of an army disc jockey well away from combat as its inspiration, *Good Morning, Vietnam* presented the conflict in cultural terms, accompanied by a period rock soundtrack. Star Robin Williams was keen to distinguish his film from previous portrayals of the war through the complexity of its Vietnamese characters, describing them as 'more fully figured and, unlike the Vietnamese in most any film I can think of, neither victims nor villains'.[6] This drive to complicate history would also figure prominently in the years ahead.

As a retelling of Elliot Ness's battles against Al Capone, *The Untouchables* made no such claims. Its significance lay in its origins as an adaptation of a television crime series that ran between 1959 and 1964. Together with Universal's *Dragnet*, released three weeks later and the fourteenth biggest hit of 1987, the Paramount production was the beginning of a trend for big-budget films based on 1960s television. In the view of Scott Rudin,

---

[6]Donald Chase, 'Radio Free 'Nam', *Los Angeles Times*, 28 June 1987, 16.

Fox's president of production at the time, 'The biggest reason to make an old television series into a movie is title identification. You have immediate presence in the marketplace.'[7] Yet with few exceptions, and despite syndication, these titles largely had meaning for audiences old enough to remember their original runs. As Julie Salamon revealed in the case of *The Untouchables*, deep into preproduction with the major roles cast – including Kevin Costner as Ness and Bob Hoskins as Capone – 'Paramount Pictures tested the film's audience potential, only to find that the names of both *The Untouchables* and Eliot Ness drew a blank from young moviegoers.'[8] Discovering youth had heard of Al Capone, the part was 'immediately upgraded' and Hoskins was replaced at considerable expense by Robert De Niro. Regardless, when the film was released and enjoyed the sixth highest opening weekend of the year, *Newsweek* reported it was due 'mostly to older (over 25) audiences'.[9]

In addition to these older audience successes, 1987 was characterized by the underperformance of several high-profile youth-oriented productions. Despite his earlier claims that he intended to lay off cinematic 'sugar', as an executive producer Spielberg had two expensive, family science fiction films in wide release, but neither caught on with audiences. **batteries not included*, about robotic aliens helping the down-on-their-luck tenants of a decrepit apartment block, finished thirty-seventh for the year. *Innerspace*, a sort of comic updating of *Fantastic Voyage* that reteamed Spielberg with Joe Dante for the first time since *Gremlins*, was the forty-seventh biggest hit. Lower still, John Hughes had his worst result for a teen film when *Some Kind of Wonderful* (which Hughes wrote and produced) finished in sixtieth place, the first time a film Hughes produced failed to make the top forty. In combination with the mature composition of the top ten, such unexpected failures led some to conclude that Hollywood's audience was changing. Sidney Ganis, president of worldwide marketing for Paramount, told *Time* in March 1988, 'Older audiences now know it's safe to go back to the movies.' Jack Valenti, always keen to highlight the importance of boomer demographics, agreed: 'The movie world no longer need be girdled round by boundaries set by the very young.'[10] *Variety*'s box office analyst Art Murphy went so far as to argue that 'the teen-age phenomenon was, in essence, a decade-long aberration that is now over'.[11]

---

[7]Aljean Harmetz, 'Hollywood Recycling Old TV Hits as Films', *New York Times*, 21 February 1987, http://query.nytimes.com/gst/fullpage.html?res=9B0DE5D61F3DF932A15751 C0A961948260.

[8]Julie Salamon, 'On the Set', *Vogue*, June 1987, 60.

[9]Anon., 'The Mob at the Movies', *Newsweek*, 22 June 1987, 68.

[10]Anon., 'Adults Also Permitted', *Time*, 3 July 1988, 72.

[11]Aljean Harmetz, 'Hollywood Welcomes Back Older Audiences', *New York Times*, 27 April 1988, 30.

Yet boomer filmmakers were not the sole driving force behind 1987's adult successes. Though the majority of the top ten had at least one boomer among their credited writers, and all had prominent boomers involved in their productions, none had boomer directors. The closest was *Good Morning Vietnam*'s Barry Levinson, born in 1942. *Beverly Hills Cop II*'s Tony Scott was born in 1944 in the UK and *The Witches of Eastwick*'s George Miller was born in 1945 in Australia. Indeed, after *The Color Purple* and in line with Legal *Eagles*, the earliest examples of prominent, established boomer directors self-consciously moving into more adult-oriented filmmaking were at best modest hits. Spielberg's *Empire of the Sun* was critically well-received, but remains one of the lowest grossing films of his career (it made $22.2 million, and came fifty-third for 1987). After the failure of *Some Kind of Wonderful*, the prolific Hughes did not return to teen life, but did have a further three films in general release by June 1988, all of which he wrote and produced and two he directed. *She's Having a Baby* (released February 1988) essentially continued the story from the point where Hughes's teen films ended: a young couple in love. It begins with the couple (played by Kevin Bacon and Elizabeth McGovern) getting married and follows them through their first jobs, homes and the run-up to their first child. Closely based on Hughes's own experiences, *She's Having a Baby* was both a critical and commercial failure, taking $16 million (sixty-third for 1988). Hughes had more luck with two films finding broad comedy in the travails of family men. In *Planes, Trains and Automobiles* (November 1987), a businessman (Steve Martin) attempts to get home to his wife and young children for Thanksgiving. In *The Great Outdoors*, Dan Aykroyd and John Candy play brothers-in-law competing to give their children a memorable holiday. Grossing $49.5 and $41.5 million respectively (and finishing twenty-first and twenty-fifth for their years), and with much lower costs than *Legal Eagles*, both could be considered successful.

With *Wall Street*, Oliver Stone carried over his star and structure from *Platoon* to address contemporary domestic themes. Charlie Sheen was again cast as a young man torn between father figures representing left-wing and right-wing ideologies, this time as a stockbroker. On the right, Michael Douglas continued his run of roles (begun in *Fatal Attraction*) examining the consequences of white male privilege and weakness that would continue well into the mid-1990s. As broker Gordon Gekko, Douglas lures Sheen's character Bud Fox into the world of insider trading, against the wishes of Fox's trade unionist dad, played by Martin Sheen. Given to grandstanding, self-justifying speeches, Gekko overwhelms the rest of the film and Douglas won the Oscar for Best Actor. Unlike *Platoon*, *Wall Street* was not nominated in any other categories and received only qualified praise from critics. It was 1987's twenty-fifth biggest hit.

Though credited as co-writer and producer rather than director, Nancy Meyers worked closely with her director husband Charles Shyer on *Baby*

Boom, a romantic comedy about J. C. Wiatt, a successful career woman (played by Diane Keaton) whose plans are derailed when she unexpectedly takes custody of a baby girl following the death of a cousin. Suddenly a single mother, J. C. discovers her firm is unsympathetic to her new responsibilities and she is forced to quit, before finding a new career manufacturing gourmet baby foods. The film received mixed notices, with critics debating the relevance of its subject and the progressiveness of its message. At the box office, it made a promising start with a limited release in 200 theatres, but faded quickly after its national expansion. Its final total of $26.7 million was only enough for forty-sixth place on the 1987 chart.

Given the time-lag between production and release, as well as the limited (compared to their earlier work) popularity of boomers' adult-oriented projects, 1988 saw something of a return to earlier trends. The year's top film – *Rain Man* – was an adult drama, but below it films such as *Coming to America* (third), *Big* (fourth), *Crocodile Dundee II* (sixth), *Die Hard* (seventh) and *Beetlejuice* (tenth) carefully balanced teen and adult appeal. Second for the year was *Who Framed Roger Rabbit*, arguably the most sophisticated, and certainly the most technically astounding of the boomers' evocations of their childhood television memories. Directed by Robert Zemeckis and, like *Back to the Future*, 'presented' by Spielberg, *Roger Rabbit* combined post-war detective noir with the golden age of animation to form a category-defying spectacle with the potential to repel or attract almost any audience. In fifth, Reitman returned to high concept comedy with *Twins*, based around Arnold Schwarzenegger and Danny DeVito playing twin brothers. Screenwriter Tim Harris remembers, 'They were all at the top of their careers and they knew it was going to be huge. Just the poster made that movie, so they were waiving their salaries [in exchange for a percentage of the gross] and Herschel and I offered to waive our salaries, begged to waive our salaries, but they wouldn't let us.' With *The Naked Gun* the Zucker brothers and Jim Abrahams went back to the free-wheeling genre parody of *Airplane* and it was the year's eighth biggest success.

For some months, *Rain Man* (which went on to win Best Picture, Director, Actor and Screenplay Oscars) had been developed as a Spielberg project, until delays forced the director to step away to fulfil his commitment to make *Indiana Jones and the Last Crusade* for a summer 1989 release. At first glance, the hits of 1989 suggest the continued dominance of action-adventure franchises. The year's biggest success by a considerable distance was Warner's *Batman*, and it was joined in the top ten by *Indiana Jones and the Last Crusade*, *Lethal Weapon 2*, *Back to the Future II* and *Ghostbusters II*. *Batman* was the logical culmination of studio production trends across the 1980s. From his comic book origins in 1939, the Batman character had appeared in many forms, including 1940s film serials and 1960s television. The big-budget film adaptation signalled its relevance to teen and adult audiences through the casting of comedian star Michael Keaton as the title character and Jack Nicholson as his adversary, the Joker. To direct the project, Warner selected Tim Burton, a young director (b.1958) whose first two features (*Pee-Wee's Big Adventure* and *Beetlejuice*) had been unexpected successes for the studio.

Burton grew up in suburban California and had trained as a Disney animator. Inspired by classic horror and science-fiction, his tastes tended towards the quirky and fantastic but on *Batman* he was limited by the frequent intervention of producer Jon Peters. Peters's priority was to ensure the project's marketability and to this end he insisted upon increases to the story's action and romance as well as the inclusion of several original songs by Warner Music artist Prince.[12] The final film was sufficiently violent and gruesome to receive a PG-13 rating and it was heavily marketed across a very broad range of media and licensed products, which positioned the movie as an inclusive, lightly gothic action adventure.[13] Audiences responded, and the film grossed $251 million domestically, the third highest total for the 1980s after *E.T.* and *Return of the Jedi*. It was mentioned by two survey respondents, both as young (male) adult memories. Respondent 158 (b.1958) listed it with *Star Wars, The Fog* and *Flash Gordon*. For respondent 110 (b.1968), the opening midnight screenings were particularly memorable: 'Not a great movie, but fun because it was an event with my friends.'

Below *Batman*, the content of other blockbusters, plus the makeup of the rest of the top twenty, shows the year was a continuation of the embrace of boomer interests. In addition to the growing adult inflection of the *Lethal Weapon* films, the teams behind both *Indiana Jones* and *Ghostbusters* changed emphasis from earlier instalments. For the third Indiana Jones movie, a major new element was the introduction of the title character's father, Henry Jones, played by Sean Connery. While the series' trademark succession of action set-pieces remained intact, it was accompanied by a story of intergenerational healing, as father and son find bonds and commonalities they had previously ignored. In keeping with the collaborative nature of the series, the inclusion of Henry Jones was first proposed by Lucas and then developed by screenwriter Jeffrey Boam (b.1946) and Spielberg.[14]

The second *Ghostbusters* also had multiple authors in its long journey to the screen. Following the success of the original film, a quick sequel seemed an obvious choice, but the project was ignored during the presidency of David Puttnam, and then further delayed by the reluctance of star Bill Murray to commit. Since *Ghostbusters*, Murray had not starred in another

[12]Griffin and Masters, *Hit and Run*, 126.
[13]See Eileen R. Meehan, 'Holy Commodity Fetishism Batman!', in Roberta E. Pearson and William Uricchio, eds, *The Many Lives of Batman* (New York: BFI-Routledge, 1991), 47–65.
[14]McBride, *Steven Spielberg*, 401.

film until *Scrooged*, released at the end of 1988. During the promotion for that film he announced a change of heart in the kinds of film he would now be making, saying, 'It sounds corny but I'd like all my stuff from here on out to be things you wouldn't be afraid to let your kids' kids discover decades from now.'[15] To get him to sign for the *Ghostbusters* sequel, Reitman, Aykroyd and Ramis agreed to a storyline that developed the romance between Murray's character Peter Venkman and Dana Barrett, played by Sigourney Weaver. When *Ghostbusters II* was released, *Variety*'s reviewer highlighted its gentler overall tone, describing it as 'baby boomer silliness as opposed to the juvenile silliness of the original'.[16]

Reconnecting with parents, adult relationships and focusing on children were all common themes in the films of 1989, and all were closely associated with boomer filmmakers. Nestled between the franchise films at the top of the charts, *Look Who's Talking*, a romantic comedy about a single woman with a new baby looking for love, was a major sleeper hit, finishing fourth for the year. Written and directed by Amy Heckerling, its unique selling point was that its baby has an adult consciousness, audible only to the audience. In interviews, Heckerling further separated her film from other recent baby-themed productions by noting her own recent experience of motherhood (her daughter was born in 1985). Asked to comment on the likes of *Three Men and Baby*, *Baby Boom* and *She's Having a Baby* she said, 'I felt like those movies were made by people who hadn't even been around children.'[17]

The makers of 1989's ninth biggest hit, *Parenthood*, also talked up their qualifications for making what producer Brian Grazer described as 'sort of an *American Graffiti* about parenthood and families'.[18] The film's press notes pointed out that between them, director Ron Howard and co-writers Lowell Ganz and Babaloo Mandel had fourteen children. Howard told *Newsweek*, 'I knew I was making an adult movie this time. I wanted something that was smarter, tougher, a little more painful in places.'[19] In the press notes he expanded on the aspects of being a parent he wanted to cover: 'At the beginning of a child's life, you have such high hopes for your kids ... Then they start going to school, talking back to you and exercising their own individuality. And when they get to the teenage years, they turn on you ... Finally, when the kids get into their 20s and 30s, you think you're done as a

---

[15]Bill Murray, quoted in Timothy White, 'The Rumpled Anarchy of Bill Murray', *New York Times*, 20 November 1988, http://www.nytimes.com/1988/11/20/magazine/the-rumpled-anarchy-of-bill-murray.html?pagewanted=all.
[16]Anon., Review of *Ghostbusters II*, *Variety*, 31 December 1988, http://variety.com/1988/film/reviews/ghostbusters-ii-1200427980/.
[17]Amy Heckerling, quoted in Tom Matthews, 'Baby Talk', *Boxoffice*, November 1989, 12.
[18]Martin A. Grove, 'Hollywood Report', *Hollywood Reporter*, 2 August 1989, 10.
[19]Ron Givens, 'The Nice Guy Rides Again', *Newsweek*, 28 August 1989, 56–7.

parent. But then a crisis comes up and it doesn't matter if your child is five or 25, you never stop being a parent.'[20]

Below the top ten a number of other hits explored aspects of adult life. Four films dwelt on the passage of time, and its impact on individuals' lives and outlooks. In each, the focus was primarily on boomer characters. *When Harry Met Sally* (eleventh) and *War of the Roses* (twelfth) are both comedies charting a couple's relationship from college to early middle age and both emphasize periods of disappointment and doubt. The former (directed by Rob Reiner and featuring Billy Crystal, Meg Ryan and Carrie Fisher) ends in romance, the latter (directed by Danny DeVito and feature Michael Douglas and Kathleen Turner) ends in divorce and death. *Steel Magnolias* (fourteenth) follows a group of female friends (including Sally Field and Dolly Parton) over several years in the Deep South. In *Born on the Fourth of July* (seventeenth), Oliver Stone returned to the subject of Vietnam, with a biopic of Ron Kovic (played by Tom Cruise), tracing his life from patriotic youth in the 1950s (Kovic, like Stone, was born in 1946) to paralysed veteran and campaigner.

Two very different films also presented men reconnecting with childhood memories of their fathers. In *National Lampoon's Christmas Vacation* (written and produced by Hughes and fifteenth for the year), Chevy Chase reprises his role as Clark Griswold, trying to recreate idealized Christmas memories. As discussed in the introduction, in *Field of Dreams*, written and directed by Phil Alden Robinson, Kevin Costner plays a farmer driven by unexplained forces to mend rifts with his dead father caused by the generational conflict of the 1960s. Citing *When Harry Met Sally* and *Parenthood* in particular, Morgan Stanley and Co. analyst Alan Kassan told the *Wall Street Journal* that the 1980s concluded with the studios 'doing a super job of changing its product development to coincide with the demographic changes of the baby boomers replacing teenagers as the heavy moviegoing group'.[21]

But just as important in 1989 was the success of two films that looked beyond the boomers to their kids. The fifth and thirteenth biggest hits of the year were *Honey, I Shrunk the Kids* and *The Little Mermaid*, both Disney releases aimed at young children with the intention of luring their parents as well. After the success of *Oliver and Company*, *The Little Mermaid* was a step up again. Its $83.4 million and thirteenth place finish was the best result for a Disney animation since *The Jungle Book* in 1967, which had been the last project Walt Disney personally oversaw. *Honey, I Shrunk the*

[20]Ron Howard quoted in Anon., 'Parenthood Production Notes, Universal Studios', from 'Parenthood' file, AMPAS Margaret Herrick library.
[21]Laura Landro, 'Late Summer Movies May Steal Thunder from Glut of Big-Budget Action Films', *Wall Street Journal*, 27 July 1990, B1.

Kids, an expensive, effects-oriented fantasy adventure, harked back to the live-action family films of the 1950s and 1960s like *20,000 Leagues Under the Sea* and *Mary Poppins*. Starring Rick Moranis as a suburban inventor who accidentally shrinks a group of children in his back garden, the film self-consciously drew upon imagery from 1950s science fiction films such as *The Incredible Shrinking Man* (1957), presenting their extreme scale contrasts with a new degree of realism and a brightly lit, lightly comic tone.

Boom (and bust) at the box office

Into the 1990s the dual trends for adult-oriented features and family films intensified, fuelled both by box office returns and the interests of powerful filmmakers. This combination of factors was particularly important in 1990, when all of the top four films of the year were unexpected hits. At number one was *Home Alone*, written and produced by Hughes and directed by Chris Columbus (b.1958). A slapstick comedy about a young boy (Macaulay Culkin) accidently left at home by his family when they go on holiday, the film became a phenomenon, taking $285.7 million, more than any other film since *E.T.* in 1982. In second place was *Ghost*, a peculiar generic hybrid of romance, comedy, thrills and supernatural fantasy. Its screenwriter, Bruce Joel Rubin (b.1943), has traced the film's origins to a period in his early twenties when he stayed in a Tibetan monastery 'to sit quietly and get to know myself': 'I knew while I was there that I was going to be able to come back with stories to tell. *Ghost* was one of the stories that came from that trip.' At Paramount, the script came to the attention of Jerry Zucker, who was looking for his first project as a director away from his brother and Abrahams ('I wasn't looking for any particular genre. I just wanted to find a good script'). When Rubin heard his work had interested the director of *Airplane*, 'I literally cried. I couldn't believe that the studio had done that to me.'[22] But Zucker had responded to Rubin's story and the two men were able to work together closely during filming. Audiences responded to the finished product to the tune of $217.6 million.

In some ways, the film in third was even more unlikely. Early in his career, Kevin Costner had featured only at the edges of the Hollywood and the baby boom story. He had a small part in Ron Howard's *Night Shift* (as Frat Boy #1) and was cut from the final version of *The Big Chill*. He had starring roles in *Silverado* and *Fandango* (produced by Spielberg's Amblin) but neither had performed to financial expectations. As the industry's tastes matured, Costner hit his stride. *The Untouchables* was his first major success,

[22]Bruce Rubin, director and writer's commentary on the *Ghost* (1990) DVD (Paramount Home Entertainment, 2001).

soon followed by Ron Shelton's baseball romance *Bull Durham* (eighteenth for 1988) and *Field of Dreams*. The star elected to use his new standing in the industry to raise the $15 million budget for a project he had wanted to make for several years, the western *Dances with Wolves*. Apart from its unfashionable genre, a number of other factors made the film a long shot: it was Costner's first film as a director, he insisted on a three-hour running time and he used it to dwell on the community and traditions of the Native American Sioux, contrasting them with the unthinking violence of white invaders. Remarkably, it found a huge audience, taking $184.2 million.

Finally, the year's fourth biggest hit was *Pretty Woman*, a romantic comedy with distinctly adult themes. In telling its tale of a prostitute and corporate raider redeeming one another after a chance encounter on Hollywood Boulevard, the film presented a carefully white-washed version of both professions but still received an R-rating. Undoubtedly aided by a star-making performance from Julia Roberts (eighteen years younger than her costar Richard Gere and who, for Janet Maslin in the *New York Times*, was 'so enchantingly beautiful, so funny, so natural and such an absolute delight that it is hard to hold anything against the movie'), *Pretty Woman* made $178.4 million.

Many of the adult-oriented hits of 1989 and 1990 were listed as boomer favourites in our survey, with the vast majority of mentions coming from female respondents. *When Harry Met Sally*, *Steel Magnolias*, *Pretty Woman* and *Ghost* each received five mentions, all but one (from respondent 789 (b.1962), who listed *When Harry Met Sally* as a favourite with *Wizard of Oz*, *Oh Brother Where Art Thou*, *Groundhog Day* and *Once Upon a Time in America*) from women. Both *When Harry Met Sally* and *Pretty Woman* were mentioned as a favourite by respondent 551 (b.1945) as 'chick flicks' she loves to rewatch alone while knitting. For respondent 294 (b.1950) *Pretty Woman* is her favourite because it shows 'we can be trashy and still have the opportunity to meet a knight in shining armor'. For respondent 218 (b.1957) the film is a 'modern day fairy tale' while for respondent 448 (b.1962) 'it is the ultimate love story that shows you can change no matter what side of the tracks you come from'. *Ghost* was singled out for the emotional experience it offers. Respondent 579, for example, said that it is 'just so beautiful and sad at the same time', adding that Whoopi Goldberg is 'just too funny'. Comments on *Steel Magnolias* highlighted the film's focus on female friendship. Respondent 255 listed it as a favourite with two other films from the period, *Fried Green Tomatoes* (1991) and *Heart and Souls* (1993) 'because of strong women characters and because of the friends I was with when I saw them; they made strong, positive memories'. For respondent 81 the film's appeal lay in 'women being nice to each other'.

Dances with Wolves received three mentions, again all from female respondents. Respondent 622 listed it with *Gone with the Wind* and *It's a Wonderful Life* and the explanation that all had made her cry. Respondent

493 associated it with *Camelot, Gladiator, Star Wars* and *Titanic* for their epic scale. *Home Alone* and *Christmas Vacation* were each mentioned as a favourite once, the former as part of a long and eclectic list of titles from respondent 388, the latter as the favourite of respondent 596. Only *Field of Dreams* featured in multiple male responses, with respondents 671, 412 and 181 all listing it as a favourite. Respondent 671 listed it with *What Dreams May Come* but added that he really couldn't explain why. Respondent 412 reported having visited the film's set while travelling in Iowa.

Unlike in 1989, the adult-oriented hits of 1990 were not crowded out of the top positions by spectacular action-adventure movies, as a number of expensive, youth-oriented productions did not live up to expectations. Among the most high profile were *Dick Tracy, Days of Thunder, Back to the Future Part III* and *Gremlins 2: The New Batch*, each of which was so expensive to produce that nothing less than blockbuster returns were considered enough. Though *Dick Tracy*, for example, made over $100 million, by January 1991, Katzenberg would conclude the film 'made demands on our time, talent and treasury that, upon reflection, may not have been worth it'.[23]

Katzenberg's reflections on *Tracy* were part of an infamous twenty-eight-page memo the Disney chairman wrote outlining his concerns and hopes for the industry's present and future. In Katzenberg's view, studios were giving too much power and money to certain stars, writers and directors, placing big names ahead of developing projects based on their conceptual and narrative strengths. The result was a loss of control and an increase in risk, as stars both in front of and behind the camera took gross participation deals, cutting into the studios' chances of profits. Such worries from one of the most powerful men in Hollywood serve to temper claims that studios comprehensively regained the upper hand over creative personnel during the 1980s. Katzenberg's complaints were not reserved for action-adventure movies. Other productions singled out as follies were clearly intended for older audiences, including 1990 releases *The Bonfire of the Vanities* at Warner Brothers, *Havana* at Universal and *The Two Jakes* at Paramount. The general consensus is that Katzenberg's words fell on deaf ears. In Thomas Schatz's view, the memo 'scarcely signalled any real change at Disney or anywhere else'.[24]

Katzenberg framed his argument in the context of the economic recession then gripping America. In 1991, the recession conclusively reached Hollywood as blockbusters again failed to catch on and breakout smaller films this time failed to provide adequate compensation. Significantly, in

[23]Katzenberg, 'The World In Changing, 12.
[24]Thomas Schatz, 'The New Hollywood', in Jim Collins, Hillary Radner and Ava Preacher Collins, eds., *Film Theory Goes to the Movies* (New York: Routledge, 1993), 28.

seeking to explain the reversal of fortune, industry commentators now began
with the assumption that another shift had occurred in how executives
saw their audiences. In the *Los Angeles Times*, Jack Mathews partially
blamed the poor summer on a lack of diversity in releases targeting specific
audiences: 'A few years ago, the studios made movies mostly for kids; today,
they're making them mostly for older (age 25+) adults.'[25]

At the end of October, Paramount's new chairman, Brandon Tartikoff
(b.1949), complained about exactly this situation to the *New York Times*.
Tartikoff had assumed control of the studio four months earlier, and
presided over the release of a string of expensive adult-oriented releases put
into production by his predecessor, Frank Mancuso (b.1933). *Regarding
Henry*, *Soapdish* and *Frankie and Johnny* all found only limited audiences
and led Tartikoff to conclude, 'While there is a place for the adult film, or
for pictures that don't necessarily have to be made for the most frequent
moviegoers – twenty five and under – you don't want an abundance of
pictures clearly tilted to viewers twenty five and up.' This was because, in
his view, 'In a recession, the people most affected will be the least frequent
moviegoers – the older audience. If you aim for this audience, you better hit
the bull's-eye, or else they say, "Hey, I'll wait for the video."'[26]

More than ten years after the introduction of Betamax, video's impact on
the industry had been simultaneously seismic and subtle. As Frederick Wasser
has shown, perhaps the biggest surprise was the sheer enormity of revenues
the format conjured up, seemingly out of nothing.[27] From 1987, video sales
began to outstrip theatres as the industry's primary source of revenue for
its theatrically released films. Contrary to the predictions of many in the
industry, this money was not at the expense of theatrical returns, which rose
steadily during the 1980s (largely thanks to ticket price inflation). In effect,
the value of being in the movie business more than doubled in a decade.

Yet the way studio heads elected to invest their new cash was less than
revolutionary. As we saw in the previous chapter, the early days of video
created something of a wild west situation, where new companies sprouted
up all over the place, hoping to seize a piece of this commercial territory. For
a brief period, the result was an overall increase in feature film production.
But as the 1980s progressed, harsh truths about the market were revealed.
In the late 1980s and early 1990s, the video market was still driven by
the tastes and needs of baby boomers. A 1991 survey conducted by the
Video Software Dealers association found VCR ownership was up 73 per
cent and 'the average vid renter is thirty nine years old and married with

---

[25]Jack Mathews, 'No Mystery: Four Real reasons moviegoing is Off', *Los Angeles Times*, 20
October 1991, 26.
[26]Bernard Weinraub, 'Tartikoff Begins Charting New Course for Paramount Films', *New York
Times*, 31 October 1991, B2.
[27]Wasser, *Veni, Vidi, Video*, 179.

children'.[28] Though video gave these boomers unparalleled opportunity to access and experience a range of cinema, sales figures demonstrated that the public gravitated towards new releases that had enjoyed extensive theatrical exposure.[29]

The new home entertainment game, therefore, was played by the old theatrical rules, for which the upstart companies lacked the experience and resources to compete. The theatrical market placed limitations on competition: the number of cinemagoers, the number of bookable screens and the promotional opportunities in national and local media were all finite. While independent companies responded to video by increasing the number of titles available, the majors instead elected to either maintain or cut their production numbers and increase the amount spent on each release. The extra money on production values and promotion widened the gap between the product of the majors and their competitors, so that even films that failed to find an audience theatrically had an advantage in terms of awareness upon their arrival in video stores. The most obvious example of a film benefitting from the additional exposure offered by video was *The Shawshank Redemption* (1994), a Columbia Pictures release. Despite strong reviews and seven Oscar nominations, the prison drama was not a box office hit, just failing to make the top fifty for its year. Yet when it was released on video in April 1995, it found a new audience and remained among the top forty video rentals for thirty-two weeks, longer than any other title released that year. In our survey, *Shawshank* was the third most mentioned film from the 1987–99 period with eleven respondents considering it a favourite, including seven born between 1943 and 1964. Respondent 242 (b.1945) said it was a film she could 'rewatch and find new messages'. Others (such as respondents 207 and 578) praised the quality of the story or performances.

It would be too simple, however, to conclude that boomers were responsible for a contraction in the range of film production. Production trends continued to be dictated by the theatrical market, and within that arena, boomers were a force for diversity. Despite Tartikoff's concerns about video, the problem for majors was less to do with getting boomers to the cinema (they were attending far more than any over-twenty-five group since the end of the Second World War), and more to do with getting them to turn out en masse for the same films with sufficient regularity to justify the incredible expense of the studios' new spending model. Among the independent distributors, firms such as New Line and Miramax who specialized in finding the gaps in the majors' theatrical output survived and sometimes thrived.

[28]Marc Berman, 'Studios Miss Boat on Vid Demographics', *Variety*, 14 September 1992, 3.
[29]Wasser, *Veni, Vidi, Video*, 183.

More than any other section of the industry, distributors operating at the 'speciality' end of the market were dependent upon the continuing theatrical attendance of the baby boomers. Miramax in particular learnt how to exploit a certain kind of upscale cinema: films that combined prestige and envelope-pushing content with popular genre and narrative. As Harvey Weinstein reportedly responded when asked how he would sell early acquisition *Erendira* (1983), 'You got a Nobel Prize winner and you got sex. You work both ends.'[30] Tellingly, the company's breakthrough success *sex, lies and videotape* was acquired without home distribution rights, which its makers had pre-sold to finance the production. Although the film contains no nudity, Miramax sold the sex angle hard, to the extent that its young writer-director Steven Soderbergh (b.1963) worried the company 'was promising way more than the movie delivered'.[31] Also flaunting the film's Palme D'Or win at Cannes, the company selected an August release date as counterprogramming against the summer blockbusters and spent $2.5 million on prints and advertising. The result was a domestic gross of $24.7 million, the forty-sixth highest return for 1989.

sex, lies and videotape is often seen as a watershed moment in independent film, an important demonstration that a small movie could compete in conglomerate Hollywood. Miramax's innovation – dating back to their experience with Cineplex Odeon and *The Secret Policeman's Other Ball* – was to aggressively expand promising films from the art house or speciality circuit into mainstream theatres. Such a strategy still relied on a positive initial reaction from art-film lovers and the art houses had remained the preserve of the baby boom. In 1991, panellists discussing the state of speciality film at a NATO/ShoWest seminar concluded that 'the challenge for the specialty film industry in the 1990s will be cultivating and re-educating college students, an audience that was once its mainstay'. Steven Rothenberg, vice president of theatrical distribution at the Samuel Goldwyn Company, told attendees, 'We're finding that young people are not as interested in specialty films, particularly foreign-language ones, as their counterparts in the 1960s and 1970s.'[32] By the end of the decade there was little evidence that the challenge had been met. A *Variety* report into the ongoing popularity of speciality cinema chains found that '[t]hough the speciality audience has remained stable over the years, it primarily comprises the baby boom generation'. Cary Jones, vice president of marketing for the Landmark chain of theatres, admitted, 'Our audience is maturing, and it's not being replaced by a younger generation.'[33]

[30]Peter Biskind, *Down and Dirty Pictures: Miramax, Sundance and the Rise of Independent Film* (New York: Simon and Schuster, 2004), 47.
[31]Biskind, *Down and Dirty Pictures*, 80.
[32]Greg Ptacek, 'Give It College Try, Exhibs Urged', *Hollywood Reporter*, 8 February 1991, 3.
[33]Richard Natale, 'Finding New Speciality Fans', *Variety*, 19 October 1999, B6.

Even within the theatrical mainstream, the early 1990s continued to hear
a number of voices expressing doubt about the wisdom of relying on the
young. In February 1992, William F. Kartozian, president of NATO, 'called
for an emphasis on movies geared for older audiences', again supported
by statistics from Jack Valenti showing that admissions of those over forty
(now bolstered by the first five years of the boom) had shot up by over
100 million tickets in a single year.[34] A June 1993 feature by David J. Fox
in the *Los Angeles Times* reported 'real anxiety' within the industry about
the state of the 13 to 25-year-old audience, relating to both the group's
declining demographic size and their interest in film. On demographics, Fox
quoted MCA chairman Tom Pollock who predicted movies 'will not be a
growth industry for the next two or three years. And absent a few variations
depending on films, the business will erode and then get better as the 13-to-
25 age group is expected to grow larger'. For Fox chairman Joe Roth habits
were more important. In his view the young had become a group 'that you
can only count on as part of the overall audience for big hits. The really dire
way of looking at it is that this is the first generation that seems to have lost
the tribal rites of going to the movies every weekend'.[35]

Certainly, what hits there were in 1991 were largely geared towards the
baby boom, a pattern that continued in 1992, 1993 and 1994. Between
1991 and 1993, major adult-oriented hits included *The Silence of the
Lambs* (fourth for 1991), *City Slickers* (fifth for 1991), *Sleeping with the
Enemy* (eighth for 1991), *Father of the Bride* (ninth for 1991), *A Few Good
Men* (fifth for 1992), *The Bodyguard* (seventh for 1992), *Basic Instinct*
(ninth for 1992), *A League of the Own* (tenth for 1992), *The Fugitive* (third
for 1993), *The Firm* (fourth for 1993), *Sleepless in Seattle* (fifth for 1993),
Indecent Proposal (sixth for 1993), *In the Line of Fire* (seventh for 1993),
The Pelican Brief (eighth for 1993) and *Schindler's List* (ninth for 1993).
Similarly successful films aimed at families with young children included
Beauty and the Beast (third for 1991), *Hook* (sixth for 1991), *Aladdin* (first
for 1992) and *Home Alone 2: Lost in New York* (second for 1992).

Even in the small number of hit action-adventure films there was a
repeated use of narratives emphasizing family life, a marked contrast from
similar projects in the 1970s and early 1980s (Spielberg's films excepted). In
Terminator 2: Judgement Day (the top hit of 1991), the first film's protagonist,
Sarah Connor, is now a mother struggling to relate to her teenage son. In
Jurassic Park (the top hit of 1993), Alan Grant, played by Sam Neill becomes
a father figure to two children as he guides them through the park. *Jurassic
Park* was an expensive commitment for Universal, prompting the studio's

---

[34]Claudia Eller and John Evan Frook, "91 BO Down, Spirits Up at Confab', *Variety*, 24
February 1992, 5.
[35]David J. Fox, 'Honey, They Shrunk the Movie Audience', *Los Angeles Times*, 8 June 1993, F1.

chairman, Tom Pollock, to comment, 'With *Jurassic Park*, we're trying for a broad audience ... I wouldn't spend that kind of money on a movie if we were only going to get a teen audience or adult audience.'[36]

Boomer attitudes and boomer films

In their efforts to prioritize family as audience and subject, these films fed into wider debates about the current state of the American family as the boomers joined Spielberg in entering their forties en masse. The late 1980s and early 1990s have often been portrayed as a period of political and social polarization in America, with the country split between conservative and liberal voting blocs closely aligned with the Republican and Democratic political parties. This picture was most vividly painted by James Davison Hunter in his 1991 book *Culture Wars: The Struggle to Define America*. Hunter saw the media, including movies, as an important 'field of conflict' in a larger war. Though he cited studies finding 'a fairly strong and consistent bias toward a liberal and progressivist point of view' among media elites, the only example he discussed is the reaction to Scorsese's *The Last Temptation of Christ*, a film hardly representative of the industry's output in the late 1980s.[37] Other studies from the same period focused on Hollywood in more detail, arguing that America was becoming increasingly divided between conservatives and liberals. Interestingly, the movies were attacked as an agent of both conservative and liberal ideology. In *Hollywood vs. America* (first published in 1992), Michael Medved accused industry leaders of an 'assault on traditional values' by producing films that 'celebrate vulgar behavior, contempt for all authority, and obscene language'.[38] In *Backlash* (1991), Susan Faludi included Hollywood in a pervasive cultural turn against feminism and gender equality that started 'among the evangelical right'.[39]

In the years since, however, there has built a substantial and convincing body of work challenging the extent of division, at least within the general population. Such work draws clear distinctions between the opinions of political leaders and activists on the one hand (which have undoubtedly polarized), and those of the vast majority of Americans on the other. For instance, studying the period from 1974 and 1994, Paul DiMaggio, John Evan and Bethany Bryson found convergence to be the dominant trend in public opinion across a range of social issues with abortion being the

---

[36]Fox, 'Honey, They Shrunk the Movie Audience', F1.
[37]James Davison Hunter, *Culture Wars: The Struggle to Define America* (New York: Basic, 1992), 225–49.
[38]Michael Medved, *Hollywood vs. America* (New York: HarperPerrenial, 1993), 10.
[39]Susan Faludi, *Backlash: The Undeclared War against Women* (New York: Vintage, 1993), xix.

sole exception.[40] This is not to say that opinion converged in one direction; trends were (and remain) complex and sometimes contradictory, and this is reflected in the films of boomer filmmakers. In the hit films we have identified already in this chapter and those slightly further down the annual charts, it is possible to identify two seemingly disparate trends associated with boomer filmmakers beginning in the late 1980s: explorations of contemporary adult life and epic historical dramas. Though vastly different in terms of tone, setting and scale, there is considerable overlap in the themes of these films. In their own ways, both are fixated on the boomers' relationship to their upbringing. Whether considering how to live in the present, or how to represent the past, boomer filmmakers begin with their own formative experiences, and struggle to reconcile the opposing messages of their 1950s childhood and 1970s youth.

In a 2001 analysis of survey results on American attitudes to family, Arland Thornton and Linda Young-DeMarco find 'very little evidence that the commitment of Americans to children, marriage, and family life has eroded substantially in the past two decades'.[41] What has 'changed dramatically' is the meaning of marriage and children, with – again – tolerance and equality being the principal themes. By the mid-1980s, 'a significant majority of Americans had egalitarian attitudes on most dimensions of sex roles' within marriage, and across all consulted surveys 'there was more expression of egalitarian attitudes and beliefs in the mid-1990s than in the mid-1980s'.[42] Over the same period, marriage and having children came to be seen as more of an option than a responsibility. Yet it is important not to confuse general principles with personal preference. Though marriage was increasingly seen as a choice, it remained the preferred choice for most Americans.[43] While a majority were in favour of equality, Thornton and Young-DeMarco also found 'a strong current of continued support of a gendered division of labour. A substantial number of Americans – more men than women – continue to believe in men having primary responsibility outside the home, with women being in charge of the home'.[44] In the late 1980s and early 1990s, this was certainly still true of the baby boom.[45]

---

[40]Paul DiMaggio, John Evan and Bethany Bryson, 'Have Americans' Social Attitudes Become More Polarized?', *American Journal of Sociology* 102, No. 3 (November 1996), 690–755.

[41]Arland Thornton and Linda Young-DeMarco, 'Four Decades of Trends in Attitudes toward Family Issues in the United States: The 1960s through the 1990s', *Journal of Marriage and Family* 63, No. 4 (2001), 1030.

[42]Thornton and Young-DeMarco, 'Four Decades', 1014.

[43]Ibid., 1017.

[44]Ibid., 1032.

[45]In 1988 and 1994, the National Survey of Families and Households asked respondents to rate a range of statements on a scale from 'Strongly Agree' to 'Strongly Disagree' and two specifically related to domestic gender roles. For the statement 'It is much better for everyone if the man earns the main living and the woman takes care of the home and family', in 1988

In the context of such tensions what is most notable about the contemporary adult boomer films of the late 1980s and early 1990s is their attempts to sincerely engage with social issues within the framework of popular genres. Crucially, ideological struggles are primarily located within families (and often within individuals) rather than between social groups. This is not to say every perspective is represented equally; reflecting extreme biases in Hollywood's workforce, the films repeatedly favour a white, male, upper-middle-class point of view. Yet to varying degrees alternative voices are heard as anxieties and doubts are aired and worked through. Between 1989 and 1993, top thirty hits to explicitly dwell on the priorities and values of contemporary American adult life included *Look Who's Talking*, *Parenthood*, *War of the Roses*, *When Harry Met Sally* and *Field of Dreams* in 1989; *Pretty Woman* and *Kindergarten Cop* in 1990; *City Slickers*, *Father of the Bride*, *Hook* and *Thelma and Louise* in 1991; and *Mrs Doubtfire*, *Sleepless in Seattle*, *Philadelphia* and *Dave* in 1993. All had boomer writers and all except *Steel Magnolias* (Herbert Ross (b.1927)), *Pretty Woman* (Garry Marshall (b.1934)), *Thelma and Louise* (Ridley Scott (b.1937, UK)) and *Sleepless in Seattle* (Nora Ephron (b.1941)) had boomer directors.

Taken as a group, perhaps the most pervasive theme is one of compromise and expectations reduced. All feature protagonists questioning their values and the directions their lives have taken, though the scale of their concerns varies considerably. In *Father of the Bride*, a remake of the 1950 Spencer Tracy vehicle, the crisis of the lead character, played by Steve Martin, is explicitly presented as irrational: the film opens with Martin directly addressing the camera to explain his behaviour in the narrative that follows as the typical overreactions of a loving father. The stakes in the film are remarkably low; Martin and his wife, played by Diane Keaton, have made a success of their lives. Both have careers they appear to enjoy and live in a large detached house in a pleasant leafy suburb. Their two children, a son in his early teens and a daughter in her early twenties, are presented as happy, sensible and close to their parents. What little narrative tension there is, is generated by Martin's concerns about the suitability of the man his daughter

---

among baby boomers 35.6 per cent either agreed or strongly agreed, 30 per cent neither agreed or disagreed and 29.5 per cent either disagreed or strongly disagreed. By 1994 those figures were 31.5 per cent, 28 per cent and 38.5 per cent. In both years, women were more likely to disagree than men, totalling 62.9 per cent of those in disagreement in 1988 and 63.6 per cent in 1994. For the statement 'Preschool children are likely to suffer if their mother is employed', in 1988 among baby boomers 37.2 per cent either agreed or strongly agreed, 25 per cent neither agreed or disagreed and 33 per cent either disagreed or strongly disagreed. By 1994, those figures were 39 per cent, 26.7 per cent and 32.2 per cent. For this question the gender splits were greater, with women accounting for 66.9 per cent of disagreeing responses in 1988 and 70.3 per cent in 1994. See James A. Sweet and Larry L. Bumpass, *The National Survey of Families and Households – Waves 1 and 2: Data Description and Documentation* (Wisconsin: University of Wisconsin-Madison, 1996).

is going to marry and the spiralling cost and scale of the wedding. Yet the film quickly makes it clear that the prospective husband is a perfect match, and while the wedding does become expensive there is never any suggestion that the family risk any degree of financial hardship. Moreover, by remaking a 1950s suburban comedy, director Charles Shyer and writer Nancy Meyers pay covert homage to the movie culture of the boomer's earliest years, and the focus on a suburban family experience bears some correlation to Meyers own family upbringing. Indeed, Meyers and Shyer – and from 2000s *What Women Want*, Meyers alone as a writer-director – would return repeatedly to 1950s movie culture, and a wealthy suburban milieu, as a touchstone in many of their future films – thereby reflecting both the youthful memories and current experiences of a boomer audience.

By contrast, Danny DeVito's *War of the Roses* presents a similar set of circumstances as the catalyst for a deadly battle of wills. Michael Douglas and Kathleen Turner play Oliver and Barbara Rose, a couple who meet and marry fresh out of college. Over years, Oliver pursues his career as a lawyer, while Barbara raises their children and restores their lavish home. Slowly, Barbara also begins to feel frustration at her homemaker role and contempt at her husband's growing arrogance and falsity. When Oliver has a health scare, Barbara realizes she needs to escape, but plans for divorce founder on who should retain the house. Neither party is prepared to budge or even temporarily move out, provoking an escalating conflict as they compete to land psychological and finally physical blows to gain the upper hand. In a climactic sequence of mutual destruction, the Roses find themselves clinging to the ornate chandelier in the ruins of their once elegant foyer and plunge to their death.

What these films – and others that fit between their respective extremes – share is a continuing engagement with debates surrounding personal social values begun in earnest during the 1960s. In *Father of the Bride*, the greatest moment of drama comes late in the film when Martin's daughter announces that the wedding is off after her fiancé gives her a gift of a blender. She explains that her reaction was based on an implicit expectation of gender roles: 'What is this, 1958? "Give the little wife a blender"?' It is left to Martin to straighten matters out with his prospective son-in-law, who concedes, 'I guess I can see her point. I mean a blender does suggest a certain 1950s reference to sexual politics but I swear it never entered my conscience at the time.' The suggestion that the sexual politics of the 1950s have been left far behind sits somewhat awkwardly in a film that in other respects serves to reinforce gender stereotypes that occasionally are untouched from the 1950 version of the story directed by Vincente Minnelli.

Weddings are presented as sources of unending excitement and fascination for the female characters and of mystery and fear for the men. Considering the extent of her star power, Diane Keaton has a thankless role in the film, either supporting the daughter or reacting in exasperation to Martin's irrationalities. Whereas Martin is repeatedly seen at work and we are shown how his ownership of a company has enabled him to fit his profession around his family life, Keaton's work is a mystery. That she works at all is only indicated by a single remark early in the film. Co-writer and co-producer Nancy Meyers explains the decision in relation to having children herself:

> I wanted to set an example to them, with the type of people who populated my movies, particularly the women. It would be hard for you to take any female character in one of my films that didn't have a job, even in *Father of the Bride*, where her work didn't have anything to do with the movie, and her character doesn't drive the movie in any way. I think in any other filmmakers' hands, she would have been a homemaker and not had a job, but I remember it just being important to mention, 'Oh, I can't go that day, I have to do inventory at the store', just a slight mention that the woman worked. So for the kids, having two daughters, always the women in my movies were purposeful women with goals.

Meyers is correct that women as homemakers were still a staple of mainstream Hollywood production. *Parenthood, Field of Dreams, Hook* and *City Slickers* all centre on married male protagonists whose wives are only seen in domestic situations. However, as the case of *War of the Roses* indicates, such representations did not go entirely unchallenged. In *Parenthood*, the central character's wife (played by Mary Steenburgen) has a lengthy speech justifying her desire to remain a stay-at-home mother (and have a fourth child), as if this was now socially frowned upon. Elsewhere in the film, Steenburgen's two sisters-in-law are both working mothers – as a teacher and bank manager – although both are pregnant by the conclusion.

Look Who's Talking more directly addresses contemporary anxieties about family and gender roles. Kirstie Alley plays a New York accountant involved in an affair with a wealthy married man. When she discovers she is pregnant, the father (played by George Segal) persuades her to keep the baby, but leaves her to pursue another affair shortly before the birth. Suddenly single, Alley must consider her priorities in light of her newborn son. Initially pushed to date fellow accountants by her parents, her options are complicated by the increasing presence of a cab driver, played by John Travolta, who becomes her babysitter and friend. It is soon apparent the pair have a romantic connection, strengthened by Travolta's affection for the child. However, between his cab and a failing ambition to be a flight instructor, Travolta has limited prospects. In one of the film's numerous idiosyncratic moments, Alley's fears are visualized in a *Honeymooners*-style fantasy sequence where she and Travolta have a large family in a filthy apartment, happy but reduced to foraging in bins for food. The film ends with Alley dismissing such concerns and having a second child, this time with Travolta as the father and, it must be assumed, with Alley as the family's primary earner.

At the same time, several of the most successful films present their male characters questioning their own priorities, specifically relating to family and career. In *City Slickers*, Billy Crystal plays Mitch, a radio advertising sales executive depressed by what he sees as a lack of purpose in his life. Addressing his son's class at a school careers presentation, Mitch has a public near-breakdown, lecturing nine-year-olds on the futility of existence. Concerned about his well-being, his wife sends him with two similarly minded friends on a cowboy experience holiday. While there, a series of adventures and conversations conclude with Mitch realizing that his life is given definition by his family and he returns home with a new sense of purpose. *Parenthood*, which shares the writing team of Lowell and Mandel with *City Slickers*, opens with the central character Gil explicitly presenting his approach to parenting as a reaction against his own childhood. Where his father considered child rearing to be 'a job, a burden, a prison rather than a playground', Gil's dream is to raise 'strong, happy, confident kids' and structures his life to achieve that goal. Yet as the narrative progresses, Gil experiences work and family crises that cause him to doubt his own abilities and to look on his father's efforts more kindly.

A shared element in *Parenthood, Father of the Bride, Look Who's Talking* and Spielberg's *Peter Pan* sequel *Hook* is playing as an ideal paternal activity. The four films feature extended sequences of fathers – or a prospective father in the case of *Look Who's Talking* – engaging in play with their young children. Playing with children is presented as more important than providing for them. *Hook* takes this concept to considerable lengths. For the last decade, Spielberg had been connected with attempts to make a live-action *Peter Pan*. As the story of a boy who never grew up, the J. M. Barrie novel had obvious resonance with Spielberg's persona, and Disney's 1953 film was clearly a boomer touchstone. Yet the version Spielberg finally made took a different approach. *Hook* begins with the premise that Pan did finally leave Neverland and become an adult. The adult Pan (named Peter Banning and played by Robin Williams) is now in mergers and acquisitions and pursuing a $6 billion land development deal to the extent of alienating his family. Early in the film, Peter's disappointed wife spells out his failings: 'Your children love you. They want to play with you. How long do you think that lasts? ... A few years, and then it's over. You are not being careful and you are missing it.' Peter is presented with a chance for redemption when his old adversary Captain Hook steals his children as an act of revenge. To win them back, Peter returns to Neverland and discovers he must reconnect with his childhood sense of wonder in order to defeat Hook.

Though *Hook* was not the outright smash its pedigree suggested (it still made $119 million, sixth for 1991), family audiences drove other films to record-breaking heights. In 1992, the top two films were Disney's animated

Aladdin and Fox's *Home Alone 2: Lost in New York*. Universal's executive vice president of marketing Perry Katz confirmed the studios' thinking: 'The one thing you don't want to have happen is to create the image that this is a film that parents just drop their kids off at as a babysitter. You want to create a campaign that is appealing to parents as well as children so they will attend as a family unit.'[46]

Outside of gender and family dynamics, the films of this period also present a largely consistent vision of American society. Overwhelmingly, the focus is on the white, upper-middle classes. Where money troubles do exist – as in *Field of Dreams, Parenthood, Look Who's Talking* and even *Pretty Woman* – they are ascribed to the personal choices of individuals rather than any underlying problem with society. Where other ethnicities and classes do appear, the dominant impression is of successful integration and harmony. In *Father of the Bride*, for example, Martin is shown to be on friendly, first-name terms with his workforce on the factory floor, several of whom are black or Hispanic.

It was possible to seriously address social inequality in studio films during the late 1980s and early 1990s, but these films generally found smaller audiences. Interestingly, the most successful film to address discrimination in contemporary America was one addressing an issue with limited public support. *Philadelphia*, directed by Jonathan Demme (b.1944), told the story of a gay lawyer named Andrew Beckett (played by Tom Hanks), who is fired when his firm learns he has contracted AIDS. As his health deteriorates, Beckett must confront homophobia in the legal profession (including from his own lawyer) to win compensation. The hostility Beckett experiences reflected wider views in American society at the time of the film's release in December 1993; Jeni Loftus reports that the early 1990s was a time of liberalization in attitudes to gays and lesbians, but the American public was still 'overwhelmingly' of the view that homosexuality was morally wrong.[47] Yet *Philadelphia*'s sympathetic portrayal of a gay man's plight was a box office hit, taking $77.4 million domestically, 1993's twelfth biggest hit.

Where films sought to expose continuing prejudices involving social groups whose campaigns for equality were supposedly more advanced, box office takings were more limited. *Thelma and Louise*, written by Callie Khouri (b.1958), just made it into the top thirty of 1991 (it was twenty-eighth, taking $45 million), and featured two female working or lower-middle-class protagonists. The film was also unusual in emphasizing (and not attempting to 'solve') the social inequalities still faced by women. *Do*

[46]Perry Katz, quoted in Martin A. Grove, 'Hollywood Report', *Hollywood Reporter*, 17 August 1994, 10.
[47]Jeni Loftus, 'America's Liberalization in Attitudes toward Homosexuality, 1973 to 1998', *American Sociological Review* 66, No. 5 (October 2001), 762–82.

the Right Thing (1989) released by Universal, *Grand Canyon* (1991) from Fox and *Falling Down* (1993) from Warner Brothers each attempted holistic portrayals of America at a particular time and place, although all three privileged male points of view.

After his breakthrough independent success with *She's Gotta Have It*, Spike Lee was courted by the major studios, first making a college-set musical *School Daze* (1988) at Columbia and then *Do the Right Thing* at Universal. For his third feature, Lee focused on exploring racial and economic tensions on a block in Brooklyn over a twenty-four-hour period. As residents try to stay cool during a summer heatwave, tempers fray and resentments come to the surface, culminating in a night of violence. Like *She's Gotta Have It*, *Do the Right Thing* began it promotion at Cannes, where it competed for the Palme D'Or but lost to *sex, lies and videotape*. From its first festival screening, the film provoked controversy, with some accusing Lee of attempting to incite riots. The director – with good reason – argued he was doing nothing of the sort and trouble did not materialize. *Do the Right Thing* made $27.5 million (forty-third for 1989), a good return on its $6.5 million budget, though perhaps disappointing given its media prominence. Lee certainly thought so, later reflecting, 'The box office was damaged by all the negative publicity. It scared white audiences away from the film.'[48]

Two years later, Lawrence Kasdan released *Grand Canyon*, which used a chance meeting and tentative friendship between a black mechanic (played by Danny Glover) and a white lawyer (played by Kevin Kline) to address divisions of race and class in Los Angeles. In publicizing the film, Kasdan said he had been moved to write the script (with his wife, Meg Kasdan) because of a 'sense of things going to hell, and not much being done about it ... One thing about LA that's more pronounced than in eastern cities is that enormous despair exists just within a few miles of enormous prosperity and hope'. He also welcomed comparison with his earlier hit, *The Big Chill*, noting that film 'expresses how I felt when I was 32 years old, and it's a lighter movie. But it's struggling with the same central issue, which is: What's the right way to be?'[49] *Grand Canyon*'s more sombre tone did not resonate with audiences to the same degree as its predecessor, talking $33 million, forty-third on 1991's domestic chart.

Also concerned with Los Angeles, 1993's *Falling Down* was a film that, according to producer Tim Harris, 'the studio did not want to make', even after the enthusiasm of star Michael Douglas pushed it into production.

---

[48]Spike Lee and Kaleem Aftab, *Spike Lee: That's My Story and I'm Sticking to It* (New York: WW Norton, 2005), 99.
[49]Lawrence Kasdan, quoted in Jeff Schwager, 'Canyon Country', *Boxoffice*, December 1991, 14.

Douglas plays a recently divorced and laid-off defence worker who reaches emotional breaking point in an LA traffic jam and sets off on foot across the city to visit his ex-wife and daughter, despite their restraining order against him. On route, he becomes embroiled in a series of increasingly violent confrontations as he rails against the unfairnesses he perceives in LA society. Like *Do the Right Thing*, ambiguities in the film's narrative provoked extensive media coverage that did not translate into ticket sales. Its gross of $40.9 million was only the thirty-seventh best total for its year

Yet for all the trouble filmmakers faced in directly confronting contemporary social issues, there was more encouragement – from studios and audiences – to explore similar themes in a historical setting. As we have described elsewhere, boomer filmmakers were the driving force behind a resurgence in Hollywood's production of dramas depicting significant events in American history. The 1980s had begun with a spate of high-profile, extremely costly historical productions (including *Heaven's Gate* (1980), *Reds* (1981) and Spielberg's *1941*) where box office returns ranged from disappointing to disastrous. For the rest of the decade studios funded only occasional forays into the past, usually at the behest of powerful creative figures. From *Out of Africa* and *Amadeus* to *The Last Emperor* and *Full Metal Jacket*, these films' varied temporal and national settings did not coalesce into a production trend. Spielberg's *The Color Purple* and *Empire of the Sun* were arguably part of this impulse, yet together with Stone's *Platoon*, *The Color Purple* was also the start of a more coherent group of features that attempted to understand history in terms of social equality and self-fulfilment popularized in the late 1960s. Not all of these films were successful, but enough were to maintain a steady stream of production well into the 1990s.

Among the productions closely associated with boomers were *Glory* and *Born on the Fourth of July* in 1989, *Dances with Wolves* in 1990, *JFK* and *The Doors* in 1991, *A League of their Own*, *Last of the Mohicans*, *Far and Away* and *Malcolm X* in 1992 and *Schindler's List*, *Tombstone* and *Heaven and Earth* in 1993. Clearly, in several respects, this is a disparate group of releases both in tone and their fidelity to the historical record. Yet the majority also share similar concerns, principally a focus on people from social groups marginalized by society. In a number of cases, the protagonists' actions do not fit within the widely accepted historical narrative; though their ultimate ambitions remain unfulfilled, the cumulative impact is to portray history as the product of choices rather than the inevitable outcome of events.[50] At the same time as these films complicate history, however, they acknowledge its allure. All go to considerable expense to recreate the

---

[50]This point is developed and discussed in more detail in William J. Palmer, *The Films of the Nineties: The Decade of Spin* (New York: Palgrave, 2009), 19–37.

environment and culture of their times, offering excitement and spectacle alongside social criticism.

All of these traits are evident in the first of these releases, *Glory*, although it was not a box office success. Its director, Edward Zwick, was born in 1952 and had started his career in contemporary drama, directing the feature *About Last Night ...* (1986), and co-producing *thirtysomething* (ABC, 1987–91) for television. With *Glory*, he turned to the civil war, filming Kevin Jarre's (b.1954) script about the fifty-fourth Massachusetts Volunteer Infantry, the first unit of the US Army to be wholly composed of African American soldiers. Based on the diaries of the unit's white commanding officer, Robert Gould Shaw, the film received some criticism for using Shaw (played by Matthew Broderick) as its protagonist, rather than a black volunteer. Jarre's script did, however, extend well beyond what was available in the historical record to create a core group of black soldiers with varied backgrounds and motives for enlisting. Building to an ill-fated assault on a Confederate fort during which all the principal characters are killed, the film serves as a powerful reminder that the civil war was not only fought for African Americans but by them. For his portrayal of an escaped slave – an invented character named Silas Trip – Denzel Washington won the Oscar for Best Supporting Actor. *Glory* also received Oscars for its cinematography and sound, but awards and largely positive reviews were not enough to secure a large audience; domestic ticket sales were $26.8 million against an $18 million budget.

The cycle of historical productions was instead inspired by the successes of Oliver Stone and Kevin Costner. As noted above, Stone's *Born on the Fourth of July* was the seventeenth biggest hit of 1989, while Costner's *Dances with Wolves* was 1990's third most successful film. It was also by some distance the most popular historical film in at least a decade.[51] Like *Glory*, Stone's and Costner's films question assumptions and blur boundaries. *Born on the Fourth of July* depicts the fraught relationship between disabled Vietnam veterans, their war and their country as they confront neglect and hostility upon their return home. *Dances with Wolves* presents a white civil war soldier (Costner) who sides with the Sioux in their fight against displacement. In each case members of the white, male establishment are shown joining with a marginalized group and attempting to give them a greater voice and presence in American society. In 1991, Costner teamed with Stone to make *JFK*, an unconventionally structured drama depicting Jim Garrison's investigation into the assassination of John F. Kennedy. In the way it introduces and explains Kennedy's importance, it also thematically fits with Stone's and Costner's earlier work. Over archival

---

[51]The last film with a period setting to enjoy comparable success was *Grease* in 1978, although as a production it was hardly similar.

footage, *JFK* begins with an authoritatively toned voiceover telling us that following his close 1960 election victory, Kennedy was 'the symbol of the new freedom of the 1960s, signifying change and upheaval for the American public'. As these words are said, the accompanying images are of civil rights demonstrations. Immediately after, Martin Luther King stating 'All men are created equal' is juxtaposed with an edited extract from Kennedy's election victory speech where he says, 'I can assure you that every degree of mind and spirit that I possess will be devoted to the cause of freedom around the world.' In this way the filmmakers recast Kennedy's presidency as primarily involved with civil rights, a heavily disputed proposition that is allowed to stand as fact and frames the many claims and counterclaims that form the subsequent narrative.

Though highly controversial for its willingness to blend fact, conjecture and outright fiction, *JFK*'s understanding of history in terms of the ebb and flow of civil rights and equality was typical of films of the period, even when such considerations were not previously seen as central to the events being retold. When Costner played Robin Hood in 1991's *Robin Hood: Prince of Thieves*, the character acquired a new consciousness of race and gender relations, causing Vincent Canby in the *New York Times* to complain that 'in Sherwood Forest, they look as anachronistic as Coke cans'.[52] Similarly, in the same newspaper, Stephen Holden took issue with the 'sociological and psychological baggage' applied to the legend of Wyatt Earp in the Kevin Jarre–scripted *Tombstone*. In particular, Holden noted the film's 'liberated' heroine and the highlighting of discrimination against Chinese workers.

In 1992, leading boomer directors were behind the release of four expensive historical productions, all dealing with inequalities in America's history. Penny Marshall's *A League of Their Own* gave a fictionalized account of the establishment of the All-American Girls Professional Baseball League, which had existed between 1943 and 1954 and was formed in response to male players joining the armed forces. Michael Mann's *The Last of the Mohicans* adapted James Fenimore Cooper's novel to emphasize the negative impact of Europeans on Native Americans' ways of life. Ron Howard's *Far and Away* detailed the class and racial discrimination that characterized many Irish people's experience of emigrating to America. Spike Lee's *Malcolm X* dramatized the life and assassination of the civil rights leader, in the process raising questions about the extent of a conspiracy in his death.

Dances with Wolves was also significant for its self-consciously epic scale, both in its extended running time and emphasis on the American landscape. Costner framed his ambitions for the film in terms of the

---

[52]Vincent Canby, 'A Polite Robin Hood in a Legend Recast', *New York Times*, 14 June 1991, http://www.nytimes.com/movie/review?res=9D0CE1DF113CF937A25755C0A967958260.

roadshow epics he remembered from his youth, citing *How the West Was Won* as a particular influence.[53] After *Dances with Wolves*, studios were more willing to entertain projects with similarly epic proportions, including Spielberg's *Schindler's List* (1993) and *Saving Private Ryan* (1998), both simultaneously personal films and grand epics seeking to encapsulate the defining events of the Second World War, which represented the clearest signs of Spielberg's much vaunted maturation. Other historical epics, such as Mel Gibson's *Braveheart* (1994) and James Cameron's *Titanic* (1997), followed suit. In every case, these movies were substantial commercial hits and critical successes which garnered Academy Awards alongside good reviews. Furthermore, each was partly inspired by memories of the epic movies that had proliferated in Hollywood when the filmmakers in question were young. Mel Gibson claimed that his Scottish medieval epic *Braveheart* was inspired by 'all the *Ben-Hurs* and all the *Spartaci* I saw as a kid'.[54] James Cameron told *American Cinematographer* that, with *Titanic*, 'I wanted to make an epic in the sense of *Doctor Zhivago*'.[55] These filmmakers were not simply revisiting the distant past, they were doing so through the prism of their own youth, crafting a vision of world history grounded in the shared cultural and political experiences of baby boomers.

Conclusion: Gump happens

In 1994, generational concerns and boomer tastes remained central to the year's key hits. That year for the first time, MPAA figures show that more tickets were bought at the domestic box office by people aged forty and over (36 per cent) than by people aged between twelve and twenty-four (35 per cent). All of the top five highest grossing releases privileged parent-child relationships and growing into maturity as key themes, often focusing on the middle-aged father as the dominant protagonist. Three – *The Lion King* and *The Santa Clause* from Disney and *The Flintstones*, produced by Steven Spielberg – were aimed at family audiences and carried a U or PG rating. James Cameron's R-rated *True Lies* mixed action with domestic comedy. The highest grossing release of the year, however, was *Forrest Gump*, essentially a picaresque epic of the baby boom experience, which grossed $329 million, more than double the takings of any other film that year except *The Lion King*.

---

[53]Kevin Costner, quoted in James Russell, *The Historical Epic and Contemporary Hollywood* (New York: Continuum, 2007), 22.
[54]Mel Gibson, quoted in Russell, *The Historical Epic and Contemporary Hollywood*, 22.
[55]James Cameron, quoted in David E. Williams, 'Captain of His Ship', *American Cinematographer*, December 1997, 52.

In several respects, *Gump* is a fitting film to mark the final year in which boomer concerns and boomer audiences truly dictated industry trends. An adaptation of Winston Groom's 1986 novel, *Gump* combined many of the features that had defined boomer filmmaking since the mid-1980s – it depicted family life, from youth to parenthood; it focused on recent history; it was infused with, and built upon, nostalgia for the formative cultural, social and political experiences of the baby boomers; and it was made by one of the leading boomer filmmakers, Robert Zemeckis. In it, Forrest Gump, a childlike idiot-savant, experiences almost all of the formative headline events of the baby boomers, from Elvis Presley's first performance and Gump's troubled upbringing in the Deep South, the film takes viewers through the civil rights movement, the counterculture, Vietnam, political radicalism and upheaval, to Reaganite consumerism. Although its vision is expressed through Gump, we are introduced to a series of boomers whose lives are transformed for good or ill over the post-war period. These include Gump's first love Jenny (played by Robin Wright), who experiences the highs and lows of the counterculture, and Lieutenant Dan (played by Gary Sinise) who loses his legs in Vietnam, but eventually finds God on the Louisiana bayou. Reviews were generally positive, and noted the film's appeal to boomers over other groups. According to Todd McCarthy in *Variety*, it offered up 'a non-stop barrage of emotional and iconographic identification points that will make the post-war generation feel they're seeing their lives passing by on-screen. Paramount's target audience is obvious, and boffo B.O. should ensue'.[56]

As Oliver Gruner has shown, at the time of its theatrical release *Forrest Gump* neatly encapsulated wider political debates about the value and meaning of the 1960s, and the counterculture, speaking to modern Americans who had only recently been asked to choose between older Republican George Bush and the first boomer president, Bill Clinton.[57] The movie expressed the same concern with parental responsibility and American history that defined many adult-oriented hits of the period, but it also carefully avoided overt endorsement of any clearly political perspective on some of the most divisive events of the boomers' formative years. As a result, critical responses to the film were mixed. For some, the movie stepped beyond ideology to tell a universal tale. In Todd McCarthy's words:

> In a part Dustin Hoffman might once have killed for, Hanks plays a kind of semi-imbecile whose very blankness makes him an ideal audience prism through which many of the key events of the 1950s through early

[56]Todd McCarthy, Review of *Forrest Gump*, *Variety*, 11 July 1994, http://variety.com/1994/film/reviews/forrest-gump-1200438040/.
[57]Gruner, *Screening the Sixties*, 155.

1980s can be viewed. Lacking any ideology or analytical powers, Gump is the immutable innocent moving in a state of grace through a nation in the process of losing its innocence, an Everyman who acts instinctively in an age defined by political divisiveness.[58]

For others, the movie offered a saccharine, or even conservative, world view that celebrated conformity over progressive change. *Entertainment Weekly* complained that the movie 'reduces the tumult of the last 30 years to a baby boomer version of Disney's America'.[59] In a key moment at an anti-war rally, Gump is asked to give his opinion on the Vietnam War. He approaches the stage, picks up the microphone, but his amplifier is sabotaged and the viewer never hears what Gump has to say. This moment reveals, in microcosm, the difficulties posed by addressing the boomers on the political ramifications of their lives, and the solutions invariably adopted by Hollywood movies. *Forrest Gump*'s success was dependent on boomer nostalgia, but Zemeckis clearly did not want to take sides in sometimes fraught ideological debates, instead offering viewers the opportunity to construct their own meaning out of a rare moment when the central character is silenced.[60]

However they interpreted it, boomers flocked to *Forrest Gump* and it was mentioned as a favourite four times in our survey, always by viewers born in the mid-1950s. Respondent 382 described it as 'very well written

IMAGE 10 *Forrest Gump (Tom Hanks) addresses an anti-war rally in* Forrest Gump *(1994).*

---

[58]McCarthy, Review of *Forrest Gump*, online.

[59]Mark Harris, Review of *Forrest Gump*, *Entertainment Weekly*, 15 July 1994 http://ew.com/article/1994/07/15/forrest-gump. See Gruner, *Screening the Sixties* for more on the reception of the film as a conservative text.

[60]Richard Maltby has argued that Hollywood movies are often defined by an inbuilt ambivalence around political issues. See Maltby, *Hollywood Cinema*, 268–310.

-and acted', while for respondent 143 it was an 'all-time favorite due to the historical content'. Respondent 542 noted that 'it has everything, including Tom Hanks (one of our best actors today)'. More than anything, *Gump* presented the historical experiences of the boomers as part of a grand narrative of social progress, with a clear structure and wider historical significance, inviting viewers to recognize moments from their youths, and indulge in bittersweet nostalgia. It remains the dominant onscreen depiction of the baby boomers, but it also marked the coming end of their dominance as suitable subjects for high-budget movies.

10

Families Forever

Despite its astounding and unanticipated success, *Forrest Gump* was the last time that boomer audiences could claim to be the primary focus of the Hollywood studios. From the mid-1990s Hollywood's attention shifted back to producing mass audience entertainments that found a place for the boomers while also prioritizing other, younger generations. Afterwards, the cultural and social preoccupations of the boomers would still inform much of Hollywood's output, but increasingly these concerns underpinned more broadly appealing films, targeted at an array of demographic groups but with renewed emphasis on the twelve—twenty-four 'youth' category that had once been synonymous with the baby boom generation. This increasingly sophisticated balancing of audience sectors was made possible by the innovations outlined in the previous chapters: a mature home entertainment market, a thriving independent film sector and the PG-13 rating. The end result was a gradual (and entirely understandable) decline in the commercial power of boomer audiences, as they finally relinquished their controlling hold on the industry, established in the late 1960s. Though the forty and over audience had briefly surpassed the twelve—twenty-four demographic in 1994, this proved to be an exception for the decade. In the late 1990s, 12- to 24-year-olds expanded their share of ticket sales, reaching 41 per cent of sales in 1999, compared with 29 per cent for those aged 40 and over.[1]

This chapter outlines the industry's steadily increasing focus on mass appeal, 'all-audience' movies from the mid-1990s onwards. The first section charts the rise of a subtly different kind of commercial blockbuster, starting with the release of *Jurassic Park* in 1993, and it focuses on the impact of the PG-13 rating. The second section examines the arrival of a new generation of filmmakers, mostly working in the independent sector during the 1990s, who were harbingers of generational change in the film industry. The third

---

[1]For MPAA audience share figures, see Appendix B.

section looks in detail at the activities of one key company, founded by some of the most influential boomers in the business – DreamWorks SKG – whose fortunes neatly capture the shifting filmmaking priorities of the 1990s, and the shifting status of the boomers themselves. The chapter concludes with a brief discussion of one of the period's biggest hits – James Cameron's *Titanic* (1997).

Seeking a new mass audience

The beginning of the loosening of the boomers' grip on Hollywood can (ironically) be found in the extraordinary success of Spielberg's *Jurassic Park*. This was a film that had been planned from its inception as an all-audience smash. Although its primary character arc was grounded in the concerns of boomer parents, the film's marketing centered on the spectacle of photo-realistic dinosaurs. *Jurassic Park* was a signal that the production trends which had first emerged in the early 1980s could not only still work, but could work better than ever. Though it was possible to overstate the similarities between them, *Jurassic Park* marked a new level of refinement of the approaches Spielberg and Universal had employed with *Jaws* nearly twenty years earlier. Both opened wide in summer and offered state-of-the-art scares and thrills. But whereas *Jaws* had opened in 409 theatres, *Jurassic Park* managed 2,404, many of which were multiplexes showing the film on several screens. The film set a new record for highest opening weekend, taking $47 million in three days and, even more impressively, dropped only 18 per cent in its second weekend. Eventually, its domestic total reached $357 million. Moreover, it achieved these levels with a PG-13 rating, raising questions about its suitability for families with younger children.

For a film to receive the PG-13 rating meant the MPAA's rating board had concluded it contained material that 'might not suitable' for children under thirteen. Not coincidentally, this was also the age at which the MPAA had previously reported that children began regularly attending films without their parents.[2] While aspects of the film – not least the inclusion of two pre-teen children as major characters – show *Jurassic Park* still had one (massive, scaly) foot in the family-friendly trend of the early 1990s, the makers' willingness to risk alienating parts of this audience with a PG-13 rating indicates their prioritizing of teen viewers. As previously noted, such an approach ran contrary to the prevailing wisdom within the industry at the time.

Between 1985 – the first full year of PG-13 – and 1992, the value and appropriate use of the rating was still in contention. Despite first being

---

[2]Motion Picture Association of America, 'Summary of Remarks by Jack Valenti', 4.

introduced to accommodate more 'adult' event movies such as *Gremlins*, it was initially used for that purpose fairly infrequently, at least with the intended degree of success. On average, just one film per year combined big-budget event movie status with a PG-13 rating and finished within the top ten releases.[3] During this period, PG-13 was much more likely to be associated with hit comedy, and even then, the rating was attached to fewer top ten releases overall (twenty-one films) than either PG (thirty films) or R (twenty-seven films). Prior to *Jurassic Park*, the only PG-13s to really trouble the all-time top grossing films were *Batman, Indiana Jones, Ghost, Dances with Wolves* and Costner's immediate *Wolves* follow-up *Robin Hood*. When Warner Brothers tried to build on their triumph with *Batman*, giving director Tim Burton an improved budget ($80 million) and greater creative control to make *Batman Returns*, it lacked the wide appeal of the original.[4] In the *New York Times*, for example, Janet Maslin felt it necessary to warn parents that 'a cartoonish spirit and a taste for toys do not make it a children's film'.[5] After a huge $45 million opening, the sequel lost more than 40 per cent of its audience on each of its subsequent four weekends, finishing with a domestic gross of $162.8 million. Though still the third highest total for the year, the *Wall Street Journal* reported that Warner were sufficiently 'worried about the steep falloff in box office receipts [from] the original *Batman*' to rethink the direction of the franchise.[6]

In this context, therefore, *Jurassic Park* was a compelling demonstration of the potential of PG-13 without necessarily offering a convincing argument for its widespread adoption. Among A-list directors, only Spielberg had proven himself repeatedly able to deliver unqualified blockbuster success using the rating. While *Jurassic Park* may have tempted studios to consider backing similar projects, there was still the chance that Spielberg's film was the unique product of a unique filmmaker, a worrying possibility given Spielberg's decision to take a break from filmmaking after his exertions on *Schindler's List*.[7] To support this conclusion, executives had to look no further than the film that came out the week after *Jurassic Park*, John McTiernan's *The Last Action Hero*. Columbia had sunk comparable resources into their comedy action film starring Arnold Schwarzenegger as Universal had invested in their dinosaurs, and had comparable expectations. However, the

[3]There were eight in eight years: *Cocoon* (1985), *The Golden Child* (1986), *Batman* (1989), *Indiana Jones and the Last Crusade* (1989), *Kindergarten Cop* (1990), *Robin Hood: Prince of Thieves* (1991), *The Addams Family* (1991) and *Batman Returns* (1992).
[4]Griffin and Masters, *Hit and Run*, 173.
[5]Janet Maslin, '*Batman Returns*; A Sincere Bat, a Sexy Cat and a Bad Bird', *New York Times*, 19 June 1992, http://www.nytimes.com/1992/06/19/movies/review-film-batman-returns-a-sincere-bat-a-sexy-cat-and-a-bad-bird.html?pagewanted=all&src=pm.
[6]John Lippman, 'Warner's Batman Forever Takes in Record $53.3 Million in First Three Days', *Wall Street Journal*, 19 June 1995, B1.
[7]McBride, *Steven Spielberg*, 442.

project struggled to find the correct tone and audiences were not convinced. Having cost $87 million to produce and another $30 in marketing, *Last Action Hero* managed to gross just $50 million at the domestic box office.[8]

In 1994 and 1995, two related developments would have given studio heads more confidence. The first was the sudden appearance of Jim Carrey as a box office draw. A Canadian comedian born in 1962, Carrey had been appearing in films and on television since the early 1980s. His career received a major boost when he joined the cast of the Fox Network's sketch comedy programme *In Living Color* (1990–4). Carrey created a number of characters that showcased his talent for high-energy physical and vocal contortion. Their popularity resulted in his casting in three PG-13 comedies. *Ace Ventura: Pet Detective, The Mask* and *Dumb and Dumber* were all released between March and December 1994. Each debuted as the top grossing film during its opening weekend, and each improved on the performance of the last, finishing as the sixteenth, ninth and sixth most successful films of the year. Commentators were in little doubt regarding who was responsible for Carrey's popularity. Before the release of *The Mask*, the *Hollywood Reporter* noted anticipation among teenagers was 'testing at the blockbuster level in prerelease surveys while adults barely budged the interest scale'.[9] In the *New York Times*, Bernard Weinraub considered Carrey 'a bankable star with a large audience, mostly teen-agers'.[10]

Carrey was important for his ability to reach teens, but also because three consecutive hits indicated the demographic might be regaining its reliability. The only comparable recent hit had been 1992's *Wayne's World*, and that film's star, Mike Myers, had been unable to repeat the film's success in either of his subsequent releases, *Wayne's World 2* (1993) and *So I Married an Axe Murderer* (1993). An indication of Carrey's significance for the industry came when Warner Brothers immediately hired him to play the Riddler in their third Batman film, *Batman Forever*. Released in June 1995, *Batman Forever* was the proof the industry needed that successful PG-13 blockbusters could be planned and manufactured. What was most remarkable about *Batman Forever* was the unremarkable nature of its creative team. Though Tim Burton was still credited as producer, he was replaced as director by Joel Schumacher (b.1939), a former set designer, who had previously specialized in mid-budget dramas and teen films such as *St. Elmo's Fire* (1985) and *The Lost Boys* (1987). According to *Newsweek*, Schumacher 'had a mission to lighten up the series'.[11] None of Burton's key collaborators, including Michael Keaton as Batman and composer Danny

---

[8]Griffin and Masters, *Hit and Run*, 362–85.

[9]Roger Cels, 'Sure to be a Mask Marvel', *Hollywood Reporter*, 29 July 1994, 2.

[10]Bernard Weinraub, 'A Comic on the Edge at $7 Million a Movie', *New York Times*, 1 August 1994, C9.

[11]Jack Kroll, 'Lighten Up, Dark Knight!', *Newsweek*, 26 June 1995, 54.

Elfman, returned for *Forever*. In addition to Carrey, the sequel highlighted its youth-oriented intent through the introduction of Batman's regular comic book sidekick, Robin, played as a moody, rebellious teenager by 25-year-old Chris O'Donnell.

Warner's tight control of the production extended to planning the release. In the days before its launch in a record-breaking 2,842 theatres, *Variety* suggested the studio's plans could bode a 'new box office era' in its aggressive pursuit of opening grosses, making a virtue of the kind of rapid declines in attendance experienced by *Batman Returns*. As described by Leonard Klady, Warner's intention was to make money fast in order to avoid competition from other studios and to free up theatres for its other releases later in the summer.[12] The studio only asked exhibitors to commit to showing the film for six weeks, but demanded up to 90 per cent of ticket sales in the first three weeks and 80 per cent for the next three weeks, with theatres expected to make their money on concessions. Though not mentioned in the article, such a strategy clearly relied upon the support of younger audiences, particularly males, who were more likely to respond to hype and had the free time and money to attend quickly.[13] Warner's efforts paid off. *Batman Forever* broke *Jurassic Park*'s opening record, taking $52 million in its first three days. By its fifth weekend, *Forever* had surpassed the final total for *Batman Returns*, and it ended the year as the second highest grossing release, with $184 million.

As Klady predicted, other studios followed Warner's lead. The following year the top three releases all sported PG-13 ratings and opened wide to take at least $40 million in their first weekends. Like *Batman Forever*, they were the work of directors with limited blockbuster track records, using the templates created by boomers but not boomers themselves. While all three still worked to include boomer angles to their narratives, such concerns were increasingly pushed to one side in the service of teen-friendly scenes of action and destruction. From Fox, *Independence Day*, about a spectacularly destructive alien invasion of Earth, was from the team of Roland Emmerich (writer/director, b.1955 in Germany) and Dean Devlin (writer/producer, b.1962) who had previously made two much lower-profile science fiction action-adventures, *Stargate* (seventeenth for 1994) and *Universal Soldier* (fortieth for 1992). Three of the film's four main characters (a Vietnam-vet president, an ecologically minded scientist and a drunken single father) were boomers, but advertising emphasized the one non-boomer, Will Smith (b.1968), and he became the breakout star.

---

[12]Leonard Klady, 'Bat Blitz Bodes New BO Era', *Variety*, 19 June 1995, 1.
[13]Tino Balio, 'Hollywood Production Trends in the Era of Globalisation, 1990–9', in Neale, ed., *Genre and Contemporary Hollywood*, 165.

Produced by Amblin and written by Michael Crichton, *Twister* functioned as a successor to *Jurassic Park* but discarded leading child characters. The film again featured scientists contending with nature out of control, although here the expensive computer-generated threat was a series of tornadoes ripping up the American Midwest. It was directed by Jan De Bont (b.1943), a Dutch former cinematographer whose only previous feature as director was the 1994 action hit *Speed*. Amid the destruction, *Twister* finds time for adult relationship drama, as its acrimoniously divorced protagonists are drawn back together. However, critics were dismissive of the relationship as mere filling in between special effects. For Todd McCarthy in *Variety*, the film conveyed 'the overwhelming impression of a mechanical entertainment, a very high concept in which the characters and their problems seem like utterly arbitrary creations'.[14]

Like many of the period's big movies, *Mission: Impossible* was rooted in boomer nostalgia. Following *Dragnet, The Untouchables, Lost in Space* (1996) and family films such as *Casper the Friendly Ghost* (1995) or *The Flintstones* (1994) it was an adaptation of a 1960s television favourite, rooted in the formative culture of the boomers. It was distributed by Paramount and directed by Brian DePalma, and so it had particularly clear creative connections to *The Untouchables*, but was far less beholden to the form and content of its inspiration than earlier adaptations. As Richard Schickel wrote in *Time*, the film version 'aside from the title, sound-track quotations from the theme song and self-destructing assignment tapes, has little to do with the old TV show'.[15] Instead, the general milieu of international espionage was used to place star/producer Tom Cruise into a series of spectacular action and suspense sequences. Characters from the series were largely ignored, with the exception of the heroic leader of the Impossible Missions Force, Jim Phelps, whom the film somehow contrived to both kill off before the opening credits and reveal as its major villain.

The trend towards PG-13 hits continued for the rest of the decade. In 1997, all of the top five were rated PG-13, including four action-adventures and another Jim Carrey comedy (*Liar, Liar* in fourth). In the six years from 1995 to 2000, thirty-two top ten hits carried the rating, compared with fifteen Rs and just seven PGs. That was more than in the previous ten years, when twenty-nine top ten films were PG-13, thirty-three were PG and thirty-five were R. The year 1997 was when the popular media caught on to the change in the industry's emphasis, and once again boomer demographics were used as an explanation. In articles such as 'Attack of the 90-Foot Teen-Agers'

---

[14]Todd McCarthy, Review of *Twister*, *Variety*, 10 May 1996, http://variety.com/1996/film/reviews/twister-2-1200445875/.
[15]Richard Schickel, 'Movie: Improbable', *Time*, 27 May 1996, http://content.time.com/time/magazine/article/0,9171,984610,00.html.

and 'Keen on Teen Green', journalists noted an increase in surprise hits that specifically targeted youth.[16] Few of these films made the upper reaches of the charts, but their low budgets made them highly profitable. Cited examples included *Clueless* (1995), *Scream* (1996), *Beavis and Butthead Do America* (1996), *Romeo and Juliet* (1996), *I Know What You Did Last Summer* (1997) and the films of Adam Sandler and Chris Farley. In the *New York Times*, Linda Lee described an 'epochal change' in the culture caused by a critical mass of boomer children reaching their teen years. As evidence, Lee noted a recent report that school enrolment in America had reached a new high of 51.7 million in 1996, breaking a record of 51.3 million set in 1971 as the 'second generation of baby boomers is now moving through high school'. The report added that numbers, bolstered by a steady increase in immigration, were expected to continue to rise until 2006.[17]

Though it is tempting to suggest the new teen-oriented films were the personal responses of filmmakers to the teenage children in their own lives, these films were usually based upon scripts by younger writers (both *Scream* and *I Know What You Did Last Summer*, for example, were written by Kevin Williamson (b.1965)) or a corporate desire to embrace the resurgent youth market. *Clueless*, considered by Lee to be 'the first expression of [the new teen] cohort's buying power', began when writer/director Amy Heckerling went to pitch an entirely different project. She later recalled being told, 'We don't want to do what you're talking about, we want you to do something about teenagers. We're tired of shows about nerdy teenagers and we want to do something about the cool kids. So I said, "Well, I could deal with that if they're, like, stupid."'[18] As she developed the project, initially as a television show, 'My daughter was an entirely separate entity. There was a studio, and a network, and what they expected us to feed to young people. And then there was this person who had entirely different taste, and no interest in becoming the kind of characters I was expected to write.'[19] In the movie Heckerling ultimately made, Elle, played by Alicia Silverstone, inhabits a heightened high school experience, where Jane Austen–inspired plotting rubs up against the real or imagined hierarchies of 1990s teen life.

---

[16]Linda Lee, 'Attack of the 90-Foot Teen-Agers', *New York Times*, 9 November 1997, http://www.nytimes.com/1997/11/09/style/attack-of-the-90-foot-teen-agers.html; Leonard Klady, 'Keen on Teen Green: Taken Unawares, H'w'd Refocuses on Youth', *Variety*, 15 January 1997, 10.

[17]Associated Press, 'Record Number of Students Expected in Fall', *New York Times*, 22 August 1996, http://www.nytimes.com/1996/08/22/us/record-number-of-students-expected-in-fall.html.

[18]Amy Heckerling, interviewed for Harold Lloyd Master Seminar, moderated by Jean Firstenberg, 14 September, 1995. Transcript available at http://famillemouroux.free.fr/Clueless.html.

[19]Noel Murray, 'Amy Heckerling', *A.V. Club*, 20 March 2008, http://www.avclub.com/articles/amy-heckerling,14217/.

And the movie, like many others during the period, clearly indicates that the experiences of young people and teenagers were returning to the centre of Hollywood's output, while boomers (represented here by teachers and parents) moved slowly to the margins of the film narrative – especially in teen horror movies such as *Scream*.

Generation X and the 'Indy' movie

Unlike the sudden splash created by the likes of Lucas and Spielberg, directors born after 1960 had a more gradual impact upon popular cinema. Notably, three of the first four to get films into the annual top thirty were African Americans. The first was Eddie Murphy (b.1961), who capitalized on his run of hits as a performer to make his directorial debut with *Harlem Nights* (1989). Though critically reviled, Murphy's presence as star (alongside his idol Richard Pryor) enabled the film to finish as the twenty-first highest grossing film of 1989. In 1991, Murphy was followed by John Singleton (b.1968), a recent graduate of USC's Filmic Writing programme whose own debut, *Boyz N the Hood*, about gang life in suburban California was twenty-third for its year. Reginald Hudlin (b.1961) had had an independent hit comparable to *sex, lies and videotape*, when his first feature, *House Party*, was distributed by New Line and made $26 million (forty-sixth for 1990). He was then selected by Murphy to direct the romantic comedy *Boomerang*, which was the eighteenth most successful film of 1992. Also that year, David Fincher nominally became the first white post-1960 director in the top thirty when *Alien 3* finished in twenty-eighth, although he has distanced himself from the version of the film Fox released.

The post-1960 filmmaker to make the top ten was Quentin Tarantino (b.1963) with *Pulp Fiction*, which was the tenth biggest hit of 1994. *Pulp Fiction*'s success (and even its very existence) was at least partially the result of the other major development of the 1990s: the major studios' co-option of independent film. During the 1980s, the limited scale of the speciality market maintained the independents' independence. Finding an audience for low budget, often difficult and controversial films required specialist knowledge, and even exceptional successes rarely grossed over seven digits. It was not worth the studios' effort to develop or acquire the necessary personnel and distribution networks. The success of *sex, lies and videotape*, and the way in which Miramax achieved it, changed that. Though the film opened in just 4 theatres, within a month it was in over 100 and peaked in its ninth week in 534. This expansion was supported by television advertising, an expense almost unheard of at that end of the industry. Theatre counts and media buys were, however, familiar to the studios and in the years that followed all of the majors involved themselves in the production and distribution of 'independent' film, using their resources to push releases to previously unimaginable visibility and profit.

Sony went first, contracting former executives from Orion, Michael Barker, Tom Bernard and Marcie Bloom to launch Sony Picture Classics in December 1991. Barker, Bernard and Bloom brought with them the rights to the Merchant Ivory production *Howard's End*, and the film became the new division's first release. While very different from *sex, lies and videotape*, it shared that film's combination of critical acclaim and outsider status (here as a British production) with accessible narrative and genre. With Sony's backing, Barker, Bernard and Bloom were able match the scale of Miramax's expansion, albeit at a slower rate. Having begun its release in March 1992 in a single theatre, *Howard's End* reached its widest point of 547 theatres in March 1993, the same weekend it won three Oscars, including Best Adapted Screenplay and Best Actress (for Emma Thompson).[20] It ultimately earned $25.9 million. Universal followed in 1992, launching Gramercy Pictures, a joint initiative with Polygram. At the time, Universal's Tom Pollock explained the decision: 'If we release three, four or five movies a year through Gramercy and they average a small profit, we've made money ... if we release them through Universal, we've lost money.'[21] Their early releases included *King of the Hill* (1993), Soderbergh's third feature, although, as Miramax had found with Soderbergh's second film, *Kafka* (1991), the director was not a commercial certainty. Collectively, the five films Soderbergh made after *sex, lies and videotape* grossed less than $3 million at the domestic box office.

Miramax had also initially struggled to match their big hit. That changed at the end of 1992 when the company released *The Crying Game*. A thriller dealing with issues of national and gender identity, Miramax expertly exploited the film's narrative twist, which happened to involve frontal nudity. It began in limited release in November 1992, but following its nomination for six Academy Awards in February, it expanded into over 1,000 theatres. By the end of its theatrical run, it had made $62.5 million, the twentieth highest total for a 1992 film. Profit of this level was impossible to ignore, and by April Miramax had been sold to Disney for $60 million. As part of the deal, the Weinsteins were to remain an autonomous unit, although the parent company retained the right to refuse productions and forbade the release of any film that received an NC-17 rating.[22] Disney's own adult-oriented divisions, Touchstone and Hollywood, were barely competitive. In his 1991 memo, Katzenberg had stressed the importance of building on Touchstone's *Pretty Woman*, but that film proved more of an ending than a

---

[20]John Pierson, *Spike Mike Reloaded: A Guided Tour across a Decade of American Independent Cinema* (New York, Hyperion Books, 2004), 194 and 203.
[21]Aljean Harmetz, 'The Little Movie Company That Might', *New York Times*, 31 October 1993, H15.
[22]Biskind, *Down and Dirty Pictures*, 205.

beginning. As Kim Masters notes, *Pretty Woman* was 'one of the last films made according to the old Disney formula'.[23] In the early 1990s only *Father of the Bride* and *Sister Act*, both eminently family friendly, were even close to being comparable hits, to the extent that by the time of the Miramax purchase, Katzenberg had 'pretty much given up on his efforts to grow his own prestige product'.[24]

Within a year, the Weinsteins had justified their price with two very different films. Just prior to the Disney purchase, Miramax had released *Like Water for Chocolate*, a Mexican film with primarily Spanish dialogue. Over time, the company nursed the film to a domestic gross of $21.6 million, breaking the record for a subtitled release in US theatres that had stood since MGM released *La Cage aux Folles* in 1979. At Disney, they quickly repeated this feat with *Il Postino*, a gentle, Italian-language love story that the company pushed to $21.8 million, aided by five Oscar nominations, including Best Picture. At the opposite end of Miramax's repertoire, the Weinsteins both financed and released *Pulp Fiction*, Tarantino's second feature. They had previously bought his debut *Reservoir Dogs*, but had failed to convert its festival notoriety into big screen popular success. *Pulp Fiction* shared a number of elements with its predecessor, including nonlinear narrative, lengthy scenes of expletive-laden chat and shocking bursts of violence. To the list of objectionable content, the new project added drug-taking and rape; but Disney's money also enabled Tarantino to employ an eclectic high-profile cast led by John Travolta and Bruce Willis, and to open up his on-screen world of low-rent Los Angeles crime.

IMAGE 11 *Butch Coolidge (Bruce Willis) and Vincent Vega (John Travolta) in* Pulp Fiction *(1994).*

---

[23]Masters, *The Keys to the Kingdom*, 235.
[24]Ibid., 292.

Like George Lucas, Tarantino was born just before the commonly accepted demographic boundary of a generation, but his upbringing and creative output were emblematic of the cultural and social forces which gave that generation its identity. Where Lucas was a product of suburban prosperity and network television, Tarantino was raised by his mother in a series of apartments around California, struggled to find employment upon leaving school at fifteen and was exposed to a considerably more diverse media landscape. Tarantino's particular voice and sensibility came out of years of employment in a video rental store. His taste incorporated the same 1950s art films as the boomers' college years, but also 1970s auteur and exploitation cinema. For Tarantino, these 1970s works had the same allure as the genre films of the 1930s and 1940s held for boomers: a still present but no longer current tradition, the pleasures of which he hoped to revive. It was his schooling in video that truly marked out Tarantino as a forerunner of generation X. Boomers may have been the first to have routine access to different eras of film, but outside of revival houses and college campuses, the past was found on the small screen and the present was confined to theatres. In a well-stocked store like Tarantino's Video Archives, such boundaries did not exist, allowing for a rapid sampling of different cultures that was reflected in his movies.

That didn't stop boomers from enjoying his films. *Pulp Fiction* was the most mentioned title from the 1987 to 1999 period in our survey. It was also an immediate hit. With Disney's backing, Miramax was able to orchestrate a national release in 1,338 theatres. *Pulp Fiction* opened as the number one film, taking $9.3 million in its first weekend and went on to gross $107.9 million. Along the way it picked up seven Oscar nominations including Best Picture. Prestige and controversy had been the twin engines of Miramax's rise, and *Pulp Fiction* had both to spare. Thereafter, however, mainstream prestige (best expressed by Academy recognition) became the company's focus. In 1996, the Weinsteins won their first Best Picture award with *The English Patient*. From *The Crying Game* in 1992 until *The Aviator* in 2004, Miramax managed to secure at least one Best Picture nomination every year, and had two further winners (*Shakespeare in Love*, 1998; and *Chicago*, 2002).

The appeal of Miramax's way of doing business for major studios was obvious and had particular implications for older audiences. Buying truly independent films, or using studio money to produce tonally equivalent work did not improve the odds of catering to adult audiences, but they did lower the stakes. *Pulp Fiction* cost Miramax around $8 million despite featuring a large number of star names – many of them iconic boomer performers, like Travolta and Willis. The cast was willing to work for greatly reduced fees because they saw the project as an artistic as much as a commercial undertaking. The understanding was that there was a likelihood that the results would not find as wide an audience as a studio production. Miramax refined a system whereby such features could find a large audience, on which occasions stars were reimbursed through profit participation deals. The same year as *Pulp Fiction*, Willis had starred in *The Color of Night*, an erotic thriller very much in the mould of *Basic Instinct*, co-produced by Disney's Hollywood Pictures and Andrew G. Vajna's Cinergi. The film cost an estimated $40 million, but only made $19.7 at the domestic box office. Through Miramax, Disney was able to continue to attract stars and offer them to audiences in adult-oriented material at a fraction of the cost of a full-scale studio production.

By the end of the decade, the remaining majors had set up similar operations. Fox launched Fox Searchlight in 1994. New Line had been purchased by Turner Broadcasting in 1994, who then merged with Warner Brothers in 1996. Lastly, Paramount created Paramount Classics in 1998. Not all of these divisions had the same commercial drive and market presence as Miramax, but all contributed to a growing understanding that explicitly adult cinema, and the demographic limitations that label implied, was outside the remit of major studio production, if not distribution. Supported by video, production costs continued to rise. By 1996, the MPAA was reporting that the average cost of making and marketing a studio feature was approaching $60 million, an increase of 148 per cent over ten years.[25] Regardless of the cushion ancillary revenues offered, such spending levels could only be justified in pursuit of breakout theatrical success. Despite the boomers' continued presence at the box office, their more diverse interests and habits meant that they alone could not be relied upon to provide the explosive launch of a *Jurassic Park* or *Batman Forever*.

This is not to say that everyone in the industry, even at the highest levels, were delighted by the situation. Confronted by the 1996 budget figures, Sherry Lansing – chairperson of Paramount, a position she held from 1992 to 2004 – told the *New York Times*, 'I'm horrified at these numbers. They don't make sense. We're killing ourselves.'[26] Studio-produced adult-oriented films continued to be made but with less frequency and, as we have seen, reduced presence in the upper reaches of the annual charts – a situation that would become even more intense in future decades.

DreamWorks SKG

In an environment of decline in directly studio-produced adult fare, the formation of DreamWorks SKG was especially intriguing. In October

---

[25]Bernard Weinraub, 'Average Hollywood Film Now Costs $60 Million', *New York Times*, 5 March 1997, http://www.nytimes.com/1997/03/05/movies/average-hollywood-film-now-costs-60-million.html.
[26]Weinraub, 'Average Hollywood Film', online.

1994, Spielberg, Katzenberg and David Geffen held a press conference in Los Angeles to announce their intention to create a new major studio. In her history of DreamWorks, Nicole LaPorte notes that each of the three men had personal motives for undertaking the colossal project. Most straightforwardly, Katzenberg had recently been overlooked for the vacant president position at Disney and effectively forced from the company. Co-owning a studio would enable him to exceed the standing and influence he had lost. For Spielberg and Geffen, already in possession of the wealth and power to realize whatever projects they wished, DreamWorks represented the opportunity to institutionalize their personal importance within the industry.[27] What was less clear was why they felt a new studio was necessary for the rest of Hollywood.

At their first press conference, Katzenberg spoke only vaguely of 'revolution'. Reading from a prepared statement, Spielberg sold DreamWorks as an artist-centred venture: 'I want to find ways to insure filmmakers, both established and new, that they have a new home, that they are free to explore and share successfully in every success.'[28] However, Spielberg complicated that vision when he juxtaposed the company's creative ambitions with the industry's past: 'Hollywood studios were at their zenith when they were driven by point of view and personalities. Together with Jeffrey and David, I want to create a place driven by ideas and the people who have them.'[29] Clearly, the opinionated personalities who drove the studios in the 1930s and 1940s were studio heads not generally considered idea creators. As studio head and leading director, Spielberg was one of only a handful of people in the history of cinema to whom both sentences could apply. Arguably, Katzenberg was another. His memo, written less than five years earlier, had also exalted ideas as the heart of the industry, but only when controlled by studio executives, not independently powerful creative personnel. Both men were certainly closely involved in the selection, development and production of DreamWorks's initial slate of releases. Their ability to impose their tastes upon their studio's output was not entirely overwhelming, but it did mean that, on balance, DreamWorks ran counter to the trend of moving away from boomer-oriented production. If anything, DreamWorks's early, 'signature' releases were grounded in nostalgia for 1950s movies and television to an unprecedented degree.

In keeping with Katzenberg's success at Disney, DreamWorks immediately poured resources into animation. Much more than Disney, however, DreamWorks animated releases seemed to court boomer parents over their

---

Nicole Laporte, *The Men Who Would Be King* (Boston: Mariner Books, 2011), 12–27.
[28]Bernard Weinraub, '3 Hollywood Giants Team Up to Create Major Movie Studio', *New York Times*, 13 October 1994, http://www.nytimes.com/1994/10/13/us/media-business-overview-3-hollywood-giants-team-up-create-major-movie-studio.html?pagewanted=all.
[29]LaPorte, *The Men Who Would be King*, 32.

offspring. Katzenberg went so far as to remark, 'Walt Disney had a mission statement: "I make movies for children and child who exists in each of us." So I say – with both a nod and a wink – my idea for DreamWorks was that we would make animated movies for adults, for the adult that exists in every child.'[30] All of the company's first four traditionally animated releases sought to recreate genres popular in the 1950s, explicitly referencing memories of boomers' childhood entertainment. The initial flagship release was *The Prince of Egypt*, a costly retelling of *The Ten Commandments*. In publicity for the film, Katzenberg stressed that the idea had originated in discussions between himself and Spielberg:

> Steven asked what the criteria would be for a great animated film and I launched into a twenty-minute dissertation about what you look for: a powerful allegory that we can relate to in our time; extraordinary situations to motivate strong emotional journeys; something wonderful about the human spirit; good triumphing over evil; music as a compelling storytelling element; and so on. Steven leaned forward and said, "you mean like *The Ten Commandments?*" and I said, "exactly".[31]

The biblical epics of the 1950s were a direct inspiration. *The Prince of Egypt* was followed by *The Road to Eldorado* (2000), a Kiplingesque historical adventure crossed with Hope and Crosby humour, whose title explicitly referenced the adventure films that Spielberg and Katzenberg grew up watching on television. Then came *Spirit: Stallion of Cimarron* (2002), an epic western told from a horse's point of view. Last, the studio released *Sinbad: Legend of the Seven Seas* (2003), which borrowed liberally from Ray Harryhausen's 1960s tales of gods and monsters. These implementations of Katzenberg's theory did not prove wildly popular with audiences. Launched with much ceremony for Christmas 1998, *The Prince of Egypt* scraped over $100 million only after it was booked back into hundreds of theatres late in its run. That milestone proved entirely beyond its successors, which topped out at $50.8 million, $73.2 million and an embarrassing $26.4 million respectively. However, over the same period, DreamWorks had also begun production of computer-generated animation, based on Katzenberg's experiences with Pixar while still at Disney. In 1995, Pixar had released the first entirely computer-generated feature, *Toy Story*, which became the top-grossing film of the year. In spring 1996, DreamWorks purchased 40 per cent of Pacific Data Images, a computer animation company, to produce a CGI film of their own. Controversially, the project selected (later titled *Antz*)

---

[30]Jeffrey Katzenberg, quoted in Russell, *The Historical Epic and Contemporary Hollywood*, 143.
[31]Katzenberg, quoted in Russell, *The Historical Epic and Contemporary Hollywood*, 139.

dealt with life in an ant colony, the exact same subject Pixar were known to be using for their *Toy Story* follow-up *A Bug's Life*.

The impact of CG animation and the roles of Pixar and DreamWorks in developing it will be discussed in the next chapter. Here, though, it is worth pointing out the much greater emphasis DreamWorks placed on adult-oriented humour and other attractions compared to their competitor. Though Pixar had used big stars Tom Hanks and Tim Allen to voice their lead characters in *Toy Story*, for *A Bug's Life* the only comparable member of the voice cast was Kevin Spacey as the lead villain. *Antz*, however, was packed with star names, most of whom were associated with decidedly adult entertainment, including Woody Allen, Sharon Stone, Sylvester Stallone, Christopher Walken and Danny Glover. Many jokes also seemed to be exclusively for adults, with frequent reference to psychoanalysis and workplace anxiety. When the lead character, Z (voiced by Allen), is asked to go to war, he responds, 'Why don't we just try to influence their political process with campaign contributions?' If anything, the attempts to ape Allen's trademark humour positioned the film as a watered down version of his own comedies that had proven influential with boomer audiences since the 1970s. Like *The Prince of Egypt, Antz* was a qualified success, its $90.7 million domestic gross approximately matching its production costs.

For DreamWorks's live action productions, Spielberg brought in the husband and wife team who had recently taken over the running of his Amblin production company at Universal. Laurie MacDonald (b.1953) had been a production executive at Columbia. Her husband, Walter F. Parkes (b.1951) began as a screenwriter, with credits including *Wargames* and *Sneakers* (1992). Under their control, a definite pattern was evident in the company's early live action releases. As Spielberg promised, DreamWorks did back new voices. During the first years of operation, a reasonably eclectic range of directors were able to make their first (Mimi Leder, Gore Verbinski, Todd Phillips and Sam Mendes) and second (Bronwen Hughes, Rod Lurie, Dean Parisot) theatrical features. For DreamWorks's most expensive and high-profile releases, the majority were entrusted to filmmakers with an existing relationship with Amblin. The studio's first release was *The Peacemaker* (1997), a seriously minded thriller starring George Clooney and Nicole Kidman. Though its director, Mimi Leder (b.1952), was making her feature debut, she had had a long career in television drama, most successfully as director and supervising producer on Amblin's medical drama, *ER* (NBC, 1994–2009).

Leder was also handed DreamWorks's first attempt at a summer blockbuster, *Deep Impact* (1998), a co-production with Paramount. In a scenario reminiscent of the *Antz/Bug's Life* clash, *Deep Impact* shared its concept (involving humanity's reaction to an impending, planet-threatening asteroid strike) with a leading Disney production, this time *Armageddon* (1998). Again, DreamWorks sought to distinguish their product as the more grown-up offering. Leder told Peter Bart, 'They would play with their *Dirty Dozen* in space. We had more serious spiritual and emotional issues to deal with.'[32] Both films were successful at the box office, but with different audiences. During *Deep Impact*'s opening weekend, it attracted 'an even mix between men and women' and 'older moviegoers outnumbered the young'.[33] Released nine weeks later, exits polls revealed *Armageddon* appealed to a 'predominantly young male audience'.[34]

Two other big-budget summer films, *Small Soldiers* (1998) and *The Haunting* (1999), were assigned to Amblin veterans, Joe Dante and Jan De Bont. These were both effects-driven movies, though neither satisfactorily courted teens or any other demographic. *Small Soldiers* in particular appeared to show the studio was ill-equipped to play the youth-oriented game. The film's premise involved children's action figures coming to life and waging war against one another. As the director of *Gremlins*, Dante should have been the ideal candidate for the material, but he was unprepared for the implications a promotional contract with Burger King held for the production. The fast food company had agreed to offer *Small Soldiers* toys with their children's meal with the understanding the film would be released with a PG rating. When early footage from Dante indicated a darker tone, Burger King demanded – and was granted – changes. The director later recalled,

I'm sure I was aware there was a tie-in with Burger King. I wasn't aware how much control they were going to be allowed over the movie. It became quite unique, I think, in the annals of moviemaking, the amount of control that ultimately was ceded to Burger King. It came out of desperation. It came out of real terror that their multi-million dollar deal was going to be blown and they might even be sued. This became a corporate problem, not an artistic problem. The artistic problem became a separate entity and much less important. This is only one movie.[35]

Eventually, Burger King's efforts proved fruitless, as *Small Soldiers* received a PG-13 rating and the now tonally confused production limped to $54.6 million at the domestic box office, forty-second for its year.

Much more successfully, long-term Spielberg collaborator Robert Zemeckis signed up to make two large-scale productions, *Cast Away* (2000) with Tom Hanks and *What Lies Beneath* (2000) starring Harrison Ford and Michelle Pfeiffer. Since *Forrest Gump*, Zemeckis had continued his journey away from jokey, juvenile material. In 1997 he had released *Contact*, an

[32]Peter Bart, *The Gross: The Hits, The Flops – The Summer That Ate Hollywood* (New York: St. Martin's Press, 1999), 170.
[33]Bart, *The Gross*, 174.
[34]Ibid., 238.
[35]Joe Dante in Bill Krohn, 'I, Robby: The Secret Life of Joe Dante', 184.

ambitious science fiction film based on the novel by Carl Sagan that put a spiritual spin on mankind's search for extraterrestrial life. In different ways, the DreamWorks films continued *Contact*'s existential questioning. In *Cast Away*, Hanks's character is stranded on an island and wrestles with the meaning of a life spent alone. *What Lies Beneath* is ultimately an exercise in generating suspense, but Zemeckis's starting point is a serious representation of a woman (Pfeiffer) simultaneously confronting a sense of loss as her daughter leaves for college and the possible existence of supernatural forces. Both were major hits, earning $233.6 and $155.5 million respectively, the second and tenth biggest hits of 2000.

Where DreamWorks did employ established filmmakers without an Amblin connection, there was still an adult emphasis. Since *The Crying Game*, Neil Jordan had made three films for Geffen Pictures (*Interview with a Vampire*, 1994; *Michael Collins*, 1996; and *The Butcher Boy*, 1997), and he brought *In Dreams* (1999), a psychological thriller about a mourning mother, to Geffen's new studio. As well as lending his voice work for *Antz*, Woody Allen signed to make three comedies, after DreamWorks bought domestic distribution rights for his 2000 comedy, *Small Time Crooks*. Since *Hannah and Her Sisters* in 1986, none of Allen's fourteen films had made more than the $18.2 million earned by *Crimes and Misdemeanors*. That record wouldn't change at DreamWorks and the director's main value to the studio was to signal their artistic friendliness without too great a budgetary outlay.

In 2000, DreamWorks released a series of films which very clearly built upon an ongoing fascination with boomers and boomer culture. One was *Almost Famous*, Cameron Crowe's semi-autobiographical account of a teenager who becomes a reporter for *Rolling Stone* magazine in the early 1970s. In reviewing the film *Variety* noted that 'boomers whose own rites of passage coincided with those so vividly captured here are sure to respond enthusiastically and in significant numbers, but ultimately the commercial fate of this production will rest upon whether or not its embraced by the under 30 public'.[36] In effect, *Variety* was beginning to express concern that films targeted too exclusively at the boomers might struggle to capture a wider American audience. The concerns proved correct, when *Almost Famous* earned only $32 million on domestic release, despite costing $60 million. To some degree, the overt nostalgia of the film, and its clear desire to recreate on-screen the specific pop cultural experiences of a minority of boomers, failed to appeal to a wide audience.

Jay Roach (b.1957), the director of Mike Myers's Austin Powers films, directed *Meet the Parents*, a broad comedy that starred boomer Robert De Niro (b.1943) as the overprotective father of an adult daughter, and

---

[36]Todd McCarthy, Review of *Almost Famous*, *Variety*, 11 September 2000, 21.

treated intergenerational relationships as a source of comedy – although the uptight, ex-CIA character played by De Niro was not a typical boomer role. On a budget of $55 million, the film earned $166 million, meriting a sequel, *Meet the Fockers* (2004), which spent more time depicting boomer parents, in a cast expanded to include Dustin Hoffman and Barbra Streisand. The sequel performed significantly better than its predecessor (despite less glowing reviews), earning $280 million domestically. By matching De Niro's straight-laced military man against Hoffman and Streisand's uproarious, new age, Jewish hippies, *Meet the Fockers* drew much of its comic inspiration from a stereotypical vision of the social, political and ethnic divisions that characterized the boomers in popular debate.

DreamWorks also released the fourth highest grossing release of the year in the form of Ridley Scott's *Gladiator*, a Roman epic that can be understood as a direct homage to the biblical epics that had proliferated during the 1950s, when the boomers were children. Although most of DreamWorks's 2000 releases have some link to the culture of the boomers, the studio's more successful movies were those that featured boomers or often derived from boomer culture but did not emphasize nostalgia to any particular degree. Indeed, *Gladiator* eschewed the grand spiritual themes of the 1950s biblical epics it referenced in favour of a revenge narrative, which emphasized family by casting the central character as a grieving father. The focus on the gladiatorial tournaments over wider political and social themes meant that the movie more closely resembled a sports movies rather than a solemn, potentially more educational or edifying, historical epic.

Most importantly for establishing DreamWorks's reputation, Spielberg himself directed two films for the studio in rapid succession. Both were R-rated historical dramas and continued his exploration of the recurring themes of his self-consciously 'adult' work: racial identity and war. *Amistad*, released in December 1997, was based on the mutiny and subsequent legal fight by a group of Africans captured for sale in America in 1839. Other than the opening shipboard confrontation, the film contained little action and DreamWorks elected for a platform release, in the hope of gradually building an audience on the back of strong reviews and award recognition. These failed to materialize in sufficient number, however, and *Amistad*'s final domestic gross of $44.2 million was considered a disappointment. *Saving Private Ryan* – a co-production with Paramount – was no easier to sell. Spielberg's ambition for the film was the capture the experience of frontline combat, in all its violence and confusion. In interviews he would later claim, 'I didn't think [the graphic violence] would be tolerable to audiences … We had kind of noble ambitions but never really any commercial ones.'[37]

---

[37]Kenneth Turan, 'Crossroads: Steven Spielberg', in Friedman and Notbohm, *Steven Spielberg Interviews*, 218.

Unlike *Amistad, Ryan* was given a wide summer launch in July 1998 and – like *Schindler's List* – was expertly marketed as a cultural event. It wound up becoming the most successful film of its year, making $216 million domestically.

All told, the major successes of DreamWorks's first four years of releasing – *Deep Impact, Private Ryan, Gladiator, Cast Away, What Lies Beneath, Meet the Parents*, plus Sam Mendes's surprise Oscar-winning hit about suburban frustration *American Beauty* – favoured boomer audiences. Yet this was an anomaly compared to the experiences of the established studios and, crucially, the established majors' hits were more numerous and often bigger. In 1997, DreamWorks's first year of operation, Spielberg directed *The Lost World: Jurassic Park* for Universal and lent his name as executive producer to Sony's *Men in Black*. These were the second and third biggest hits of their year, taking $250 and $229 million, respectively. Above them, by an unprecedented margin, was the biggest cultural event of all, James Cameron's *Titanic*.

Conclusion

Titanic represented the apex of baby boomer filmmaking in the 1990s, but also reinforced the importance of youth demographics for big-budget productions. Written and directed by Canadian wunderkind James Cameron, the movie had cost $200 million, making it the most expensive production in Hollywood's history, and its focus on romance was not a usual topic for high-budget movies. *Variety* described it as 'the biggest roll of the dice in cinema history', but Cameron's gamble paid off to an unprecedented degree: *Titanic* earned $658 million at the US box office, and a further $1.5 billion overseas.[38] In retrospect it is easy to see that the movie grew out of a burgeoning trend for high-budget epics, infused with nostalgia for the big-budget spectacles of the 1950s and 1960s, which characterized boomer filmmaking in the late 1990s. Like several other historical films from the period, the film was structured around the act of reminiscence, and positioned an older figure telling a story in the present as a mechanism to reveal some hidden truth about the past, a device which also featured in *Forrest Gump* and *Saving Private Ryan*. The film's central romance narrative took place mostly in the past and focused on two young lovers, played by young stars Kate Winslet and Leonardo DiCaprio (born in 1975 and 1974, respectively), who meet on the doomed Titanic before it sinks in 1912. Its blend of teen romance, computer-enhanced spectacle and boomer nostalgia appears to have captured all moviegoing demographics. In our

---

[38]Todd McCarthy, 'Spectacular *Titanic* a Night to Remember', *Variety*, 3 November 1997, 7.

survey it was mentioned by thirteen respondents, four male and nine female, eleven of whom born between 1946 and 1964. Ten respondents listed it as a favourite, stressing its story and epic scale.

Titanic's success transformed Cameron from a successful action director into a highly regarded, Oscar-winning public figure. Consequently, Cameron's journey mirrored his baby boomer contemporaries, and while it was an exceptional release in terms of scale and expense, *Titanic*'s historical setting, genre pleasures and cross-demographic appeal seem to embody the competing trends that defined film production at the end of the 1990s.

Boomer filmmakers continued to release successful movies after the millennium, often by revisiting the thematic terrain of their earlier hits using new digital technologies. And Hollywood followed *Titanic* and Spielberg's war movies with a cycle of related releases, including Ridley Scott's Roman epic *Gladiator*, released by DreamWorks in 2000. But the market for adult-oriented films, and the age demographic of Hollywood's key production personnel, entered a period of sustained change after 2000 as new generations of filmgoers and filmmakers emerged.

PART FIVE

Legacy

11

Franchise Hollywood

By the end of 2000, *Variety* already identified 2001 as a potentially transformative year in the industry's history, explaining:

> The studios have already slotted some thirty pics for next summer, more than half the usual release schedule. Despite all the industry talk about cost-saving, the summer fare is pricier than ever and heavier with special effects. Summer 2001 is shaping up with some major trends: Remakes and sequels. ... Heavy hitters [identified as Spielberg's *AI* and Bruckheimer/Bay's *Pearl Harbor*]. ... Animation ... and adaptations of videogames. While the lineup appears particularly rich, it comes at a stunning negative cost. At least 10 of the titles have budgets in the $100 million range.[1]

While not all of the films identified as potential hits would go on to set the box office alight, the trends identified in *Variety* – expensive, effects heavy serialized releases – would indeed become the sine qua non of post-2000 production. Most significantly, after 2000, these films increasingly catered for child as well as teen audiences. Teen films, historical films and adult dramas remained part of Hollywood's output, but diminished in commercial significance, as movies based on comic books, theme park rides, children's fiction or fondly remembered children's television shows continued to proliferate, reaching new heights of commercial success by the end of the decade.

Initially, these productions were directed or produced by boomer filmmakers and approved by boomer executives, building on the trends for populist, commercial entertainment grounded in nostalgia that they themselves had started earlier in their careers. Christopher Columbus, a protégé of Spielberg and director of *Home Alone*, was given directing duties for *Harry Potter and the Sorcerer's Stone* (2001); in addition to his own directorial work, Spielberg produced a series of movies based on Hasbro's

---

[1]Dana Harris and Dade Hayes, 'Can Studios Survive Tentpole Traumas?', *Variety*, 23 October 2000, 1.

line of Transformers toys; Ron Howard directed *The Grinch* in 2000; Sam Raimi (b.1959) directed *Spider Man* in 2001; George Lucas wrote, directed and produced a series of prequels to his Star Wars movies (before selling the rights to future movies to Disney); and in 2008 Marvel Studios was established in an effort to adapt comic book stories that had first gained popularity with baby boomers in the 1960s, with great success. These kinds of blockbusters generated box office returns that would have been unthinkable previously, often topping $1 billion in global revenues, by appealing to younger generations of viewers in America, and much larger international audiences.

As the decade rolled on, the primacy of the baby boomers within Hollywood was also challenged, as new directors, producers and studio heads emerged to steer the industry towards new markets. This chapter looks at the production conditions of films at and after the millennium, and it begins by tracing the turnover of creative staff in Hollywood, charting the gradual decline of the baby boomers as the architects of Hollywood's biggest movies. It also explores the priorities and concerns of a new generation of younger filmmakers, most drawn from generation X – the smaller generation that had grown up in the 1980s and 1990s. The chapter then looks in more detail at the key releases of the post-2000 period, which were increasingly aimed at children alongside adult viewers, before focusing on the fortunes of the Disney Company once again.

While the direct creative influence of many key boomer filmmakers declined during this period, they cast a long shadow over Hollywood's modes of operation. Many of the most successful films released during the post-2000 period continued to be firmly grounded in the popular culture, and social experiences, of the baby boomers. Furthermore, the growing commercial significance of high-budget, family-friendly releases must be understood as a key part of the boomers' legacy. From the very beginning, these were the kinds of movies that the most influential and successful boomer filmmakers had wanted to make. While their priorities changed with age, the industry's dependence on tent pole releases only intensified.

The filmmakers

The highest grossing movie of 1999, with domestic returns of $431 million, was George Lucas's *Star Wars Episode 1: The Phantom Menace*, a revival of the *Star Wars* franchise that drew in huge swathes of viewers, despite mixed critical responses. While the movie represented Lucas's triumphant return as a writer-director, other top grossing films of the year indicated that the baby boomers were being superseded by younger generations of filmmakers. The second highest grossing release of the year was M. Night Shyamalan's

The Sixth Sense, which earned an equally spectacular (in the context of its budget) $293 million in the United States, followed by several sequels (*Toy Story 2* and *Austin Powers: The Spy Who Shagged Me*) and other key hits including *The Matrix*, written and directed by the Wachowski siblings, and *The Blair Witch Project*, written and directed by Edouardo Sanchez and Daniel Myrick. A high proportion of these were breakthrough projects from relatively unknown filmmakers who, like Lucas, both wrote and directed their most iconic movies. All were born either in the final years of the baby boom, or afterwards. Shyamalan was born in 1970, the Wachowskis in 1965 and 1967 respectively, Edouardo Sanchez in 1968 while Myrick and comedian Mike Myers were both born in 1963.

These were not the first gen X-ers to create highly successful movies; Michael Bay (b.1965) and Brett Ratner (b.1969) had preceded them as directors, while the comedian Adam Sandler (b.1966) was one of the first true generation X stars to consistently headline successful high-budget comedy movies.[2] By contrast, the year 2000 marked something of a retrenchment for the boomers. Ron Howard's *The Grinch Who Stole Christmas* was the highest grossing movie of the year, with domestic grosses of $260 million. It was followed by new releases from Robert Zemeckis, Nancy Meyers and Jay Roach. Nevertheless, the tide had turned. Between 2000 and 2005 boomer directors were responsible for half of the top ten highest growing movies released every year on average. Between 2006 and 2015, boomer directors were responsible for two of the top ten highest grossing films of the year, on average.

The decline that had begun in the 1990s but escalated quickly after 2000 can be attributed to a combination of changing audience tastes and changing priorities for the filmmakers. Jack Epps Jr, who together with his partner Jim Cash had written *Top Gun*, *The Secret of My Success* and *Dick Tracy*, found writing for a new generation of audiences and executives difficult: 'After the 1980s, things got snarkier. The term people used was "edgy". They wanted more edgy material, and our material was not edgy. ... That's part of what we were struggling with in the 1990s.' Similarly, Tim Harris, who with Herschel Weingrod was one of the leading comedy writing teams of the 1980s, also saw a decline in demand during the 1990s. After 1991's unsuccessful *Pure Luck*, the pair had only one credit during the decade, on another project steeped in nostalgia for the children's entertainment from the 1940s and 1950s, regular collaborator Ivan Reitman's *Space Jam* (1997). Harris remembers:

All through that period we were writing spec scripts of the kind that we wanted to see made, that nobody was offering us. And then, I'm not sure

[2]Whalley, *Saturday Night Live*, 161–86.

how long after *Space Jam*, we just ended up getting all these rewrites on dreadful movies, about monkeys and stuff, and by the end I just got fed up. So it wasn't that I dropped Hollywood, it was Hollywood that dropped me. I got old. Comedy is very much a young person's game, more than any other genre.

Others found the creative and commercial pressures of success equally difficult to navigate. After *Field of Dreams* and directing and co-writing *Sneakers*, Phil Alden Robinson attempted to use his standing to interest studios in projects dealing with social issues:

I thought, 'OK, these two films in a row were both commercially successful. I'm now in a position – I felt – where I can get films made that might otherwise not get made.' And my focus changed from 'Do something that means something deeply to me', to 'Do something that means deeply to me, but also, wouldn't get made if I didn't do it.' And I felt that was a responsible thing to do.

Robinson spent years writing and researching two films, one addressing the contemporary conflict in Sarajevo, the other a history of the civil rights movement in America. The Sarajevo film, *The Age of Aquarius*, was almost made in the late 1990s with Harrison Ford as star, but the production collapsed. 'Turns out I couldn't do it. ... I overestimated my ability to get the system to embrace something it didn't want to embrace. The films I'd made were successful, but not that successful.' The civil rights project *Freedom Song* (TNT, 2000) was eventually made for television.

I intended that to be a feature film, but we couldn't get any studio to finance a feature film about a bunch of African American teenagers in the Sixties, in the movement. They just didn't think it had any foreign potential. I'm guessing they didn't think it had a lot of domestic potential either, but they would always say, 'We can't sell this film foreign', that's what the studios said.

For Jerry Zucker, in the wake of the runaway success of *Ghost*, the problem was not the nature of the projects that interested him, but whether to direct again at all:

It was a culmination of things, actually. One is that I had young kids and because I didn't have to work, I could spend a lot of time with the family. When I shoot I'm really gone; even if it shoots in Los Angeles, where I live, my mind is on the film. It wasn't a conscious decision not to direct, but when I got scripts, I weighed them. ... There was a while when I was offered a tonne of scripts, after *Ghost*, but it's hard to find great material.

I didn't really want to go back and do satire again, I'd done a lot of that. David and Jim have kept doing a lot of great satire. It was hard for me.... And the last reason is that sometimes a big hit can mess you up. It sort of puts you in a position where ... the choice of your next [film] becomes a big deal, because all eyes are on you.

Eventually, Zucker selected *First Knight* (1995), a big-budget retelling of Arthurian legend, as his next picture. Later he would wonder if it was 'not the best idea for me to be directing a movie about the Arthur legend, being as I never cared much for it and never had much interest in medieval film'. Instead, he had been attracted by the themes of duty and romance in the screenplay and 'the idea of doing something completely different'. *First Knight* was neither popular with audiences nor critics (nor even Zucker, who describes it, humorously, as 'a debacle') and it would be another six years before Zucker directed again.

In each case, many of those filmmakers who had achieved commercial success seem to have found that family commitments, other interests and charity work began taking precedence over making movies as they entered late middle age. Even James Cameron, who wrote, directed and produced the most successful films of the 1990s and 2000s, spent most of his time pursuing highly personal deep sea diving projects, developing new diving and filmmaking technology along the way. In May 2013, Cameron was awarded the Nierenberg Prize for Science in the Public Interest by the Scripps Institution of Oceanography. At the ceremony in San Diego, he explained that he had come to see himself primarily as an oceanographic explorer. 'I think where people get messed up is they think that I was doing these dives to find inspiration for movies', he said. 'That's not the case. I make the movies to pay for the dives.'[3]

By 2005, the relatively small group of boomer directors who continued to produce culturally and commercially significant films worked at a more leisurely pace than ever before. Steven Spielberg remained the foremost filmmaker of his generation, and continued to make interesting, challenging and ambitious movies. However, he arguably lost much of his unerring connection to American culture after 1998, and seemed happy to pursue more personal and unusual projects, from the downbeat sci-fi of *AI* (2001) and *Minority Report* (2002), through to the historical dramas *War Horse* (2011) and *Lincoln* (2012). Almost all of these are undeniably impressive movies – perhaps some of his best work – but none were 'events' in the same fashion as Spielberg's earlier releases.

[3]James Cameron, quoted in Anon., 'James Cameron Honored with Scripps Nierenberg Prize', *Scripps Institute of Oceanography News*, 15 May 2013, https://scripps.ucsd.edu/news/5230.

Spielberg's long-time collaborator George Lucas directed more films in the 2000s than he had in the 1980s and 1990s put together. After he completed a highly commercially successful 'prequel trilogy' of Star Wars films in 2004, he again retreated to the Lucasfilm ranch, overseeing the expansion of Star Wars into a branded entity aimed primarily at young children, before selling Lucasfilm to the Disney Company in 2012. The other boomer directors still working with notable success of by the end of the 2000s were Robert Zemeckis, Ivan Reitman, Ron Howard, James Cameron, Sylvester Stallone (amazingly) and Nancy Meyers. Although Cameron only made one film that received a general release in the 2000s, it was the most commercially successful film of all time – *Avatar* (2009) – and so marks him out as a special case.

By the end of the decade, then, only a small handful of boomers retained positions as Hollywood's most successful directors (although as we will see many boomers moved to occupy more senior positions as studio executives, retaining considerable influence and control at a corporate level). As the boomers began to decline in terms of creative relevance, new generations of filmmakers appeared to take their place.

In 2001 DreamWorks appointed former New Line Pictures executive Michael DeLuca as president of production. The trade press reported that DeLuca 'will become the first person to hold a title at DreamWorks, which has always disdained a corporate structure. He will now be the man expected to help the mini studio push its output towards major studio level'.[4] DeLuca was born in 1965, and was thirty-five years old at the time. While the studio would continue to be led by boomers at the most senior level, production was no longer in the supervisory control of a boomer. DeLuca was already one of the youngest executives in the business, having occupied the same role at New Line from the age of twenty-seven. Under his control, New Line had specialized in low and mid-budget movies, but had broadened its focus to make production and distribution deals with the majors, and to invest in high-budget projects too. DeLuca brought a similar strategy for expansion to DreamWorks.

As a member of generation X, DeLuca was still very much an anomaly, and boomers continued to dominate executive positions, but those executives were increasingly looking to new generations to replenish their talent pools. At Warner Bros, Terry Semel and Robert Daly (b.1943 and 1937, respectively) were replaced in 2001 as chairman and president of production by Alan Horn and Lorenzo DiBonaventura (b.1943 and 1957, respectively). Almost immediately, the pair increased production levels,

---

[4]Michael Fleming, 'DreamWork's DeLuca Makes Executive Decision', *Variety*, 11 June 2001, 10.

started developing more family-friendly projects and 'put ... the accent on more eclectic fare and younger directors'.[5]

This 'new generation' of directors was already visible in the independent sector. According to *Variety*'s Charles Lyons:

> They fashion themselves as maverick storytellers. Their names are by now familiar – David O. Russell, Kimberly Pierce, Paul Thomas Anderson, Alexander Payne, Spike Jonze and Wes Anderson. These filmmakers and a few more like them delight in dancing between the studio and independent worlds; but they are less interested in fat, long term studio pacts than they are in creating movies with resonance.
>
> If the 1980s and 1990s were a time of the studio director for hire, these new millennium helmers are looking increasingly like the filmmakers of the counter-cultural 1970s.[6]

With the exception of Alexander Payne (b.1961) and David O. Russell (b.1958), all of these directors were gen-Xers born in the late 1960s and early 1970s. For Michael DeLuca at DreamWorks they represented the future of American movies, because 'these new directors are looked upon as pioneers because many are at the beginning of their careers and nobody knows what the next years will bring'.[7]

Reporting on this group, *Variety* observed, 'In their headlong search for the Next Big Thing, the studios are granting untested directors more opportunities than they have since the late 1960s. This comes at a time when the perils of such ventures – for the studios and the talent – are greater than ever. Today's rookies are ambitious young turks who want to stand at the vortex of a $50 million production.'[8] The filmmakers coming under the microscope who wanted to work with the studios included Robert Luketic (b.1973), Joseph 'McG' McGinty (b.1968) and Michael Bay (b.1965). Other, related, figures were Bryan Singer (b.1965), director of several *X-Men* films and *Superman Returns* (2004); Chris Nolan (b.1970 in the UK, but holds dual British and American citizenship), writer/producer/director of *Inception* (2010) and the *Dark Knight* movies; and J. J. Abrams (b.1966), director of the reworked *Star Trek* and most recent *Star Wars* movies.

An equally slow yet inescapable turnaround occurred at the level of performers. The most commercially successful stars of the early 2000s were Tom Cruise, Tom Hanks, Jim Carrey and George Clooney, all technically boomers (although Cruise and Carrey – both born in 1962 – are perhaps

---

[5]Dana Harris and Dade Hayes, 'WB Revs Up Movie Machine', *Variety*, 7 May 2001, 1.
[6]Charles Lyons, 'Helmers Let Out a Rebel Yell', *Variety*, 18 June 2001, 1 and 53.
[7]Lyons, 'Helmers', 53.
[8]Jonathan Bing, 'Pix Bet on Frosh, by Gosh', *Variety*, 23 July 2001, 1.

more closely associated with generation X). But younger stars such as
Matt Damon (b.1970), Will Smith (b.1968), Reese Witherspoon (b.1976),
Drew Barrymore (b.1975), Angelina Jolie (b.1975) and Leonardo DiCaprio
(b.1974) had been headlining major releases pretty consistently from the
mid-1990s onwards. As they grew in status, they were also setting up their
own production companies, which ensured that these 'young stars are
getting more deals than ever', according to *Variety*.[9] In the second half of the
decade, successful stars also came to include Robert Downey Jr (b.1965),
Christian Bale (b.1974, UK), Bradley Cooper (b.1975) and Johnny Depp
(b.1963). Certain key boomers clearly remained important box office in the
2000s and 2010s, usually men. Tom Hanks and, to a lesser extent George
Clooney, graduated from youthful roles in the 1980s to playing figures of
seniority and authority by the late 1990s, while Tom Cruise, whose filmic
identity had been predicated around his youthfulness, was always more
closely associated with youthful roles, and struggled to retain his popularity
with mass audiences. Johnny Depp, who was born at the very end of the
baby boom, and achieved mainstream stardom later in his career, was even
more closely associated with youth culture in the 1990s and 2000s, and is
best understood as a generation X star.

Alternatively, *Forbes* Magazine's annual list of the most highly paid
actors and actresses included some much younger figures. In 2013, the
highest paid male star was Robert Downey Jr, followed by young gen-
Xer Channing Tatum (b.1980) and Mark Wahlberg (b.1974). The highest
paid actress was millennial Kristen Stewart (b.1990), in a list which also
included Angelina Jolie and Charlize Theron (b.1975, South Africa).[10] And
in 2016, Tom Cruise, Johnny Depp and Brad Pitt continued to earn high
pay, but the highest paid actors were Dwayne Johnson (b.1972) and Kevin
Hart (b.1979).[11] In terms of pay, the most well-remunerated stars skewed
younger, reflecting the film industry's willingness to develop and reward
young stars who might reasonably appeal to a younger audience over and
above older performers.

As all of these changes occurred, boomers moved increasingly from
positions of creative primacy – where they dominated creative roles, and
their interests determined the content of mainstream movies – to corporate
seniority. In effect, boomers controlled the industry at one remove after

[9]Dana Harris, 'H'Wood's Kiddie Litter', *Variety*, 20 August 2001, 1.
[10]Kristina Acuna, 'Robert Downey Jnr Tops Forbes List of Highest Paid Actors', *Business Insider*, 17 July 2013, http://www.businessinsider.com/forbes-highest-paid-actors-2013-2013-7?IR=T.
[11]Natalie Robehmed, 'The World's Highest-Paid Actors 2016: The Rock Leads with Knockout $64.5 Million Year', *Forbes*, 25 August 2016, http://www.forbes.com/sites/natalierobehmed/2016/08/25/the-worlds-highest-paid-actors-2016-the-rock-leads-with-knockout-64-5-million-year/#1ab9b59f45da.

the mid-2000s, employing younger stars, writers and directors to develop projects grounded in the culture and filmmaking sensibilities of the baby boomers, but reworked for an audience that was presumed to be younger, reinforcing the trends begun in the mid-1990s with the likes of *Mission: Impossible*.

Movies and the movie market after 2000

The period after 1999 was marked by intensifying changes in the nature of the film and media market. Chief among these was the ongoing expansion of the DVD market, which became Hollywood's largest source of revenue by the mid-2000s. 'For a time', wrote Marc Graser, 'it seemed as if studios were printing money, with an explosion on DVD sales reaching some $24 billion in 2006'.[12] The trend for home viewing, which had emerged in the 1980s became the standard mechanism for watching Hollywood films for many millions of viewers, and sales of DVDs (which were higher than sales of videos had ever been) concomitantly became a dominant revenue stream for the major studios.

However, the DVD market rapidly retracted in the face of new competition from online viewing and subscription services towards the end of the decade, leading to a sharp drop in revenues from home viewing. One can gauge a sense of the decline by comparing the bestselling DVD of 2003, Pixar's *Finding Nemo*, which sold twenty-eight million copies (making it the highest selling DVD of all time), to the bestselling DVD of 2014, Pixar's *Inside Out*, which sold five million copies on Blu-ray and DVD formats combined.[13] As we will see in the conclusion, over the course of the 2000s, DVD sales surged, spiked and then declined in the face of new online viewing technologies. While most of the major studios had entered into new mergers or takeovers at the start of the decade in order to better exploit the possibilities of growing internet penetration and usage, the web nonetheless challenged and undermined Hollywood's standard modes of operation throughout the 2000s.

As early as 2001, some in the industry had identified the internet as a viable means of delivering content (rather than simply 'data') to audiences. In a 2001 profile for *Vanity Fair*, boomer agent and former Disney chief Michael Ovitz discussed his long-standing plans for a new kind of film and television delivery services: 'I had a very strong vision from day one

---

[12]Marc Graser, quoted in Tino Balio, *Hollywood in the New Millennium* (London: BFI, 2012), 2.
[13]Anon., Top-Selling DVDs in the United States 2015', *The Numbers*, http://www.the-numbers.com/home-market/dvd-sales/2015.

that it [the web] is going to deliver digital goods … programs that can be downloaded onto TVs, computers, even cell phones, and which may be sponsored, 1950s style, by targeted advertisers whose products will be used in the shows.'[14] Ovitz had attempted to develop such technologies in the 1990s with Ivan Seidenberg, who would go on to become CEO of Verizon, but, in Seidenberg's words, 'He was ten years too early. He's constantly seeing the future ahead of the rest of us.'[15] In the years between Ovitz's vision and its final realization, the internet caused far more problems than it solved.

The clearest example was Time-Warner's costly takeover by internet service provider America Online (AOL), which managed to acquire Time-Warner in 2000, creating a new conglomerate, AOL-Time-Warner, intended to capitalize on growth in the 'new' media sector. Instead, the links between AOL's service provision business model and Time-Warner's media focus failed to materialize, and the company collapsed when the dot-com bubble of the early 2000s burst, and AOL-Time-Warner reported losses of $100 million in 2002.[16]

It was only towards the end of the decade that the internet's potential as a mechanism for the distribution and viewing of filmed content was fully realized, but it should be emphasized that the ongoing growth in home viewing and widespread adoption of the internet contributed to shifts in the production ecology of the major studios, who increasingly favoured movies that would play as well at home as they did in theatres. Another key shift in the market for American movies was ongoing growth in the overseas market for Hollywood produced films. Foreign ticket sales had first outpaced domestic sales in 1994, but, according to Tino Balio, by 2010 overseas audiences consistently made up over 60 per cent of Hollywood's business.[17] New markets, such as China, promised further growth in years to come. As with home viewing in the United States, the growth in significance of overseas viewers meant that the film industry increasingly favoured movies which it was thought would play well in key overseas markets – thereby diminishing the decision-making power of American viewers at least to some degree, including the ageing boomers.

Taken in combination with the changing demographics of Hollywood's key talent (and, as we will see in the final chapter, its audience), the factors outlined above contributed to a number of changes in the nature of Hollywood's core product. After 2000, the US film industry became more reliant than ever before on high-budget tent-pole releases, often conceived

---

[14]Need Zeman, 'Michael Ovitz Take Two', *Vanity Fair*, April 2001, 231.
[15]Zeman, 'Michael Ovitz Takes Two', 233.
[16]Balio, *Hollywood in the New Millennium*, 18.
[17]Ibid., 10.

of as part of ongoing franchises, frequently aimed at younger viewers (and international audiences), though still constructed out of boomer juvenilia (especially comic books, television shows and remakes of earlier hits from boomer directors). While these family-oriented movies of all kinds had been a key part of Hollywood's output since the boomers assumed positions of prominence, and sequels or series had been common productions for far longer, the 'intensity of implementation was different' after 2000, in the words of Balio.[18] In this regard, George Lucas's PG-rated *Star Wars Episode 1: The Phantom Menace* was a harbinger of the coming changes, although it took several years for the industry to catch up.

The Phantom Menace was sometimes criticized for privileging child viewers over older fans. The *New York Post*'s review identified new character Jar Jar Binks as 'annoying, but he'll appeal to *Star Wars*' primary audience: kids'.[19] *Variety* observed that 'those most looking forward to the first new Star Wars instalment in sixteen years are mostly people – now in their thirties – who were kids when episodes four through six were released. If anything, Lucas has tilted *Phantom* away from this audience and aimed it directly at a new crop of children.[20]' Lucas appears to have assumed that by addressing the presumed tastes of children his movie would attract a broad demographic cross-section of viewers, both young and old, and he was largely correct. *The Phantom Menace* earned $474 million in the United States and Canada, and a further $552 million overseas, making it easily

IMAGE 12 *A young Anakin Skywalker (Jake Lloyd) is the focus of* Star Wars Episode 1: The Phantom Menace *(1999).*

[18]Ibid., 25.
[19]Thelma Adams, Review of *The Phantom Menace*, New York Post, 18 May 1999, http://nypost.com/1999/05/18/sexless-says-thelma-adams/.
[20]Todd McCarthy, Review of *The Phantom Menace*, Variety, 10 May 1999, http://variety.com/1999/film/reviews/star-wars-episode-i-the-phantom-menace-1117499730/.

the highest grossing release of the year, and one of the highest grossing movies of all time. In its address to children over 'youth', the movie was unlike many of the key tent pole movies of the late 1990s, but closer in spirit to Lucas's hits in the early 1980s. *The Phantom Menace,* therefore, hinted at changes in content and appeal that would come to define the movies of the 2000s.

Outside of the top ten highest grossing movies of the year, 1999 and 2000 saw the release of many films which built upon the hits of the 1990s, by focusing on historical events that might be deemed significant to baby boomers, or on the contemporary experiences of boomers themselves. Away from the DreamWorks productions discussed in the previous chapter, a good example is *Thirteen Days* (2000), a dramatized account of the Cuban Missile Crisis starring Kevin Costner and directed by Australian Roger Donaldson for New Line. The film was aimed at 'serious minded adult viewers', according to *Variety*.[21] Despite very good reviews, it grossed $66 million domestically, failing to cover its relatively high production budget of $80 million, and thus can be understood as a solid performer, but a commercial flop in pure financial terms. As such, *Thirteen Days* was one of several releases at the time of the millennium that suggested that boomer history would no longer prove viable for high-budget investment.

The highest grossing release of 2000 provided further evidence that child audiences were now a far more lucrative proposition than adults. In November, *Variety* predicted that the forthcoming Dr Seuss adaptation *How the Grinch Stole Christmas*, directed by Ron Howard, was 'likely to fade after Christmas', and might struggle to recoup its reported $175 million production cost.[22] In fact, the movie was a box office sensation despite poor reviews, earning over $260 million domestically, thereby becoming the highest grossing movie of the year.

How the Grinch Stole Christmas combined a number of developing trends. Although the film was fundamentally grounded in boomer culture – in that it was an adaptation of one of Theodore 'Dr Seuss' Geisel's most iconic children's stories of the 1950s – the content remained fundamentally child-friendly, despite the casting of teen-lure Jim Carrey. Todd McCarthy of *Variety* described the film as 'shrill, strenuous and entirely without charm', while Steven Holden wrote in the *New York Times* that it was 'so clogged with kooky gadgetry and special effects and glitter and goo that watching it feels like being gridlocked at Toys 'R' Us during the Christmas rush'.[23]

---

[21]Todd McCarthy, Review of *13 Days*, *Variety*, 4 December 2000, 21.
[22]Dade Hayes, 'Are There Legs Enough in Whoville?' *Variety*, 20 November 2000, 7.
[23]Todd McCarthy, Review of *The Grinch*, *Variety*, 16 November 2000, http://variety.com/2000/film/reviews/dr-seuss-how-the-grinch-stole-christmas-1200465392; Stephen Holden, Review of *The Grinch*, *New York Times*, 17 November 2000, http://movies.nytimes.com/movie/review?res=9E06E1D9153BF934A25752C1A9669C8B63.

Many reviewers agreed that the film had little to offer adult viewers, but it became a hit at least partially because it honed in on the tastes of younger viewers – millennials aged fourteen or, more likely, significantly younger – alongside adults. *How the Grinch Stole Christmas* can therefore be seen as an early example of a film type that became more commonplace as the 2000s rolled on. In fact, many of the criticisms levelled at the movie ultimately represented a complaint that the film was too exclusively addressed at children, in a way that adults might find tiresome. As with *The Phantom Menace*, such complaints were counteracted by the movie's colossal commercial success. Together, Lucas's and Howard's films indicated that addressing children in films which paid little apparent regard to the presumed tastes of adults, but drew upon their cultural memories, might appeal to huge audiences of millennials, gen-Xers and boomers.

At the same time, Hollywood was continuing to abandon the sort of issues-driven mid-budget movies that had once been its principal output. At the end of 2001, *Variety* identified a series of mid-budget flops as a sign that the industry did not quite understand its audience. The flops, which included Robert Redford's *The Last Castle* and *The Legend of Bagger Vance* (both DreamWorks releases) were noteworthy because they 'contradict the vow of every studio regime to make only two kinds of pics: mega budget tentpoles and $25 million niche titles. Yet here they are again, stuck in the middle with ego-driven fare, priced at well over $50 million and desperately in search of an audience'.[24] The article continued:

A false truism is that summer is the time for teenagers and kids, but autumn moviegoing is geared to adults – as if young people stop going to films once school starts. This thinking can prove a handicap as studios often stumble when they target only over 25s in their marketing. Among adults, critics play a significant role. But the few remaining critics with influence in a culture rife with blurbmeisters and web wonks often stump for arthouse releases in the fall. That leaves expensive titles with artistic pretensions – if not execution – out in the cold.[25]

The authors praised the movie *Training Day*, a police drama starring boomer Denzel Washington (b.1954) and directed by gen-Xer Antoine Fuqua (b.1966), for finding a youth audience, and concluded by drawing one other conclusion from the movie's success: 'A hip-hop soundtrack will trump a Baby Boomer ploy (even Bob Dylan) any day of the week.'[26] Here, the trade press called out studios for investing too much money in

---

[24]Dade Hayes, 'Non-Legends of the Fall', *Variety*, 12 November 2001, 1.
[25]Hayes, 'Non-legends', 1 and 46.
[26]Ibid., 46.

vanity projects, often from boomers, and targeting boomers too intensely. It suggested that studios would do better to focus on tent poles with family appeal, or niche releases – and that the boomer audience did not warrant and could not support the sort of serious releases that had become common a decade earlier. Further evidence to support such claims was provided by Warner's 2001 adaptation of J. K. Rowling's first Harry Potter novel.

Early in 2001, *Variety* noted that 'Harry Potter's generation spanning popularity has opened the floodgates at other studios and a new wave of young adult material is pouring into story departments around town'.[27] Where previously children's films had been low-budget affairs, produced almost exclusively by the Disney Company, 'modern films that aim to capitalise on a widespread hunger for stories of children and magic are a major investment. Their success rests on pricey digital effects, merchandising and multi-platform release plans – all facets of a synergistic entertainment economy that didn't exist in the days of the old Disney classics'.[28] *Variety*'s review of *Harry Potter and the Sorcerer's Stone* (2001) described it as 'a product more than a film', but nonetheless noted that 'that will have little bearing on how many times youngsters or even adults will return to this high flying entertainment that looks poised to become one of the biggest grossing films of all time'.[29] Earlier in the same month, *Variety* had complained that the industry was making too many films that targeted only over-twenty-fives and failed to make back their budgets. *Harry Potter* seemed like a corrective – ostensibly a film for children, but also somehow a film for adults too. *Variety*'s prediction proved correct, and the first Harry Potter film was the highest grossing release of the year, earning $317 million domestically and a further $657 million overseas. Later entries in the franchise performed even better commercially, and the series of eight Potter movies paved the way for more adaptations of young adult fiction such as the Twilight and Hunger Games movies.

Within a week of Potter's release, the trade press had moved on to focus on the forthcoming premier of another very similar movie, produced by Warner Brothers affiliate New Line – Peter Jackson's *The Lord of the Rings: The Fellowship of the Ring* (2001). *Variety* asked 'Can *Rings* be hotter than *Potter?*' and quoted one New Line 'insider', who said, 'Warner has concocted a more Disney-esque property with *Harry Potter*. It's a good film but it's for kids. Ours is hipper, cooler. It's the best of independent cinema.'[30] While the company tried to claim the movie was an 'indie' fantasy blockbuster from

---

[27]Jonathan Bing, 'Harry-ed Hollywood Hunting Kid Fodder', *Variety*, 29 January 2001, 9.
[28]Bing, 'Harry-ed Hollywood', 10.
[29]Todd McCarthy, 'Wizard of Awes Will Conjure Gigantic BO', *Variety*, 12 November 2001, 32 and 27.
[30]Dana Harris and Adam Dawtry, 'Can BO Postman Ring Twice?' *Variety*, 26 November 2001, 70.

obscure Kiwi horror director Peter Jackson, it was promoted as if it was very much a children's film: '*Rings* is attached to more than 40 licensed products, including videogames, toys, collectables, trading cards, even swords.'[31] Unlike the first *Harry Potter* film, which was rated PG, *The Fellowship of the Ring* was rated PG-13, which would become much more commonly applied after 2001. While a PG-13 rating suggested that the content of Jackson's film was more suited to slightly older viewers, it also represented part of a gradual shift in the application and wider cultural meaning of the PG-13 rating, which has increasingly come to be associated with relatively child-friendly films – including later entries in the Harry Potter and Star Wars franchises and superhero films.

Lord of the Rings may not have had quite the cultural traction that the Harry Potter novels had acquired in the late 1990s, but, much like *The Grinch*, it was derived from a literary property with a special meaning to boomer audiences. Kristen Thompson observes that 'the flower child generation in particular made Tolkien's books part of their culture', and to some degree, New Line's adaptation relied on the relationship between the boomers and the stories of J. R. R. Tolkien in order to ensure it was greenlit, and in order to ensure it connected with a substantial audience base.[32] Ultimately, the film would go on to become the second highest grossing release of 2001, earning $313 million at home, and $555 overseas.

DreamWorks enjoyed similar levels of success in 2001 with a child-friendly movie about a misunderstood, misanthropic green-skinned monster, in the form of the CGI animation *Shrek*, which grossed $267 million on US release and a further $216 million overseas, making it the third highest grossing release of the year. The movie, very loosely based on a children's book by William Steig, was a parody of fairy tale conventions, and by association the popular image of DreamWorks's key rival, Disney. *Shrek* was better received by mainstream critics than *The Grinch*, but both nonetheless shared a proclivity for anarchic humour. In his review for the *New York Times*, Elvis Mitchell described the movie as 'a blistering race through pop culture, and what the movie represents is a way to bring the brash slob comedy of *The Simpsons* and *South Park*, as well as the institutional irreverence of *Saturday Night Live*, to a very young audience'.[33] In this way, the multilayered comedy of *Shrek* provided older viewers with a point of access into a fantasy movie ostensibly targeted at children.

---

[31]Harris and Dawtry, 'Can BO Postman', 70.

[32]Kristen Thompson, *The Frodo Franchise: The Lord of the Rings and Modern Hollywood* (Berkeley: University of California Press, 2007), 7.

[33]Elvis Mitchell, 'So Happily Ever After, Beauty and the Beasts', *New York Times*, 16 May 2001,http://www.nytimes.com/movie/review?res=9F00E3DD153AF935A25756C0A9679C 8B63.

The top three hits of 2001, therefore, provided definitive evidence that child-friendly material, and by association children, were now the most important audience demographic of the age, leading *Variety* to declare, at the start of 2002:

> Hollywood has found its inner child. *Shrek, Harry Potter* and *The Lord of the Rings* ruled the box office like playground bullies in 2001, generating close to 10% of the year's overall $8 billion take and kicking off lucrative pic franchises. All three appealed to nearly every age group and as Disney/Pixar's *Monster's Inc* also proved, the market for family films is as robust as ever.[34]

The piece went on to note that studios were acquiring the rights to children's literature with abandon and claimed that 'the run on kiddie-lit owes something to demographics and marketing trends; chiefly films skewing towards a younger mass audience and studio execs jumping on the Potter bandwagon... For the vertically integrated congloms that own the studios, kiddie properties aren't just a popular fad; they're perfect fuel for the synergy machine'.[35] *Variety* saw this as a relatively new phenomenon, but one with roots in the 1950s, when 'Walt Disney's empire was founded on his success leveraging kid's content into feature films, TV programming and theme park rides'.[36] In a separate piece exploring the same phenomenon, staff writer Charles Lyons wrote that 'while the family film is by no means new, studios have discovered lately that the upside of such pics can be more significant than that of teen-driven event movies'.[37]

In effect, industry commentators quickly recognized that targeting films at children, rather than teens or adults, could result in enormous box office returns. In the 1950s, Hollywood had pretty much ignored the child audience and treated children's films as a minor subset of its output. In the 2000s, the studios proved much more responsive to the emergent 'millennial' generation than they ever had to the boomers. Most remarkable of all was the growing, and apparently accurate, belief that audiences of all ages would attend child-oriented movies in large numbers. Though the twelve to twenty-four demographic had increased its audience share in the late-1990s, in the 2000s, the over-forty audience consistently retained an audience share of 32 per cent or higher. By making films ostensibly for kids, but with access points for older viewers, the studios hit upon a formula that would come to define their business practices to the present day. At long last, the majority of distributors came to accept practices that had previously

[34]Jonathan Bing and Cathy Dunkley, 'Kiddy Litter Rules H'Wood', *Variety*, 7 January 2002, 1.
[35]Bing and Dunkley, 'Kiddy Litter', 1.
[36]Ibid., 1.
[37]Charles Lyons, 'Family Pix Get a Fix', *Variety*, 7 January 2002, 69.

only been associated with outlying, exceptional figures: Walt Disney in the 1930s and 1950s, George Lucas and Steven Spielberg in the early 1980s.

The growing viability of high-budget children's films was proven again in 2002 when Sony scored a colossal hit with *Spider Man*. The film, directed by Sam Raimi, featured a comic book character who had first appeared in 1962. The high school kid of Marvel's early comic book titles had proven hugely popular with boomer readers, and the 2002 film adaptation built upon the appeal of this iconic boomer figure – played by Tobey Maguire as a teenager in contemporary New York – transforming him into a superhero whose appeal bridged boomer nostalgia, teen angst and child-friendly pulp heroics. The film was the highest grossing release of 2002, earning $403 million in North America, and a $418 million overseas. Other key hits of the year included new entries in the Harry Potter and Lord of the Rings franchises, alongside George Lucas's *Star Wars Episode II: Attack of the Clones* (2002), all of which adopted a similar strategy and succeeded with a similar audience. Kids films were, and would remain, consistently the most reliable commercial propositions of the age.

The ongoing Star Wars, Potter and Lord of the Rings series were bolstered by a growing trend for comic book adaptations. Following the success of *X-Men* in 1999 and *Spider-Man* in 2002 the trade press reported that 'Hollywood is scouring comic publishers' vaults for more movie-worthy characters'.[38] Bob Levin, MGM's president of marketing and distribution, explained at the time, 'When they're successful, you're dealing with a compelling character in chapter stories. Then it's very easy to spin that character into another chapter for a sequel.'[39] At the end of the decade, comic book adaptations superseded children's fantasy as the most popular source material for high-budget movies, and the period since 2008 has been marked by the astounded commercial performance of interconnected superhero franchises, which repeatedly gross over a billion dollars on worldwide release. The success of Marvel Studios (the film production wing of the comic book company) and Legendary Entertainment (a hedge fund which specializes in funding and producing comic book adaptations and related genre releases) provides a particularly striking example of the primacy that superhero movies now enjoy. Marvel's most popular characters mostly originated in the 1960s and 1970s, and found their first audience with baby boomers. Their current success is a testament to the boomer-era nostalgia that underpins the key releases of the post-2000 period. Boomer-age characters receive relatively little screen time in movies such as Legendary/Warner's *The Dark Knight* (2008) or Marvel's *Iron Man 3* (2012), but the characters at the centre of these films were a key part of the boomers' early cultural experience, and

---

[38]David Bloom, 'Comic Caper Captivate Studios', *Variety*, 24 June 2002, 9.
[39]Bob Levin, quoted in Bloom, 'Comic Caper', 9.

the high-budget, family-friendly films in which they feature owe a clear debt to the early filmmaking predilections of figures such as Spielberg and Lucas.

To some extent, Hollywood has been recycling the past, in the form of either historical films, remakes or revived genre production, for much of its history. Nostalgia, which Paul Grainge has described as 'a yearning... a form of idealized remembrance... claiming a vision of stability or authenticity in some conceptual "golden age"', certainly underpinned many of the early films released by key baby boomer filmmakers.[40] George Lucas's *American Graffiti* and Robert Zemeckis's *Back to the Future* were sold on the faux naïf appeal of 1950s and 1960s youth culture, while the science fiction, adventure and comedy movies of Lucas, Spielberg, Landis and others explicitly revisited the popular culture of the 1950s. It is probably no surprise that this era of cinema history would encourage yet another wave of nostalgia in future generations, grounded as ever in the commercial imperatives of the film industry. Before selling Lucasfilm to the Disney Company, George Lucas effectively reformulated his *Star Wars* franchise as an essentially nostalgic media brand, and in 2008 he teamed up with Steven Spielberg once more to produce a new entry in the Indiana Jones franchise, *Indiana Jones and the Kingdom of the Crystal Skull* (2008). Unlike other Indiana Jones movies, the latest entry was set in the 1950s, and filled with explicit references to the cultural touchstones of the early boomers – teenage bikers, UFOs, Cold War paranoia and, in one eerie sequence, the dangers that nuclear conflagration posed to the American suburban idyll.

The year before, Steven Spielberg had teamed up with director Michael Bay to produce *Transformers* (2007), based on a popular toy line from the early 1980s. This was followed in 2009 by director J. J. Abrams' *Star Trek*, a reworking of the 1960s series, and Abrams would go on to direct an explicit Spielberg homage in the form of the science fiction drama *Super 8* in 2011 (produced by Spielberg himself). Later, Abrams directed the first entry in the Star Wars series to be produced without George Lucas's involvement, *Star Wars: The Force Awakens* (2015), which, far more so than Lucas's prequels, played upon a nostalgia for the iconography and narrative terrain of the original movies. Like the most recent Indiana Jones film, it featured Harrison Ford returning in one of his most iconic roles, and the story was focused on a new generation investigating the legendary accomplishments of an older generation. Other remakes and sequels of iconic boomer-era movies included *Jurassic World* (2015) and *Ghostbusters* (2016).

Ultimately the nostalgia which motivates these productions has as much to do with brand recognition as any great creative agenda. Nonetheless, the growth of remakes, reboots and belated sequels provide an insight into

---

[40]Paul Grainge, 'Nostalgia and Style in Retro America: Moods, Modes and Media Recycling', *Journal of American Culture* 23, No. 1 (2000), 28.

the status and legacy of the baby boomer filmmakers today, whose creative influence continues to resonate, even if their recent creative contributions do not.

The Disney Company and the limits of nostalgia

Just as it had in the early 1980s, it took the Disney Company's production arm some time to catch up with the shifting trajectory of the wider film industry. The company had enjoyed success throughout the 1990s with a series of highly performing animated movies, starting with *The Little Mermaid* in 1989. By the early 2000s, Disney's feature animations were stalling in the face of external competition from DreamWorks, and internal competition from Pixar, whose films Disney distributed but did not fully own. Nevertheless, Disney's senior management recognized the shifting currents of audience demand. Peter Schneider, briefly in tenure as Disney's head of production following the departure of Joe Roth in 1999, told *Variety* in 2000 that his goal was to reshape Disney as 'an even more family friendly studio that centers on resurrecting the Walt Disney Pictures brand for the entire family, not just for kids'.[41] Many of Schneider's strategies involved attempts to reduce costs and streamline production, but the two core goals he set himself neatly described the trajectory of the post-2000 period: 'make dramatic films that will play for the whole family', and 'think franchise'.[42] In the end, Schneider spent relatively little time in the role before departing in 2001, but his aims – to focus on an all-age audience (with children very much at its centre), and develop franchises rather than standalone movies – would become central for all studios in the 2000s.

While Schneider's plan, to emphasize all-age blockbuster entertainment, was already being adopted by other studios – especially Warner Bros – Disney was struggling to reach its core audience in the early 2000s. *Variety* identified a series of 'migraine inducing' problems for the company:

> Chief among them, the theme park business is ailing; Disney stores profits are down; the internet division was closed last year at a loss to the company of over $500 million; ABC network could finish fourth this year, and then there is the company's flagship feature animation division which has been in decline. Meanwhile, other studios are crowding in on what was once a Disney stronghold – the youth [here meaning children] market.[43]

---

[41]Charles Lyons, 'New Mickey Mouse Club', *Variety*, 9 October 2000, 1.
[42]Lyons, 'New Mickey Mouse Club', 1.
[43]Cathy Bunkly and Charles Lyons, 'Pics get tricky for Mickey', *Variety*, 17 December 2001, 1.

The studio was kept afloat by its buoyant DVD and home viewing operations. *Variety* recognized this in 2000, when it ran a lead editorial with the following 'scoop':

> OK, here's the real inside dope on Hollywood. The biggest hit of the year was not *The Grinch* or *MI:2* but rather *Tarzan*. Yes *Tarzan*. And Universal did not really threaten Disney's market share. The Mouse House had the top three money makers of the year. And if you want to talk about real blockbusters, how about *The Little Mermaid II: Return to the Sea*. Of course we're talking about the vid world here [which] hit $20 billion for the first time – nearly triple the domestic box office. And the key factor powering this boom is DVD.[44]

Tarzan reportedly earned $268 million in retail DVD and video sales, compared to its $172 million gross at the US box office.[45] The success of the aforementioned *The Little Mermaid II: Return to the Sea* clearly demonstrated the extent to which the DVD market could be relied upon for family-oriented product. Throughout the DVD boom, Disney was able to produce a series of highly lucrative sequels and spin-offs intended exclusively for the home market. The studio came to realize that 'if it were possible to sell over 10 million copies of a movie such as *The Lion King* ... the same consumers [would] buy a branded property that was not released to theatres'.[46]

The studio's connection with theatre audience got back on track with movies such as the Pirates of the Caribbean franchise, which were able to compete directly with *Harry Potter* and *Lord of the Rings*. As with other key franchises developed after this time, *Pirates of the Caribbean: Curse of the Black Pearl* (2001) was an inherently nostalgic proposition. Pirates of the Caribbean was one of the company's best-known theme park rides, which provided an atmospheric journey below the 'New Orlean's Square' area of Disneyland. The ride opened at Disneyland in Anaheim in 1967, very shortly after Disney's death. It built upon the popular image of the pirate that featured in many films during the 1950s and 1960s, including Disney releases such as the live action version of *Treasure Island* (1950), *Peter Pan* (1952), *The Swiss Family Robinson* (1960) and *Blackbeard's Ghost* (1968), as well as Warner Bros' *Captain Horatio Hornblower RN* (1951) Columbia's *The Crimson Pirate* (1950) and Fritz Lang's *Moonfleet* (1955). Marty Sklar, president of the Imagineering division for many years,

---

[44]Scott Hettrick, 'Tarzan Puts Grinch in Vidlock', *Variety*, 8 January 2001, 1.
[45]Hettrick, 'Tarzan Puts Grinch', 79.
[46]Ulin, *The Business of Media Distribution*, 182.

has described it as 'Disney's quintessential, signature attraction. We measure everything we do against Pirates of the Caribbean'.[47]

A movie adaptation was tentatively developed over many years by screenwriters Ted Eliot (b.1961) and Terry Rossio (b.1960), both long-standing Disney staff members responsible for many of the studio's animated hits in the late 1980s and early 1990s. The pair were, apparently, seeking to write a 'pirate movie in the grand swashbuckling tradition of Captain Blood and The Crimson Pirate', but, in their words, 'nobody was making sword-fighting movies anymore'.[48] Disney eventually appointed producer Jerry Bruckheimer to oversee the project. Bruckheimer, too, claims to have been inspired by the pirate movies of his youth, 'I loved watching pirate pictures as a kid. Treasure Island, Captain Blood and The Black Pirate were some of my favorites. Errol Flynn and Douglas Fairbanks were formidable, and although their movies are still exciting and very watchable today, I thought we could add some extra pizzazz.'[49] Bruckheimer and Disney then appointed Gore Verbinski (b.1964) to direct. Almost all of the talent involved were 'late' boomers, if they can be considered boomers at all, who would have been children when the ride first opened. This includes star Johnny Depp who was born in 1963. Verbinski was a young filmmaker who had gotten his big break at another studio very closely tied to the boomer filmmaking traditions of the 1980s and 1990s – DreamWorks, which released his feature debut Mousehunt in 1997 and his follow-up crime drama The Mexican in 2001.

Despite the fact that the project was grounded in Disney lore, it did not receive unanimous support. Michael Eisner, then COO and CEO of the company, 'disliked Pirates of the Caribbean, and was afraid association with the theme park ride would hurt the movie with the key teenage demographic, who would assume the movie was for children', according to James B. Stewart.[50] As we have seen, Eisner's thinking was typical of studio executives from the 1960s until 2000. Nevertheless, the movie was distributed by Disney, rather than its Touchstone label, with a PG-13 rating and Eisner's fear that teens might be deterred by the association with Disney's brand proved misguided. The movie earned $305 million on domestic release, making more on DVD, and generated a series of increasingly successful sequels. Stewart attributes the somewhat unexpected success of the film to 'how unerringly [Johnny] Depp's performance taps into the irreverent instincts of many moviegoing teenagers', and reports that 'many teenage boys saw it multiple times'.[51]

---

[47]Marty Sklar, quoted in Jason Surrell, Pirates of the Caribbean: From the Magic Kingdom to the Movies (New York: Disney, 2006), 52.
[48]Both quoted in Surrell, Pirates of the Caribbean, 113.
[49]Surrell, Pirates of the Caribbean, 116.
[50]James B. Stewart, Disneywar (London: Pocket Books, 2006), 437.
[51]Stewart, Disneywar, 440.

Other attempts to apply the same filmmaking template failed for Disney, most notably in the form of its 2013 movie *The Lone Ranger*, which was made by the same team as the earlier Pirates movies – director Gore Verbinski, producer Jerry Bruckheimer, writers Eliot and Rossio and star Johnny Depp – and was based on an iconic character from the 1930s and 1950s. If anything, the film was more explicitly nostalgic, but it failed to find an audience in a year crowded with highly budgeted science fiction movies and comic book adaptations. It generated $88 million in the United States and $150 overseas, on a £215 million budget, making it a substantial flop. Many reviewers suggested that the movie was unappealing because there was little nostalgia among younger viewers for *The Lone Ranger* or westerns in general. In the *New York Times*, A. O. Scott wrote that

> *The Lone Ranger* belongs to the ancient pop culture of the Great Depression and the early baby boom. His adventures were heard on radio, starting in the 1930s, and seen on television from 1949 to 1957, but unlike some of his cape-wearing peers, he has mostly stayed in the past, an object of fuzzy nostalgia and mocking incredulity, a symbol of simple pleasures and retrograde attitudes.[52]

The movie ultimately pointed to the limits of nostalgia, in a market where filmmakers and audience were more interested in the cinematic heritage of the 1980s rather than ever more distant 1950s. While *Pirates of the Caribbean* was one part of the puzzle, Disney only really regained its preeminent position in US media culture when Michael Eisner was replaced as president by Bob Iger (b.1951) in 2005. Iger had worked in television for much of his career, and began to rise through the ranks of the Disney Company after it bought the ABC network in 1996. One of Iger's central strategies when he ascended to the most senior position at Disney was to acquire family-oriented media brands developed elsewhere or held at one remove from Disney's main business (Pixar, Lucasfilm and Marvel Studios), and to hire those staff members who had beaten Disney at its own game earlier in the 2000s – such as Alan Horn, who had overseen the Harry Potter and Dark Knight franchises at Warner Bros. In effect, Iger reconstructed the Disney brand and broadened its corporate portfolio to bring family-friendly productions under the company's aegis rather than develop them in house. 'We used to have huge volatility in our movie studio. It could make $200m one year and $800m the next', he told the *Financial Times* in 2016. 'Now, there will be some fluctuation, like a big *Star Wars* movie in a given year,

---

[52]A.O. Scott, 'Hero rides again, with big boots to fill', *New York Times*, 2 July 2013, http://movies.nytimes.com/2013/07/03/movies/in-the-lone-ranger-tonto-takes-center-stage.html?partner=rss&emc=rss&_r=1&.

but [the returns] are going to be much more steady. And they will deliver to our bottom line.'[53]

Unlike Eisner, Iger also appears to have recognized the potency of Disney's brand with older viewers in the post-2000 period. While Eisner used the Touchstone label in the 1980s to release movies without invoking the family-friendly connotations of the Disney brand, Iger restricted use of the Touchstone label, which is today only used for R-rated movies and to distribute movies produced by DreamWorks SKG (which had entered into a short-term distribution partnership with Disney in 2015). In this regard, Iger appears to have recognized that the route to commercial success lies in appealing to the child audience first.

Disney's relationship with Pixar Animation Studios was another factor in its growing move to dominance. Pixar had started as a part of Lucasfilm's computing division, which had been sold to Apple mogul Steve Jobs in 1986. The company had started making computer animated shorts and advertisements in the late 1980s, and had moved into film production when a production agreement with Disney was signed in 1991. Disney invested $26 million for the right to distribute three full-length Pixar movies, starting with *Toy Story* in 1995. The film proved a major success, earning $191 million in North America and a further $170 million overseas, making it the highest grossing release of the year. From then on, Disney and Pixar enjoyed a profitable but fractious relationship.

Throughout this time Pixar was led by John Lasseter (b.1957 in LA), an animation buff who got his first break in Hollywood when he enrolled on the Disney-sponsored Character Animation Programme at California Institute of the Arts Film School in the late 1970s. He started as an animator at Disney in 1979, was fired and then moved to Lucasfilm's computer division in 1984. As a younger boomer, Lasseter was inspired both by 1950s and 1960s Americana, and the work of the pioneering boomer filmmakers who preceded him:

There are a few moments in my life that had focused why I do what I do. And one of them was in May 1977 at the Chinese Theatre on Hollywood Boulevard, seeing *Star Wars* for the first time. I'd won a place at CalArts so I already wanted to be an animator – but after standing in line for six hours and being in this first week crowd in this huge theatre. ... I was shaking by the end, I was so excited. It entertained the audience on another level: people were screaming, having so much fun. And I looked at this audience and thought to myself that animation could do that to.[54]

---

[53]Matthew Garrahan, 'Bob Iger Broadens Disney's Horizons in Age of Disruption', *Financial Times*, 7 March 2016, http://www.ft.com/cms/s/0/e0e70758-e21d-11e5-96b7-9f778349aba2. html#axzz4EBhZhM2W.
[54]Quoted in Anon., 'A Night to Remember', *Time Out London*, 27 February 2001, 14.

Under his management, Pixar's movies pushed Hollywood towards the family audience in the 1990s, and transformed animation into an even more commercially viable mainstream form. The company's films were also infused with the same nostalgia for childhood and for the cultural experiences of the baby boom that were writ large across the rest of the industry.

A good example can be seen in Pixar's Toy Story films, which focus on the concerns of a group of toys who come to life when their owner, Andy, leaves the room. In part the films provide quintessential juvenile fantasy, in that they invite children to wonder what their toys would do and say if they could speak and move. However, the narrative gains considerable thematic complexity and resonance because the toys are aware of their status as toys, and for the most part, their concerns are prosaic, middle-class and middle American. Several are voiced by iconic boomer stars, most notably Tom Hanks as the cowboy Woody, and Tim Allen as the astronaut Buzz Lightyear. The first film is a slapstick comedy which focuses on Buzz's realization that he is a toy. The second includes many more references to events of the baby boom.

Toy Story 2, released in 2000, reveals that Woody is a family heirloom, passed down across several generations, who was originally featured on a 1950s television series. His show 'Woody's Round Up' was cancelled following the success of the space programme: 'Once the astronauts went up', Woody is told, 'children only wanted to play with space toys'. In these moments, Toy Story 2, more than any other entry in Pixar's back catalogue, marries its nostalgia for childhood and toys to a keen sense of the boomer's formative cultural years. Woody is emblematic of an earlier era in children's movie culture, one familiar to parents or grandparents in the auditorium. A similar nostalgia for 1960s car culture, and 1960s spy movies, informs Pixar's Cars movies, also directed by Lasseter. The first of these, 2006's Cars, was a highly nostalgic homage to small-town Americana. Bizarrely, Cars 2 (2011) is equally nostalgic, this time for the James Bond films of the 1960s and their many imitators. The same nostalgia for 1960s spy movies informs Pixar's The Incredibles (2004), which is set in a glamorized and idealized milieu of post-war American suburbia. Meanwhile in Up (2009) the central character is an elderly suburbanite, seeking a life of adventure in South America, following the death of his wife. In all of these Pixar movies, intergenerational relationships, usually between parents and their children, form the basic elements of the plot.

In January 2006, Pixar's often fractious relationship with Disney was transformed when Disney acquired Pixar outright in a deal worth $7.4 billion, and Lasseter became chief creative officer of Disney animation, tasked with reviving the company's flagging department. The success of animated movies such as Tangled (2011), Wreck It Ralph (2012) and Frozen (2013) clearly owe some debt to Lasseter's management. These films are less infused with nostalgia than Pixar's releases (although *Wreck It Ralph* harks back to a 'golden age' of videogames in the 1980s and 1990s), but they nonetheless provide compelling evidence of Lasseter's creative influence. With John Lasseter, Robert Iger, Kathleen Kennedy, Alan Horn and others occupying positions of corporate pre-eminence at Disney, the company reached new heights of commercial success, dominating the film production landscape by 2016.

Conclusion

By 2016, the baby boomers' position within Hollywood was complex and contradictory. While boomers continued to occupy executive roles, many directors, writers and producers had willingly or unwillingly retired from active filmmaking. (When approached to contribute to this book in 2013, George Lucas's office responded that he was 'currently enjoying his retirement'.) The boomers' formative experiences continued to provide rich source material for Hollywood productions, but relatively few of these projects originated with active boomer filmmakers. Those boomers who continued to make movies with frequency occupied positions on the edge of mainstream trends, but nonetheless seemed able to retain some creative control over their movies as a result of their reputation. These directors, notably Spielberg, Howard and Zemeckis, mostly focused on making the kinds of issues-based entertainment movies that they had begun to favour in the 1990s, and exhibited a restrained ambivalence about current, higher budget franchise releases.

Lawrence Kasdan, speaking shortly after he had begun work on J. J. Abrams's *Star Wars: The Force Awakens*, told us that

> I want [the new Star Wars films] to be more human. The original Star Wars saga is a metaphor for people losing their humanity and fighting to get it back, and the people who lose their humanity become machines. They become Darth Vader. The same thing has happened to the movies. Movies that used to be based on emotion are now based on sensation. Emotion has been completely denigrated and characters have been denigrated and our patience has been denigrated, because you can't take any time to do anything, except take 40 minutes to destroy a city and you're going out of your mind with boredom – but they won't take 2 minutes to create a character or have a quiet moment.

Kasdan implied that movies had changed at a formal and structural level in the years after the release of Lucas's original Star Wars trilogy, and his comments fell very much into the same lines as wider critical debates that had emerged in academia in the 1990s. Warren Buckland has neatly summarized such claims in his observation that 'narrative complexity is sacrificed on the altar of spectacle' in many modern films.[55]

The extent to which modern blockbusters represent a break with past conventions is debatable, because so many seem built on a combination of nostalgia and a drive to entertain that defined the boomer's influence on Hollywood more generally. Moreover, such films do still coexist with more intimate independent dramas. Perhaps a more significant change has been a broad move away from funding mid-budget movies, in favour of either very low or very high-budget productions, which numerous boomer filmmakers have found an impediment to their filmmaking projects. Jerry Zucker described the situation by saying:

> Studios now would rather be in the business of spending $200 million to make $2 billion on a comic book title, than they would spending $25 million on the hope it might gross $80. Because those big films are actually more resilient, because when you look at it, they hit at a much higher percentage. There seems to be no end to the public appetite, particularly outside the United States, for those kind of films. A lot of movies that didn't do that well here did big business in other places. China is an emerging huge market. And it helps that those movies are not United States based. Even if they take place here, they're not about the US, they're simply located there. They're otherworldly.

As a result, filmmakers seeking to develop issues-based movies, or mid-budget entertainment films, have struggled to elicit the kind of financial support they had previously depended on, especially in the 1990s. Nancy Meyers told us in 2013:

> I'm trying to figure out the landscape. It seems to me that the people running the studios are on very short leashes right now, profits are not up and people are confused about what to make. The options are just not there anymore. And if I'm going through this, and I've had this really good long streak, I can't imagine what it's like for people who haven't had movies made recently, who have wonderful ideas and great scripts that they're sitting on. It's very tough right now.

In comparing his own filmmaking career to that of his son, Jason (b.1977), Ivan Reitman explained:

> Jason decided on a whole different tack. I'm a refugee and an immigrant, and struggled somewhat, although I never thought of it as a struggle. So

---

[55]Warren Buckland, 'A Close Encounter with *Raiders of the Lost Ark*: Notes on Narrative Aspects of the New Hollywood Blockbuster', in Steve Neale and Murray Smith, eds, *Contemporary Hollywood Cinema* (London: Routledge, 1998), 167.

I've always been an entertainment guy. Jason never thought that. His ideas, his audience is the film festival audience, the independent group. His most expensive movie cost $25 million. Most of his films have cost between $10 million and $15 million.

The overwhelming triumph of the ultra high-budget, child-oriented franchise movie is the defining story of American cinema after 1999, and it represents the culmination of a decades-long journey. In the 1950s, when the baby boomers first became a significant audience, the American film industry purported to make movies for viewers of all ages, but most commonly focused on adult-oriented stories with some elements targeted at children. Disney was left to define the features of the family-friendly blockbuster, largely untroubled by competition from the other major distributors, who catered increasingly to occasional cinemagoers, attracted by spectacular event movies. Throughout the 1970s and into the 1990s, Hollywood's core audience fragmented, as filmmakers pursued the baby boomers and then other demographics, with more targeted releases aimed at families, teens or adults.

By the end of the 2010s, Hollywood appears to have come full circle, as a process which had begun with baby boomer filmmakers like Spielberg and Lucas, who were sometimes accused of juvenalizing American movies in the 1980s, permeated production plans. Almost all of the franchise movies developed during this period were greenlit by boomers in executive roles, and derived either from the shared popular culture of the boomers or from a growing nostalgia for the early film works of boomers themselves. What makes this new generation of blockbusters distinctive is that they have been targeted at younger viewers, but with some elements for teens and adults, a reversal of 1950s practice but with the same intention of finding a universal audience. Early in 2017, the *Hollywood Reporter* outlined a situation that sounded strikingly familiar to debates which had raged throughout the 1950s. It explained that

> in the US, children younger than 18 make up 25 per cent of the population. Worldwide, more than 25 per cent are under age 15. Kids also are going to the movies more frequently than other sectors of the populace, according to the MPAA. Though nearly every demo of moviegoers declined in 2015, two did not: those ages 2-to-11 and those ages 25-to-39 – kids and their parents – and that audience is especially lucrative when it comes to home entertainment.[56]

The piece went on to quote box office analyst Paul Dergarabedian, who argued that preferred ratings were changing in response to these shifts, and

[56]This and subsequent quotation, Pamela McClintock, 'Why PG Has Become the New Go-To Rating for Movies', *Hollywood Reporter*, 31 March 2017, http://www.hollywoodreporter.com/news/why-pg-has-become-new-go-rating-studio-movies-986239.

that targeting this new generation of children might assure wider box office appeal: 'PG has become the new go-to rating. From a business perspective, the rating is perfect because you can grab everyone from little kids to Grandma.' Where such logic was ignored after the 1950s, targeting a PG-13 or PG rating underpinned the strategies of almost all the major Hollywood distributors in the 2010s, which, to a greater or lesser extent, have broadly adopted a business model developed by Disney in the 1950s. It has taken seventy years, and the entire life cycle of the boomers, for Hollywood to effectively respond, at least in commercial terms, to shifting demographics that first disrupted its relationship with its audience in the 1950s. Boomers still appeared in these films, and still watched them in droves, but the film industry no longer paid as much attention to them as a demographic group when planning its release strategies. The boomers became a source of creative inspiration. They had crafted a legacy and moved on.

Conclusion: A Legacy

While their status as working filmmakers gradually declines, the boomer filmmakers discussed throughout this book have, today, largely reached a point where their legacy and influence is more substantial than their ongoing work. For example, Steven Spielberg's *The BFG* performed poorly at the domestic box office in 2016, but his influence could be felt in a huge range of family-friendly blockbusters, such as 2015's *Jurassic World* and in television shows like Netflix's *Stranger Things* (2016), which directly invoked nostalgia for the early films of the boomers. In this conclusion, we ask, how have the boomer filmmakers sought to craft a wider legacy, on and off the screen? Moreover, how do boomer audiences understand the cinemagoing experience today? And finally, how does Hollywood now depict the ageing boomers?

Passing the torch

A number of the filmmakers we have discussed throughout this book got their start at the University of Southern California's (USC) School of Cinematic Arts, and in recent years, the school has come to bear the imprint of their legacy very clearly. Although in the 1960s, George Lucas's tutors had been sceptical about the ability of their students to find a place in the film industry – as we saw in Chapter 6 – the school increasingly evolved into a centre for industry-focused training, and many boomers found their education at USC closely enmeshed with the priorities of the industry. In 1984, Stephen Farber wrote of the school's development:

> USC operated along the lines of a trade school. The purpose of its curriculum was specifically to train students to work in the movie business; the studios even offered apprenticeships and fellowships to USC graduates. In addition, the kind of student film project encouraged by the USG cinema department was the traditional narrative film with a strong story and slick production values.[1]

---

[1]Stephen Farber, 'The USC Connection', *Film Comment* 20, No. 3 (May 1984), 34–5.

More than that, USC also acted as a site where young filmmakers could network and share ideas:

> USC fostered a kind of young-boys network designed to help its graduates … 'USC was how I cracked into the film business,' says Robert Zemeckis, who was there from 1971 to 1973. 'I made a student film that won a lot of awards, so I would just call the USC graduates and say to them, "I'm a USC student, and I made this student film. Would you take a look at it?" John Milius, George Lucas, Hal Barwood, and Matthew Robbins were all really receptive to SC film students.'
> Zemeckis also met Steven Spielberg through film school. 'The last day of the semester they said we were going to meet with a young director, Steven Spielberg. After the class I hung back and said to him, "I have this student film. Would you like to see it?" He set up a screening, and we became close friends.'[2]

As we have seen in this book, the first group of filmmakers associated with USC, almost all of them boomers, changed the direction of American filmmaking more than once. They skewed the content and commercial performance of mainstream Hollywood film production via their preoccupation with entertainment, which itself was frequently grounded in the cultural baggage of their own childhood. As they grew older, and their early preoccupations with youth audiences and youth culture came to dominate American movies, they also sought to foster a cinematic legacy grounded in socially conscious filmmaking, which combined entertainment with edification. And as they hit old age, and many retired from active filmmaking or came to occupy positions of operational control at the major studios, their films became a cultural touchstone for new generations of filmmakers.

USC was one of the places where this culture was forged, and it is perhaps no surprise that some of the most influential boomer filmmakers have seen it as a place where their legacy might take physical form. In 1980, George Lucas 'donated $4.7m to his alma mater, the University of SoCal, to assist in the construction of a new five-building complex for the division of Cinema and TV', laying the groundwork for a department that would increasingly come to celebrate the achievements of its most famous alumni and their colleagues.[3] In later years, Lucas and his peers would make increasingly generous donations to USC, but would also use their contributions to shape the school more and more directly. In 2001 the *Los Angeles Times* reported that Robert Zemeckis was 'going back to the future

[2]Farber, 'The USC Connection', 35.
[3]Anon., '£4.7 million for USC from Lucas', *Hollywood Reporter*, 21 November 1980, 1.

with the creation of the Digital Arts complex at the USC school of Cinema and Television, his alma mater'.[4]

In 2006, Lucas provided a far larger donation, and consequently took on a more substantial role in shaping the design and overall ethos of the school.

> Motion-picture magnate George Lucas sought to recreate the ambience [of 1920s Californian-Mediterranean architecture] in providing the creative vision and nearly half of the funding for a new six-building, $170 million complex for his alma mater, the University of Southern California's School of Cinematic Arts. Mr. Lucas contributed $75 million for the buildings and $100 million for SCA's endowment.[5]

He later told *Business Week*, 'Why pick now to give one of the largest gifts ever to a film school? I always told them, "wait until I'm sixty" ... So, when I finished with the last Star Wars and I decided to more or less retire, I decided this was the time.'[6]

The complex's crown jewels are the George Lucas Building and the Steven Spielberg building, which sit alongside the Robert Zemeckis Center for Digital Arts, the Marilyn and Jeffrey Katzenberg Center for Animation, the John Williams Soundstage and many other similar spaces. Elsewhere on the USC campus is Spielberg's Survivors of the Shoah archive, a repository of filmed Holocaust survivor testimonies that has its roots in the production of *Schindler's List*.

The Cinematic Arts complex at USC is a concrete example of these boomers' attempts to cement their legacy. Jack Epps Jr, now professor of Cinematic Arts at USC, explains:

> We feel a deep legacy to the motion picture industry. It started in 1929 with Douglas Fairbanks and the Academy of Motion Picture Arts and Sciences. The people who work here believe that we're part of a tradition of filmmaking in Hollywood; we're not just a film school. So our goal is very much to educate the next generation of filmmakers, but also to allow them to tell their story their way.

That sense of tradition extends from the curriculum to the architecture, which is grounded in George Lucas's fascination with the largely abandoned architectural styles of the 1920s. The faculty can also then be understood

---

[4]Bill Desowitz, 'Digital Cinema Gets a Push', *Los Angeles Times*, 4 March 2001, 82.

[5]Catesby Leigh, 'What George Lucas Wrought', *Wall Street Journal*, 2 June 2010, http://www.wsj.com/articles/SB10001424052748703460404575244732489548088.

[6]Ronald Grover, 'The Many Gifts of George Lucas', *Business Week*, 11 October 2006, https://www.bloomberg.com/news/articles/2006-10-09/the-many-gifts-of-george-lucasbusinessweek-business-news-stock-market-and-financial-advice.

as an attempt to safeguard the legacy of the baby boomers (rooted as it has frequently been in nostalgia), by linking them to a much longer history of Hollywood filmmaking, and also positioning them as mentors for a new generation of aspiring filmmakers. Not content with seeing themselves as entertainers or craftsmen, the USC campus reveals the extent to which Spielberg, Lucas, Zemeckis and various others have, in recent years, finessed their status as the architects and elder statesmen of the wider American film industry.

A cursory glance at the position of boomer-related movies in 2016 reveals both their cultural reach and the limitations of their status. Spielberg, Zemeckis and Ron Howard were the most high-profile boomer directors with movies on release, but *The BFG*, *Allied* and *Inferno* (a child-oriented Roald Dahl adaptation, a Second World War romantic thriller and a Dan Brown adaptation) performed poorly in the domestic market, earning $55 million, $38 million and $34 million respectively, on domestic release at the time of writing. But the year's highest grossing releases were the Pixar animation *Finding Dory*, *Captain America: Civil War* and *Rogue One: A Star Wars Story*. All had generation X directors – Andrew Stanton (b.1965); Joe and Anthony Russo (b.1971 and 1973); Gareth Edwards (b.1975) – and all bore some debt to the filmmaking predilections of the baby boomers. *Finding Dory* was an animated family adventure which paid narrative homage to Steven Spielberg's early work; *Captain America* was yet another Marvel movie built upon the pop culture of the 1960s; and *Rogue One* was a direct prequel to Lucas's first *Star Wars* film. *Finding Dory* and *Rogue One* were also produced by boomers, John Lasseter and Kathleen Kennedy, who occupy key positions as heads of Pixar and Lucasfilm respectively. Remarkably, all three were also distributed by the Walt Disney Company, headed by boomer Robert Iger. By the end of the year, it was clear that the boomers' influence, and the wider legacy of their most iconic films, was far greater than the individual success of the movies they still made as writers or directors.

Furthermore, the Walt Disney Company's transformation over the previous seventy years was another potent confirmation of the boomers' power as filmmakers and, more importantly, as film viewers. Walt Disney was one of the few in Hollywood who had recognized the commercial value of the baby boomer audience in the 1950s. Although its commercial reach had waxed and waned over the years, by the 2010s, Disney had cemented its position as Hollywood's leading distributor, and its reputation in recent years has been built upon nostalgia for the youth culture of the baby boomers (in the form of Disney's back catalogue and also the strain of retrograde Americana that inform its parks, as well as key movie brands such as Marvel and Star Wars). Reporting on the 2016 annual shareholders' meeting, the *New York Times* observed that even today, 'the Disney brand in many ways turns on nostalgia'.[7] While Disney's core consumers today, and the wider audience for movies in America, are no longer principally made up of baby boomers, their tastes nonetheless underpin much of Disney's output, not least because for so long they were the company's most important audience. In its theme parks and other ventures during the 1950s, Disney 'created mockups of his own childhood memories and fantasies which he invited others from his own generation to share with their children and grandchildren'.[8] A similar process is at play in the Disney company's movie output today, which mines the memories of boomer audiences but also gen-Xers and millennials raised on the movies of boomer filmmakers. But what role does the boomer audience play in this new moviemaking culture?

Audiences

According to the MPAA, admissions to North American movie theatres have fallen slightly across the 2000s. In 2003, the business experienced a record high of 1.52 billion admissions in the United States and Canada.[9] By 2015, admissions had fallen to 1.32 billion. Admissions have fluctuated throughout this period, with 2011 seeing the steepest drop to 1.28 billion, but box office revenues have consistently risen, from $9.2 billion in 2003 to $10.8 billion in 2012, and $11.1 billion in 2015. Ticket price rises, and the added cost of 3D (which has made up 10–20 per cent of all sales since 2009), mean that box office revenues have still increased while domestic audiences have actually declined. Increasingly the kinds of high-budget blockbusters that appear to dominate US production are targeted at international markets, which in 2015 accounted for 71 per cent of worldwide ticket sales.

Perhaps the most remarkable trend within this data has been the relative reliability of the boomer audience, who visit movie theatres less often than in their youth, but who continue to generate a substantial volume of overall ticket sales. Since 1999, over-forties have consistently made up a third of the total moviegoing audience.[10] In 2011, the proportion of tickets sales to over-forties (39 per cent) once again overtook the twelve to twenty-four demographic (34 per cent) for the first time since 1994. This time, however,

---

[7]Brooks Barnes, 'At Disney's Annual Meetings, Cruise Ships and Questions from Kids', *New York Times*, 3 March 2016, http://www.nytimes.com/interactive/2016/03/03/business/media/disney-bog-iger-shareholder-annual-meeting.html?_r=0.
[8]Gary Cross, *Consumed Nostalgia: Memory in the Age of Fast Capitalism* (New York: Columbia University Press, 2015), 206.
[9]All data in this paragraph is derived from Motion Picture Association of America, *Theatrical Market Statistics 2015*, available online via http://www.mpaa.org/wp-content/uploads/2016/04/MPAA-Theatrical-Market-Statistics-2015_Final.pdf.
[10]For MPAA age demographics, see Appendix B.

they retained, and even extended, their lead in subsequent years, buying 40 per cent of tickets in 2013 and 41 per cent in 2015. Also in 2011, there was a notable shift within the over-forty group, as over-sixties bought a larger share of tickets than either the forty to forty-nine or the fifty to fifty-nine demographic for the first time. These figures indicate that older viewers have not abandoned moviegoing to a younger audience. Instead, the post-2000 audience has been more evenly distributed in terms of age than at any time in the film industry's history.

Consequently, the logic of targeting large-scale films at younger viewers is not grounded in any radical change in audience demographics. As we have seen in the previous chapter, Hollywood became intensely fixated on child and family viewers after 1999 for two reasons. First, such films play well in international markets where age demographics are less important than class and brand awareness, and where spectacle, alongside a global or fantastical setting, can appeal more generally than smaller, American-set stories. Secondly, Hollywood has found that films ostensibly aimed at children in the first instance could attract a surprisingly broad audience. Peter Krämer identified this trend in the 1990s, and called them 'family adventure' movies.[11] More recently Noel Brown has described these blockbusters as 'kidult' entertainment.[12] The majority of such films receive a PG or PG-13 rating, which, according to Brown has become 'almost a prerequisite for live-action blockbuster success. More than 60 per cent of the top 30 films of all-time fall into PG-13'.[13] From *Stars Wars: The Phantom Menace*, through Harry Potter and the Pirates of the Caribbean to the current crop of superhero movies, child-friendly material has generated higher revenues much more consistently than adult-oriented content.

Films with mature themes aimed at mature moviegoers continue to make up an important part of Hollywood's output, to make money and to dominate awards ceremonies today. Some even generate substantial returns, such as Spielberg's *Lincoln* (2012), which earned $182 million on domestic release. The value of the boomers remains curtailed by their status as senior citizens, who pay less for tickets, and who watch in different ways. Hence Kevin Costner's complaint, at the very start of this book, that 'it's very hard to get a gross from baby boomers'.[14] But the truth is that boomers remain very likely to attend the kinds of high-budget blockbusters favoured by the industry because so many are rooted in boomers' own cultural memories, while dramas and films focused on the concerns of older viewers have less commercial power.

---

[11]Peter Krämer, 'Would You Take Your Child', 305.
[12]Brown, *The Hollywood Family Film*, 192.
[13]Ibid., 5.
[14]Christie D'Zurilla, 'Kevin Costner at AARP Gala', online.

Also, boomers have remained avid consumers of movies in the home. We have already seen that video sales and rentals helped to stabilize revenue streams for many Hollywood studios in the 1980s. Boomers had been largely responsible for driving growth in the video market, not least because they had the purchasing power to afford a VCR, even if many of the videos rented or purchased were viewed by other members of the household. At the end of the 1990s, videocassettes were being superseded by DVDs, which allowed a relatively high-quality movie transfer to be stored on a cheaply produced, CD-sized disc. For various reasons, Americans consumed far more DVDs than they ever had videos. To give some examples, total videocassettes sales in 1998 stood at 626 million units, and in the same year, 34.3 million DVDs were sold.[15] Therefore, 660.3 million copies of movies were sold for consumption at home in 1999, across both formats. By 2003, 1.096 billion DVDs were sold alongside 293.6 million videos, making a grand total of 1.38 billion home entertainment sales, more than twice as many as in 1999. Furthermore, the astounding growth of the DVD market occurred at the same time as consumers increasingly chose to buy, rather than rent, their home viewing selections. Ulin goes on to explain that 'by the time the DVD market had reached its peak in 2004–2005, the percentage of sales for sell though had shifted to close to 70%, whereas only a few years before the split was even'.[16]

The growth of the sell-through DVD market was driven by a range of interrelated factors, notably falling product prices, increased investment in marketing for certain titles and a growing trend for treating videos, and especially DVDs, as collectable items.[17] Growth of the DVD market cut across age divisions, and so older boomers were as likely to purchase DVD players and DVDs as anyone else. In some ways, DVDs offered older viewers choices and viewing possibilities that video had not. The availability of 'extras', and studios' willingness to re-master and rerelease old movies may well have encouraged viewers of all ages to develop a seemingly 'curated' collection of well-presented movies from within particular periods or genres.[18] David Bishop, chief of MGM home entertainment, observed in 2001 that 'VHS never offered the opportunity to canonize big titles like this format does. It's now all about a collector's mindset'.[19] Older films were identified as

---

[15] All statistics relating to DVD sales in this paragraph are taken from 2003 MPA Market Statistics, 30, reproduced in Russell, *The Historical Epic and Contemporary Hollywood*, 175.
[16] Ulin, *The Business of Media Distribution*, 170–1.
[17] Ibid., 173.
[18] See Barbara Klinger, *Beyond the Multiplex: Cinema, New Technologies and the Home* (Berkeley: University of California Press, 2006), 54.
[19] David Bishop, quoted in Michael Seier and Scott Hettrick, 'DVD Disc Jockeying', *Variety*, 3 September 2001, 56.

big potential releases in the future, and much of this 'collector's mindset' appealed principally to an older audience.

On a much more basic level, the easy access to closed captioning on the format made it a much more viable home viewing choice for older viewers with limited hearing abilities. Discussing video sales of Taylor Hackford's 2004 biopic *Ray*, *USA Today* described it as 'one of a growing number of films that performed better on DVD than they did in theaters, primarily because they appeal to older movie fans'.[20] Although DVD provided older viewers with better access to movies than ever before, the DVD market was ultimately subject to the same demographic shifts as the cinema market. While ageing boomers were clearly an important demographic for DVD sales, the industry seems to have felt that from relatively early on in the DVD boom, children and families formed the core audience.

While DVD certainly did appeal to older moviegoers, and offered boomers the opportunity to continue watching films long after they had lost interest in regularly attending multiplex movie theatres, the DVD market did not differ in terms of hits and flops from theatrical box office trends. If anything, the conditions of the DVD market encouraged production of the sort of family-oriented franchise releases discussed above. The DVD market reached its peak sales levels in 2006, and since then DVD sales and attended revenues have steeply declined, as we saw in Chapter 11, leaving behind a substantial gap in studio revenue sheets.

So, on the one hand, the growing DVD market offered boomers the opportunity to consume more and more movies at home, at a time in their lives when they were more likely to stay away from movie theatres anyway. On the other hand, the nature of the DVD market, where children's films proved even more successful than at theatres, provided further impetus for studios to shift production away from more serious-minded, adult-oriented fare that might directly concern the boomers, to focus on family-friendly projects.

Our survey respondents provide a compelling snapshot of how boomers' attitudes to the moviegoing experience have evolved as they enter their fifties and sixties. In terms of how and where our sample consumes movies, their current habits are broadly consistent with those of their childhoods. Just as when they were young, our boomers (respondents born between 1946 and 1964) are much more likely to watch films at home than in a theatre. To the extent change has taken place, the most noticeable trends are a move away from regular cinema attendance, and an embrace of home video technology, particularly DVD. While individuals' levels of engagement with films varies enormously, thanks to home viewing the number of respondents who see fewer than two films per year remains as low now as it did in the past.

---

[20]Russell, *The Historical Epic and Contemporary Hollywood*, 177.

	Twice a week or more	Weekly	Monthly	A few times per year	Yearly or less
On cinema	12 (2.1%)	101 (17.8%)	165 (29.1%)	175 (30.9%)	114 (20.1%)
On television	208 (37.7%)	192 (34.8%)	57 (10.3%)	56 (10.2%)	38 (6.9%)

FIGURE 6 *Childhood Viewing Habits, Survey.*

	Twice a week or more	Weekly	Monthly	A few times per year	Yearly or less
On cinema	9 (1.6%)	33 (6%)	91 (16.5%)	215 (39.1%)	202 (36.7%)
On TV	185 (33.4%)	166 (30%)	96 (17.3%)	68 (12.3%)	39 (7%)
On VHS	17 (3.3%)	18 (3.5%)	31 (6%)	81 (15.7%)	368 (71.5%)
On DVD	84 (15.3%)	114 (20.7%)	138 (25.1%)	132 (24%)	82 (14.9%)
Online	51 (9.5%)	50 (9.3%)	63 (11.8%)	73 (13.6%)	298 (55.7%)

FIGURE 7 *Current Viewing Habits, Survey.*

Asked to describe how their viewing habits had changed compared to earlier points in their lives, 220 respondents reported watching films more, with 31 respondents specifying the cinema (such as respondent 747 (b.1959): 'As I became an adult, I was able to spend more so from the late 1980s, I have gone to the movies weekly.') and 161 respondents watching more films at home (such as respondent 588 (b.1960), who reported, 'I now watch 99 per cent of movies at home. I have a home theatre system with high definition sound and blu-ray. I watch movies with my wife. My favorite types of movies are sci-fi, superhero, action and to a lesser degree, comedy and animated movies.'). Thirty-one respondents said there had been no change in their viewing habits; 192 respondents said they watched films less than they used to, with 151 of them specifying fewer cinema visits. In a separate question we asked respondents how they felt the cinemagoing experience of today compared to earlier times in their lives. The most frequent responses were negative: 179 respondents said that a trip to the cinema was now too expensive, 91 respondents said there was too much noise from other patrons and 47 respondents felt the experience as a whole had become less of an event. More positively, 48 respondents praised advances in technology and 40 said modern theatres were more comfortable. Respondent 592's (b.1962) answer addressed many of these factors: 'Audiences are noisier, less considerate than I remember; often not a pleasant experience. Sometimes chairs are more comfortable but not always. Not too crazy about multiplexes. Rather love the old, well-appointed cinemas with chandeliers and wall sconces and such.'

Fifty respondents said that the types of films they watch had changed, including respondent 622 (b.1958) who said 'As I've gotten older, I've come to prefer the older movies and classics more'; and respondent 317 (b. 1960) who 'stopped looking for *Movies* and started to try and find *Films* that had a deeper meaning than just being entertained'. As in earlier chapters, multiple respondents made clear that personal circumstance could be a bigger factor in their film consumption than taste. To give two examples, respondent 414 (b.1961) told us, 'As a young adult, I watched a ton of movies (sometimes more than one a day) on television, with friends, because I had a job that required being ready to respond on a moment's notice. Now, I watch a movie about twice a year with my wife, usually on television. I don't care much for movies.' For respondent 572 (b.1962), 'Our family circumstances, unfortunately, lend us to enjoy movies at home on Netflix or using Redbox. Going to the movies is very expensive for a family of five (incl. three teens). We have a child fighting leukaemia and the medical bills are staggering!'

Our respondents were asked their opinion on how movies released today compare to those of the past, and their answers were similarly wide ranging, from the enthusiastic 'much better!' of respondent 349 (b.1947), to the dismissive 'they stink' from respondent 792 (b.1958). Several recurring themes emerged, and again the overall tone was more negative than positive. Ninety-four respondents noted improvements in special effects (respondent 322 (b.1961): '[I] love the effects of today'), although forty-three respondents felt that the emphasis on effects had become excessive (respondent 132 (b.1949): 'Too many dollars are wrapped up in special effects, at the expense of human feelings'). Fifty-seven respondents were of the opinion that recent films lacked originality, and there was repeated criticism of the industry's fondness for remakes. Sixty-six respondents said that scripts or stories were of a lower quality than in earlier periods. Interestingly, given baby boom audiences' central role in introducing explicit content to Hollywood productions in the late 1960s, sixteen respondents praised the increased realism of modern productions, but sixty-nine said films now contained too much sex, and one hundred and ten said there was too much violence. Examples include respondent 250 (b.1963): 'I miss the simplicity of black-and-white, and the less brutal culture depicted prior to the 1970s. Movies are reflecting our more brutal and simultaneously more sentimental natures, which worries me', and respondent 686 (b.1958): 'Don't care for most, too many political messages, too much profanity, nudity, sex. Not near enough family films are produced by main film companies/studios.' Respondent 388's (b.1952) thoughtful answer summarizes the prevailing opinions we encountered:

In many ways they're better technologically – sound, visually, production values and the locations are amazing. Many of the independent and art films are provocative and enjoyable. I find the modern action movies to be either extremely sexist, racist and xenophobic or very condescending for children. The violence goes beyond the moral limits I was raised with, which is understandable in today's culture but does not motivate me to pay for or even watch as much. Animation has changed drastically. I loved the old animation, which I'm told is fiscally impossible to have done today. But there have been technological improvements in animation, too. Though I enjoy animation & its influence most animated features that would have been family fare when I was growing up are now witless and boring. *Shrek* was a notable exception, along with the *Cars* & *Toy Stories* – which were enjoyable for my nieces and nephews as well as the teen and young adults and me. In summary, movies today have improved technologically, and I would enjoy watching them except for the violence and one-dimensional story lines. For example all the *Die Hards* and many of the action movies are simply for teenage boys.

But if our survey suggests boomer dissatisfaction with contemporary Hollywood, what do movies today have to say about the boomers?

Depictions of the boomers today

Throughout their life cycle, the baby boomers have been condemned as often as they have been celebrated, and such impulses continue to define their image in the new millennium. Tom Wolfe argued in 1976 that the baby boomers ushered in 'the greatest age of individualism in American history!'[21] In the 1990s, a growing preoccupation with the boomers' parents, the so-called Greatest Generation, was grounded in an implicit critique of the boomers – who, by association, had not suffered or triumphed in the same manner as the generation who had lived through the Second World War (a position refuted by Leonard Steinhorn in his 2006 book about the boomers, *The Greater Generation*). In his satirical account of the baby boom, *Balsamic Dreams*, published in 2000, Joe Queenan wrote, 'Everything I had ever learned as a baby boomer had oriented me in a single direction: further into myself. We were appalling. We had appalling values.'[22] In Christopher Buckley's 2007 political satire, *Boomsday*, he depicts a world where the boomers are given tax breaks for killing themselves before they become too great a burden on the state. As they grew older, the boomers were seen in many sectors of the American media as a problem. Buckley's book, in

---

[21]Wolfe, 'The Me Decade', online.
[22]Joe Queenan, *Balsamic Dreams: A Short but Self-Important History of the Baby Boom Generation* (New York: Picador, 2002), 6.

particular, echoed wider debates which framed the ageing boomers as a financial and political burden on the rest of America, especially the young.

On the one hand, boomers have been criticized for taking advantage of opportunities that were not available to younger generations: cheap college education, lower house prices and reliable employment. Boomers are also often perceived as having gained wealth at the expense of gen-Xers or millennials. Conversely, boomers' lack of financial security is also considered a major financial problem by commentators. The first boomers began to reach retirement age (sixty-five years old) in 2011, prompting concerns over a retirement crisis, when it transpired that many members of the 'me generation', had not managed to accrue sufficient savings over their working lives to fund retirement.[23] Boomers are both 'the wealthiest generation in U.S. history', according to Bloomberg, and too poor to retire.[24]

Politically, the boomers have always been divided, and appear to have drifted further to the right as they have headed towards old age. In 2015, a slim majority of boomers (44 per cent) identified as conservative, despite their reputation for social liberalism.[25] In some accounts, it appears that the boomers have come to represent a common-sense, and clichéd, image of what older people are generally 'like' – a wealthy conservative group, politically opposed to the more progressive generations beneath them, but increasingly dependent on younger generations for financial support. This picture fails to address the diversity of experience, wealth and opinion that really defines the baby boom generation – as it always has – but it is one useful shorthand for understanding how boomers are now perceived. But as these discourses have circulated how have the boomers and their lives been depicted over the past fifteen years? What role has Hollywood played in shaping our perception of the baby boomers?

Boomer performers appear in a huge array of movies, but Hollywood films featuring boomers (and the cultural experiences of the boomers) at their centre have become relatively rare, and fall into several broad categories: mid-budget action movies featuring ageing male stars such as Liam Neeson, Tom Cruise and Sylvester Stallone (*Taken*, 2008; *The Expendables*, 2010; *Red*, 2010; *Captain Phillips*, 2013; the Mission: Impossible and Jack Reacher movies); comedies about ageing groups of men seeking to revisit their youth, or entering into some kind of comedic conflict with younger people (*Last*

[23]Dan Kadlec, 'Why Retirement Reality Is Finally Sinking in for the Boomers', *Time*, 11 April 2016, http://time.com/money/4287851/retirement-reality-boomers/.
[24]Ben Severman, 'The Richest Generation in US History Just Keeps Getting Richer', *Bloomberg*, 12 July 2016, http://www.bloomberg.com/news/articles/2016-07-12/the-richest-generation-in-u-s-history-just-keeps-getting-richer.
[25]Jeffrey M. Jones, 'U.S. Baby Boomers More Likely to Identify as Conservative', *Gallup* Online, 29 January 2015, http://www.gallup.com/poll/181325/baby-boomers-likely-identify-conservative.aspx.

Vegas, 2013; *Wild Hogs*, 2007; *Old Dogs*, 2009; *Meet the Parents, Meet the Fockers, Why Him?*, 2016; *The Intern*, 2015); comedies or dramas about the romantic travails of ageing middle-class Americans, many of which feature iconic boomer star Meryl Streep (*Mamma Mia!*, 2008; *It's Complicated*, 2009; *Hope Springs*, 2012; *Parental Guidance*, 2012; *August: Osage Country*, 2013; *Darling Companion*, 2012); and high-budget franchise releases featuring boomers in roles as mentors or elder statesmen (*Star Wars: The Force Awakens, Indiana Jones and the Kingdom of the Crystal Skull, Tomorrowland*, 2015; *Man of Steel*, 2013; *Ant Man*, 2015).

Obviously, these movies present the lives of the older boomers in a fairly diverse variety of ways. In many, boomers are presented as members of an 'uptight' older generation. Often those depictions are dependent on a star's particular popular image, or persona. So in *Meet the Parents* and *The Intern*, Robert De Niro plays an older man defined by self-control, resilience and conservatism. The same might be said of Liam Neeson in the *Taken* films and its various imitators, where he plays a gruff boomer father, whose taciturn exterior conceals a CIA operative with a 'very particular set of skills.' Many such comedies, action movies or franchise releases do not seem interested in making any kind of statement about the experiences of the boomers. Rather, boomers feature by default as older characters, who espouse a blandly conservative ethos if any kind of political or ideological world view at all is expressed.

Others engage more directly with the lives of boomers. In Nancy Meyers's *It's Complicated*, Alec Baldwin and Meryl Streep feature as a divorced middle-class Californian couple who reconnect after years of separation and start an affair at their daughter's graduation. In the movie, Baldwin plays a successful but boorish attorney, who provides many of the film's laughs, but is eventually passed over by Streep's character in favour of a

IMAGE 13 *Jake Adler (Alec Baldwin) and Jane Adler (Meryl Streep) reconnect in* It's Complicated *(2009).*

more sensitive architect played by Steve Martin. Many critics noted that the film maintained Meyers's long-standing focus on middle-class and middle-aged lives. Manohla Dargis in the *New York Times* noted,

> One of the most interesting things about Ms. Meyers's romances is that they are pitched at a niche demographic, by which I mean women over 40. Ms. Streep looks sensational, but she and her crinkles also look close enough to her real age (60) to reassure you that she hasn't resorted to the knife. That may sound grotesque and petty. But in an industry in which actresses whittle themselves down to nothing so they can have a little screen space only to fade away once they hit a certain age, there's nothing trivial about a movie that insists a middle-aged woman with actual breasts and hips and wrinkles can be beautiful and desirable while also fully desiring.[26]

The world depicted in *It's Complicated* features some trappings of the liberal permissive values associated with the boomers – the three leads share a joint, and Streep and Baldwin watch iconic boomer movie *The Graduate* with their children. For Meyers, that movie in particular is relevant because it cut to the core of the movie's themes:

> The son had just graduated from college, and the father had used bad judgement in showing it, because he always had bad judgement: it was a movie about somebody having an affair within the family and the kids don't know. The daughter in *The Graduate* doesn't know, and these kids didn't know that their parents were having an affair. And then I showed Alec absolutely enjoying it because he's a thoughtless person and Meryl's sitting in a chair, just dying. They are having completely different experiences with the movie. So they're just seeing it as comedy, and the kids, of course, are innocent because they don't know and she's squirming because it so reflects what's going on within their family.

Alternatively, comedy movies such as *Parental Guidance* do seek to engage to some extent with the culturally liberal popular image of the boomers. In the movie Billy Crystal and Bette Midler play grandparents whose permissive approach to childrearing clashes with the more disciplined attitude of younger parents. The films bears comparison to 2004's *Meet the Fockers*, discussed in Chapter 10, and like Barbra Streisand and Dustin Hoffman in that movie, the central couple are closely associated with the cultural values of the 1960s. But again, the boomers are ultimately presented as

---

[26]Manohla Dargis, 'A September-September Romance', *New York Times*, 24 December 2009, http://www.nytimes.com/2009/12/25/movies/25complicated.html.

members of a wealthy, privileged cultural elite. Like so many depictions of the boomers, these movies ultimately provide a fantasy, an idealized account of the boomer experience that focuses on the privilege of the few over the struggles of the many. As a result, they largely adhere to representational codes that have defined Hollywood's depiction of the boomers over the past seventy years. The scale and diversity of the baby boom generation escapes the limits of our vision, on-screen at least.

Over the course of this book, we have seen the many ways that those struggles have resulted in a profoundly transformed movie industry, which is not the same as saying that Hollywood today is radically different from its earlier iterations. If anything, the legacy of the boomer filmmakers and boomer audiences has found continuities with the past, a process made concrete in the George Lucas building at USC. In the 1950s and 1960s, many of the movies that boomers watched at matinees and on television originated in an earlier period of Hollywood's history, and as they began to make movies of their own, boomer filmmakers blended an interest in the strikingly new with influences from own their childhood. That process continues today, as the whole American movie industry is now built upon nostalgia: nostalgia for the youth of the boomers and the pop culture of those formative years; nostalgia for the films they made in the 1970s and 1980s; and also nostalgia for childhood itself. These are powerful forces that show no obvious signs of abating. It would appear that, while this history has reached its conclusion, the history of Hollywood and the baby boom extends into the foreseeable future.

Appendix A: The Survey

Our audience survey was undertaken in the spirit of experimentation. The huge size of the baby boom generation meant that we were less interested in generating quantitative data than in gaining some insight into the ways that audience members might reflect on the roles that movies and moviegoing have played in their lives. As a result, we amended the questions we asked and our methods in reaching participants over time.

In devising the survey, our aim was to give respondents as much freedom as possible to tell us about their engagement with film in their own words while also encouraging them to consider different periods in their lives. To this end, we initially broke the survey into seven pages, each featuring questions addressing a different life stage or theme. On page one, we asked a series of multiple choice questions relating to the respondents' identities. The second page dealt with respondents' childhoods, defined as the period up to and including the age of twelve. The third page then moved forward to focus on the period we termed the respondents' 'teens and young adulthood', defined as from thirteen until their 'early twenties'. The final pages addressed the respondents as adults.

A guiding principle in our publicizing of the survey was to focus on ordinary filmgoers rather than academics and the process of getting people to take the survey ultimately involved three stages: First, an initial exploratory period where we attempted to engage online communities through forum postings; second, a period of advertising the survey via Facebook and Google; third, the decision to purchase some responses from Survey Monkey, the provider of our survey software.

We initially enjoyed considerable success by approaching users of online forums targeted at older Americans. Some of these were easy to access, while others placed restrictions on external users seeking to take advantage of their user base for profit or research. Fortunately, administrators of the forum The Straight Dope granted us permission to post a link, for which we are extremely grateful. The Straight Dope is a syndicated column by Cecil Adams (a pseudonym) in which Adams answers readers' questions on any topic. The column began in the *Chicago Reader* in 1973 and, according to its website, is currently syndicated in more than thirty newspapers across the United States and Canada.

In many respects the early data was excellent: of the first 256 responses, completion rate was nearly two-thirds (64 per cent) and many respondents gave full and thoughtful answers. Gender was almost evenly split (54 per cent male) and responses came from forty-two states (with California the highest with 37 or 15 per cent). In other ways, however, considerable biases were evident. Most glaring was the almost total lack of ethnic diversity. Fully 96.7 per cent of the 246 respondents who answered the question on racial identity identified themselves as white. Other biases were less extreme but still marked. In terms of education, 65 per cent of respondents said that they had at least a bachelor's degree and 33 per cent had a graduate degree. By contrast, only 4 per cent reported a high school degree or equivalent as their highest level of education and no one said that they hadn't finished high school. On religion, more than half (53.7 per cent) said they had no religious belief, compared with just 19 per cent giving their religious affiliation as Protestant Christian, the next most popular response. Similarly, more than half (51.8 per cent) of respondents said that generally speaking they considered themselves Democrats, with only 10 per cent considering themselves to be Republicans (the rest were either Independents or 'something else'). In short, our audience of forum users, the vast majority of whom were users of the Straight Dope message board, was primarily white, highly educated, not religious and Democratic.

In order to reach a broader demographic, we elected to begin using paid advertisements using the websites that – theoretically at least – promised access to the widest general audience. Using Facebook, we ran an advert specifically targeted to users in the United States aged over forty-eight. The advert text ran: 'Take Our Movie Survey. Born between 1946 and 1964? A new university study needs your movie memories.' In total advertising through Facebook resulted in 274 clicks taking users to our website. Using Google adwords we ran an advert that featured both on specified search results and more generally on Google's Display Network. The ad (which had a lower word limit than on Facebook) read, 'Take Our Movie Survey. Born between 1946 and 1964? New study needs your movie memories.' In total, the Google campaign resulted in 308 clicks through to our website. At this time, we also took the decision to simplify and streamline the survey. Shortly after beginning the Facebook campaign we noted that whereas our overall completion rate from forum users had held around 65 per cent, once respondents began clicking through from Facebook, the completion rate quickly dipped to 61 per cent. A total of 126 people began the shorter survey.

As we monitored the nature of the advertised responses, we decided that the most effective way to boost our demographic reach in a controlled manner was to engage the services of Survey Monkey, who offer a 'panel' of respondents to their users so that completed responses from specific demographic groups can be purchased for a fixed price. For our purposes, Survey Monkey Audience had obvious advantages and drawbacks. In addition to helping us achieve a more balanced range of responses that better reflected the demographic identity of the United States, this approach also fit with our determination to reach an audience with no declared special interest in film, which is to say, 'ordinary' viewers. Survey Monkey rewards its audience with charitable donations and entries into prize draws based upon the number of surveys they complete. Unfortunately, this has the disadvantage of creating an audience whose primary motivation is to complete as many surveys as possible, rather than to put maximum time and effort into each response. This was a compromise we felt was acceptable given the aforementioned gains. We arranged to purchase 300 responses divided equally between those from general boomer-age (1946–64) respondents, from boomers whose racial identity was other than 'white' and from boomers without college education. Because of the way in which Survey Monkey makes surveys available to its audience panel, it is always highly likely that somewhat more than the requested number of surveys will be completed and these are given at no extra charge to the user. Therefore, we ended up with 406 responses, of which 269 (90.9 per cent) were complete.

As requested, the Survey Monkey Audience responses provided a very different demographic profile to our initial forum group. Here, 49 per cent of responses were male, responses came from forty-eight states, and 66 per cent identified themselves as white. Of the respondents, 7 per cent were black or African American, 2 per cent American Indian or Alaskan Native, 2 per cent Asian, 1 per cent Native Hawaiian or other Pacific Islander and 22 per cent from multiple races. Following the example of the US census, we asked separately if respondents were part of a Spanish, Hispanic or Latino group; 31 per cent said that they were, with Mexican American (with 10 per cent of responses) being the most common. Twenty-seven per cent of responses came from people whose highest level of education was a high school degree or less, with a further 25 per cent having attended college without attaining a college degree. Notably, although we were not able to specify political or religious affiliation, both were more evenly spread than the earlier forum responses. Of Survey Monkey Audience respondents, 24 per cent generally thought of themselves as Republican, compared with 39 per cent Democrat and 37 per cent Independent or something else. While 'No religion' was still the single most popular response to religious affiliation (with 33.5 per cent), it was much more closely followed by Roman Catholic (28 per cent), Protestant Christian (27 per cent) and Evangelical Christian (7.1 per cent).

The survey text

Key:

*   long version only
^   short version only
~   not asked to Survey Monkey Panel

Section one: General information

1. In what year were you born?

1930–42:	13 (1.6%)
1943–5:	32 (4%)
1946–50:	131 (16.2%)
1951–5:	155 (19.2%)
1956–60:	214 (26.5%)
1961–4:	166 (20.6%)
1965–70:	90 (11.2%)
1971+:	6 (0.7%)

ONLY 1946–64 responses included in all subsequent answers

2. Are you male or female?

Male	329 (49.8%)
Female	332 (50.2%)

3. Are you White, Black or African American, American Indian or Alaskan Native, Asian, Hawaiian Native or other Pacific Islander, or some other race?

White	518 (78.8%)
Black or African American	33 (5%)
American Indian or Alaskan Native	8 (1.2%)
Asian	8 (1.2%)
Hawaiian Native or other Pacific Islander	4 (0.6%)
From multiple races	86 (13.1%)

4. Are you Mexican, Mexican American, Chicano, Puerto Rican, Cuban, Cuban American or some other Spanish, Hispanic or Latino group?

I am not Spanish, Hispanic or Latino	511 (80.3%)
Mexican	14 (2.2%)
Mexican-American	43 (6.8%)
Chicano	9 (1.4%)
Puerto Rican	18 (2.8%)

Cuban	1 (0.2%)
Cuban-American	3 (0.5%)
Some other Spanish, Hispanic or Latino group	27 (4.2%)
From multiple Spanish, Hispanic or Latino groups	10 (1.6%)

5. In what type of environment have you lived for the majority of your life?

City	227 (34.4%)
Suburban	291 (44.2%)
Rural (small town/village)	119 (18.1%)
Rural (isolated)	22 (3.3%)

6. In what state or US territory do you live?

7. Have you ever lived outside the United States

Yes	151 (22.8%)
No	510 (77.2%)

If yes, please give details

8. What is the highest level of school you have completed or the highest degree you have received?

Less than high school degree	9 (1.5%)
High school degree or equivalent (e.g. GED)	116 (18.5%)
Some college but no degree	178 (26.9%)
Associate degree	71 (10.7%)
Bachelor degree	145 (21.9%)
Graduate degree	135 (20.4%)

9. Which of the following categories best describes your employment status?

Employed, working 1–39 hours per week	109 (16.5%)
Employed, working 40 or more hours per week	346 (52.3%)
Not employed, looking for work	48 (7.3%)
Not employed, NOT looking for work	26 (3.9%)
Retired	87 (13.1%)
Disabled, not able to work	46 (6.9%)

10. Generally speaking, do you usually think of yourself as a Republican, a Democrat, an Independent or something else?

Republican	144 (21.9%)
Democrat	272 (41.3%)
Independent	172 (26.1%)
Something else	71 (10.8%)

11. What is your religious affiliation?

Protestant Christian	174 (27.3%)
Roman Catholic	149 (23.4%)
Evangelical Christian	33 (5.2%)
Jewish	15 (2.4%)
Muslim	3 (0.5%)
Hindu	2 (0.3%)
Buddhist	7 (1.1%)
No religious affiliation	255 (40%)

~12. How important are the following to your sense of who you are?

	Very important	Somewhat important	Not an issue
Religion	61 (21.7%)	54 (19.2%)	166 (59.1)
Ethnicity	21 (7.5%)	76 (27.2%)	182 (65.2%)
Age	27 (9.7%)	119 (42.8%)	132 (47.5%)
Occupation	51 (18.5%)	103 (37.5%)	121 (44%)
Politics	50 (18.2%)	114 (41.5%)	111 (40.4%)

*Section two: Childhood

*This section is an attempt to understand the role that movies played in your life when you were a child. We'd like to know how you watched movies, and who you watched them with, but we are also interested in hearing about any memories you have, or films you loved, that seemed important to you when you were a child (under thirteen years).

Section 2: Childhood and youth

This section focuses on the role that movies played in your childhood and youth up to your early twenties. We'd like to know how you watched movies, and who you watched them with, but we are also interested in hearing about any memories you have, or films you loved, that seemed important to you when you were young.

13. How often did you watch movies as a child?

	Twice a week or more	Weekly	Monthly	A few times per year	yearly or less
On cinema	12 (2.1%)	101 (17.8%)	165 (29.1%)	175 (30.9%)	114 (20.1%)
On television	208 (37.7%)	192 (34.8%)	57 (10.3%)	56 (10.2%)	38 (6.9%)

14. In what circumstances did you watch movies as a child?

	Usually	Occasionally	Rarely	Never
With family	371 (64.1%)	147 (25.4%)	52 (9%)	9 (1.6%)
With friends	122 (22.9%)	257 (48.2%)	110 (20.6%)	44 (8.3%)
On your own	105 (19.7%)	173 (32.5%)	154 (28.9%)	101 (18.9%)

*15. What kinds of movies did you enjoy as a child? If possible, please give examples.

*16. What specific movies or movie-viewing experiences stand out in your memory from your childhood? What made them particularly memorable?

^15. What kinds of movies or movie-viewing experiences did you particularly enjoy as a child? If possible, please give examples.

^16. How did your movie-viewing habits change during your teens/young adulthood? Do any movies/experiences stand out?

*Section three: Teen/young adult

*This section invites you to reflect on the role that movies played in your life once you became a teenager and then headed into your early twenties. We're interested in how your moviegoing habits and preferences might have changed as you grew up, and, again, in any memories that stand out from this period of your life.

*17. Returning to your movie-viewing habits (how often you watch movies, where you watch them and who you watch them with), how did these habits change during your teens/young adulthood?

*18. What kinds of movies did you enjoy as a teenager/young adult? Again, please give examples.

*19. What specific movies or movie-viewing experiences stand out in your memory from your teenage years/early adulthood, and what made them memorable?

*20. Do you have children?

     Yes
     No

*Section four: Parenthood

*You have told us something about the role that movies played in your own childhood, but here we are interested in how movies might have featured in your relationship with your own kids, and what role you think movies seem to play in their lives.

*21. How did having children affect your movie-viewing habits and preferences?

*22. As a parent, how do you think your children's experience of movies compares to your own childhood experiences?

Section five: Adulthood

Following on from the last few sections, these questions bring the story up to the present, and invite you to provide some details about your moviegoing habits and preferences today.

23 (long survey)/17 (short survey). Returning again to your movie-viewing habits (how often you watch films, where you watch them and who you watch them with), how have these habits changed during your adult life?

24/18. How often do you watch movies at present?

	Twice a week or more	Weekly	Monthly	A few times per year	Yearly or less
On cinema	9 (1.6%)	33 (6%)	91 (16.5%)	215 (39.1%)	202 (36.7%)
On television	185 (33.4%)	166 (30%)	96 (17.3%)	68 (12.3%)	39 (7%)
On VHS	17 (3.3%)	18 (3.5%)	31 (6%)	81 (15.7%)	368 (71.5%)
On DVD	84 (15.3%)	114 (20.7%)	138 (25.1%)	132 (24%)	82 (14.9%)
Online	51 (9.5%)	50 (9.3%)	63 (11.8%)	73 (13.6%)	298 (55.7%)

*25. In what circumstances do you watch movies at present?

	Usually	Occasionally	Rarely	Never
With family	41 (38%)	33 (30.6%)	21 (19.4)	13 (12%)
With friends	5 (5%)	37 (36.6%)	39 (38.6%)	20 (19.8%)
Alone	57 (51.8%)	31 (28.2%)	17 (15.5%)	5 (4.5%)

^20. If you have children, how do you think their experience of movies compares to your own childhood experience?

Section six: Attitudes

This section offers you the opportunity to reflect on your answers. We're interested in finding out what you think about the role that movies might have played in your life, but also what you think about the role that movies have played more generally in American society. If you have strongly held opinions on cinema or the media, this is the place to put them.

26/21. What do you think of the movies being produced today compared to those being made at earlier times in your life?

*27. Would you say that movies (this could also include filmmakers, stars, advertising, soundtracks, etc.) have played an important role in your life? Please explain your answer.

28/23. How would you compare the role of movies in your life to that of other media such as music, books or television? Has this changed over time?

*29. Do you think movies play an important role in American society? Please explain your answer.

Section seven: Watching movies

30/22. How do you think the experience of going to see a film at the theatre has changed in your lifetime?

*31. Approximately when did your household first get home video?

1970–5	2 (1.9%)
1976–80	20 (18.7%)
1981–5	51 (47.7%)
1986–90	24 (22.4%)
1991–5	5 (4.7%)
1996–2000	3 (2.8%)
2001–5	0
2006+	1 (0.9%)
Never had it	1 (0.9%)

*32. Approximately when did your household first get a DVD player?

1997–2000	33 (30.8%)
2001–5	53 (49.5%)
2006–10	20 (18.7%)
No DVD	1 (0.9%)

*33. How often do you use home video/DVD for the following:

	Often	Occasionally	Rarely	Never
Watching new releases	24 (22.6%)	35 (33%)	30 (28.3%)	17 (16%)
Watching old favorites	36 (33.6%)	46 (43%)	21 (19.6%)	4 (3.7%)
Watching older films you'd missed	30 (28.3%)	46 (43.4%)	26 (24.5%)	4 (3.8%)

34/19. When deciding which new movies to watch, how would you rate the following influences, with '5' being very important and '1' being unimportant?

	1	2	3	4	5
Print reviews	177 (32.2%)	91 (16.6%)	109 (19.9%)	105 (19.1%)	67 (12.2%)
Online reviews	142 (25.8%)	93 (16.9%)	117 (21.3%)	123 (22.4%)	75 (13.6%)
Print advertising	197 (36.1%)	128 (23.5%)	132 (24.2%)	58 (10.6%)	30 (5.5%)
Trailers	81 (14.8%	61 (11.1%)	120 (21.9%)	163 (29.7%)	123 (22.4%)
Opinion of friends	51 (9.4%)	40 (7.4%)	120 (22.2%)	176 (32.6%)	153 (28.3%)

35/24. ... and finally, what would you consider to be your favorite movies, and why?

Appendix B: MPAA Age Demographics

Since the Yankelovich report in 1967, the Motion Picture Association of America (MPAA) has regularly released statistics regarding the demographic composition of ticket sales in the United States and Canada. We have compiled the following table of their ticket sales age statistics from two sources: MPAA press releases (found either in the Margaret Herrick Library's 'Audience' clipping file, or for more recent years online), and reproductions of the MPAA's data in the Quigley Publishing Company's annual *International Motion Picture Almanac*. In recent years (post-2010), the MPAA has begun reporting sales to the 2- to 11-year-old age group. In order to keep figures comparable with earlier periods, we have excluded this group (which accounts for around 11 per cent of sales each year) and adjusted the shares of the remaining groups accordingly.

	12-15	12-24	16-20	21-24	16-24	25-29	30-39	25-39	40-49	50-59	60+	40+
1969	18	65	31	16	47	12	10	22	6	3	4	13
1970	16	59	27	16	43	13	12	25	8	6	2	16
1973	14	60			46	14	13	27	8	4	2	14
1975	14	60	32		46	14	12	26	8	3	3	14
1976	14	60			46	16	13	29	5	3	3	11
1977	16	57			41	17	13	30	6	4	3	13
1979	20	63			43	13	11	24	6	5	2	13
1981	16	55	24	15	39	13	17	30	6	5	4	15
1982	12	51	25	14	39	13	16	29	8	5	6	19
1983	13	53	25	15	40	15	17	32	7	4	4	15
1984	13	54	23	18	41	13	18	31	8	4	3	15
1985	14	53	21	18	39	14	18	32	7	4	4	15
1986	14	52	21	17	38	14	20	34	8	3	3	14
1987	11	47	21	15	36	15	18	33	10	5	5	20
1989	11	44	19	14	33	16	18	34	12	4	7	23
1990	11	42	20	11	31	14	20	34	12	5	7	24
1991	12	43	19	12	31	12	19	31	13	5	8	26
1992	13	40	16	11	27	11	19	30	15	7	8	30

Year												
1993	9	36	17	10	27	13	19	32	15	7	11	33
1994	10	35	14	11	25	10	18	28	16	8	12	36
1995	9	36	16	11	27	12	20	32	16	7	10	33
1996	11	38	16	11	27	11	18	29	16	8	8	32
1997	9	37	17	11	28	12	19	31	15	9	9	33
1999	11	41	20	10	30	12	18	30	14	7	8	29
2000	10	38	17	11	28	12	18	30	14	10	8	32
2001	12	38	16	10	26	9	19	28	17	9	8	34
2002	10	39	17	12	29	11	17	28	15	8	9	32
2003	11	39	16	12	28	9	19	28	14	11	8	33
2004	11	38	17	10	27	9	18	27	16	10	9	35
2005		38				11	17	28	15	10	9	34
2006		37				10	18	28	17	9	9	35
2007		38				14	15	29	15	9	9	33
2010		36						28	12	12	12	36
2011		34						27	13	11	15	39
2012		35						27	15	10	13	38
2013		34						26	14	12	14	40
2015		34						25	13	12	16	41

BIBLIOGRAPHY

Abramowitz, Rachel. *Is That a Gun in Your Pocket? Women's Experience of Power in Hollywood*. New York: Random House, 2000.

Acuna, Kristina. 'Robert Downey Jnr Tops Forbes List of Highest Paid Actors'. *Business Insider*, 17 July 2013.

Adams, Thelma. 'Review of *The Phantom Menace*'. *New York Post*, 18 May 1999.

Allen, Robert C. 'Home alone together: Hollywood and the 'Family Film" In *Identifying Hollywood's Audiences: Cultural Identity and the Movies*, edited by Melvyn Stokes and Richard Maltby. London: BFI, 1999.

Alpert, Hollis. 'Now the Earlier, Earlier Show'. *New York Times Magazine*, 11 August 1963.

Anderson, Christopher. 'Disneyland'. In *Television: The Critical View*, edited by Horace Newcomb. Oxford: Oxford University Press, 2000.

Anderson, Christopher. *Hollywood TV: The Studio System in the Fifties*. Austin: University of Texas Press, 1994.

Anon. '$17,000,000 Disneyland Preview'. *Variety*, 13 July 1955.

Anon. '£4.7 million for USC from Lucas'. *Hollywood Reporter*, 21 November 1980, 1.

Anon. '1987 Video Grosses Outstrip Theatrical By Nearly 2-1'. *Boxoffice*, March 1988.

Anon. '5000 Films Yearly on TV Here'. *Hollywood Reporter*, 9 July 1951.

Anon. '53 Kids in Bus – $1 Admission'. *Variety*, 9 June, 1954.

Anon. 'Adults Also Permitted'. *Time*, 3 July 1988.

Anon. 'AIP Sets Now Generation'. *Variety*, 16 August 1967.

Anon. 'Big pix profits in bull market: Many new film millionaires'. *Variety*, 12 December 1945.

Anon. 'Everything follows the films'. *Variety*, 9 January 1946.

Anon. 'Exhibs, Distribs yell foul play'. *Variety*, 4 September 1944.

Anon. 'Film Grosses up 15% over '45'. *Variety*, 13 February 1946.

Anon. 'Films fill 50 pct. of TV Time'. *Hollywood Reporter*, 3 July 1951.

Anon. 'Getting Involved with your Machine'. *Variety*, 17 June 1981.

Anon. 'How old is your audience'. *Variety*, 16 February 1955.

Anon. 'H'wood's Biggest Whodunnit'. *Variety*, 21 January 1953.

Anon. 'H'wood Poppin' to Sound of Music With 16 Film Tuners Set by Majors'. *Variety*, 1 February 1967.

Anon. 'James Cameron Honored with Scripps Nierenberg prize'. *Scripps Institute of Oceanography News*, 15 May 2013.

Anon. 'Kid Film Library Evaporates'. *Variety*, 16 March 1955.

Anon. 'Kid Library Wiggle Tests Films'. *Variety*, 19 May 1954.

Anon. 'Lectures Townspeople in Film benefits'. *Variety*, 13 January 1954.

Anon. 'Little Family features too Costly, say distribs'. *Variety*, 24 November 1954.

Anon. 'The Mob at the Movies'. *Newsweek*, 22 June 1987.

Anon. 'Moppet-aimed Easter bookings'. *Variety*, 17 March 1954.

Anon. 'More Pix but not releases means new high in inventories'. *Variety*, 19 December 1945.

Anon. 'More Roadshows to lick costs,' *Variety*, 9 July 1947.

Anon. 'MPAA Ratings To Now: G(43), M(29), R(22); Puzzle: X for Birds But R For The Fox'. *Variety*, 4 December 1968.

Anon. 'Name a Movie He Didn't Write'. *LA Herald Examiner*, 17 May 1984.

Anon. 'A Night to Remember'. *Time Out London*. 27 February 2001.

Anon. 'Pix Must 'Broaden Market''. *Variety*, 20 March 1968.

Anon. 'Polk ('Now' Generation) Begins; McLuhan-Quoter, Gal-Charmer'. *Variety*, 15 January 1969

Anon. 'Prods. could – if they would'. *Variety*, 24 November 1954.

Anon. 'Record Jobs and BO Boomer'. *Variety*, 16 July 1947.

Anon. 'Review of *Cinderella'*. *Variety*, 13 December 1949.

Anon. 'Review of *Ghostbusters II'*. *Variety*, 31 December 1988.

Anon. 'Star Wars Shunned G Rating As Uncool For Young Crowd'. *Variety*, July 1 1977.

Anon. 'Survey Says Vid Rentals No Big Drain on Pic BO'. *Variety*, 27 March 1989.

Anon. 'Taking Note Of Youth-Slanted Clicks Of Others, Fox Eager About 5 Newbies'. *Variety*, 13 Aug. 1969.

Anon. 'Top Drawer industry leaders accent staggering production costs but fear B.O. dip'. *Variety*, 8 January 1947.

Anon. 'UA's Midnight Cowboy Most Costly Film To Be Marked X For Youth'. *Variety*, 21 May 1969.

Anon. 'Universal Bathes in Youth Fountain'. *Variety*, 10 December 1969.

Anon. 'Upped Grosses and Reduced taxes Bulling Almost Every Picture Stock'. *Variety*, 5 December 1945.

Anon. 'US Films as Old Guy's Biz'. *Variety*, 24 November 1964.

Anon. 'US Suburbia's Big Pix Role'. *Variety*, 5 August 1953.

Anon. 'Valenti Sez Sex Becoming Old Hat In Pix, But There's No Family Audience'. *Variety*, 15 October 1969.

Anon. 'Video Retailers Receive Stone's Thanks, Warnings'. *Variety*, 19 August 1987.

Anon. 'Visual Mod & Verbal Crix: Kubrick's Sure 2001 To Click'. *Variety*, 10 April 1968.

Anon. 'W7 Stress Upon Youth'. *Variety*, 6 December 1967.

Anon. 'Wall St lag despite big BO'. *Variety*, 20 February, 1946.

Anon. 'Wanted: 25,000,000 pix addicts'. *Variety*, 12 March 1947.

Anon. 'When 'Youth' Pix Bore Young: Metro's Rule is Forget It Fast'. *Variety*, 26 August 1970.

Anon. 'Wise up to Why's of BO dip'. *Variety*, 20 December 1950.

Anon. 'Youth Film Market A BO Mirage'. *Variety*, 29 November 1970.

Armstrong, Ned. 'Suburbia – Key to Legit Future?'. *Variety*, 23 January 1952.

Associated Press. 'Record Number of Students Expected in Fall'. *New York Times*, 22 August 1996.

Babitz, Eve. 'Taking a Change on Love: The New Wave'. *Vogue*, September 1984.

Balio, Tino. *Hollywood in the New Millennium*. London: BFI, 2012.

Balio, Tino. 'Hollywood Production Trends in the Era of Globalisation, 1990-99'. In *Genre and Contemporary Hollywood*, edited by Steve Neale. London: BFI, 2002.

Balio, Tino. *United Artists: The Company that Changed the Film Industry*. Madison: University of Wisconsin Press, 1987.

Barker, Martin and Brooks, Kate. *Knowing Audiences: Judge Dredd, its Friends, its Fans and its Foes*. Luton: University of Luton Press, 1998.

Barker, Martin and Mathijs, Ernest eds. *Watching The Lord of the Rings: Tolkien's World Audiences*. Oxford: Peter Lang, 2007.

Barnes, Brooks. 'At Disney's annual meetings, cruise ships and questions from kids'. *New York Times*, 3 March 2016.

Bart, Peter. 'Better Laid Than Never'. *Variety*, 1 May 2000.

Bart, Peter. *The Gross: The Hits, The Flops – The Summer That Ate Hollywood*. New York: St. Martin's Press, 1999.

Baxter, John. *George Lucas: A Biography*. London: Harpercollins, 2000.

Belushi-Pisana, Judith and Colby, Tanner. *Belushi: A Biography*. New York: Ruggedland Books, 2005.

Berman, Marc. 'Studios Miss Boat on Vid Demographics'. *Variety*, 14 September 1992.

Bing, Jonathan. 'Harry-ed Hollywood hunting kid fodder'. *Variety*, 29 January 2001.

Bing, Jonathan. 'Pix Bet on frosh, by gosh'. *Variety*, 23 July 2001.

Bing, Jonathan and Dunkley, Cathy. 'Kiddy Litter rules H'Wood'. *Variety* 7 January 2002.

Biskind, Peter. *Down and Dirty Pictures: Miramax, Sundance and the Rise of Independent Film*. New York: Simon and Schuster, 2004.

Biskind, Peter. *Easy Riders, Raging Bulls: How the Sex, Drugs and Rock 'n' Roll Generation Saved Hollywood*. New York: Bloomsbury, 1999.

Bloom, David. 'Comic Caper Captivate Studios'. *Variety*, 24 June 2002.

Bobrow, Andrew C. 'Filming *The Sugarland Express*: An Interview with Steven Spielberg'. In *Steven Spielberg Interviews*, edited by Lester D. Friedman and Brent Notbohm, 2000.

Boddy, William. *Fifties Television: The Industry and Its Critics*. Chicago: University of Illinois Press, 1993.

Bodroghkozy, Aniko. 'Reel Revolutionaries: An Examination of Hollywood's Cycle of 1960s Youth Rebellion Films'. *Cinema Journal* 41, No. 3 (Spring 2002): 38–58.

Borneman, Ernest. 'United States Vs Hollywood: The Case Study of an Anti-Trust suit'. In *The American Film Industry*, edited by Tino Balio. Madison: University Of Wisconsin Press, 1985.

Boucher, Jeff. 'Forrest J. Ackerman Ailing'. *Los Angeles Times*, 4 November 2008.

Brown, Noel. *The Hollywood Family Film*. London: I. B. Tauris, 2012.

Bryson, Bill. *The Life and Times of the Thunderbolt Kid*. London: Random House, 2007.

Buckland, Warren. 'A Close Encounter with *Raiders of the Lost Ark*: Notes on Narrative Aspects of the New Hollywood Blockbuster'. In *Contemporary Hollywood Cinema*, edited by Steve Neale and Murray Smith. London: Routledge, 1998.

Bunkly, Cathy and Lyons, Charles. 'Pics get tricky for Mickey'. *Variety*, 17 December 2001.

Cameron, Julia. 'The Panic Faded, Hollywood Comes to Grips with the Brave New VCR World'. *Chicago Tribune*, 3 November 1985.

Canby, Vincent. 'Butch Cassidy and the Sundance Kid'. *New York Times*, 26 September 1969.

Canby, Vincent. 'Film View; When Movie Theaters and Patrons are Obnoxious'. *New York Times*, 7 February 1982.

Canby, Vincent. 'A Polite Robin Hood in a Legend Recast'. *New York Times*, 14 June 1991.

Canby, Vincent. 'Real Butter and Big Bucks'. *New York Times*, 13 December 1987.

Caulfield, Deborah. 'Cineplex- A Medley of Movies'. *Los Angeles Times*, 14 July 1982.

Cels, Roger. 'Sure to be a Mask Marvel'. *Hollywood Reporter*, 29 July 1994.

Champlin, Charles. '$1 Billion in Grosses? It Takes Gumption'. *Los Angeles Times*, 28 December 1994.

Chase, Donald. 'Radio Free "Nam"'. *Los Angeles Times*, 28 June 1987.

Clinton, Bill. *My Life*. New York: Arrow, 2005.

Cohen, Lizabeth. *A Consumer's Republic: The Politics of Mass Consumption in Post-War America*. New York: Vintage, 2004.

Cohn, Lawrence. 'All-Time Film Rental Champs'. *Variety*, 10 May 1993.

Collins, Glenn. 'Spielberg Films *The Color Purple*'. In *Steven Spielberg Interviews*, edited by Lester D. Friedman and Brent Notbohm. Jackson: University Press of Mississippi.

Combs, Richard. 'Primal Scream: An Interview with Steven Spielberg'. In *Steven Spielberg Interviews*, edited by Lester D. Friedman and Brent Notbohm. Jackson: University Press of Mississippi.

Conant, Michael. *Antitrust in the Motion Picture Industry: Economic and Legal Analysis*. Berkeley: University of California Press, 1960, 115.

Conant, Michael. 'The Paramount Decrees Reconsidered'. In *The American Film Industry*, edited by Tino Balio. Madison: University of Wisconsin.

Cook, David A. *Lost Illusions: American Cinema in the Shadow of Watergate and Vietnam*. Berkeley: University of California Press, 2000.

Cowie, Peter. *Coppola: A Biography*. New York: Da Capo, 1994.

Cross, Gary. *Consumed Nostalgia: Memory in the Age of Fast Capitalism*. New York: Columbia University Press, 2015.

Crowther, Bosley. 'Bonnie and Clyde'. *New York Times*, 14 April 1967.

Crowther, Bosley. 'Run, Bonnie and Clyde'. *New York Times*, 3 September 1967.

Cullen, Jim. *The American Dream*. New York: Oxford University Press, 2003.

D'Zurilla, Christie. 'Kevin Costner at AARP gala'. *Los Angeles Times*, 3 February 2015.

Dargis, Manohla. 'A September-September Romance'. *New York Times*, 24 December 2009.

Davison Hunter, James. *Culture Wars: The Struggle to Define America*. New York: Basic, 1992.

Desowitz, Bill. 'Digital cinema gets a push'. *Los Angeles Times*, 4 March 2001.

DiMaggio, Paul, Evan, John and Bryson, Bethany. 'Have Americans' Social
    Attitudes Become More Polarized?' *American Journal of Sociology* 102, No. 3
    (November 1996): 690–755.
Doherty, Thomas. *Teenagers and Teenpics: The Juvenilization of American Movies
    in the 1950s*. Philadelphia: Temple University Press, 2002.
Dunne, John Gregory. *The Studio*. London: Vintage, 1998.
Ebert, Roger. 'Butch Cassidy and the Sundance Kid'. *Chicago Sun-Times*, 13
    October 1969.
Ebert, Roger. 'Review of *Field of Dreams*'. *Chicago Sun-Times*, 21 April 1989.
Edmunds, Jane and Turner, Bryan S. *Generations, Culture and Society*.
    Buckingham: Oxford University Press, 2002.
Eller, Claudia and Frook, John Evan. "91 BO Down, Spirits Up at Confab'. *Variety*,
    24 February 1992.
Epstein, Edward Jay. *The Big Picture: Money and Power in Hollywood*. London:
    Random House, 2006.
Evans, Robert. *The Kid Stays in the Picture*. New York: Hyperion, 1994.
Faludi, Susan. *Backlash: The Undeclared War Against Women*. New York: Vintage,
    1993.
Farber, Stephen. 'The USC Connection'. *Film Comment* 20, No. 3 (May 1984): 34–9.
Farr, Louise. '*Rocky*: It Could Be A Contender'. *New York*, 18 October, 1976.
Finler, Joel W. *The Hollywood Story*. London: Wallflower, 2003.
Fishman, Arnold. '*Catch 22* Telephone Survey 1970, Report Date February 30,
    1970,' in 'Communikon audience test reports,' file 2.f-3, AMPAS Margaret
    Herrick library.
Fishman, Arnold. '*The Godfather* – Catch-22 Telephone Awareness Survey,'
    February 1970, '*Catch-22*' File f.3, AMPAS Margaret Herrick library.
Fishman, Arnold and Gladstein, Lin. 'Communikon Audience Survey Conducted at
    the Annual Congress of the U.S. National Student Association in El Paso, Texas,
    August 20 through August 26, report date 29 October 1969,' in 'Communikon
    audience test reports,' file 2.f-15, AMPAS Margaret Herrick library.
Fleming, Charles. *High Concept: Don Simpson and the Hollywood Culture of
    Excess*. New York: Bloomsbury, 1999.
Fleming, Michael. 'DreamWork's DeLuca Makes Executive Decision'. *Variety*, 11
    June 2001.
Forsberg, Myra. 'Spielberg at Forty, The Man and the Child'. In *Steven Spielberg
    Interviews*, edited by Lester D. Friedman and Brent Notbohm. Jackson:
    University Press of Mississippi.
Fox, David J. 'Honey, They Shrunk the Movie Audience'. *Los Angeles Times*, 8
    June 1993.
Frank, Thomas. *The Conquest of Cool: Business Culture, Counterculture and the
    Rise of Hip Consumerism*. Chicago: University of Chicago, 1998.
Frederick, Robert B. '*Star Wars*; What Else Was News in 1977'. *Variety*, 4 January
    1978.
Friedman, Lester D. and Notbohm, Brent. eds. *Steven Spielberg Interviews*.
    Jackson: University of Mississippi Press, 2000.
Gabler, Neal. *Walt Disney: The Autobiography*. London: Aurum, 2008.
Garrahan, Matthew. 'Bob Iger broadens Disney's horizons in age of disruption'.
    Financial Times, 7 March 2016.

Gelman, Morrie. 'No Place For Advertising on Homevid Agenda'. *Daily Variety*, 5 March 1982, 16.

Gillon, Steve and Singer Olaguera, Nancy. *Boomer Nation: The Largest and Richest Generation Ever, and How it Changed America*. New York: Free Press, 2004.

Gitlin, Todd. *The Sixties: Years of Hope, Days of Rage*. London: Bantam, 1993.

Givens, Ron. 'The Nice Guy Rides Again'. *Newsweek*, 28 August 1989.

Goetz, William. 'What does the public want?' *Variety*, 2 January 1952.

Gold, Ronald. 'US Can't Get On The Offbeat. But Majors Take the 'Risk' Abroad'. *Variety*, 10 May 1967.

Golden, Herb. 'Family Pix as BO backbone'. *Variety*, 6 September 1950.

Golden, Herb. 'Hollywood's 33 Top Hits' *Variety*, 25 September 1946.

Goldman, William. *Adventures in the Screen Trade: A Personal View of Hollywood*. London: Abacus, 1996, 40.

Gomery, Douglas. *The Hollywood Studio System: A History*. London: BFI, 2005.

Gomery, Douglas. 'Motion Picture Exhibition in the 1970s'. In *Lost Illusions: American Cinema in the Shadow of Watergate and Vietnam*, edited by David A. Cook. Berkeley: University of California Press, 2000.

Gomery, Douglas. *Shared Pleasures: A History of Movie Presentation in the United States*. Madison: University of Wisconsin Press, 1992.

Gomery, Douglas and Pafort-Overduin, Clara. *Movie History: A Survey*. London: Routledge, 2011.

Grainge, Paul. 'Nostalgia and style in retro America: Moods, modes and media recycling'. *Journal of American Culture* 23, No. 1 (2000).

Green, Abel. 'Godfather Boon to All Pix'. *Variety*, 5 April 1972.

Green, Abel. 'Pix Production's Dipsy Doodle'. *Variety*, 5 February 1947.

Griffin, Nancy and Masters, Kim. *Hit and Run: How Jon Peters and Peter Guber Took Sony for a Ride in Hollywood*. New York: Simon & Schuster, 1996.

Grove, Martin A. 'Hollywood Report'. *Hollywood Reporter*, 2 August 1989.

Grove, Martin A. 'Hollywood Report'. *Hollywood Reporter*, 17 August 1994.

Grover, Ronald. 'The Many Gifts of George Lucas'. *Business Week*, 11 October 2006.

Gruner, Oliver. *Screening the Sixties: Hollywood Cinema and the Politics of Memory*. New York: Palgrave MacMillan, 2016.

Hall, Sheldon and Neale, Steve. *Epics, Spectacles and Blockbusters: A Hollywood History*. Detroit: Wayne State University Press, 2010.

Hardy, Phil. ed. *Aurum Film Encyclopedia of Science Fiction*. London: Aurum, 1983.

Harmetz, Aljean. 'Hollywood Recycling Old TV Hits as Films'. *New York Times*, 21 February 1987.

Harmetz, Aljean. 'Hollywood Welcomes Back Older Audiences'. *New York Times*, 27 April 1988.

Harmetz, Aljean. 'The Little Movie Company That Might'. *New York Times*, 31 October 1993.

Harris, Dana. 'H'Wood's Kiddie Litter,' *Variety*, 20 August 2001.

Harris, Dana and Dawtry, Adam. 'Can BO postman ring twice?' *Variety*, 26 November 2001.

Harris, Dana and Hayes, Dade. 'Can studios survive tentpole traumas?' *Variety*, 23 October 2000.

Harris, Dana and Hayes, Dade. 'WB revs up movie machine'. *Variety*, 7 May 2001.

Harris, Mark. 'Review of *Forrest Gump*.' *Entertainment Weekly*, 15 July 1994.

Hart, Warren. 'Review of *Old Yeller*.' *Motion Picture Daily*, 14 November 1957.

Hawkins, Robert F. 'Youth Slant' As Accident: Producer Often Quite Surprised". *Variety*, 3 September 1969.

Hayes, Dade. 'Are there legs enough in Whoville?' *Variety*, 20 November 2000.

Hayes, Dade. 'Non-Legends of the Fall'. *Variety*, 12 November 2001.

Hendra, Tony. *Going Too Far: The Rise and Demise of Sick, Gross, Black, Sophomoric, Weirdo, Pinko, Anarchist, Underground, Anti-Establishment Humor*. New York: Doubleday, 1987.

Herbstman, Mandel. Review of *Cinderella*. *Motion Picture Daily*, 13 December 1949.

Hettrick, Scott. 'Tarzan puts Grinch in Vidlock'. *Variety*, 8 January 2001.

Hift, Fred. 'Mature BO no Myth'. *Variety*, 28 April 1954.

Hobbs, Frank and Stoops, Nicole. *Demographic Trends in the 20th Century*. Washington: U.S. Government Printing Office, 2002.

Holden, Stephen. 'Review of *The Grinch*'. *New York Times*, 17 November 2000.

Hollinger, Hy. 'Studios aloof to Exhib Grief,' *Variety*, 10 March 1954.

Horowitz, Joy. 'From Slapstick to Yuppie Fantasy'. *New York Times Magazine*, 15 June 1986.

Hughes, John. 'Vacation '58'. *National Lampoon*. September 1979.

Jackson, Kenneth T. *Crabgrass Frontier: The Suburbanization of the United States*. Oxford: Oxford University Press, 1985.

Jones, Jeffrey M. 'U.S. Baby Boomers More Likely to Identify as Conservative'. *Gallup* Online, 29 January 2015.

Jones, Landon. 'A Booming Baby Explosion'. In *The Baby Boom*. edited by Stuart A. Kallen. San Diego: Greenhaven Press, 2002.

Jones, Landon. *Great Expectations: America and the Baby Boom Generation*. New York: Coward McCann, 1980.

Kadlec, Dan. 'Why retirement reality is finally sinking in for the boomers'. *Time*, 11 April 2016.

Kael, Pauline. 'Bonnie and Clyde'. *New Yorker*, 21 October 1967.

Kaplan, Mike. 'Exhibs sour on formula pix'. *Variety*, 21 June 1950.

Kashner, Sam. 'The Making of *The Graduate*'. *Vanity Fair*, March 2008.

Katzenberg, Jeffrey. 'The World is Changing: Some Thoughts on Our Business' Unpublished Internal Memo. 11 January 1991.

Kauffmann, Stanley. *A World on Film: Criticism and Comment*. New York: Harper and Row, 1966.

Keegan, Rebecca. *The Futurist: The Life and Films of James Cameron*. Three Rivers Press: New York, 2010.

Kendrick, James. *Darkness in the Bliss-Out: A Reconsideration of the films of Steven Spielberg*. London: Bloomsbury, 2014.

Kildare, Gregg. 'Film-maker, 23, throws scares into the monster biz'. *Los Angeles Times*, 13 December 1973.

Kildare, Gregg. 'Sampling a Cinematic Smorgasbord'. *LA Herald-Examiner*, 30 July 1982.

King, Stephen. *On Writing*. New York, Pocket, 2000.

Klady, Leonard. 'Bat Blitz Bodes New BO Era'. *Variety*, 19 June 1995.

Klady, Leonard. 'Keen on Teen Green: Taken Unawares, H'w'd refocuses on youth'. *Variety*, 15 January 1997.

Klein, Herbert S. *A Population History of the United States*. Cambridge: Cambridge University Press, 2004.

Klinger, Barbara. *Beyond the Multiplex: Cinema, New Technologies and the Home*. Berkeley: University of California Press, 2006.

Knight, Bob. 'Love Conquers All, Lifting ABC to No. 1 in Third Week'. *Variety*, 11 October 1972.

Konow, David. 'Remembering the Wonders in Famous Monsters Magazine'. *Tested*, 25 November 2014.

Kramer, Eric Mark. 'Who's afraid of the Virgin Wolf Man'. In *Horror at the Drive-In: Essays in Popular Americana*, edited by Gary D. Rhodes. Jefferson: McFarlane, 2003.

Krämer, Peter. *2001: A Space Odyssey*. London: BFI, 2010.

Krämer, Peter. 'The Best Disney film Disney never made': Children's Films and the family audience in American Cinema Since the 1960's'. In *Genre and Contemporary Hollywood*, edited by Steve Neale. London: British Film Institute, 2002.

Krämer, Peter. *The New Hollywood: From Bonnie and Clyde to Star Wars*. London: Wallflower Press, 2005.

Krämer, Peter. 'Would you take your child to see this film'. In *Contemporary Hollywood Cinema*, edited by Neale Steve and Murray Smith. London: Routledge, 1998.

Krohn, Bill. 'I, Robby: the Secret Life of Joe Dante'. In *A Gremlin in Hollywood: Joe Dante in Context*, edited by Bill Krohn and Jonathan Rosenbaum. July 1999.

Kroll, Jack. 'Lighten Up, Dark Knight!' *Newsweek*, 26 June 1995.

Kuhn, Annette. *An Everyday Magic: Cinema and Cultural Memory*. London: I. B. Tauris, 2002.

Landro, Laura. 'Late Summer Movies May Steal Thunder From Glut of Big-Budget Action Films'. *Wall Street Journal*, 27 July 1990.

Landry, Robert J. 'UA Bridges Generation Gap: Every Age Group Has Understudy'. *Variety*, 13 November 1967.

Laporte, Nicole. *The Men Who Would Be King*. Boston: Mariner Books, 2011.

Lee, Linda. 'Attack of the 90-Foot Teen-Agers'. *New York Times*, 9 November 1997.

Lee, Spike and Aftab, Kaleem. *Spike Lee: That's My Story and I'm Sticking to It*. New York: W. W. Norton, 2005.

Leibman, Nina. *Living Room Lectures: The Fifties Family in Film and Television*. Austin: University of Texas Press, 1995.

Leigh, Catesby. 'What George Lucas Wrought'. *Wall Street Journal*, 2 June 2010.

Lev, Peter. *The Euro-American Cinema*. Austin: University of Texas Press, 1993.

Lev, Peter. *Transforming the Screen: The Fifties*. Berkeley: University of California Press, 2003.

Levine, Joseph. 'I Do Believe in Stars, 1967 Press Release from Embassy Pictures,' in 'Tom Miller' file 6-f.81, AMPAS Margaret Herrick library.

Lewis, Jon. *American Film: A History*. New York: W. W. Norton, 2008.

Light, Paul C. *Baby Boomers*. New York: W. W. Norton, 1988.

Lippman, John. 'Warner's Batman Forever Takes In Record $53.3 Million in First Three Days'. *Wall Street Journal*, 19 June 1995.

Loftus, Jeni. 'America's Liberalization in Attitudes toward Homosexuality, 1973 to 1998'. *American Sociological Review* 66, No. 5 (October 2001).

Lyons, Charles. 'Family pix get a fix'. *Variety*, 7 January 2002.

Lyons, Charles. 'Helmers Let Out a Rebel Yell'. *Variety*, 18 June 2001.

Lyons, Charles. 'New Mickey Mouse Club'. *Variety*, 9 October 2000.

Mack. 'The Kentucky Fried Movie'. *Variety*, 3 August 1977.

Maltby, Richard. *Hollywood Cinema*. 2nd ed. Oxford: Blackwell, 2003.

Maltby, Richard. *Hollywood Cinema*. 2nd ed. Oxford: Blackwell, 2006.

Maslin, Janet. '*Batman Returns*; A Sincere Bat, a Sexy Cat and a Bad Bird'. *New York Times*, 19 June 1992.

Maslin, Janet. Review of *The Color Purple*. *New York Times*, 18 December 1985.

Masters, Kim. *The Keys to the Kingdom: The Rise of Michael Eisner and the Fall of Everyone Else*. New York: Harper, 2001.

Mathews, Jack. 'No Mystery: Four Real reasons moviegoing is Off'. *Los Angeles Times*, 20 October 1991.

Matthews, Tom. 'Baby Talk'. *Boxoffice*, November 1989.

Mayer, William G. *The Changing American Mind: How and Why American Public Opinion Changed between 1960 and 1988*. Ann Arbor: The University of Michigan Press, 1992.

McBride, Joseph. *Steven Spielberg: A Biography*. London: Faber and Faber, 1998.

McCarthy, Todd. 'Spectacular *Titanic* a Night to Remember'. *Variety*, 3 November 1997.

McCarthy, Todd. 'Wizard of Awes will conjure gigantic BO'. *Variety*, 12 November 2001.

McCarthy, Todd. 'Review of *13 Days*'. *Variety*, 4 December 2000.

McCarthy, Todd. 'Review of *Almost Famous*'. *Variety*, 11 September 2000.

McCarthy, Todd. 'Review of *Forrest Gump*'. *Variety*, 11 July 1994.

McCarthy, Todd. 'Review of *The Grinch*'. *Variety*, 16 November 2000.

McCarthy, Todd. 'Review of *The Phantom Menace*'. *Variety*, 10 May 1999.

McCarthy, Todd. 'Review of *Twister*'. *Variety*, 10 May 1996.

McClintock, Pamela. 'Why PG Has Become the New Go-To Rating for Movies'. *Hollywood Reporter*, 31 March 2017.

McNary, Dave. 'CinemaCon: Boomers Keeping Filmgoing Buoyant, Says Researcher'. *Variety*, 16 April 2013.

Medved, Michael. *Hollywood vs. America*. New York: HarperPerrenial, 1993.

Meehan, Eileen R. 'Holy Commodity Fetishism Batman!' In *The Many Lives of Batman*. edited by Roberta E. Pearson and William Uricchio. New York: BFI-Routledge, 1991.

Merkin, Daphne. 'Can Anybody Make a Movie for Women?' *New York Times*, 15 December 2003.

MGM Pictures, *Ben-Hur* Press Kit.

Mitchell, Elvis. 'So Happily Ever After, Beauty and the Beasts'. *New York Times*, 16 May 2001.

Monaco, Paul. *The Sixties*. Berkeley: University of California Press, 2003.

Mosby, Aline. 'Lone Ranger to cry Hi-Yo on the Silver Screen'. *NY World Telegram and Sun*. 9 September 1955.

Mosley, Leonard. *Zanuck: The Rise and Fall of Hollywood's Last Tycoon*. London: Granada, 1984.

Motion Picture Association of America, *Theatrical Market Statistics* 2015.

Motion Picture Association of America. Summary of Remarks by Jack Valenti, President, Motion Picture Association of America to the Convention of National Association of Theater Owners. October 3 1975.

Murf. 'Review of *Earthquake*'. *Variety*, 13 November 1974.

Murphy, A.D. 'The Graduate'. *Variety*, 20 December 1967.

Murray, Noel. 'Amy Heckerling'. *A.V. Club*, 20 March 2008.

Nadel, Alan. *Flatlining on the Field of Dreams*. Durham: Rutgers, 1997.

Natale, Richard. 'Finding New Speciality Fans'. *Variety*, 19 October, 1999.

National Center for Health Statistics, *Vital Statistics of the United States, 1988, Vol. 1, Natality*. Washington: Department of Health and Human Services, 1990.

Neale, Steve and Smith, Murray. eds. *Contemporary Hollywood Cinema*. London: Routledge, 1998.

Nowell, Richard. *Blood Money: A History of the First Teen Slasher Film Cycle*. New York: Bloomsbury, 2010.

O'Donnell, Victoria. 'Science Fiction Films and Cold War Anxiety'. In *Transforming the Screen: The Fifties*, edited by Peter Lev. Berkeley: University of California Press, 2003.

Ohmer, Susan. *George Gallup in Hollywood*. New York: Columbia, 2006.

Orth, Maureen. 'Hollywood's New Power Elite: The Baby Moguls'. *New West*, 18 June, 1978.

Owram, Doug. *Born at the Right Time: A History of the Baby Boom Generation*. Toronto: University of Toronto Press, 1996.

Palmer, William J. *The Films of the Nineties: The Decade of Spin*. New York: Palgrave, 2009.

Paramount Pictures, *Samson and Delilah* Press Kit, 1949, AMPAS Margaret Herrick library.

Paramount Pictures, *The Ten Commandments* Press Kit, 1956, AMPAS Margaret Herrick library.

Pastier, John. 'Losing It at the Movies'. *Los Angeles Weekly*, 14 August 1987.

Paul, William. *Laughing Screaming: Modern Hollywood Horror and Comedy*. New York: Columbia University Press, 1994.

Philips, Julia. *You'll Never Eat Lunch in this Town Again*. New York: Random House, 1991.

Pierson, John. *Spike Mike Reloaded: A Guided Tour Across a Decade of American Independent Cinema*. New York: Hyperion Books, 2004.

Pollock, Arthur. Review of *The Crimson Pirate*. *Daily Compass*, August 28 1942.

Pollock, Dale. 'Spielberg Cuts 1941 17 Mins. Also Reduces Trade Guess on Cost - He is Sanguine About His Next Six Pix'. *Variety*, 17 December 1978.

Prince, Stephen. *A New Pot of Gold: Hollywood Under the Electronic Rainbow*. Berkeley: University of California Press, 2000.

Prince, Stephen. ed. *American Cinema of the 1980s: Themes and Variations*. New York: Berg, 2007.

Pryor, Thomas M. 'Youth With 'Em, Exhibs Grin: Clergy Helps On Film Morals'. *Variety*, 13 November 1968.

Ptacek, Greg. 'Give it college try, exhibs urged'. *Hollywood Reporter*, 8 February 1991.

Queenan, Joe. *Balsamic Dreams: A Short but Self-Important History of the Baby Boom Generation*. New York: Picador, 2002.

Quinn, Bob. 'Easy Rider Preliminary Analysis' January 27 1969, in 'Easy Rider Promotion' file 3.f-128, AMPAS Margaret Herrick library.

Radden Keefe, Patrick. 'Spitballing Indy'. *New Yorker*, 25 March 2013.

Redelings, Lowell. Review of *The Crimson Pirate*. *Hollywood Citizen News*, 27 September 1952.

Reisman, David. *The Lonely Crowd*. 1961. New Haven: Yale University Press, 2001.

Rhodes, Gary D. ed. *Horror at the Drive-In: Essays in Popular Americana*. Jefferson : McFarlane, 2003.

Rinzler. J. W. *The Making of Star Wars: The Definitive Story Behind the Film*. London: Aurum, 2002.

Rinzler, J. W. *The Making of Star Wars: The Empire Strikes Back*. New York: Del Rey, 2010.

Rinzler, J. W. and Bouzereau, Laurent. *The Complete Making of Indiana Jones: The Definitive Story Behind all Four Films*. New York: Del Rey, 2008.

Rivera Brooks, Nancy. 'Video Stores – a Record Revolution'. *Los Angeles Times*, 30 June 1986.

Robehmed, Natalie. 'The World's Highest-Paid Actors 2016: The Rock Leads With Knockout $64.5 Million Year'. *Forbes*, 25 August 2016.

Russell, James. 'Debts, disasters and mega-musicals: The decline of the studio system'. In *Contemporary American Cinema: US Cinema Since 1960*, edited by Linda Ruth Williams and Michael Hammond. New York: McGraw-Hill, 2006.

Russell, James. *The Historical Epic and Contemporary Hollywood*. New York: Continuum, 2007.

Salamon, Julie. 'On the Set'. *Vogue*, June 1987.

Sammond, Nicholas. *Babes in Tomorrowland: Walt Disney and the Making of the American Child 1930-1960*. Durham: Duke University Press, 2005.

Sayles, John and Smith, Gavin. *Sayles on Sayles*. London: Faber and Faber, 1998.

Scammon, Richard M. and Wattenberg, Ben J. *The Real Majority*. New York: Coward, McCann & Geoghegan, 1971.

Scanlon, Paul. 'George Lucas: The Wizard of Star Wars'. *Rolling Stone*, August 25, 1977.

Schary, Timothy. *Generation Multiplex: The Image of Youth in Contemporary American Cinema*. Austin: University of Texas Press, 2002.

Schatz, Thomas. *The Genius of the System: Hollywood Filmmaking in the Studio Era*. New York: Faber and Faber, 1988.

Schatz, Thomas. *Hollywood: Critical Concepts in Media and Cultural Studies*. London: Routledge, 2003.

Schatz, Thomas. 'The New Hollywood'. In *Film Theory Goes to the Movies*, edited by Jim Collins, Hillary Radner and Ava Preacher Collins. New York: Routledge, 1993.

Schickel, Richard. 'Movie: Improbable'. *Time*, 27 May 1996.

Schwager, Jeff. 'Canyon Country'. *Boxoffice*, December 1991, 14.

Scott, A.O. 'Hero rides again, with big boots to fill'. *New York Times*, 2 July 2013.

Seagrave, Kerry. *Drive-In Theaters: A History from their Inception in 1933.* Jefferson: McFarlane, 1992.

Seier, Michael and Hettrick, Scott. 'DVD Disc Jockeying'. *Variety*, 3 September 2001.

Severman, Ben. 'The Richest Generation in US History Just Keeps Getting Richer'. *Bloomberg*, 12 July 2016.

Spilker, Eric. 'Majors Staff Up For Youth.' *Variety*, 24 June 1970.

Steinhorn, Leonard. *The Greater Generation: In Defense of the Baby Boom.* New York: Thomas Dunne, 2006.

Stewart, James B. *Disneywar.* London: Pocket Books, 2006.

Stokes, Melvyn and Maltby, Richard eds. *Identifying Hollywood's Audiences: Cultural Identity and the Movies.* London: BFI, 1999.

Surrell, Jason. *Pirates of the Caribbean: From the Magic Kingdom to the Movies.* New York: Disney, 2006.

Sweet, James A. and Bumpass, Larry L. *The National Survey of Families and Households - Waves 1 and 2: Data Description and Documentation* Center for Demography and Ecology. Wisconsin: University of Wisconsin-Madison, 1996.

Tarbox, Aubrey. 'Universal Act of Faith in 'Youth' Slants: Frank Perry, Mike Cimino Get Remarkably Free Pacts'. *Variety*, 28 January 1970.

Taylor, Frank J. 'Big Boom in Outdoor Movies'. *Saturday Evening Post*, 15 September 1956.

Thomas, Bob. *Walt Disney: An American Original.* New York: Disney Editions 1976.

Thompson, David and Christie, Ian. eds. *Scorsese on Scorsese.* London: Faber and Faber, 1996.

Thompson, Kristen. *The Frodo Franchise: The Lord of the Rings and Modern Hollywood.* Berkeley: University of California Press, 2007.

Thornton, Arland and Young-DeMarco, Linda. 'Four Decades of Trends in Attitudes Toward Family Issues in the United States: The 1960s Through the 1990s'. In *Journal of Marriage and Family* 63, No. 4 (2001).

Turan, Kenneth. 'Crossroads: Steven Spielberg,' In *Steven Spielberg Interviews*, edited by Friedman, Lester D. and Notbohm, B.

Tusher, Will. 'VCR's Picture Getting Brighter'. *Variety*, 14 May 1986.

Tzioumakis, Yannis. *American Independent Cinema: An Introduction.* Edinburgh: University Press, 2006.

Various Authors, 'Top Industry Leaders stress need for more creative films'. *Variety*, 7 January 1948.

Verrill, Addison. 'MGM Thinks Young and Big: 18-25 Features A Year As Goal'. *Variety*, 8 April 1970.

Verrill, Addison. 'Oracles Edgy, Buffs Scoff: As Old Format Films Big BO'. *Variety*, 15 April 1970.

Warga, Wayne. 'Facts of Life About Movie Audiences'. *Los Angeles Times*, 29 December 1968.

Warner Brother Pictures, *Lone Ranger* Press Kit, in '*Lone Ranger*,' file, Warner Brothers Archives, University of Southern California.

Wasser, Frederick. *Veni, Vidi, Video: The Hollywood Empire and the VCR.* University of Texas Press: Austin, 2002.

Watts, Stephen. *The Magic Kingdom: Walt Disney and the American Way of Life*. Columbia: University of Missouri Press, 1997.

Weaver, William R. 'Family appeal Vital to Combat Video: Binyon'. *Motion Picture Herald*, 5 February 1949.

Weinraub, Bernard. '3 Hollywood Giants Team Up To Create Major Movie Studio'. *New York Times*, 13 October 1994.

Weinraub, Bernard. 'A Comic on the Edge at $7 Million a Movie'. *New York Times*, 1 August 1994.

Weinraub, Bernard. 'Average Hollywood Film Now Costs $60 million'. *New York Times*, 5 March 1997.

Weinraub, Bernard. 'Tartikoff Begins Charting New Course For Paramount Films'. *New York Times*, 31, October 1991.

Wertham, Fredric. *The Seduction of the Innocent*. New York: Rhinehart, 1954.

Whalley, Jim. *Saturday Night Live, Hollywood Comedy, and American Culture: From Chevy Chase to Tina Fey*. New York: Palgrave, 2010.

Whit. Review of *Old Yeller*. *Variety*, 14 November 1957.

White, Timothy. 'The Rumpled Anarchy of Bill Murray'. *New York Times*, 20 November 1988.

Whitehead, J.W. *Appraising The Graduate: The Mike Nichols Classic and Its Impact in Hollywood*. Jefferson: McFarland, 2010.

Whyte, William. *The Organisation Man*. 1956. Philadelphia: University of Pennsylvania Press, 2002.

Williams, David E. 'Captain of his Ship'. *American Cinematographer*, December 1997.

Williams, Dick. 'Editorial'. *LA Mirror*, 18 May 1951.

Willman, Chris. 'The Kids Are Alright'. *Bam*, 29 March 1985.

Wolfe, Tom. 'The Me Decade'. *New York Magazine*, August 1976.

Yablans, Frank. 'Bold Approach To Pix BO, And TV's Production Virility Yet to be Tested'. *Variety*, 3 January 1973.

Yankelovich, Daniel. *The New Morality: A Profile of American Youth in the 1970s*. New York: McGraw Hill, 1974.

Zehr, Leonard. 'Screen Giant'. *Wall Street Journal*, 16 March 1987.

Zeman, Need. 'Michael Ovitz Take Two'. *Vanity Fair*, April 2001.

Zumburge, Marianne. 'Kevin Costner Rallies Baby Boomers at AARP Movies for Grownups Awards'. *Variety*, 3 February 2015.

INDEX

NOTE: Page numbers specified in italics referred to figures in the text respectively.